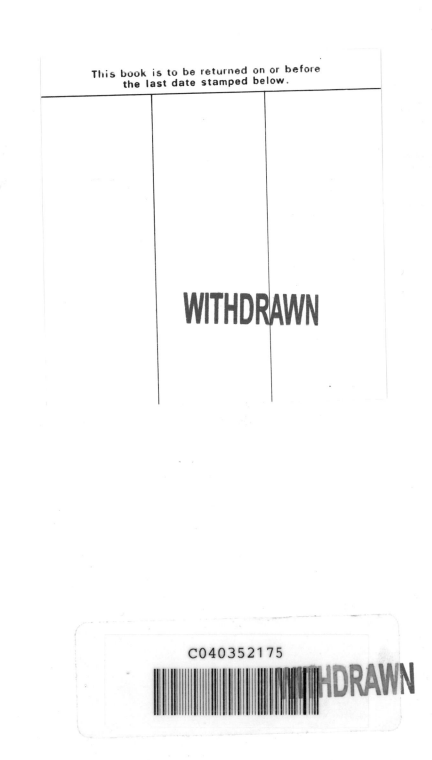

THE VALUE OF A POUND

PRICES AND INCOMES IN BRITAIN 1900–1993

THE VALUE OF A POUND
PRICES AND INCOMES IN BRITAIN 1900–1993

COMPILED BY OKSANA NEWMAN AND ALLAN FOSTER
Manchester Business School Library and Information Service

 **Gale Research International Ltd.**

An International Thomson Publishing Company

I(T)P

NEW YORK • LONDON • BONN • BOSTON • DETROIT • MADRID
MELBOURNE • MEXICO CITY • PARIS • SINGAPORE • TOKYO
TORONTO • WASHINGTON • ALBANY NY • BELMONT CA • CINCINNATI OH

Copyright © 1995 by Gale Research International Ltd
        P.O. Box 699
        Cheriton House
        North Way
        Andover
        Hants   SP10 5YE

ISBN 1-873477-31-7

Published in the United Kingdom by Gale Research International Limited

Member: European Association of Directory Publishers
Adhérent: Association Européenne des Editeurs d'Annuaires
Mitglied: Europäischer Adressbuchverleger-Verband

DPA
DIRECTORY PUBLISHERS
ASSOCIATION
ASSOCIATE MEMBER

I(T)P   Gale Research International Ltd., an International Thomson Publishing Company.
        ITP logo is a trademark under license.

A CIP catalogue record for this book is available from the British Library.

Typeset by Hodgson Associates, Tunbridge Wells
Printed in the United Kingdom by Ipswich Book Company

Contents

Contents

Contents

Preface

This book is about practical economy: how much people in certain professions have earned in Britain this century and what items have cost them. *The Value of a Pound* is a unique guide comparing the changes in real earnings against those in real retail prices through the 20th century.

In *The Value of a Pound*, statistics on earnings for a number of professions – for example, coal miners, teachers, doctors, clerical workers – are followed by prices for food and general items, making possible comparisons between what people earned and what they could afford with their wages as the century progressed. Certain regional variations are taken into account where information is available. To give a wider context to the information, national statistics are given on unemployment and employment, on consumer expenditure, on personal finance, and on the balance of payments. A number of stocks, commodities, and foreign currencies' exchange rates are also charted across the century. Interesting miscellaneous tables have been added at the end of many chapters. In all, the book presents a unique view of British earnings and prices, and hence of British society, through the 20th century.

Organization

The book contains eleven chapters, divided by period. The chapter periods are:

1900 – 1913	1950 – 1959
1914 – 1918	1960 – 1969
1919 – 1929	1970 – 1979
1930 – 1938	1980 – 1989
1939 – 1945	1990 – 1993
1946 – 1949	

All of the chapters follow a standard format.

Historical Introduction – A background essay describing the major social and economic forces of the period.

Historical Snapshot – A chronology of key economic and historic events.

Earnings and Employment – This section is divided into subsections on:

Earnings, Standard Table(s): which give(s) a selection of national average weekly or annual earnings paid for spe-

cific jobs or within particular professional areas, traced annually.

Regional Earnings by Selected Occupation: the tables up to 1968 give statistics by town and by specific industry. From 1970 the statistics are by region.

Incomes, Miscellaneous: includes data on women's earnings, certain industry sectors, and in a few cases a certain company, some miscellaneous regional earnings, and in the later chapters, details on high earners.

Employment comprises unemployment and employment figures, and regional information (as available).

Consumer Expenditure – Includes:

Consumer Expenditure, Standard Table: shows annual consumer expenditure figures in the UK, divided into ten areas of expenditure.

Regional Household Expenditure: from chapter 7 this table reports on the variations of expenditure between regions. In chapter 7 the table covers average weekly household expenditure, average weekly expenditure per capita, and average weekly expenditure on housing. The table in chapter 8 covers the above, and average weekly income by household and by person. Chapters 9, 10 and 11 cover the UK regions by areas of expenditure.

Households with Certain Durable Goods: This table features in chapters 10 and 11, and shows the proportion of households in the regions of the UK possessing durable goods such as a television, a telephone, central heating, a video, a home computer, etc.

Prices – This section includes tables on food prices followed by tables on general articles.

Food Basket: a report of a standard food basket. The pricing is compiled from information supplied for the Cost of Living Index which started in 1914, and then for the Index of Retail Prices, which replaced the Cost of Living Index from 1956. Some items featured change over the century, reflecting food fashions and availability.

Miscellaneous Food Prices Tables: includes food budgets for types of families and regional food prices.

Prices, General Articles: a selection of representative items tracked annually, allowing the reader to trace price fluctuations. During the century, new brands appear and disappear. An effort was made in the gathering of this information to trace products over long periods of time.

Prices, Selected: features a table of priced items selected from advertisements and catalogues of the given period. In the main, the prices are cited from advertisements in magazines, newspapers, sales catalogues, and on posters, or come from company archives. The items are divided first alphabetically by subheadings according to type. The order within these subheadings is then according to the year of the publication in which the items feature, and within the year of publication, the order is alphabetical by title. Where available there is a description of each item and the source of the advertisement provides indications of geographical differences in prices. The date of the advertisement in which the price was offered is provided in the sources column. This section can be used both to track standard items across periods, for example telephone tariffs, and to look at miscellany which reflect the particular concerns of the period, such as a gas mask container in the war. To a certain extent the items covered reflect the range of goods available in each given period and the changing interests of and possibilities for the consumer across the century. These sections can be used to encourage students to pick out basic items in a household budget.

Finance and Economic Data – Provides data on personal finance, stocks and shares and government data.

Finance, Personal: provides details of annual changes in income tax rates, old age pension, base interest rates, and child benefit.

Highest Closing Price of UK Major Stocks: monitors a selection of 12 large UK companies' stocks.

Commodities: tracks a selection of six important commodities: coal, cotton, gold, sugar, wheat and wool.

Foreign Exchange Rates: features annual sterling exchange rates against the mark, the franc, and the dollar. An exchange rate against the mark was not available during some of the war years.

Balance of Payments

Gross National Product (GNP) at Factor Cost and Its Component Incomes at Current Prices: national accounts compiled by the Central Statistical Office.

Miscellaneous – This section contains tables with data that does not fit into the above categories but that may be interesting to the reader or student. The table headings explain the contents, for example giving details on savings, or on rationing during the war.

Sources

A wide number of sources, from government statistics to company archives, has been used and cited in *The Value of a Pound*. Until 1944, the collation of government statistics was in its infancy. Newspapers, magazines, and some government reports served as the primary resources for this period. During the war years less information was available, therefore less is reported than in other chapters.

Users

The Value of a Pound will be of interest to students and teachers of economic history, and to school classes studying 20th-century British history, economics and society.

Specialized researchers and members of the public wishing to study how prices and expenditure have changed in comparison to incomes over different time spans, from generation to generation, and from profession to profession this century should find much of value in the book.

The Value of a Pound will therefore be of wide interest and of particular assistance to students searching for comparative statistics on earnings and prices.

Acknowledgements

This book has been put together from government statistics, company archives, books, magazines, and newspapers. I would like to thank the various individuals, companies, government departments, and museums who have helped me, by sending information and photocopies of old catalogues and price lists. There are many people who have been very helpful with their contributions. I should like in particular to thank Fiona Swales of the CWS Library, Anne Jones of the Manchester Science and Industry Archives and Miles Lambert, the assistant keeper of the Museum of Costume in Manchester. Fred Redding from Selfridges Archives provided useful prices on clothing, and Peter Gaskell from the Swan Hotel at Holmes Chapel those for beer. Rob Day prepared the figures for the *Purchasing Power of the Pound* in the Appendix. I would also like to give special mention to the staff of the Manchester Business School Library for their assistance and in particular to Evelyn Simpson for her help with the data management tasks.

This is the first edition of *The Value of a Pound*. Any suggestions for sources to use and material to include in future editions would be gratefully received and should be sent to the publisher's address.

Oksana Newman
Manchester Business School

The publisher would like to add its thanks to Aruna Vasudevan for her contributions to *The Value of a Pound*.

Abbreviations

b.h.p.	brake horsepower		HR	Human Resources
BT	British Telecom		ICI	Imperial Chemical Industries
c.	circa		in.	inch
cl.	centilitre		kg.	kilogram
cm.	centimetre		km.	kilometre
CUP	Cambridge University Press		lb.	pound
CWS	Cooperative Wholesale Society		m.	metre or million pounds
cwt.	hundredweight		mg.	milligram
d.	old penny		ml.	millilitre
doz.	dozen		mm.	millimetre
DTI	Department of Trade and Industry		n/a	not applicable
DVLA	Driving Vehicle Licensing Authority		oz.	ounce
EEC	European Economic Community		PO	Post Office
EMS	European Monetary System		p.p.	per person
EOC	Equal Opportunities Commission		s.	shilling
ERM	Exchange Rate Mechanism		SIC	Standard Industrial Classification
fl.	fluid		sq.	square
ft.	foot		t.	tonne, metric
g.	gram		TUC	Trades Union Congress
GB	Great Britain		UK	United Kingdom
GCE	General Certificate of Education		USA	United States of America
gn.	gallon		wk.	week
HMSO	Her Majesty's Stationery Office		yd.	yard
h.p.	horsepower			

Weights and Measures

Measurements of Length
Imperial Units
mile
yard (yd.)
foot (ft.)
inch (in.)

Metric Units
kilometre (km)
metre (m)
centimetre (cm)
millimetre (mm)

Measurements of Area
Imperial Units
square yard (sq.yd.)
square foot (sq.ft.)

Metric Units
hectare
square metre (m^2)

Measurements of Volume
Imperial Units
gallon
quart (¼ gallon)
pint (½ quart)
gill (¼ pint)
fluid ounce (fl. oz.)

Metric Units
litre (l)
centilitre (cl)
millilitre (ml)

Measurement of Weight or Mass
Imperial Units
pound (lb.)
ounce (oz.)
ounce troy

Metric Units
tonne, metric tonne (t)
kilogram (kg)
gram (g)
carat (metric)
milligram (mg)

Obsolescent Units of Measurement
Certain units of measurements may no longer be used for trade although the measure may still be used. For instance, it is legal to sell a 112 lb. quantity of a commodity but it must be referred to in invoices as 112 lb., not as 1 cwt. These units are defined as follows:

Measurements of Length
furlong = 220 yards
chain = 22 yards

Measurements of Area
square mile = 640 acres
square inch = ¹⁄₁₄₄ square foot

Measurements of Mass or Weight
ton = 2240 pounds
hundredweight (cwt.) = 112 pounds
quarter = 28 pounds
stone = 14 pounds
dram = ¹⁄₁₆ ounce

– One –
1900–1913

The Edwardian Heritage

PRIME MINISTERS
Marquess of Salisbury (Conservative)
Arthur Balfour (Conservative), July 1902–December 1905
Sir Henry Campbell-Bannerman (Liberal), December 1905–April 1908
Herbert Asquith (Liberal), April 1908–May 1915

CHANCELLORS OF THE EXCHEQUER
Sir M. Hicks-Beach
C. Ritchie, August 1902–October 1903
A. Chamberlain, October 1903–December 1905
H. Asquith, December 1905–April 1908
D. Lloyd George, April 1908–May 1915

During the Edwardian period, British exports accounted for a substantial part of the world market: total exports were worth £291 million in 1900 and £525 million in 1913. Britain produced approximately half of the world's pig iron in the 1870s; by 1914 this had fallen to one-eighth. Comparatively, its rate of growth in production was lower than both the US and Germany; by 1914 both countries had overtaken it in steel production. Only in shipbuilding and shipping did Britain retain its enormous market advantage.

Britain's general price level had risen since 1898, creating an atmosphere of optimism within the business community. However, this was not reflected in other areas of the country. The extravagance of the aristocracy contrasted badly with the misery of the 'sweated trades', and the increasing militancy of a working class affected by rising prices (the average wage in 1914 was just over 30 shillings a week – insufficient to maintain the average family). The violence of the suffragette movement, the battle between the House of Lords and the House of Commons, and the growing conflict in Ireland added to the sense of tension and the need for change.

Living conditions had not altered greatly among the working class since 1900 when Seebohm and Rowntree conducted their social survey in York and found that the average household did not possess a bath. Rowntree estimated that the subsistence wage needed to support a family of five was 21s.8d. However, in 1906 a Government Earnings Enquiry indicated that the average weekly wage in the cotton trade was 29s.6d., in public utilities 28s.1d., and in agriculture approximately 20s. It was not surprising that the charitable workhouses established during the Victorian era were still very popular.

Although the infant mortality rate had fallen from its average of 15 per cent of live births per annum between 1841 and 1870, it was still high at 10 per cent of live births in 1910. However, in areas of concentrated population and deprivation, such as the East End of London, this figure was much higher. The novelist Jack London asserted, in *People of the Abyss* (1903), that 55 per cent of children died before the age of five in the East End, compared to 18 per cent in the West End of London.

The Booth and Rowntree surveys indicated that almost one-third of the population was unable to afford enough to eat. Similarly, L.C. Money, in his book *Riches and Poverty*, estimated that almost half of National Income went to one-ninth of the population. The building boom of the latter half of this period slightly alleviated chronic overcrowding, but the great urban poverty found in most of Britain's towns and cities was an inescapable fact.

However, the Edwardian period was also important in the rise of the middle class, and in the growth of suburban living. Family life became centred around the semi-detached house; employment was found in the clerical sections of the expanding banking and financial sectors; and practically every middle-class household had servants, most of whom were aware of their 'place' in the existing social hierarchy.

On the political front, the Conservative Party lost its seat in the House of Commons in the General Election of 1905; it was succeeded by the Liberal Party. However many of the proposed Liberal reforms were overruled by the predominantly Conservative House of Lords. Traditional Conservatives ('Tories') could not accept the level and rate of change. The notions of meritocracy or that David Lloyd George, the son of a village schoolmaster, brought up by a shoemaker uncle, could become a Cabinet Minister, were completely unacceptable. The subsequent election of 1910 saw the Liberals return with an even larger majority.

Thus the period 1900–1913 was one of great change and development. The contrast between the extravagance of the aristocracy, and the poverty of the working-class majority was exacerbated by the rise in prices and fall in the standard of living for most of the population. The women's movement and the rise of trade union activity indicated that large sections of the population were unhappy with the paternalism and class consciousness of British society.

However, it was with the advent of war and in the years that followed that the nation experienced substantial social and economic change. As Olive Heseltine wrote in *Lost Continent* (1948) 'although the high noon of Victorian greatness was past, sunshine still glowed on its afternoon tea. Not for a moment could they [the upper and middle classes] have dreamed that their civilization, so slowly and painfully elaborated, so orderly, respectable and enlightened, would twice be mortally assailed; that their grand-daughters, slumbering peacefully in their perambulators, would find themselves maids of all work in unheated houses, cooking, sweeping, scrubbing, minding babies, tending sick-beds, standing eternally in queues; whilst their grandsons, who had faced death in African deserts, Asiatic jungles and Arctic seas, discharged from hospitals, from mental homes, from German prison camps, returned at last to help wash dishes, black the boots, and carry up the coals... '.

1.1 Historical Snapshots

1.1 Historical Snapshots

1899–1902	Boer War between UK and Boers in South Africa.
1900	Labour Representation Committee formed, precursor to the Labour Party, to represent trade unions and socialist societies in Parliament.
	First long-distance bus services in UK begin.
	Coca-Cola goes on sale for the first time in UK.
1901	Queen Victoria dies.
	The Imperial Tobacco Co. Ltd. capitalized at £11,957,022 making it the UK's largest company.
1902	Petition demanding votes for women is presented to Parliament by over 37,000 women textile workers.
	Edward VII is crowned.
1903	A regular news service using the Marconi wireless system begins.
	Henry Ford sets up his own car company in the USA.
1904	Courtauld & Co. buys the patent rights covering the making of rayon.
	First electric main-line train runs from Liverpool to Southport.
	Tobacconists protest at a 3d. increase on the tobacco tax.
1905	Footballers' first maximum wage fixed at £4 a week.

1906	Twenty six MPs elected to re-named Labour Party.
1907	Channel Tunnel Bill is defeated in Parliament.
1908	Nine suffragettes arrested after incidents at the homes of cabinet ministers.
	Lord Northcliffe, formerly Alfred Harmsworth, buys *The Times*.
	Government proposes a weekly old age pension of five shillings for single people over 70.
	Ernest Rutherford wins the Nobel prize for chemistry for his work on atoms.
	Henry Ford launches his Model T Ford in the USA at a price of $850.
1909	Selfridges Department Store opens.
1910	The new labour exchanges are besieged by job-hunters.
1911	MPs' annual salaries set at £400.
1912	The Post Office takes over the National Telephone Company.
	The House of Commons pass the Coal Miners' Bill giving miners a minimum wage.
1913	The first payments are made under the National Insurance Act.

Chronicle of Britain, J.L. International Publishing, 1992; Williams T.I. *Invention and Discovery in the 20th Century*. Harrap, 1990; Galsworthy, M. *Encyclopaedia of Association Football*.

Events occurred in the UK, unless otherwise stated.

1.2 Earnings and Employment

1.2.1 Earnings, Standard Tables

1.2.1a Incomes and Wages

	1900	1901	1906	1911	1913
Solicitor		£1,500 (a)		£1343(a)	£568 (a)
Police Constable	24s. 0d.	25s. 8d.		27s. 0d.	
General Practitioner		£265 8 (a)			
Teacher		147 10 (a)		£176 00 (a)	154 (a)
Clerical Worker		286 (a)		229 00 (a)	
Train Driver			119 (a)		
Coal Miner		34s. 4d.	31s. 5d.	32s. 2d.	
Fitter		44 7		48 0	
Bricklayer's Labourer		17 9		18 0	
Compositor		35 5		37 5	
Farm Worker	14 10	14 11			
Cotton Weaver			19 3		26 3

British Labour Statistics 1886–1968, HMSO, 1971; Bowley, A.L. *Wages and Incomes in the UK since 1860*, Cambridge University Press, 1937; Routh, G. *Occupation and Pay in Great Britain, 1906–79*, Macmillan Press, 1980; Williamson, J.G. 'The Structure of Pay in Britain, 1710–1911', *Research in Economic History*, 7, 1982.

Blank space denotes no available data. Wages are weekly rates for men unless otherwise stated. (a) – annual; (m) – male.

1.2.1b Average Weekly Earnings

	Men (20 years and over)	Lads and Boys	Women (18 years and over)	Girls	All Work People
	s. d.	s. d.	s. d.	s. d.	s. d.
Bricks, Pottery, Glass and Chemicals	29 2	11 6	11 10	7 0	23 6
Metals, Engineering and Shipbuilding	33 11	10 4	12 8	7 4	27 4
Textiles	28 1	10 5	15 5	8 11	17 6
Clothing	30 2	9 8	13 6	5 9	15 1
Food, Drink and Tobacco	26 4	10 0	11 5	6 6	19 0
Paper and Printing etc.	34 4	8 11	12 2	6 4	20 0
Building and Woodworking	32 0	9 6	12 11	6 10	26 7
Miscellaneous Trades	27 11	10 1	12 4	6 9	23 2
Public Utility Services[1]	28 1	11 10			27 3
Railway Service	26 9	11 11			25 5

British Labour Statistics, 1886–1968, HMSO, 1971.

Blank space denotes no available data. [1]Includes tramways and omnibus services and certain employees in local government. Earnings taken from a report carried out by the Board of Trade in 1906/7.

1.2.2 Regional Earnings by Selected Occupation

		London	Manchester	Newcastle	Leeds	Glasgow
		s. d.	s. d.	s. d.	s. d.	s. d.
Bricklayer (hourly)	1900	10	10	10	8½	9
	1906	10½	10	9½	9	10
	1910	10½	10	9½	9½	9½
Bricklayer's Labourer (hourly)	1900	7	6	n/a	7	5½
	1906	7	6	6¼	6½	5½
	1910	7	6	6¼	6½	n/a
Compositor (weekly)	1900	38 0	35 0	33 6	34 0	32 6
	1906	39 0	35 0	35 0	35 6	34 0
Engineering; Fitter and Turner (weekly)	1900	38 0	36 0	n/a	n/a	36 0
	1906	39 0	36 0	n/a	n/a	36 0
	1910	40 0	37 0	n/a	n/a	36 0

British Labour Statistics 1886–1968, HMSO, 1971.

1.2.3 Incomes, Miscellaneous

1.2.3a Women's Earnings, 1906

Industries	Average Full Time Weekly Earnings
	s. d.
All paper, printing, etc. trades	12 2
Bookbinding	12 10
Printing	12 3
Cardboard, canvas etc. box manufacture	12 3
Paper stationery manufacture	11 11
Paper manufacture	11 11
All pottery, brick, glass and chemical	11 10
Explosives	13 1
Soap and candle	12 5
Porcelain, china and earthenware	11 11
Brick, tile, pipe, etc.	11 5
All food, drink and tobacco	11 5
Tobacco, cigar, cigarette and snuff	12 0
Cocoa, chocolate and sugar confectionery	11 9
Preserved food, jam, pickle, sauce etc.	10 11
Biscuit making	10 10
Aerated water, etc. manufacture and bottling	9 7

Hutchins, B.L. *Women in Modern Industries*, 1915, p. 225.

1.2.3b UK Railway Earnings

	Number of men	Amount paid in wages to the men	Average earnings per head	
		£	s.	d.
1900	440,347	551,942	25	0¾
1901	440,557	551,114	25	0¼
1902	448,429	559,179	24	11¼
1903	448,321	558,819	24	10½
1904	445,577	557,820	25	0½
1905	449,251	568,338	25	3½
1906	457,942	582,207	25	5¼
1907	478,690	618,304	25	10
1908	459,120	574,059	25	0
1909	459,444	582,782	25	4½
1910	463,019	596,342	25	9

Cooperative Wholesale Society People's Year Book, 1922, p. 257.

Original source Board of Trade.

1.2.3c North British Locomotive Company Wages

Year	Average wages per man per week	
	s.	d.
1904	n/a	
1905	27	11
1906	28	2¼
1907	30	4
1908	28	3
1909	25	8¼
1910	26	4¾
1911	29	7¼
1912	29	7½
1913	31	9½

Business History, Vol. XX, No. 2, July, 1978, p. 231.

Original source, *North British Locomotive Company Papers* in Mitchell Library, Glasgow.

1.2.3d Wages of Actors at His Majesty's Theatre

1900s			average 30.4 shillings
60s.	Gladys Cooper		
40s.	Owen Nares		
25s.	Winifred Fortescue	Basil Dean	
21s.	Matheson Lang	Ernest Thesiger	Ben Iden Payne

1910–1914			average 36 shillings
70s.	Fay Compton		
50s.	Edith Evans	Robertson Hare	
40s.	Henry Kendall		
31s. 6d.	Noel Coward		
30s.	Cedric Hardwicke	Harold French	
25s.	Maud Gill		
21s.	Hesketh Pearson		
13s. 4d.	Norah Nicholson		

Business History, Vol. XXVII, No. 2, July, 1985, p. 199.

Extracted from the business records of Sir Herbert Beerbohm Tree.

1.2.4 Employment

1.2.4a Unemployment

	Membership at end of June of unions reporting	Percentage unemployed	
		Mean for year, %	End of December, %
1900	525,000	2.5	3.5
1901	531,000	3.3	4.2
1902	538,000	4.0	5.0
1903	550,000	4.7	6.3
1904	567,000	6.0	7.1
1905	569,000	5.0	4.5
1906	586,000	3.6	4.4
1907	661,000	3.7	5.6
1908	689,000	7.8	9.1
1909	698,000	7.7	6.6
1910	703,000	4.7	5.0
1911	759,000	3.0	3.1
1912	834,000	3.2	2.3
1913	922,000	2.1	2.6

Cooperative Wholesale Society People's Year Book, 1922, p. 257.

Figures are for those entitled to unemployment benefit. Original source *21st Abstract of Labour Statistics*.

1.3 Consumer Expenditure

1.3.1 Consumer Expenditure, Standard Table

	Food	Alcoholic Drink	Tobacco	Housing	Fuel and Light	Clothing	Durable Household Goods	Motor Cars and Motor Cycles	Other Goods	Other Services	Total Consumer Expenditure
	£m	£m	£m	£m	£m	£m	£m	£m	£m	£m	£m
1900	464	187	27	167	75	153	61	2	97	390	1,637
1901	473	185	28	174	71	162	62	2	98	402	1,677
1902	481	183	29	180	70	153	62	2	101	405	1,686
1903	496	179	30	186	68	149	61	2	102	413	1,699
1904	499	173	30	191	67	154	63	4	105	420	1,719
1905	502	172	31	194	63	157	63	4	108	430	1,736
1906	507	171	32	198	64	161	63	5	113	440	1,766
1907	510	171	33	201	74	162	68	5	118	457	1,811
1908	515	163	33	203	70	168	67	4	113	462	1,813
1909	525	154	34	211	68	174	63	3	115	469	1,831
1910	534	163	37	211	67	178	63	8	119	479	1,877
1911	551	169	38	212	70	195	66	8	122	489	1,936
1912	576	168	39	215	74	202	79	10	128	508	2,006
1913	586	175	40	220	76	210	79	12	134	521	2,070

Mitchell, B.R. *British Historical Statistics*, Cambridge University Press, 1988.

Original source Feinstein, C.H. *National Income, Expenditure and Output of the UK, 1855-1965*, Cambridge University Press, 1972.

1.4 Prices

1.4.1 Food Prices

1.4.1a Food Basket

Article (per lb. unless otherwise stated)	s.	d.
Butter	1	2
Sugar	0	3
Flour	1	5
Yeast (per ¼ lb.)	0	2
Tea	1	6
Potatoes (20lb.)	0	10
Peas	0	2½
Cheese	0	6
Bacon	0	9
Onions	0	1½
Eggs (per dozen)	1	0
Biscuits	0	8
Currants	0	5
Sultanas	0	7
Salmon (tin)	0	9
Rice	0	3
Lard	0	7
Jam	0	5½
Syrup (per 2lb.)	0	6½
Apples	0	3
Milk (6 quarts)	0	3
Meat	0	10

The Producer, October 1923, p. 373.

Retail prices of certain articles of food taken from a family order at Eccles Cooperative Retail Society in 1905.

1.4.1b Cost of Food in Workmen's Families

Limits of weekly income	Under 25s.	25s. and under 30s.	30s. and under 35s.	35s. and under 40s.	40s. and above	All incomes
Number of Returns	261	289	416	382	596	1,944
Average weekly family income	21s. 4½ d.	26s.11¾ d.	31s.11¼ d.	36s. 6¼ d.	52s. 0½ d.	36s.10d.
Average number of children living at home	3.1	3.3	3.2	3.4	4.4	3.6

Cost	s. d.	s. d.	s. d.	s. d.	s. d.	s. d.
Bread and Flour	3 0½	3 3¾	3 3½	3 4¼	4 3¾	3 7
Meat (bought by weight)	2 8	3 4¾	4 3½	4 5½	5 10½	4 5½
Other meat (including fish)	0 7½	0 8¾	0 10	1 0	1 4	0 11¾
Bacon	0 6¾	0 9	0 10¼	0 11½	1 3¾	0 11½
Eggs	0 5¾	0 8½	0 11	1 0	1 4¾	1 0
Fresh milk	0 8	0 11¾	1 3¼	1 4½	1 7¾	1 3¼
Cheese	0 4¾	0 5½	0 6	0 6	0 8	0 6½
Butter	1 2	1 7	1 10¼	2 0	3 0½	2 1½
Potatoes	0 8¾	0 9¾	0 10½	0 10½	1 1¾	0 11
Vegetables and fruit	0 4¾	0 7	0 10	0 11¾	1 3¾	0 11
Currants and raisins	0 1½	0 1¾	0 2¼	0 3	0 3¾	0 2¾
Rice, tapioca and wheatmeal	0 4½	0 5	0 6	0 5¾	0 7	0 6
Tea	0 9¼	0 11¼	1 0¾	1 1¼	1 5	1 1½
Coffee and cocoa	0 2	0 3¼	0 3½	0 4¼	0 5½	0 3¾
Sugar	0 8	0 10	0 10¾	0 11¼	1 3	0 11¾
Jam, marmalade, treacle and syrup	0 4¼	0 5¼	0 6	0 6½	0 8¾	0 6½
Pickles and condiments	0 2	0 2¼	0 3¼	0 3½	0 4¼	0 3¼
Other items	1 0½	1 3¾	1 6½	1 10½	2 6¼	1 9½
Total expenditure on food	14 4¾	17 10½	20 9¼	22 3½	29 8	22 6
Percentage of family income spent on food	67.3%	66.2%	65.0%	61.0%	57.0%	61.1%

British Labour Statistics, Historical Abstract, 1886-1968, HMSO, 1971.

Figures are for urban districts in 1904. Report of an enquiry by the Board of Trade.

1.4.1c Farm Labourers' Earnings and Retail Prices

	Bread, 4lb.	Butter, 1lb.		Margarine, 1lb.	Sugar, 1lb.	Tea, 4oz.	Flour, 7lb.	Bacon, 1lb.	Cheese, 1lb.	Farm Labourers' Earnings, 1907	
	s. d.	s.	d.	s. d.	s. d.	s. d.	s. d.	s. d.	s. d.	s.	d.
Oxfordshire	5½	1	3	6	2	4½	11	8	n/a	14	11
Berkshire	5½	1	2½	6	2	4¼	11	8	9	16	8
Essex	6	1	0	7¾	2	4½	11	7¾	9	16	4
Leicestershire	5¾	1	3	6	2½	4¼	11½	10	9	18	9
Yorkshire East Riding	n/a	1	4	5½	2¼	4¼	10½	n/a	n/a	19	3
Yorkshire West Riding	n/a	1	0	8	2½	5	10½	10	8½	20	0
Yorkshire North Riding	n/a	1	2½	6	2¼	4½	10¼	10	9½	19	7

Hunt, E. *Regional Wage Variations in Britain 1850–1914*, Clarendon Press, 1973.

Earnings are for 1907 and prices for rural areas, 1912–1913. Original source Rowntree, B.S. and Kendall, M. *How the Labourer Lives*, 1963.

1.4.1d Board of Trade Standard Working-Class Budget

	s.	d.
Bread and Flour	3	7
Meat (bought by weight)	4	5½
Other meat (including fish)	0	11¾
Bacon	0	11½
Eggs	1	0
Fresh milk	1	3¼
Cheese	0	6½
Butter	2	1½
Potatoes	0	11
Vegetables and Fruit	0	11
Currants and Raisins	0	2¾
Rice, Tapioca and Oatmeal	0	6
Tea	0	1½
Coffee and Cocoa	0	3¾
Sugar	0	11
Jam, Marmalade, Treacle and Syrup	0	6½
Pickles and Condiments	0	3¼
Other Items	1	9½
Total	22	6

Cooperative Wholesale Society People's Year Book, 1922.

Budget for 1904.

1.4.2 Prices, General Articles

	1900	1901	1902	1903	1904	1905	1906	1907	1908	1909	1910	1911	1912	1913
	s. d.	s. d.	s. d.	s. d.	s. d.	s. d.	s. d.	s. d.	s. d.	s. d.	s. d.	s. d.	s. d.	s. d.
Aspirin								1 0					9	
Beer (1 pint as served in a public bar)	2	2	2	2	2	2	2	2	2	2	2	2	2½	2½
Cheddar Cheese (1 lb.)						10					6½			
Colmans Mustard (1 lb. of double superfine)								1 4	1 7					
Colmans Starch									1					
Daily Mail	½	½	½	½	½	½	½	½	½	½	½	½	½	½
Guinness Extra Stout (1 pint)	3					3			3					
Inland Letter Post	1	1	1	1	1	1	1	1	1	1	1	1	1	1
Pears Transparent Soap (3 bars)	1 0					1 3					6			
Petrol (1 gallon)													1 7	
Red Label Tea (1 lb.)				1 6							1 6			
Scotch Whisky (standard bottle)	1 3½ duty	1 8½ duty												
Swan Vestas Matches (100)	1	1	1	1	1	1	1	1	1	1	1	1	1	1
The Times	3	3	3	3	3	3	3	3	3	3	3	3	3	3

The Boots Company; British Library; Burmah Castrol; Colmans of Norwich; Guinness Brewing GB; Royal Mail; Sainsbury's Archives; The Scotch Whisky Association; Unilever Historical Archives.

Blank space denotes no available data.

1.4.3 Prices, Selected

Item	Source	Description	Price £	s.	d.
Alcoholic Drink					
Wines	*Army & Navy Catalogue*, 1907	Champagne	4	18	0 (per doz. bottles)
		Claret	2	10	0 (per doz. bottles)
		Port	1	14	0 (per doz. bottles)
		Sherry	2	2	0 (per doz. bottles)
Appliances: Domestic and Electrical					
Chopper	*Pryce Jones Ltd*, Newtown, 1907	Enterprise Meat Chopper		5	3
Cleaner	*Army & Navy Stores Catalogue*, 1907	Empress Electric Aspirator Air Suction Cleanser	23	2	0
Kettle		Three Pint Electric Kettle	2	3	6
Iron		Electric Iron	1	3	0
Washing Machine		Bradford Vowel A Washing Machine	3	3	9
Vacuum Cleaner		Pneumatic Dust Extractor	5	5	0
	J & N Philips & Co, Manchester, 1913	Daisy Vacuum Cleaner	3	13	6
Clothing and Footwear:					
Children's					
School Uniform	*Queen*, London, 1900	Boy's Westminster Suit		19	0
Suit		Boy's Wool Suit		13	9
Shirt	*John Noble Ltd*, Manchester, 1902	Boy's Cotton Shirt		6	3 (up to 12/6)
Knickers		Boy's Navy Blue Serge Knickers		1	6½
Suit		Boy's Norfolk Suit		9	3 (up to 17/6)
Boots	*Affleck & Brown*, Manchester, 1903	Children's Boots		2	11
Flannels		Baby's Night Flannels		1	6 (up to 2/6)
		Baby's Day Silk Flannels		3	6 (up to 8/6)
Coat	*Affleck & Brown*, Manchester, 1906	Girl's Coat	1	1	0
Frock	*Pryce Jones Ltd*, Newtown, 1907	Girl's Serge School Frock		2	8 (up to 3/10)
Dress		Knockabout Dress for Girls		2	4 (up to 5/3)
Overall		Brown Holland Overall		2	3 (up to 3/6)
Men's					
Tie	*Affleck & Brown*, Manchester, 1900	Gent's Tie			1 (up to 9¾)
Collars		Gent's Collars			4½
Cuffs		Gent's Cuffs			6¾ (up to 9¾)
Shirt	*John Noble Ltd*, Manchester, 1902	Gent's Cotton Shirt		3	6 (up to 5/6)
Jacket		Engineer's Jacket		2	6
Suit		Man's Drill Suit		6	11
Trousers		Man's Cord Trousers		7	11
Collars	*Affleck & Brown*, Manchester, 1903	Gent's Collars			4
Cuffs		Gent's Cuffs			9½
Collars	*Affleck & Brown*, Manchester, 1904	Gent's Collars			9¾
Cuffs		Gent's Cuffs			6
Tie	*Affleck & Brown*, Manchester, 1905	Gent's Silk Tie			9¾
Collars		Gent's Collar			4
Cuffs		Gent's Cuffs			9¾
Suit	*Charles H Cook*, Macclesfield, 1907	Made to Measure Lounge Suit	2	15	0
Umbrella	*Affleck & Brown*, Manchester, 1908	Gent's Umbrella		4	11 (up to 21/0)

Continued

1.4.3 Prices, Selected *continued*

Item	Source	Description	Price		
			£	s.	d.
Women's					
Stockings	*Queen*, London, 1900	Ladies Plain Black Cashmere Hose		1	0 (up to 1/5)
Gloves	*Affleck & Brown*, Manchester, 1900	Ladies Kid Gloves		1	0 (up to 1/6)
Nightdress		Ladies Cotton Nightdress		1	10½
Shirt		Ladies Poplin Shirt		4	11
Corsets		Ladies Boned Corsets		4	11
Shoes		Ladies Kid Shoes		4	6
Nightdress	*Affleck & Brown*, Manchester, 1901	Ladies Cotton Nightdress		1	10½
Coat	*John Noble Ltd*, Manchester, 1902	Ladies Cashmere Coat		11	9
Shirt		Ladies Cashmere Shirt		5	9
Gloves	*Affleck & Brown*, Manchester, 1903	Ladies Kid Gloves		1	0
Umbrella		Ladies Umbrella		3	11
Corsets		Ladies Boned Corsets		3	11 (up to 15/9)
Nightdress		Ladies Cotton Nightdress		4	11
Shirt	*Dickins & Jones*, London, 1904	Ladies Cambric Shirt		6	6
		Ladies Silk Shirt		19	6
Shoes		Ladies Calf Leather Shoes	1	1	9
		Ladies Kid Leather Shoes		15	9
Nightdress	*Affleck & Brown*, Manchester, 1904	Ladies Cotton Nightdress		2	10½
Corsets		Ladies Boned Corsets		10	6 (up to 15/9)
Shoes		Ladies Shoes		5	11
Coat and Skirt	*Queen*, London, 1905	Exquisite Coat and Skirt by Fenwick	6	6	0
Gloves	*Affleck & Brown*, Manchester, 1905	Ladies Kid Gloves		1	0
Nightdress		Ladies Cotton Nightdress		3	6
Shoes		Ladies Glacé Kid Gloves		4	6
Coat		Ladies Winter Coat		19	11 (sale price)
Nightdress	*Affleck & Brown*, Manchester, 1906	Ladies Cotton Nightdress		3	9
Gloves		Ladies Kid Gloves		1	0
Dress	*Pryce Jones Ltd*, Newtown, 1907	Women's Serge Dress for Cottage or Servants Wear		8	6
Cloak		Women's Stout Waterproof Melton Cloak		12	6
Shoes	*C & J Clark Ltd*, 1907	Black Goat One Bar		4	6
		Ladies Walking Boots in Glacé Kid		8	0
Nightdress	*Affleck & Brown*, Manchester, 1908	Ladies Cotton Nightdress		6	11 (up to 14/0)
Gloves		Ladies Kid Gloves		1	3
Umbrella		Ladies Umbrella		2	11 (up to 16/9)
Gloves	*Affleck & Brown*, Manchester, 1909	Ladies Kid Gloves		1	0
Coat		Ladies Fur Lined Motor Coats	2	2	0
Boots		Ladies Boots		12	11
Nightdress	*Sellers & Sellers*, London, 1909	Ladies Nightdress		1	11¾
Corsets		Ladies Corsets		1	11¾
Hat		Ladies Felt Hat		4	11 (up to 8/11)
Gloves		Ladies Long Suede Gloves		1	6¾
Shoes		Ladies Leather Shoes		7	11
Coat and Skirt	*Harrods*, London, 1910	Coat and Skirt in Best Quality Velveteen	4	4	0

Continued

1.4.3 Prices, Selected *continued*

Item	Source	Description	Price £	s.	d.
Coat and Skirt *cont.*		Tailor Made Coat and Skirt in Reversible Silk	18	18	0
		Stylish Coat and Skirt in French Corded Suiting	7	7	6
Boots	*C & J Clark Ltd*, 1911	Ladies Boots in Glacé Kid		8	6
Shoes		Ladies Wessex Shoe in Fine Chrome Patent		9	0
Food Products					
Tea	*Queen*, London, 1900	Loose Tea		1	4 (per lb.)
Baby Food	*Queen*, London, 1902	Savory & Moores Infant Food		1	0 (up to 10/0 according to size of tin)
		Frame Baby Food		1	0 (per tin)
Sugar	*CWS Annual*, 1905	Foreign Refined Sugar			½ (per lb.)
		English Colonies Refined Sugar			½ (per lb.)
Cheese	*J Sainsbury*, 1903	Cheddar Cheese			10 (per lb.)
Tea		Red Label Tea		1	6 (per lb.)
Butter		Loose Butter		1	0
Eggs		Six Medium Eggs			5
Bacon		Unsmoked Back Bacon			10½ (per lb.)
Chocolate	*Queen*, London, 1903	Caillers Milk Chocolate			1 (up to 3d. per tablet)
Coffee	*Army & Navy Catalogue*, 1907	Good Household Roasted Ground Coffee		1	0½ (per lb. tin)
		Vera Paz After Dinner Ground Coffee		1	10 (per lb. tin)
Currants		Selected			4½ (per lb.)
Custard Powder		Birds Custard Powder			4 (per packet)
		Lyons			4 (tin)
Cornflour		Brown & Polsons			6 (packet)
		CWS			4 (packet)
Cream		Devonshire Clotted Cream			6 (per jar)
Biscuits	*CWS Annual*, 1907	Cream Crackers			1 (per lb.)
		Garibaldi Biscuits			1 (per lb.)
Drink		Marmite			1½ (2oz. jar)
		Bovril		1	10 (4oz.)
Honey		Honey			2½ (per lb.)
Oatmeal		Scots Oatmeal			1 (per lb.)
Semolina		Semolina		1	1 (7lb.)
Fish		Cod			3 (per lb.)
		Plaice			3 (per lb.)
Treacle		West Indian			6 (per 2lb.)
Confectionery		Acid Drops			5 (per lb.)
		Barley Sugar			7 (per lb.)
		Plain Chocolate		1	2 (per lb.)
		Nougat		2	8 (per lb.)
Cheese	*J Sainsbury*, 1910	Cheddar Cheese			6½ (per lb.)
Tea		Red Label Tea		1	6 (per lb.)
Butter		Loose Butter		1	0 (per lb.)
Eggs		Six Medium Eggs			5

Continued

1.4.3 Prices, Selected *continued*

Item	Source	Description	Price		
			£	s.	d.
Bacon		Unsmoked Back Bacon		1	1 (per lb.)
Baby Food	*Boots*, 1912	Merseals Food		1	0 (per tin)
		Robinsons Barley and Groat			6 (up to 1/0)
Furniture					
Bedroom	*Queen*, London, 1900	Five Piece Bedroom Suite	4	15	6
Drawing Room		Settee and Two Elbow Chairs	19	19	0
Chair	*Queen*, London, 1905	Hampton Easy Chair	2	15	0
Solid Hardwood Bedstead		3ft. wide x 6ft. 6in. long	1	1	0
		3ft. 6in. wide x 6ft. 6in. long	1	7	6
		4ft. wide x 6ft. 6in. long	1	12	6
		4ft. 6in. wide x 6ft. 6in. long	1	17	6
Carpet	*Affleck & Brown*, Manchester, 1908	Axminster Carpets		5	6 (up to 5/9 sq. yd.)
Coal Box	*J & N Philips & Co*, Manchester, 1913	Coal Box		13	4
		Coal Cabinet	1	5	9
Table		Occasional Table		7	11
		Whist Drive Card Table		3	9
		Dining Table with Cypress Top and Turned Legs	2	6	3
Sideboard		Fumed Oak Sideboard	13	6	8
Mantlepiece		Overmantel with Solid Walnut Frame	1	14	8
Settee		Woven Velvet Covered Couch	17	15	7
Suite		Three Piece Suite in Tapestry	12	12	0
Settee		Chesterfield Settee, One Drop End with Spring Seat	5	10	0
Bedstead		Combined Bedstead and Mattress		15	0 (up to 16/6)
Chair		Baby Chair in Birch Polished Walnut	1	2	3
Cot		Premier Baby Cot in Birch		15	11
Bookcase		Inlaid Mahogany Revolving Bookcase	2	10	8
		Fumed Oak Bureau and Bookcase	7	2	3
Garden Equipment and Supplies					
Lawn Mower	*Army & Navy Catalogue*, 1907	Victoria Chain Lawn Mower	2	0	0 (up to 141/3)
		Victoria Ball Bearing Lawn Mower	1	17	0 (up to 60/0)
Lawn Sprinklers		Patent Hose Reel and Lawn Sprinkler combined		12	9
Garden Sprinkler		New Revolving Garden Sprinkler		2	6
Garden Syringe		Cooper's Patent Protection Syringe		15	10
Hose Reel		Wrought Iron Frame and Galvanised Reel		9	3
Garden Chair	*J & N Philips & Co*, Manchester, 1913	Folding Hammock Chair with Canvas Seat		3	3
Hammock		Patent Woven Wire Garden Hammock		12	6
Heat and Light					
Candles	*CWS Annual*	Candles			4½ (per lb. box)
Coal		Coal		10	9 (ton) in 1906
Electricity		Electricity			2 (per unit)

Continued

1.4.3 Prices, Selected *continued*

Item	Source	Description	£	s.	d.
Firelighters		Firelighters			6 ½ (250)
Hotel Rates					
Armfields South Place Hotel, London	*Bradshaws ABC Railway Guide*, 1910	Bed, Breakfast, Bath and Attendance		5	6
Opera Hotel, London		Double Bed		4	6
Edelweiss Hotel, Manchester		Very Superior Board and Residence		5	0
Household Goods					
Bulbs	*Army & Navy Catalogue*, 1907	Ediswan Light Bulbs		11	0 (doz.)
Strainer		Household Triturating Strainer		16	9
Cooking Utensils	*Pryce Jones Ltd*, Newtown, 1907	Saucepan with Lid		2	0 (2 pint)
		Deep Stewpan with Lid		2	9 (8 inches)
		Preserving Pan		5	0 (13 inches)
		Lipped Saucepan		1	7 (7½ inches)
		Frying Pan		2	3 (11 inches)
		Kettle		4	0 (6 pint)
Seeder		Raisin Seeder		3	3
Milk Boiler		Patent Seamless Aluminium Milk Boiler		5	2 (3 pints)
Houses					
Houses	*CWS Annual*	1913 Semi-detached House in London	600	0	0
		1913 Semi-detached House in the Provinces	450	0	0
Solicitor's Fees		Vendor's Solicitor's Fees	1	0	0 (for the first £1000)
Jewellery					
Diamond Ornaments	*Army & Navy Stores Catalogue*, 1907	Fine Diamond Heart Pendant	55	10	0
		Diamond Fine Lace Brooch	2	18	0
		Diamond Tiara	123	16	0
		Diamond Star Brooch	8	12	0
Gem Jewellery		Triple Row Crescent Brooch	53	0	0
		Fine Diamond Necklet	100	15	0
		Diamond Cluster Ring	18	5	0
		Fine Diamond Dragon Fly Brooch	48	11	0
		Single Stone Diamond Earrings	75	0	0
Musical Instruments					
Piano	*Queen*, London, 1900	Semi-Grand Piano	20	0	0
	Army & Navy Catalogue, 1907	Bechstein Concert Grand Piano	330	0	0
	J & N Philips & Co, Manchester, 1913	Upright Iron Grand	28	0	0
		Steinhoff High Class German Overstrung Piano	42	13	4
Personal Care Items					
Medicine	*Bradshaws ABC Railway Guide*, 1900	Jamaica Sarsparilla		5	6 (bottle)
		Bates Boil Plasters		1	1½ (box)
		Midgleys Bronchial Cough Mixture		2	0 (bottle)

Continued

1.4.3 Prices, Selected *continued*

Item	Source	Description	£	s.	d.
Medicine *cont.*		Capsicum Ointment for Coughs and Chest Affections		1	1½ (up to 2/3)
		Wills Hygeia Salt			5 (tin)
Curlers	*Queen*, London, 1900	Twelve Hair Curlers			6 (box)
Soap	*Queen*, London, 1902	Wrights Coal Tar Soap			4 (tablet)
Pills		Carters Little Liver Pills		1	1½ (40)
Shampoo		Calverts Shampoo Soap		1	0
Brush		Baileys Bath Brush		5	0
Haircut		Scalpette Partings, Cycling and Yachting Fringes	1	1	0
Soap	*Unilever Archives*, 1902	Pears Unscented Transparent Soap			6 (tablet)
		Pears Hospital Transparent Soap			6 (tablet)
	Unilever Archives, 1905	D & W Gibbs Real Carbolic		8	0 (¼ doz. boxes)
	Unilever Archives, 1906	Watsons Royal Windsor			2 (tablet)
	Unilever Archives, 1909	Atkinsons Transparent Glycerine Soap		8	0 (doz. tablets)
	Army & Navy Catalogue, 1909	Pears Glycerine Soap		1	3 (box of 3 tablets)
Shaving Stick		Erasmic Shaving Stick			10½
Pills	*Boots*, 1912	Aspirin			9 (25)
Sanitary Towels		Packet of 12 (size 3)		1	2
Shampoo		Box of 6 Powdered Sachets			6
Soap		Pears Transparent Soap			6
		Boots Bath Size Soap			4½
Publications					
Books	*Queen*, London, 1900	Cloth Books		6	0
	Queen, London, 1901	Popular Novels		6	0
		Romeo and Juliet		3	6
Magazines	*Queen*, London, 1903	Ladies Gazette			1 (weekly)
		Cornhill Magazine		1	0 (monthly)
		Ladies Home Magazine			6 (monthly)
		Pall Mall Magazine			6 (monthly)
Services					
Passport	*Henry Blackelock & Co Ltd*, London, 1900	Cost of Passport and Fee		5	0
Visa		Cost of Visa		2	0
Licence	*DVLA*, Swansea, 1909	1st Road Fund Licence	6	6	0
Telephone Tariffs	*British Telecom Archives*, 1912				
London		Annual Residential Rental	17	0	0
Provinces			8	0	0
London		Annual Business Rental	17	0	0
Provinces			10	0	0
Call Charges (7 am – 7 pm)		Up to 25 miles			3 (per 3 minutes)
		25 to 50 miles			6
		50 to 75 miles			9
		75 to 100 miles		1	0
		Each additional 40 miles			6

Continued

1.4.3 Prices, Selected *continued*

Item	Source	Description	Price £	s.	d.
Parcel Postage Rates	*Post Office Archives*, 1906	1lb. weight			3
		5lb. weight			6
		10lb. weight			10

Sewing Equipment and Supplies

Item	Source	Description	Price £	s.	d.
Fabric	*Queen*, London, 1900	Macclesfield Silk		1	0 (yard)
Sewing Machine		Hand Sewing Machine	1	19	0
	Army & Navy Catalogue, 1907	Chain Stitch Machine with Accessories	1	2	6
		Auto Hand Machine	2	12	6
		Stand and Table for Above	1	2	6
Haberdashery	*Housekeepers Diary & Haberdashery Guide*, 1910	Porcupine Pin Box			6½ (¼ lb. pins)
		Peri-Lusta 100 yds. Cotton Reels			1
		Hooks and Eyes			1 (per card)
		Black Cotton Elastic			2½ (per yard)
		Collar Support			3 (per card of four)
		Dress Fasteners			6½ (up to 9½ per card of 36)
Sewing Machine	*J & N Philips & Co*, Manchester, 1913	Hand Sewing Machine	3	0	0
		Treadle Machine	5	0	0
Haberdashery		Safety Pins		3	11 (per 108)
		Curtain Hooks			9 (per gross to 2/6 per gross)

Sports and Hobbies

Item	Source	Description	Price £	s.	d.
Camera	*Queen*, London, 1900	Kodak Camera		5	0 (up to 147/0)
Games	*Army & Navy Catalogue*, 1907	Poker Dice		2	6 (set of five)
		Roulette Board	1	5	0 (12 inch)
		Brass Roulette Rake		3	0
		Bacton Board Game with Balls	3	3	0
		Game of Shuvette		14	0
Sports Equipment		Four Golf Clubs and Bag	1	9	3
		Golf Balls	1	4	0 (dozen)
		12ft. Billiards Table with Balls and Cues	109	10	0
		14ft. Spruce Dinghy	23	5	0
		Football		10	0

Tobacco Products

Item	Source	Description	Price £	s.	d.
Cigarettes	*Army & Navy Catalogue*, 1907	W.D. & H.O. Wills, Three Castles		15	0 (1000, in tins of 50)
		Ogden's Guinea Gold		13	6 (1000, in tins of 50)
		Virginia Mild	1	7	0 (1000)
Tobacco		Army & Navy Evening Glow Mixture		3	6 (1lb. sold in ¼ lb. tin)
		Lambert & Butlers Gold Flake		3	(1lb. sold in ¼ lb. tin)
		J. Player & Sons Navy Mixture		3	0 (1lb. sold in ¼ lb. tin)
Cigars		Army & Navy Mexican & Havana Blend		14	9 (100)
		Darvel Bay Aguilas	1	2	6 (100)
Cigarettes	*Tatler*, 1909	Turkish Cigarettes		9	0 (up to 11/0 per 100)
		Black Cat			3 (10)

Continued

1.4.3 Prices, Selected *continued*

Item	Source	Description	Price		
			£	s.	d.
Cigarettes *cont.*	*Scottish CWS Ltd*, 1911	Virginia Cigarettes		6	0 (per lb.)
Cigars		Lord Byron Havanas	1	6	6 (100)
Cheroots		Compania General Manila		17	0 (100)
Snuffs		Princes Mixture		3	11 (lb.)
		Irish Blarney		5	2 (lb.)
Pipes		Horse shoe, Heart and Hand, Branch Rifle		1	4 (per gross)
Toys					
Doll	*Army & Navy Catalogue*, 1909	18½ inches high Dressed Doll		6	11
Transport and Vehicles					
Bicycle	*Queen*, London, 1900	Raleigh cycle	10	0	0
		Humber cycle	10	10	0
Rail Fares	*Bradshaws ABC Railway Guide*, 1900	Manchester to London Return	1	10	11 (up to 49/0)
		Manchester to London Single		15	5½ (up to 24/6)
Vehicle	*Ford Motor Co. Archives*, 1905	Model T Ford	175	0	0
	Tatler, 1905	8 h.p. Rover Two-Seater	200	0	0
Rail Fares	*Bradshaws ABC Railway Guide*, 1905	Manchester to London Return	1	10	11 (up to 49/0)
		Manchester to London Single		15	5½ (up to 24/6)
Bicycle	*Army & Navy Catalogue*, 1907	Standard Raleigh Bicycle (Ladies or Gents)	8	10	0
		Triumph Standard Gentleman's	6	15	0
		Triumph Standard Lady's	7	0	0
		Rudge-Whitworth Gentleman's Tricycle	16	13	0
		Rudge-Whitworth Lady's Tricycle	17	2	0
		Army & Navy Juvenile Boys Bicycle	5	17	6
		Army & Navy Juvenile Girls Bicycle	6	0	0
Rail Fares	*Tatler*, 1909	London to Brighton Return		12	9 (first class)
		London to Isle of Wight Return	1	1	6 (first class)
	Bradshaws ABC Railway Guide, 1910	Manchester to London Return	1	10	11 (up to 49/0)
		Manchester to London Single		15	5½ (up to 24/6)
Motor Bike	*Army & Navy Catalogue*, 1911	Triumph 3½ h.p. Roadster	48	15	0
Travel					
Tourism	*Bradshaws ABC Railway Guide*, 1900	Manchester to Isle of Man (Train and Steamer)		18	0 (first class)
	Thomas Cook Archives, 1900	Week Tour of Lucerne, Switzerland	5	5	0 (from London)
		Week in the English Lakes	6	0	0 (inc. travel and hotel)
		Fortnight in Isle of Man	5	10	0 (from London)
	Thomas Cook Archives, 1903	27 Day Excursion to Port Florence via Mombasa	7	6	0 (first class)
		27 Day Excursion from London to Entebbe	50	2	9 (first class)
	Thomas Cook Archives, 1913	Week Tour of Lucerne	5	5	0 (from London)
		10 Day Tour to Medieval Chateaux of France	7	5	0
		7 Day Tour of Paris or Brussels	7	7	0

Continued

1.4.3 Prices, Selected *continued*

Item	Source	Description	Price £	s.	d.
Miscellany					
Luggage	*Bradshaws ABC Railway Guide*, 1900	Finigans Gladstone Bag in Heavy Leather 26 inches	4	4	0
Timber (per foot)	*Producer*, 1916	Birch		2	0 (before war)
		Oak		3	0
		Walnut		3	9
		Mahogany			4 (up to 6)
		Pine			3
Upholstery Material (per yard)		Moquette		4	0
		Velvet		3	0
		Flocks (per ton)	12	0	0

1.4.4 Prices, Miscellaneous

1.4.4a Rents for Accommodation

Location	Price range
Birmingham	3s. 6d. to 5s.
Bristol	4s. 0d. to 5s.
Leeds	3s. 6d. to 4s. 6d.
Manchester	4s. 6d. to 5s. 6d.
Newcastle	5s. 3d. to 6s. 6d.
Sheffield	3s. 9d. to 4s. 6d.
Taunton	3s. 6d. to 4s. 6d.
London	6s. 0d. to 9s.

Hunt, E.H. *Regional Wage Variations in Britain 1850–1914*, Clarendon Press, 1973.
Rents are for three rooms in 1905, except for Bristol and Taunton figures which are for four rooms.

1.4.4b Manchester Corporation Tramways: Comparative Table

Year	Traffic Receipts £	Working Costs £	Car Mileage Miles	Revenue per Car Mile d.	Working Costs per Car Mile d./mile	Passengers Carried
1909	774,035	508,072	17,316,753	10.72	7.04	155,011,884
1910	777,219	511,070	17,161,774	10.86	7.14	159,049,096
1911	810,094	519,142	17,367,200	11.19	7.17	165,800,077
1912	856,789	530,069	18,076,999	11.37	7.04	174,424,237
1913	887,647	557,738	18,768,259	11.35	7.13	187,675,183

Garcke Manual of Electrical Undertakings and Directory of Officials, 1913.

1.5 Finance and Economic Data

1.5.1 Finance, Personal

	1900	1901	1902	1903	1904	1905	1906	1907	1908	1909	1910	1911	1912	1913
	s. d.	s. d.	s. d.	s. d.	s. d.	s. d.	s. d.	s. d.	s. d.	s. d.	s. d.	s. d.	s. d.	s. d.
Income Tax Rates[1]	8	1 0	1 2	1 3	11	1 0	1 0	1 0	1 0	1 0	1 2	1 2	1 2	1 2
Old Age Pension[2]									5 0	5 0	5 0	5 0	5 0	5 0
Basic Interest Rate in percent[3]	5%	5%	3½%	3½%	4%	3%	4%	5%	6%	3%	4%	4%	5%	5%

Mitchell, B.R. *British Historical Statistics*, Cambridge University Press, 1988; Bank of England; CWS People's Year Book.

[1]Standard rate in the pound. The rates apply to years ended 5th April. [2]The old age pension was introduced in 1908. [3]The rates apply to January of each year.

1.5.2 Financial Markets

1.5.2a Highest Closing Price of UK Major Stocks[1]

	1910	1911	1912	1913
Barclays Bank				9⅛
Boots the Chemist	42/6	41/6	41/0	42/0
Burmah Oil	6¾	4⁵⁄₃₂	3²⁹⁄₃₂	3¹⁵⁄₁₆
Courtaulds				37/0
Guinness	480⅝	458¾	410	387½
Lever Brothers	11⅝	11¹¹⁄₁₆	11¾	11⁹⁄₁₆
Reckitt and Sons	87¹¹⁄₂	5¹⁄₃₂	6¹⁄₃₂	5⁹⁄₃₂
Schweppes			26/9	27/0
Viyella	14	12¼	10¹¹⁄₁₆	9½
Whitbread and Co.	60¾	64½	59¾	63½

Mathieson, F.C. and Sons, *Stock Exchanges Ten Year Record of Prices and Dividends*.

[1]Fractions are quoted as parts of £1=32. Blank space denotes no available data.

1.5.2b Commodities

	Best Coal (price per ton)		Raw Cotton (price per lb.)	Gold (average market)	Sugar (annual average world prices)	Wheat (per imperial quarter)		Wool (average import value per lb.)
	s.	d.	old pence (d.)	£ per troy oz.	£ sterling per metric ton	s.	d.	pence per lb.
1900	23	6	5.50	3.887	12.221	26	11	9.5
1901	20	0	4.75	3.887	10.417	26	9	7.5
1902	18	6	4.88	3.887	7.874	28	1	7.5
1903	16	6	6.03	3.892	9.268	26	9	8.3
1904	16	3	6.60	3.887	10.827	28	4	8.7
1905	15	6	5.09	3.887	12.139	29	8	9.3
1906	16	6	5.95	3.887	9.760	28	3	10.2
1907	19	9	6.55	3.887	10.335	30	7	10.3
1908	18	0	5.72	3.892	11.237	32	0	9.3
1909	17	6	6.33	3.887	11.647	36	11	9.5
1910	17	3	8.00	3.887	12.958	31	8	10.2
1911	17	9	7.04	3.887	13.370	31	8	10.0
1912	21	9	6.45	3.887	12.795	34	9	9.9
1913	21	6	7.01	3.887	10.252	31	8	10.3

Mitchell, B.R. *British Historical Statistics*, Cambridge University Press, 1988· World Gold Council; Czarnikow Sugar.

Original source, Sauerbeck, A. *Prices of Commodities and the Precious Metals, Journal of the Statistical Society.*

1.5.2c Foreign Exchange Rates

	Hamburg[1] Marks per £1	Paris Francs per £1	New York Dollars per £1
1900	20.72	25.38	4.872
1901	20.62	25.35	4.879
1902	20.61	25.33	4.876
1903	20.63	25.36	4.868
1904	20.61	25.33	4.872
1905	20.62	25.31	4.866
1906	20.71	25.37	4.857
1907	20.78	25.43	4.867
1908	20.66	25.32	4.868
1909	20.66	25.36	4.876
1910	20.71	25.45	4.868
1911	20.71	25.49	4.866
1912	20.75	25.50	4.870
1913	20.78	25.56	4.868

Mitchell, B.R. *British Historical Statistics*, Cambridge University Press, 1988

[1] Berlin from 1909.

1.5.3 Balance of Payments and GNP

1.5.3a Balance of Payments

	Merchandise Exports[1]	Merchandise Imports	Overall Visible Balance	Exports of Services	Imports of Services	Property Income from Abroad[2]	Property Income Paid Abroad[3]	Balance of Current Transfers	Overall Invisible Balance	Overall Current Balance[4]
	£m	£m	£m	£m	£m	£m	£m	£m	£m	£m
1900	356	485	-129	111	50	112	8	-2	+163	+34
1901	349	485	-136	109	55	115	9	-5	+155	+19
1902	350	491	-141	110	46	119	10	-8	+165	+24
1903	361	505	-144	118	38	122	10	-5	+187	+43
1904	372	512	-140	120	39	124	11	-2	+192	+52
1905	409	527	-118	126	40	135	12	-3	+206	+88
1906	462	568	-106	139	43	148	14	-3	+227	+121
1907	519	603	-84	152	46	160	16	-4	+246	+162
1908	457	550	-93	140	46	168	17	-2	+243	+150
1909	470	581	-111	145	47	175	17	-3	+253	+142
1910	536	632	-96	155	51	189	19	-4	+270	+174
1911	559	634	-75	156	51	197	20	-3	+279	+204
1912	600	694	-94	168	54	209	22	-4	+297	+203
1913	637	719	-82	179	58	224	24	-4	+317	+235

Mitchell, B.R. *British Historical Statistics*, Cambridge University Press, 1988

[1]Including re-exports. [2]Net of foreign taxes paid by UK residents. [3]Net of taxes paid by non-residents. [4]Equals net investment abroad plus acquisition of gold and foreign exchange reserves.

1.5.3b GNP at Factor Cost and Its Component Incomes at Current Prices

	Income from Employment	Income from Self Employment	Gross Trading Profits of Companies[1]	Gross Trading Surplus of Public Enterprises[1]	Rent[2]	Gross Domestic Product	Net Property Income from Abroad	Gross National Product	Capital Consumption	National Income
	£m	£m	£m	£m	£m	£m	£m	£m	£m	£m
1900	909	322	229	8	209	1,677	104	1,781	96	1,685
1901	908	304	216	8	213	1,649	106	1,755	96	1,659
1902	899	315	224	10	217	1,665	109	1,774	97	1,677
1903	908	287	209	11	221	1,636	112	1,748	98	1,650
1904	893	286	205	14	225	1,623	113	1,736	100	1,636
1905	913	311	230	13	227	1,694	123	1,817	103	1,714
1906	952	334	260	14	230	1,790	134	1,924	109	1,815
1907	1,008	350	274	15	233	1,880	144	2,024	115	1,909
1908	975	313	245	15	235	1,783	151	1,934	114	1,820
1909	987	317	249	17	237	1,807	158	1,965	116	1,849
1910	1,027	332	265	17	239	1,880	170	2,050	120	1,930
1911	1,065	358	278	18	243	1,962	177	2,139	125	2,014
1912	1,114	371	314	21	246	2,066	187	2,253	134	2,119
1913	1,162	372	332	20	249	2,133	200	2,333	141	2,192

Mitchell, B.R. *British Historical Statistics*, Cambridge University Press, 1988.

[1]Before providing for depreciation and stock appreciation. [2]Including the imputed charge for consumption of non-trading capital, which was not identified separately prior to the 1977 Blue book. The figures are for before providing for depreciation.

1.6 Miscellaneous

1.6.1 Life Assurance Figures, 1906

	Prudential	Refuge	Pearl	Britannic	
	£	£	£	£	
Industrial Life Insurance					
Premiums	6,499,028	1,429,794	1,297,485	871,516	
Interest	873,432	40,513	61,655	47,151	
Income	7,372,460	1,470,307	1,359,140	918,667	
Claims and Surrenders	2,376,863	599,110	457,556	386,380	
Commission and Expenses	2,640,436	702,013	584,993	370,033	
Total Premiums					10,097,823
Total Interest					1,022,751
Paid Policyholders					3,819,909
Paid Management Expenses					4,297,475
Ordinary Life Assurance					
Premiums	4,290,271	589,317	217,643	174,019	
Interest	1,131,980	89,034	36,159	25,920	
Claims and Surrenders	2,285,129	193,493	52,879	89,150	
Expenses and Commission	373,556	58,931	31,176	35,636	
Total Premiums					5,271,252
Total Interest					1,283,093
Paid Policyholders					2,620,651
Paid Expenses and Commission					499,299

Cooperative Wholesalers Society Ltd. Annual, 1908, p. 229+.

1.6.2 Accommodation and Travel Prices

	Five Days			One Week		
	£	s.	d.	£	s.	d.
Third Class (via Dieppe)	3	16	11	4	16	9
Third Class (via Folkestone)	4	1	1	5	0	11
Second Class (via Dieppe)	4	3	11	5	3	9
Second Class (via Folkestone)	4	13	1	5	12	11

The Wheatsheaf, July, 1900, p. 2.

Prices are for Cooperators to the Paris Exhibition of 1903. If three or four more persons occupied the same room, the price would have been 17s. 6d. less per person for a five day visit and £1 1s. less per person for a week's visit.

– Two–
1914–1918

The Carnage and the Peace

PRIME MINISTERS
Herbert Asquith (Coalition), May 1915–December 1916
David Lloyd George (Coalition), December 1916–January 1919

CHANCELLORS OF THE EXCHEQUER
R. McKenna, May 1915–December 1916
A. Bonar Law, December 1916–January 1919

Britain declared war on Germany on 4th August 1914, officially because Germany had violated a joint treaty obligation to respect the neutrality of Belgium. However other reasons also came into play: it was Britain's traditional defence strategy to make sure that the low countries were not dominated by a hostile power; the naval agreements with France made it morally necessary to stand by the French in case of war; and finally a deep-rooted fear of German naval power impelled Britain to avoid isolation in a world of international fear and tension.

However, the immense loss of life and expenditure on munitions during 1915 brought home to the British public that this was an entirely different kind of war. The concept of *total warfare*, in which professional fighting men were the spearhead and the framework for an all-out national effort in a life or death struggle, was too new to be easily accepted. At first, Britain, like most other nations involved in the war estimated the fighting would be over in six months but no-one anticipated the political deadlock that followed. War of this kind had not happened before.

There were an unprecedented number of deaths and casualties. Britain and the member countries of the Empire lost 1.1 million men and women; 1.5 million people from France and its colonies died; and some 2 million Germans were killed. Between 1914 and 1917 Russia experienced almost as many losses as all of the Allies put together.

On the political front, Asquith's Coalition Government (a mixture of Conservative and Liberal Party politicians) struggled to control these cataclysmic events. A century of near peace had not prepared the British political (or military) machine for this kind of situation. Asquith was a skilled parliamentarian but was unfit in both temperament and experience to conduct a war. At the end of 1916 Asquith was ousted from power by David Lloyd George. The change was justified by the need to reorganize the central machinery of government. Lloyd George created the War Cabinet to simplify decision making and shorten lines of responsibility. A much closer relationship developed between the political decision-makers and the senior military leaders, presided over by the Prime Minister. On the whole, David Lloyd George was responsible for the machinery and the development of central government during this period.

Once victory had been achieved by the Allies (the German Kaiser abdicated on 9th November 1918 and an armistice was signed two days later) the cost of war proved much greater than had originally been envisaged in 1914. Throughout the war years taxes met less than 30 per cent of the Government's expenditure. Loans were raised on unnecessarily expensive terms. Until the last 18 months of the war financial policy was highly inflationary in its effects. When the war ended purchasing power was roughly one-third of what it had been in 1914. The price of victory continued during the post-war years: in heavy taxes, economic tensions and crises, and international frictions.

The war had interrupted the natural path of social change. While, temporarily at least, bringing more women in the labour force, it also helped to contract the process of natural thought and intellectual development. The highly successful use of propaganda and the promotion of nationalism helped to introduce a spirit of conformity and an intolerance of individuality and of social and cultural deviation.

2.1 Historical Snapshots

2.1 Historical Snapshots

1914	First World War begins.
	Suspension of Gold Standard by Britain.
	20,000 builders go on strike.
	Railway and mine workers join builders on strike.
	Two million workers are now unemployed.
	First bomb is dropped on the city of London.
1915	London Stock Exchange, closed since the start of the war, reopens for trading.
	Women first employed on permanent staff at Scotland Yard.
	Einstein completes his general theory of relativity.
1916	Two million more women are employed now than a year ago.
1917	Call for the decimalisation of British currency.
1918	All men over 21 and women over 30 get the vote.
	London County and Westminster Bank announces merger with Parr's Bank as Westminster Bank.
	Government announces rationing of coal, gas and electricity.
	War ends leaving the UK with war debts of £7,100 m.

Chronicle of Britain, J.L. International Publishing, 1992.

2.2 Earnings and Employment

2.2.1 Earnings, Standard Table

2.2.1a Incomes and Wages

	1914	1915	1916	1917	1918
Police Constable					30–40s
Train Driver	40 s. 6d.				
Fitter	38 11				
Turner	38 11				
Bricklayer	40 7				
Bricklayers' Labourer	27 0	5s.5d.[1]	6s.0d.[1]	6s.11d.[1]	7s.11d.[1]
Compositor	35 8				
Farm Worker	16 9			30 6	
Baker	30 1				
Cotton Weaver	1 8 (f)				

British Labour Statistics 1886–1968, HMSO, 1971; Bowley, A.L. *Wages and Incomes in the UK since 1860*, Cambridge University Press, 1937; Brown, H.P.and Hopkins S.V. *Seven Centuries of Building Wages*, *Economica 22*, 1955; Routh, G. *Occupation and Pay in Great Britain 1906-1979*, Macmillan Press, 1980.

Blank space denotes no data available. Wages are weekly unless otherwise stated. [1]The figures are per 10 hours. (f) – female.

2.2.2 Regional Earnings by Selected Occupation

		London	Manchester	Newcastle	Leeds	Glasgow
		s. d.	s. d.	s. d.	s. d.	s. d.
Bricklayer (hourly)	1914	11½	10½	10	10	10½
Bricklayer's Labourer (hourly)	1914	8	6½	6¾	7	6½
Compositor (weekly)	1914	39 0	38 6	36 6	37 0	38 0
Fitter and Turner (weekly)	1914	40 0 or 40 6	39 0	n/a	n/a	38 3

British Labour Statistics 1886-1968, HMSO, 1971.

2.2.3 Incomes, Miscellaneous

2.2.3a Earnings in the Textile Trades

Trades	Lads and Boys		Women		Girls	
	s.	d.	s.	d.	s.	d.
Cotton	11	6	18	8	10	1
Woollen and Worsted	8	10	13	10	8	4
Linen	7	8	10	9	6	7
Jute	10	11	13	5	9	8
Silk	8	2	11	2	6	4
Hosiery	9	5	14	3	7	9
Lace	12	8	13	5	7	1
Fustian and Cord Cutting	9	8	10	10	8	1
Bleaching and Dyeing	10	8	12	4	8	2
Dress and Millinery	9	11	15	5	6	4
Tailoring (Ready Made)	8	11	11	10	5	1
Tailoring (Bespoke)	6	11	14	2	5	5
Shirt, Blouse, Underclothing	8	9	13	4	6	9
Boot and Shoe	10	4	12	4	6	9
Silk Hat and Felt Hat	12	7	16	4	7	8
Dyeing and Cleaning	10	7	13	10	7	2
Laundry (factory)	8	9	12	10	6	6
Laundry (workshop)	9	4	12	9	6	7

CWS Annual 1915, p.429.

Earnings are weekly for 1914.

2.2.3b Wages for John Brown and Co., Shipbuilders

Year	Average Number of Men per Week	Average Pay Bill			Average Wages per Man per Week		
		£	s.	d.	£	s.	d.
1914	9,260	16,947	16	2	1	16	7
1915	10,088	24,050	4	2	2	7	8
1916	10,031	24,166	8	6	2	8	2
1917	9,444	25,868	6	5	2	14	9
1918	9,209	32,894	10	4	3	11	5

Business History, Vol. XIX, No.2, July, 1977, p. 204.

Compiled from *Abstract Wages Books, John Brown & Co., Clydebank, 1914-1938*.

2.2.4 Employment

	Membership at end of June of unions reporting figures	Percentage Unemployed	
		Mean for Year %	End of December, %
1914	993,000	3.3	2.5
1915	922,000	1.1	0.6
1916	939,000	0.4	0.3
1917	950,000	0.7	1.4
1918	1,117,000	0.8	1.2

The People's Year Book, 1922, p. 257.

Figures are for those entitled to claim unemployment benefit. Original source, *21st Abstract of Labour Statistics*.

2.3 Consumer Expenditure

2.3.1 Consumer Expenditure, Standard Table

	Food	Alcoholic Drink	Tobacco	Housing	Fuel and Light	Clothing	Durable Household Goods	Motor Cars and Motor Cycles	Other Goods	Other Services	Total Consumer Expenditure
	£m	£m	£m	£m	£m	£m	£m	£m	£m	£m	£m
1914	557	188	42	224	74	173	77	9	131	526	2,074
1915	724	179	49	227	83	193	84	4	151	538	2,384
1916	846	207	57	227	100	169	81	1	177	531	2,581
1917	1,012	201	65	229	108	212	105	1	211	564	2,979
1918	1,132	232	80	237	122	364	141	3	273	683	3,600

Mitchell, B.R. *British Historical Statistics*, Cambridge University Press, 1988.

Original source, Feinstein, C.H. *National Income, Expenditure and Output of the UK, 1855-1965*, Cambridge, 1972.

2.4 Prices

2.4.1 Food Prices

2.4.1a Food Basket

Article (per lb. unless otherwise stated)	July, 1914 s.	d.
Beef, home-killed:		
Ribs		10
Thin flank		6½
Beef, chilled or frozen:		
Ribs		7¼
Thin flank		4¾
Mutton, home-killed:		
Legs		10½
Breast		6½
Mutton, frozen:		
Legs		6¾
Breast		4
Bacon, streaky		11¼
Flour (per 7lb.)		10½
Bread (per 4lb.)		5¾
Tea	1	6¼
Sugar, granulated		2
Milk (per quart)		3½
Butter:		
Fresh	1	2½
Salt	1	2¼
Cheese		8
Margarine		7
Eggs, fresh (each)		1¼
Potatoes (per 7lb.)		4¾

British Labour Statistics, 1886–1968, HMSO, 1971.

The table was compiled from information supplied for the "Cost of Living Index" by over 5,000 retailers in approximately 500 towns.

2.4.1b Comparison of Food Prices

	1867		1917	
	s.	d.	s.	d.
Currants		4	1	4
Candy Peel		10	1	2
Coffee	1	6	1	10
Best Sugar		5½		6½
Golden Syrup		3	1	2
Tea	2s.–3s.4d.		2s.–3s.8d.	
Butter	1	3	2	5
Cheese		10	1	4
Rice		3		8
Ham		10	2	2
Sago		3½		9
Tapioca		5		9

The Producer, November 19th, 1917, p. 4.

Original source *Jubilee Volume of Coventry Cooperative Society*. Prices for 1917 taken from a grocery bill.

2.4.1c Food Prices Before and During the War

Article (per lb. unless otherwise stated)	Before the War		January 1, 1917	
	s.	d.	s.	d.
Milk (quart)		4		5½
Potatoes (20lb.)		10	2	6
Eggs (each)		2		4
Beef, lean		10	1	4
Mutton		9	1	2
Pork, fat		7½	1	2
Cheese, Cheddar		8½	1	2
Lentils		2½		4
Peas		3½		6
Haricot Beans		3		5

The Producer, February 15th, 1917, p. 113.

Prices taken from Burton-on-Trent Cooperative Society.

2.4.1d Regional Grocery Prices

Article (per lb. unless otherwise stated)	Glasgow s.	d.	Bradford s.	d.	Alloa s.	d.	West Riding s.	d.	Midlands s.	d.	Ipswich s.	d.
Bread		3¼		4		2¼		4		1½		2¾
Flour		2⅛		n/a	10	(7lb.)		2½		6		2
Cheese	1	0		10		10		10		9		8
Butter	1	8	1	6	1	3	1	5	1	4	1	1
Bacon	1	4		11½		n/a	1	0		10		10
Currants		6		5		6		5		4		4
Rice		1½		3		n/a		3		2		2
Oatmeal		1⅞		1¾		1¾		2		2		n/a
Tea	1	6	2	4	2	2	2	4	1	4	1	8
Cocoa	1	4	1	8		n/a	3	0	1	4		n/a
Sugar		1¾		2¼		2¼		2¼		2		1¾
Jam		6½		6		8	1	0		11		4½
Lard		6		n/a		7		8½		9		8
Eggs (per dozen)	1	10		n/a	1	4		n/a		n/a		n/a
Potatoes (stone)		n/a		6½		8		n/a		n/a		9
Meat		10	5	10 (7lb.)		10		11		8		8
Milk (per pint)		1¾	2	0½ (quart)		1½		4		1½		2
Coal (2 cwt)	1	0	2	5		n/a	22	0 (ton)	1	0	2	0
Soap		3½		n/a		n/a		3½		3½		3

The Producer, April, 1923, p.166+.

Prices taken from Cooperative Societies in Glasgow, Bradford, Alloa, West Riding, Midlands and Ipswich in 1914.

2.4.1e Regional Cost of Bread

Place	Cooperative Prices OTC	Dlvd	Place	Cooperative Prices OTC	Dlvd	Place	Cooperative Prices OTC	Dlvd
London	8½	9	Liverpool	9	9	Wolverhampton	8½	8½
Birmingham	9	9½	Manchester	9	9	Aberdeen	9	9
Bristol	9	9	Middlesbrough	9	9	Dundee	9	9½
Cardiff	8½	9	Norwich	9	9	Edinburgh	9	9
Derby	9	9½	Nottingham	9	9	Glasgow	9	9
Ipswich	9	9	Portsmouth	9	9	Belfast	9	9½
Leeds	9	9	Southampton	8½	9	Dublin	8½	9
Leicester	9	9	Stoke-on-Trent	9	9			

The Producer, October 15th, 1917, p. 397.

On September 17th, 1917, the sale of bread at the controlled maximum price of 9d. for cash over the counter began. This table was compiled by *The Producer* and the places selected are those which appear in the *Labour Gazette*. OTC – Over the counter price; Dlvd – Delivered price.

2.4.2 Prices, General Articles

	1914		1915		1916		1917		1918	
	s.	d.	s.	d.	s.	d.	s.	d.	s.	d.
Aspirin										
Beer (1 pint as served in a public bar)		3		3		3		3		3
Cheddar Cheese (1 lb.)			1	0						
Daily Mail		½		½		½		½		½
Guinness Extra Stout (1 pint of bottled/draught)				4						
Inland Letter Post		1		1		1		1		1½
Pears Transparent Soap	1	0	1	0	1	0	1	0	1	0
Petrol (1 gallon)	2	1					4	1		
Red Label Tea (1 lb.)			2	0						
Scotch Whisky (standard bottle)									9	0
Swan Vestas Matches (100)		1		1		1½		1½		1½
The Times		3		3		3		3		3

The Boots Company; British Library; Burmah Castrol; Colmans of Norwich; Guinness Brewing GB; Royal Mail; Sainsbury's Archives; The Scotch Whisky Association; Unilever Historical Archives.

Blank space denotes no prices available.

2.4.3 Prices, Selected

Item	Source	Description	Price		
			£	s.	d.
Baby Equipment					
Prams	*Bradshaws ABC Railway Guide*, 1915	Baby Cars, "The Roma"	2	10	0
Clothing and Footwear:					
Children's					
Coat	*Harrods Elegancies and Economies*, 1915	Useful Coat for the Little Girl of 6–12 years	1	5	6
Vest		Children's Vest in Fine Ribbed Wool		1	9½ (up to 3/0)
Frock	*Harrods*, London, 1917	School Girl's Useful Frock in Stripes and Plaids		12	6
Coat	*D.H. Evans & Co.*, 1918	Girl's Warm Tweed Coat	4	17	6
Suit		Boy's School Suit in Dependable Tweeds	3	5	0 (upwards depending on size)
Shirt		Negligee Shirts in Union Flannel		12	6 (up to 17/6)
Raincoat	*Civil Service Supply Association*, 1918	Boy's Raincoat	1	12	0
Shoes		Child's Walking Shoes		10	9 (up to 14/9)
Men's					
Suit	*Bradshaws ABC Railway Guide*, 1915	Beaty Bros Summer Suits in Cheviot Fine Worsteds	2	5	0 (up to 52/6)
	Civil Service Supply Association, 1918	Men's Lounge Suit	2	16	0
Raincoat		Men's Raincoat	2	7	6
Jacket		Men's Sports Jacket	1	11	6
Women's					
Shoes	*C & J Clark Ltd.*, 1915	Ladies Wessex Shoe in Glacé Kid		5	9
		Ladies Glacé One Bar		4	9
		Dancing Sandal in Glacé Kid		4	2
	Harrods Elegancies and Economies, 1915	Patent Walking Shoe	1	10	0
Socks		Knitted Scotch Woolley		3	11
Stockings		Pure Silk Stockings		3	11
Shoes	*Harvey Nichols & Co Ltd*, London, 1915	Smart Canvas Tennis Shoes	1	1	9
Skirt		Soft Black Satin Skirt	6	6	0
Socks		Fine Silk Wool Hose in Black and Shades of Grey		7	6
		Plain Black Cashmere Hose		4	6 (up to 4/11)
Hat		Practical Felt Hat	1	1	9
Umbrella		Coloured Umbrella	1	17	6
Coat	*Harrods*, Spring, 1917	Blanket Coat in Spring Colours	3	3	0
Skirt		Useful Skirt for Any Occasion	2	9	6
Suit		Smoothly Cut Walking Suit in Worsted Suiting	5	5	0
Blouse	*D.H. Evans & Co.*, London, 1918	Silk Georgette Blouse	1	9	6
Laces		Best Quality Silk Mixture Shoe Laces		3	3 (up to 3/6 doz.)
Shoes		Tan Willow Calf Oxford Shoes	2	5	9
Socks		Cashmere Half Hose Socks		4	6 (up to 4/11)
Wrap		Fleecy Wool Motor Wrap		18	6
Bag	*Civil Service Supply Association*, 1918	Shopping Bag		7	9
Boots		Ladies Glacé Button boots	1	13	0 (up to 36/9)
Case		Ladies Blouse Case in Brown Leather	2	8	0

Continued

2.4.3 Prices, Selected *continued*

Item	Source	Description	£	s.	d.
Handbag		Dainty Handbag in Morocco Leather	1	11	0
Handkerchiefs		Ladies Hemstitched Embroidered		2	6 (for 6)
Shirt		Useful Shirt in Washed Jap Silk		16	6
Umbrella		Fox's Paragon Frame, Pure Silk Bordered Cover	1	13	0
Boots	*Dickins & Jones*, c1919	Black Cloth Top Boots	3	15	0
Gloves		Ladies Fur Gloves	1	19	6
Food Products					
Bacon	*J Sainsbury Archives*, 1917	Bacon, Unsmoked Back		1	2
Bread	*Producer*, 1917	4lb. Loaf			8½
Butter	*J Sainsbury Archives*, 1917	Loose Butter		1	4 (lb.)
Cheese		Cheddar Cheese		1	0 (lb.)
Eggs	*Producer*, 1917	Medium Size			6 (each)
Beans		Haricot Beans			5 (lb.)
Lentils		Red Lentils			4 (lb.)
Milk		Milk			5½ (quart)
Mutton		Mutton		1	2 (lb.)
Peas		Peas			6 (lb.)
Potatoes		Red Potatoes		2	6 (lb.)
Tea	*J Sainsbury Archives*, 1917	Red Label Tea		2	0 (lb.)
Heat and Light					
Electricity	*CWS Annual*	Electricity per unit			3½
Gas		Gas per therm			2
Coal		Coal per ton	1	6	2½
Hotel Rates					
St. Catherine's Private Hotel, Cornwall	*Bradshaws ABC Railway Guide*, 1915	Dinner, Bed and Breakfast	2	5	0
Warne's Hotel, Worthing		All inclusive		10	6 (a day)
Household Goods					
Towels	*Producer*, 1914	Turkish Towels		4	6 (per doz.)
Tablecloth		Bleached Linen Tablecloth		4	6
Cloths		Typed Kitchen Cloths		4	8 (per doz.)
Bedding		Plain Pillow Cases		3	3 (per doz.)
		Wool Blankets		15	6 (pair)
	D.H. Evans & Co., Manchester, 1918	Fine Cotton Sheets (72in. x 3 yds.)	1	12	6 (pair)
		White Cotton Bedspread		16	9 (up to 21/6)
Tablecloth		Irish Damask Tablecloth 54in. x 54in.		7	6
Towels		White Bath Towels with Wide Hem Ends		2	3½ (up to 4/11)
Hot Water Bottles		Hot Water Bottles with Cover		4	9 (up to 5/11)
Cutlery	*Pryce & Jones*, 1918	Handsome Case containing 6 Silver Handled Knives		1	0
		Xylonite Handles, Rustless Steel Blades Knives		2	6 6 (per doz.)

Continued

2.4.3 Prices, Selected *continued*

Item	Source	Description	Price £	s.	d.
Cutlery *cont.*		Case of Afternoon Tea Spoons and Tongs in Silver	1	12	0
		Jam Spoon and Butter Knife in Silver		3	9 (each)
		Hard White Nickel Forks		13	6 (per doz.)
Jar		Wedgewood Heather China Biscuit Jar	1	1	0
Cake Basket		Silver Plated Cake Basket	1	4	6
Teapot		1½ Pint Teapot	1	15	6
Coffee Pot		Silver Plated Coffee Pot	1	16	0
Houses					
Houses	*CWS Annual*, 1918	New House in Scotland	350	0	0
Solicitor's Fees		For the first £1000	1	0	0
Jewellery					
Watch	*Pryce & Jones*, 1918	Swiss Silver Watch 10 Jewels	2	5	9
		Ingersoll Waterbury Regular Dial		18	6
		Ingersoll Junior	1	0	0
Ring		Ladies Dress Ring in Gold	2	5	0
		Ladies Dress Ring with Real Opals	2	5	0
Brooch		9 ct. Gold Brooch		14	9
Bracelet		9 ct. Gold Curb Flexible Bracelet	1	18	6
Pendant		9 ct. Gold Pendant		10	0
		9 ct. Gold Pendant with Peridots and 12 Pearls	1	11	0
Hat Pin		Silver Mounted Hat Pin and Ring Stand		5	6
Vase		Solid Silver Vase		7	3
Personal Care Items					
Soap	*Unilever Archives*, 1915	Pears Wash Balls No 1 Size			8 (each)
		Pears Oval Tablets No 1 Size			8 (each)
Shaving Stick		Pears Round Shaving Cakes No 1 Size			8 (each)
		Pears Round Shaving Stick			8 (each)
Hairdressing	*Harrods*, London, 1917	Haircutting		5	0
		Hair Dyeing	1	1	0
		Henna Shampooing		5	6
Beauty Treatment		Manicure		1	0
Cream	*Civil Service Supply Association*, 1918	Perlean Skin Cream			10½
Mirror	*Pryce & Jones*, 1918	Plain Design Silver Mirror	2	7	0
Combs		Plain Design Silver Dressing Combs		6	6
	Civil Service Supply Association, 1918	Real Horn Combs		1	11½ (each)
		Pretty Black Comb		3	3
Publications					
Books	*Producer*, 1917	Low's New Novels		2	6
		Jeffery Farnol's Popular Works		2	0
		The Exploitation of Plants		2	6
		The Cooperative Movement in Russia		2	6

Continued

2.4.3 Prices, Selected *continued*

Item	Source	Description	Price £	s.	d.
Services					
Cinema	*Producer*, 1917	Admission Price to the Electric Cinema			4 (up to 10d.)
					1d. (for children at Sat. Matinee)
Licence	*DVLA*, 1915	Cars to 6½ h.p.	3	3	0
		Cars to 12 h.p.	4	4	0
		Cars to 16 h.p.	6	6	0
		Cars to 26 h.p.	8	8	0
Telephone Tariffs					
London	*British Telecom Archives*, 1915	Annual Residential Rental	20	0	0
Provinces			8	0	0
London		Annual Business Rental	20	0	0
Provinces			12	0	0
7 am to 7 pm charge for 3 minutes		Up to 25 miles			4
		25 to 50 miles			8
		50 to 75 miles		1	0
		75 to 100 miles		1	4
		Each additional 40 miles			8
Parcel Postage Rates	*Post Office Archives*, 1915	1lb. weight			4
		5lb. weight			7
		10lb. weight			11
Sewing Equipment and Supplies					
Fabrics	*Producer*, 1914	50in. Casement Cloth			6⅞ (per yard)
		White Calico			4 (per yard)
		Wool Shirting		1	2 (per yard)
Haberdashery		Coats 200yds. Sewing Cotton	1	6	0 (per gross)
		Linen Buttons		7	6 (per gross)
	Civil Service Supply Association, 1918	Whitehall Bunch of Tapes			11½ (1 doz. of assorted widths)
		Gairs Perfection Patent Blouse Grip			11½
		Crescent Mending Wool			9 (per ball)
		Lippon Sleeve Protector			11½ (per pair)
		Card of Linen Buttons			9½ (per card)
		Hussifs fitted for Soldiers		2	3
		Crescent Companion Tape Measure			9
Tobacco Products					
Cigarettes	*Scottish CWS Ltd*, Glasgow, 1916	Pure Virginia		2	0 (packet of 10)
		Turkish "Queen of the Earth"		2	6 (carton of 10)
Cigars		Manilla	1	2	6 (bundles of 10)
		Merchant Gem "Whiffs"		9	2 (per lb.)
Cheroots		Manilla, Large	1	2	6 (per lb.)
		Moulmein, No 2		16	6 (per lb.)
Snuff		High Toast		6	9 (per lb.)
		Morton Mixture		5	11 (per lb.)
		London Brown		5	4 (per lb.)

Continued

2.4.3 Prices, Selected *continued*

Item	Source	Description	Price		
			£	s.	d.
Transport and Vehicles					
Bicycle	*What it Cost the Day Before Yesterday*	Bicycle	6	0	0
Car		Family Car Medium Size	200	0	0
Bus Fares		Paddington to Mansion House (4 miles)			4
	Museum of Transport, Manchester 1915	Average Length of Penny Stages 3 miles			1
Rail Fares	*Bradshaws ABC Railway Guide*, 1915	Manchester to London Return	1	10	11 (up to 49/0)
		Manchester to London Single		15	5 (up to 24/6)
Travel					
Regular Daily Sailings	*Bradshaws ABC Railway Guide*, 1915	Liverpool Belfast Service Single		12	6 (saloon)
		Liverpool Belfast Service Return	1	1	0 (saloon)
Hotel Rudyard, Staffordshire		North Staffordshire Green Fees		2	6
		Day's Fishing on Rudyard Lake		1	0
Miscellany					
Purse	*Civil Service Supply Association*, 1918	Suede Guard Purse	1	1	11½ (each)
Laces		Artificial Silk Shoe Laces			8½ (pair)
Cement	*People's Year Book*, 1918	Cement per ton	3	10	6
Lime		Lime (Buxton) per ton	1	12	6

2.4.4 Prices, Miscellaneous

2.4.4 Regional Costs of Coal

Distribution Costs (per ton)	Manchester	Newcastle	London	Total
	d.	d.	d.	d.
1914	1.8	1.5	2.8	2.0
1915	2.1	1.4	3.1	2.3
1916	2.1	1.4	3.1	2.4
1917	2.1	1.8	4.1	2.5
1918	2.4	2.1	5.4	3.1
Five Years' Average	2.1	1.6	3.6	2.4

Average Price of Coal (per ton)	s.	d.	s.	d.	s.	d.	s.	d.
1914	15	10	17	3	18	2	16	9
1915	18	4	19	0	22	9	19	10
1916	21	1	21	7	24	10	22	2
1917	22	2	22	8	25	8	23	2
1918	25	11	26	3	29	8	26	11
Five Years' Average	20	7	21	4	23	10	21	7

The Producer, April 21st, 1919, p. 130.

Figures are for CWS coal.

2.5 Finance and Economic Data

2.5.1 Finance, Personal

	1914	1915	1916	1917	1918
	s. d.	s. d.	s. d.	s. d.	s. d.
Income Tax Rates [1]	1 2	1 8	3 0	5 0	5 0
Old Age Pension	5 0	5 0	5 0	5 0	5 0
Base Interest Rates in percent [2]	4½%	5%	6% (July 13)	5½%	5%

Mitchell, B.R. *British Historical Statistics*, Cambridge University Press, 1988; Bank of England; CWS People's Year Book.

[1]The rates apply to years ended 5th April. [2]The rates apply to January of each year.

2.5.2 Financial Markets

2.5.2a Highest Closing Price of UK Major Stocks

	1914	1915	1916	1917	1918
Barclays Bank	$9^{11}/_{16}$	$9^7/_{16}$	$8^3/_8$	$7^{15}/_{16}$	$8^{1}/_2$
Boots the Chemist	42/0	38/6	35/0	35/0	34/0
Burmah Oil	$7^{95}/_{12}$	$8^5/_8$	$4^{25}/_{32}$	$7^{15}/_{16}$	$9^5/_{16}$
Courtaulds	50/0	60/3	$7^{13}/_{32}$	$7^9/_{16}$	$8^3/_8$
Guinness	390	297½	280	310	·375
Lever Brothers	$11^7/_8$	$10^{29}/_{32}$	$9^{15}/_{16}$	9½	$9^3/_8$
Reckitt and Sons	95/1½	$4^{29}/_{32}$	$4^{13}/_{16}$	107/0	$5^{27}/_{32}$
Schweppes	27/6	26/9	24/6	22/7½	23/1
Viyella	$8^{11}/_{16}$	6¼	$6^{15}/_{16}$	$6^{25}/_{32}$	8
Whitbread	65	48	53	55½	57

Mathieson, F.C. and Sons, *Stock Exchanges Ten Year Record of Prices and Dividends*.

Blank space denotes no available data. Fractions are quoted as parts of £1=32

2.5.2b Commodities

	Best Coal (price per ton)	Raw Cotton (per lb.)	Gold (average market price)	Sugar (annual average world price)	Wheat (per imperial quarter)	Wool (average import value)
	s. d.	old pence(d.)	£ per troy oz.	£ sterling per metric ton	s. d.	pence per lb.
1914	21 3	6.41	3.887	9.843[1]	34 11	10.5
1915	30 9	5.87	3.887	18.865	52 10	10.9
1916	27 6	9.00	3.887	21.407	58 5	14.6
1917	27 6	16.55	3.887	26.492	75 9	19.1
1918	33 7	22.30	3.887	24.197	72 10	21.1

Mitchell, B.R. *British Historical Statistics*, Cambridge University Press, 1988; World Gold Council; Czarnikow Sugar.

Original source, Sauerbeck, A. *Prices of Commodities and the Precious Metals, Journal of the Statistical Society*, continued annually in that journal. [1]Average Jan/July, 1914.

2.5.2c Foreign Exchange Rates

	Berlin Reichsmarks[1] per £1	Paris Francs per £1	New York Dollars per £1
1914		25.16	4.876
1915		26.51	4.748
1916		28.04	4.766
1917		27.47	4.764
1918		26.72	4.765

Mitchell, B.R. *British Historical Statistics*, Cambridge University Press, 1988.

[1]There were no dealings with Germany during the war.

2.5.3 Balance of Payments and GNP

2.5.3a Balance of Payments

	Merchandise Exports	Merchandise Imports	Overall Visible Balance	Exports of Services	Imports of Services	Property Income from Abroad	Property Income Paid Abroad	Balance of Current Transfers	Overall Invisible Balance	Overall Current Balance
	£m	£m	£m	£m	£m	£m	£m	£m	£m	£m
1914	540	660	-120	145	80	215	25	-1	+254	+134
1915	500	840	-340	250	130	190	25	n/a	+285	-55
1916	630	980	-350	370	160	230	30	+30	+440	+90
1917	620	1,040	-420	465	220	235	40	+30	+470	+50
1918	540	1,170	-630	400	230	240	65	+10	+415	-275

Mitchell, B.R. *British Historical Statistics*, Cambridge University Press, 1988.

Original source, Feinstein, C.H. *National Income, Expenditure and Output of the UK 1855-1965*, Cambridge, 1972.

2.5.3b GNP at Factor Cost and Its Component Incomes at Current Prices

	Income from Employment	Gross Trading Profits of Companies	Gross Trading Surplus of Public Enterprises	Rent	Stock Appreciation	Gross Domestic Product	Net Property Income from Abroad	Gross National Product	Capital Consumption
	£m	£m	£m	£m	£m	£m	£m	£m	£m
1914	1,260	689	21	252	50	2,172	190	2,362	145
1915	1,556	876	26	259	200	2,517	165	2,682	165
1916	1,858	1,175	31	272	350	2,986	200	3,186	198
1917	2,340	1,348	49	278	250	3,765	195	3,960	235
1918	2,881	1,482	71	281	100	4,615	175	4,790	281

Mitchell, B.R. *British Historical Statistics*, Cambridge University Press, 1988.

Original source, Feinstein, C.H. *National Income, Expenditure and Output of the UK 1855-1965*, Cambridge, 1972.

2.6 Miscellaneous

2.6.1 Post Office Savings Bank

| | Due to Depositors | Number of Accounts | | Average Accounts due to each Depositor | |
		Active	Dormant	Active	Dormant
	£	£	£	£ s. d.	£ s. d.
1914	190,533,208	9,281,370	4,233,444	20 9 8	0 2 0
1915	186,327,584	9,971,675	4,208,411	18 12 10	0 2 0
1916	196,655,159	10,555,626	4,191,195	18 11 10	0 2 0
1917	203,262,059	11,037,277	4,178,547	18 7 7	0 2 0
1918	234,633,323	11,829,651	4,168,724	19 16 0	0 2 0

Cooperative Wholesale Society People's Year Book, 1922, p. 325.

2.6.2 Trustee Savings Bank

	Due to Depositors	Number of Accounts	Average Amount due to each Depositor
	£		£ s. d.
1914	53,943,271	1,917,944	28 2 6
1915	51,412,370	1,966,730	26 2 10
1916	53,783,998	2,015,894	26 13 7
1917	52,349,367	2,046,996	25 11 6
1918	60,983,309	2,128,628	28 13 0

Cooperative Wholesale Society People's Year Book, 1922, p. 325.

See also tables 4.6.1 for 1930/37 figures and 11.6.1. for 1990/92 figures.

2.6.3 Cost of Materials and Labour in the Building Trades

Price of Building Materials	Govt. Controlled Price Oct 1918			July 1914		
	£	s.	d.	£	s.	d.
3 x 9inch Swedish A/G Redwood (per standard)	49	0	0	12	0	0
2½ x 7 inch	48	0	0	10	0	0
3 x 7 x 8 inch Spruce (per standard)	49	0	0	9	5	0
3 x 9 inch	50	0	0	9	15	0
Floorings (Swedish and Norwegian) per standard	54	0	0	11	0	0
Pitchpine 12 x 12inch, per cubic foot	0	10	0	0	2	3
Bricks (Accrington facing) per 1,000	4	7	6	2	10	0
Cement (in truck loads) per ton	3	10	6	1	17	6
Lime (Buxton) per ton	1	12	6	0	16	6

Slates, 60 to 70% increases

Glass, 100 to 200% increase

Wages in the Building Trades	Rate per Hour, Oct 1918		Rate per Hour, July 1914	
	s.	d.		s. d.
Bricklayers	1	5		10½
Masons	1	6		11
Plasterers	1	5		11
Plumbers	1	6		10
Slaters	1	5		10
Carpenters and Joiners	1	5		10½
Painters	1	5		9½
Labourers (General and Navvies)	1	2½		6½

Cooperative Wholesale Society People's Year Book, 1919, p. 197.

2.6.4 World Exchange Rates for a Sovereign

	July 30th, 1914[1]		Nov. 11th, 1918[2]		June 28th, 1919[3]		Sept. 5th, 1919	
	s.	d.	s.	d.	s.	d.	s.	d.
Argentina	19	10	18	6	18	7	17	3
Belgium	19	11	n/a		24	5	28	0
Brazil	22	11	25	10	24	7	25	0
Canada	20	4	20	0	19	6	17	9
Denmark	20	2	19	8	21	5	21	1
Finland	20	2	n/a		44	7	52	4
France	19	9	20	6	23	6	27	6
Germany	20	2	n/a		n/a		92	1
Greece	19	11	n/a		19	4	19	7
Holland	20	1	18	11	19	5	18	7
Italy	20	10	24	0	29	1	32	1
Japan	20	2	17	10	18	7	17	1
Norway	20	2	19	4	20	3	20	1
Portugal	23	8	34	4	35	6	39	9
Spain	20	7	19	1	18	5	17	6
Sweden	20	2	18	11	19	8	18	11
Switzerland	20	0	19	0	19	10	18	9
USA	20	4	19	7	18	11	17	1

Cooperative Wholesale Society People's Year Book, 1921, p. 56.

Original source, *Food Journal*. [1]Before the declaration of war. [2]At the Armistice. [3]On the signing of peace.

2.6.5 Prices of Imported Tea

	1914–15	1915–16	1916–17	1917–18	1918–19
Tea from:	d.	d.	d.	d.	d.
British East Indies	9.36	11.29	11.88	15.02	14.99
Ceylon	9.35	11.44	11.97	14.94	14.89
China	9.06	10.41	11.69	13.12	13.78
Other countries	8.83	10.70	11.43	15.35	14.63

Producer, August 16, 1920, p. 304.

Drawn from Customs and Excise.

2.6.6 Prices of Tate's Standard Granulated Sugar

	Wholesale Price		Retail Control Price per lb.		Sugar Tax per cwt.	
	s.	d.	s.	d.	s.	d.
July 30, 1914	16	4	n/a		1	10
August 12, 1914	30	0		4	1	10
October 24, 1914	30	0		4	1	10
June 11, 1917	47	1		5¾	14	0
April 22, 1918	57	9		7	25	8
November 3, 1919	66	0		8	25	8
March 22, 1920	80	0		10	25	8
May 17, 1920	112	0	1	2	25	8
November 1, 1920	96	0	1	2	25	8
November 15, 1920	96	0	1	0	25	8
November 29, 1920	80	0		10	25	8
December 27, 1920	72	0		9	25	8
February 21, 1921	67	6		9	25	8

Producer, March, 1921, p. 145.

– Three –
1919–1929

Change and Contraction

PRIME MINISTERS
David Lloyd George (Coalition), December 1916–October 1922
Stanley Baldwin (Conservative), May 1923–January 1924
J. Ramsay MacDonald (Labour), January 1924–November 1924
Stanley Baldwin (Conservative), November 1924–June 1929
J. Ramsay MacDonald (Labour), June 1929–August 1931

CHANCELLORS OF THE EXCHEQUER
A. Chamberlain, January 1919–April 1921
Sir R.S. Horne, April 1921–October 1922
S. Baldwin, October 1922–August 1923
N. Chamberlain, October 1923–January 1924
P. Snowden, January 1924–November 1924
W.S. Churchill, November 1924–June 1929

World War I forced people out of traditional and conventional patterns of peace time existence. From sleepy hamlets, comfortable suburban households, and the festering slums of the big cities, six million men had gone to fight in conditions which went far beyond their wildest nightmares. From the sheltered family environment, women had to drive trams or work in the munitions factories. Patterns of behaviour, expectations, and morals were changed by this experience. Whatever the nostalgic older generation of the time desired, these changes could never be reversed.

The years preceding the war had been marked by great industrial unrest and even violence. With the outbreak of World War I the trade unions (which had been growing gradually in membership and strength) called an industrial truce. The Government, for its part, was forced to acknowledge the vital part the working class had played in the war effort. The enforcement of arbitration in certain key industrial disputes in this period involved an unprecedented recognition of the rights and status of labour. The influence of the advance of the Labour movement can be seen in trade union membership figures which rose from 4 million in 1913, to 6.5 million in 1918, and 8.5 million in 1920.

The post-war economic boom, led by major change and development in certain sectors of the economy such as banking and transportation, reached its peak in the spring of 1920 with a fevered burst of speculation. This brief boom diverted capital away from the industries most in need of re-equipment and expansion to the traditional sectors of textiles and shipbuilding in which pre-war Britain had been most prosperous. There was insufficient development of new industries (electricity, cars, plastics, patent foods etc.). Inflation followed the boom, with prices rising quickly in 1919 and 1920. In March 1920 the price index stood at 323, against 100 in July 1914. Wages rose as well, but more slowly, and for many workers real wages declined compared with pre-war levels. The acute housing shortage continued long after Lloyd George's promise of 'homes fit for heroes'.

The subsequent crash preceded the long cycle of depression which lasted until World War II. However, there was a temporary recovery in 1923–4 when the French occupation of the Ruhr brought a cessation of German coal exports, and modest economic progress was made from 1924 to 1929. The realities of the long-term decline were, to some extent, concealed. Furthermore, the worst of the unemployment was confined to certain localized depressed areas, all far from London. The wealthy were still able to enjoy the privileges of the 'Glorious Twenties'.

The most obvious characteristic of the economic slump was the high level of unemployment. By March 1921 it had reached 1.5 million or 10 per cent of the working population. It remained at this figure throughout the twenties, until the crisis brought it up to almost 3 million in 1930. Unemployment was particularly concentrated in Lancashire, Tyneside, Cumberland, Scotland, and South Wales, where it hovered around 50 per cent or more.

The Government's economic management in the face of these pressures was profoundly deflationary. The reduction of both public and private expenditure led to less consumer spending power and, in turn, less demand for goods. The first Labour Government, elected in 1924 under the leadership of Ramsay MacDonald lacked an economic policy to deal with this situation. The Conservatives gained power in the hastily called General Election of November 1924 and with Stanley Baldwin praying for industrial 'peace in our time' there was a brief period of stability.

The blow which shattered this paper-thin accord, and which led to the country's only General Strike in 1926, was the restoration of the Gold Standard. The effects of this led to coal owners announcing their intention to impose longer working hours and smaller wages on their workers. Following prolonged negotiations, the Trades Union Congress (TUC) eventually called the General Strike which began at midnight on 3rd May 1926. Within its limitations the strike was successful and there was practically no return to work before it officially ended at noon on 12th May 1926. The miners, who believed they had been 'sold out' by the TUC leadership, fought on until the winter of 1926 when starvation drove them back to work.

The collapse of the General Strike put a significant brake on the post-war militancy of the British trade unions. It brought disillusionment and a drastic drop in membership, which in 1927 fell below 5 million for the first time since 1916. Industrial relations in the late 1920s became pervaded by the ideas of cooperation and 'peace in industry'.

Despite the depression and the defeats, which meant that 1 in 10 of the entire working population was earning less than the minimum wage needed to support a family, the British working man had not entirely lost the advantages of the post-war period. Wages had almost doubled their pre-war level to average three pounds per week, and hours had dropped from an average of about 55 to 48 per week. Although prices had kept up with wages, there was still disposable income available for 'luxuries' or for saving.

Innovation, freedom, and scepticism were the characteristics of British Society in the 1920s. The gaiety which accompanied the latter was not simply confined to the wealthier classes. Much of the employed working class was materially better off than ever before. Life in many ways was becoming easier. The growth of science, philosophy, and artistic creation was notable and internationally recognized. Mass communication expanded in a dramatic fashion. The establishment of the British Broadcasting Corporation in 1922 and its utilization of first radio and then television profoundly shaped British society. For the first time, a clearly marked 'mass culture', based on growing standardization and commercialization (and an increased American influence), began to appear. On a political level, universal suffrage was at last established when women over 21 were given the vote in 1929.

The curious anomaly which gave businessmen and university graduates two votes remained.

3.1 Historical Snapshots

3.1 Historical Snapshots

1919	Treaty of Versailles signed between the Allies and Germany.
1920	Regular public radio broadcasts begin in the UK.
	New air mail service to Amsterdam starts.
1921	1,640,000 are unemployed.
1922	Proposal accepted for footballers to receive a maximum wage of £8 a week.
	The budget cuts 1s. off income tax; 4d. off a pound of tea and lowers postal and telephone charges.
	London bank lending rates are cut to 3 per cent, the lowest since 1914.
1923	Cox's Bank announces its merger with Lloyds Bank.
	Government spends £50million on unemployment relief.
	First transatlantic broadcast to USA is made.
	The general election returns eight women MPs.
1924	Dock strike paralyses every part of the country.
	The BBC begins broadcasting to schools.
	Government rejects the idea of a channel tunnel.
1925	Introduction of widows and orphans benefits.
	The Distillers Whisky Group is formed.

1926	General Strike in the UK is called by Trade Union Congress (TUC) in support of miners' strike.
	Large quantities of food are imported as the coal strike enters its third month.
	Formation of Imperial Chemical Industries (ICI) is announced.
	15.4million tons of coal are imported in the pit strike, which has lost the industry £300 million.
1927	BBC broadcasts its first programmes.
	Morris Motors buys Wolseley Motors for £730,000.
1928	Women in the UK given vote on equal terms with men.
	Harrods buys the retailer D. H. Evans.
	Morris Motors launch their latest model, the Morris Minor.
	Elastoplast sticking plasters first made in Hull.
	First pound and ten shilling notes come into circulation.
	J.L. Baird gives first transatlantic television transmission and demonstrates colour TV.
	First working robot built.
	Fleming discovers penicillin.
1929	Wall Street Crash.

Chronicle of Britain, J.L. International Publishing, 992; Williams, T.I. *Invention and Discovery in the 20th Century*, Harrap, 1990; Galsworthy, M. *Encyclopaedia of Association Football*.

3.2 Earnings and Employment

3.2.1 Earnings, Standard Tables

3.2.1a Incomes and Wages

	1919	1920	1921	1922	1923	1924	1925	1926	1927	1928	1929
Solicitor		£1,096 (a)									
General Practitioner		£756 (a)									
Police Constable	70–90s.										
Teacher		£500 (a)			£500 (a)		£480 (a)				
Clerical Worker		£152 (m/a)									
Train Driver					72–90s.	72–90s.	72–90s.	72–90s.	72–90s.	70s. 2d.	70s. 2d.
Coal Miner		16s. 6d. (per shift)	9s. 1¾ d.	10s. 1d.		10s. 7¾ d	10s. 6d.	10s. 5d.	10s. 0¾ d.	9 3½	9 2¾
Fitter and Turner						56 6	56 6	56 6	58 1	58 9	58 9
Bricklayer						73 5	73 8	73 10	74 1	72 6	72 4
Bricklayer's Labourer						55 6	55 8	55 10	55 11	54 3	54 1
Compositor						73 9	73 10	73 10	73 10	73 10	73 10
Farm Worker	30s. 6d.	37 10½	43s. 0½ d	46 10½	28 0	28 0	30 1	31 6	31 8	31 8	31 8
Baker						64 10	64 10	64 10	64 4	64 2	64 1
Cotton Weaver		36 10					37 8				

British Labour Statistics, HMSO, 1971; Bowley, A.L. *Wages and Incomes in the UK since 1860*, Cambridge University Press, 1937; Routh, G. *Occupation and Pay in Great Britain, 1906–1979*, Macmillan Press, 1980.

Wages are weekly unless otherwise stated. Blank space denotes no available data. (a) – annual; (m) – male.

3.2.1b Average Weekly Earnings

	Males	Females
	s.	s.
Bricks, Pottery and Glass	55.1	22.4
Metals	56.4	25.2
Textiles	51.0	28.6
Clothing	54.8	26.9
Food, Drink and Tobacco	58.0	27.9
Paper and Printing	70.7	28.0
Building	59.0	26.3
Total Miscellaneous	63.5	28.0
Local Government	51.6	27.8
Railway Works	69.3	n/a
Average Full-Time Earnings	58.9	28.4

Bowley, A.L. *Wages and Incomes in the UK since 1860*, Cambridge University Press, 1937, p. 51.

Original source, *Ministry of Labour Gazette*.

3.2.2 Regional Earnings by Selected Occupation

		London		Manchester		Newcastle		Leeds		Glasgow	
		s.	d.	s.	d.	s.	d.	s.	d.	s.	d.
Bricklayer (hourly)	1920	2	4	2	4	2	4	2	4	2	4
	1924	1	8	1	7½	1	7½	1	7½	1	7½
	1926	1	9½	1	8	1	8	1	8	1	8
Bricklayer's Labourer (hourly)	1920	2	1	2	0	2	1	2	1	1	11¼
	1924	1	3	1	2¾	1	2¾	1	2¾	1	2¾
	1926	1	4½	1	3¼	1	3¼	1	3¼	1	3¼
Compositor (weekly)	1920	85	0	82	6	79	6	79	6	82	6
	1924	89	0	71	6	74	6	71	6	77	6
	1926	89	6	77	6	74	6	74	6	77	6
Fitter and Turner (weekly)	1920	89	11¼	84	11¼	n/a		n/a		85	1
	1924	60	11	56	0	n/a		n/a		56	1½
	1926	60	11	56	0	n/a		n/a		56	1½
Labourer (weekly)	1920	71	5¼	64	8¼	n/a		n/a		68	0
	1924	43	3½	38	0	n/a		n/a		40	11¼
	1926	43	3½	38	0	n/a		n/a		40	11¼

British Labour Statistics, 1886–1968, HMSO, 1971.

3.2.3 Incomes, Miscellaneous

3.2.3a Coal Miners' Earnings per Shift

	Durham		UK	
	s.	d.	s.	d.
1920 (Jan–March)	14	7½	15	1½
1921	15	4¾	15	11
1922	9	1	9	11¾
1923	9	11	10	1
1924	10	2	10	7¾
1925	9	11¼	10	6
1926 (Jan–April)	9	11¼	10	5
1927	9	2¼	10	0¾
1928	8	1½	9	3½
1929	7	11½	9	2¾

Garside, W.R. *The Durham Miners 1919–1960*, 1971.

Original source, *Reports of H.M. Inspectors of Mines, 1920–1938*.

3.2.3b North British Locomotive Company Wages

	Average Wages per Man per Week	
	s.	d.
1920	80	10
1921	67	0
1922	41	0½
1923	50	5¾
1924	47	9
1925	53	7½
1926	46	8
1927	52	11½
1928	51	5
1929	50	1

Business History, Vol.XX, No.2, July, 1978, p. 231.

Original source, *North British Locomotive Company Papers* in Mitchell Library, Glasgow.

3.2.3c Wages for John Brown and Co., Shipbuilders

Year	Average Number of Men per Week	Average Pay Bill			Average Wages per Man per Week		
		£	s.	d.	£	s.	d.
1919	9,049	33,520	8	4	3	14	1
1920	9,297	38,072	16	6	4	1	11
1921	6,322	23,274	6	1	3	13	8
1922	3,653	9,883	2	2	2	14	1
1923	3,404	8,219	10	3	2	8	4
1924	5,181	13,686	15	0	2	12	10
1925	4,353	12,341	1	6	2	16	8
1926	4,150	10,724	8	0	2	11	8
1927	5,372	14,566	8	9	2	14	3
1928	7,626	21,743	1	11	2	17	0
1929	6,675	18,428	12	7	2	15	3

Business History, Vol.XIX, No.2, July, 1977, p. 204.

Compiled from *Abstract Wages Books,* John Brown & Co., Clydebank, *1914–1938*.

3.2.4 Employment

3.2.4a Unemployment

	Membership at end of June of unions reporting	Percentage Unemployed Mean for Year, %	End of December, %
1919	1,334,000	2.4	3.2
1920	1,603,000	2.4	6.0
1921	1,235,000	14.8[1]	16.2
1922	1,360,000	15.2	13.8
1923	1,145,000	11.3	9.3
1924	1,084,000	8.1	9.2
1925	978,000	10.5	11.0
1926	833,000	12.2[1]	12.2[1]

British Labour Statistics, 1886-1968, HMSO, 1971.

Figures are for those entitled to unemployment benefit. Original source, *21st Abstract of Labour Statistics*.
[1]Affected by general coal mining stoppages.

3.2.4b Employment by Region

	1923 000's	1924 000's	1925 000's	1926 000's	1927[1] 000's	1927[1] 000's	1928 000's	1929 000's
London	2,004	2,011	2,082	2,110	2,150	2,091	2,147	2,214
South East	756	785	815	846	876	849	868	894
South West	767	777	792	813	833	807	816	840
Midlands	1,682	1,710	1,748	1,771	1,783	1,733	1,750	1,793
North East	1,964	1,981	2,003	2,016	2,025	1,962	1,969	1,986
North West	2,071	2,092	2,117	2,141	2,149	2,090	2,094	2,120
Scotland	1,268	1,299	1,320	1,324	1,306	1,268	1,264	1,270
Wales	618	625	623	629	629	608	592	583
Great Britain	11,150	11,280	11,500	11,650	11,750	11,408	11,500	11,700
Northern Ireland	253	258	266	266	254	249	251	258
UK	11,403	11,538	11,766	11,916	12,004	11,657	11,751	11,958

British Labour Statistics 1886-1968, HMSO, 1971.

Figures are at each mid-year for those covered by insurance. [1]Persons aged 65 and over ceased to be covered by the Unemployment Insurance Acts after January 1928. Two sets of figures are therefore given for 1927, one for insured persons aged 16 and over and one for insured persons aged 16-64.

3.3 Consumer Expenditure

3.3.1 Consumer Expenditure, Standard Table

	Food	Alcoholic Drink	Tobacco	Housing	Fuel and Light	Clothing	Durable House hold Goods	Motor Cars and Motor Cycles	Other Goods	Other Services	Total Con- sumer Expen- diture
	£m	£m	£m	£m	£m	£m	£m	£m	£m	£m	£m
1919	1,327	391	115	254	151	670	217	35	307	943	4,535
1920	1,624	474	127	285	183	827	149	41	556	953	5,246
1921	1,405	409	116	317	169	485	119	19	422	858	4,315
1922	1,196	356	112	329	158	434	109	28	378	748	3,842
1923	1,204	332	109	323	148	409	107	31	353	713	3,717
1924	1,213	337	112	322	160	418	107	39	352	730	3,777
1925	1,241	338	116	325	158	432	113	51	362	753	3,878
1926	1,216	323	117	336	144	417	113	47	371	762	3,833
1927	1,193	320	124	349	166	424	120	44	382	784	3,887
1928	1,209	310	131	356	152	435	125	41	394	804	3,939
1929	1,204	311	136	365	162	439	130	38	397	817	3,983

Mitchell, B.R. *British Historical Statistics*, Cambridge University Press, 1988.

Original source, Feinstein, C.H. *National Income, Expenditure and Output of the UK, 1855–1965*, Cambridge, 1972.

3.4 Prices

3.4.1 Food Prices

3.4.1a Food Basket

Article (per lb. unless otherwise stated)	1920	
	s.	d.
Beef, home-killed:		
Ribs	1	10¼
Thin flank	1	4
Beef, chilled or frozen:		
Ribs	1	3¾
Thin flank		9¾
Mutton, home-killed:		
Legs	1	11¼
Breast	1	3¼
Mutton, frozen:		
Legs	1	3½
Breast		7
Bacon, streaky	2	6¾
Flour (per 7lb.)	1	10
Bread (per 4lb.)	1	0¼
Tea	2	10¼
Sugar, granulated		11½
Milk, (per quart)		9¼
Butter:		
Fresh	2	11¼
Salt	2	11¼
Cheese	1	8½
Margarine	1	1½
Eggs, fresh each		4½
Potatoes (per 7lb.)	1	1¾

British Labour Statistics, 1886–1968, HMSO, 1971.

The table was compiled from information supplied for the "Cost of Living Index", by over 5,000 retailers in approximately 500 towns.

3.4.1b Weekly Grocery Bill[1]

	1915		1919	
	s.	d.	s.	d.
1 stone of flour	2	5	2	8
1lb. rice		3		6
¼ stone oatmeal	3	0	5	1
1 stone potatoes		8	1	3
2lb. sugar		3¾		7
½ lb. currants		5		10
½ lb. tea	2	2	2	8
½ lb. best coffee	1	8	2	4
1lb. butter	1	6	2	6
½ lb. lard		7	1	8
½ lb. cheese	1	0	1	6
8 eggs		2		3½
1lb. bacon	1	1	2	0
1lb. green peas		3½		7
1lb. cream crackers		7	1	2
2lb. jar of jam	1	0	1	11
2oz. yeast		10	1	4
1 tin of salmon		11	1	11
1lb. soap		4		8
½ lb. starch		5		10
2 boxes of matches		3	1	0
1 tin black pelaw polish		2½		5½

Producer, May 19th, 1919, p. 168.

[1]Bill for a family of four in Carlisle. Table prepared by the Carlisle South End *Cooperative Society.*

3.4.1c Regional Grocery Prices

Article (per lb. unless otherwise stated)	Glasgow	Bradford	Alloa	West Riding	Midlands	Ipswich	Liverpool
	s. d.	s. d.	s. d.	s. d.	s. d.	s. d.	s. d.
Bread	4½	4	4½	5	2¼	3¾	n/a
Flour	4	2 4 (stone)	1 4½ (7lb.)	3½	9½	3½	1 0 (7lb.)
Cheese	1 4	1 9	1 6	1 9	1 4	1 3	10
Butter	2 0	2 3	2 4	2 3	2 2	2 0	1 9
Bacon	2 0	1 9	n/a	1 8	1 2	2 1	1 6
Currants	10	10	10	11	9	4	9
Rice	2¼	6	4	5	4	n/a	4
Oatmeal	2½	3½	2½	3	3½	n/a	n/a
Tea	1 8	3 4	3 4	3 4	2 8	2 8	3 4
Cocoa	1 8	2 0	n/a	7½	2 0	n/a	n/a
Sugar	6½	6	7	7	7	6½	6½
Jam	11¼	1 1	11	11½	1 8	1 0	10½
Lard	10	n/a	10	9	9	1 0	8
Eggs (per dozen)	2 10	n/a	6	n/a	n/a	n/a	1 0 (7)
Potatoes (5lb.)	n/a	8	5	n/a	n/a	9	5½
Meat	1 6	n/a	1 4	1 6	1 2	1 8	2 0
Milk (pint)	3½	n/a	3½	7 (quart)	3	3½	5
Coal (2 cwt.)	n/a	4 8	n/a	46 0 (ton)	2 2	2 9	1 9
Soap	6½	6½	n/a	6½	6	6½	5

The Producer, April, 1923, p. 166+.

Prices taken from Cooperative Societies in Glasgow, Bradford, Alloa, West Riding, Midlands, Ipswich and Liverpool in 1923.

3.4.2 Prices, General Articles

	1919	1920	1921	1922	1923	1924	1925	1926	1927	1928	1929
	s. d.	s. d.	s. d.	s. d.	s. d.	s. d.	s. d.	s. d.	s. d.	s. d.	s. d.
Aspirin (100)						1 6					1 6
Beer (1 pint as served in a public bar)	3	3	3	5	5	5	5	5	5	5	5
Cadbury's Chocolate (½ lb. bar)		6½	6½	7	7	10	10	9½	9½	9½	10
Cheddar Cheese (1 lb.)		1 6			1 6						
Colmans Mustard (1 lb. Double Super-fine)								2 10			
Colmans Starch (tin)								1			
Daily Mail	1	1	1	1	1	1	1	1	1	1	1
Guinness Extra Stout (1 pint)		10					1 0				
Inland Letter Post	1½	1½	1½	1½	1½	1½	1½	1½	1½	1½	1½
Pears Transparent Soap	1 0				1 0						1 3
Petrol (1 gallon)	3 0½	4 3½	3 5½					1 7½		1 0½	1 4¾
Red Label Tea (1 lb.)		2 8			2 4						
Scotch Whisky (standard bottle)	10 6	12 6					12 6				
Swan Vestas Matches (100)	1½	1½	1½	1½	1½	1½	1½	1½	1½	1½	1½
The Times	4	4	4	4	4	4	4	4	4	4	4

The Boots Company; British Library; Burmah Castrol; Cadbury Ltd.; Colmans of Norwich; Guinness Brewing GB; Royal Mail; Sainsburys Archives; The Scotch Whisky Association and Unilever Historical Archives.

Blank space denotes no prices available. Inclusion of Cadbury's Dairy Milk Chocolate from 1920.

3.4.3 Prices, Selected

Item	Source	Description	Price £	s.	d.	
Alcoholic Drink						
Spirits	*Harrods Ltd*, London 1929	Johnnie Walker Red Label Scotch Whisky		12	6	
		Teachers Highland Cream Scotch Whisky		12	6	
		Harrods Irish Whisky		12	0	
		Old Bushmills Irish Whisky		12	6	
		Fine Old Jamaica Rum		12	0	
Hollands		De Kuyper in Glass		13	6	
Gin		Booths Dry Gin		12	0	
Wines		Harrods Australian Burgundy	1	16	0	(per dozen bottles)
		Stone's Green Ginger Wine	1	14	0	(per dozen bottles)
British Cordials		Ginger Gin		11	0	
		Cherry Brandy		12	6	
Appliances: Domestic and Electrical						
Gramophone	*Producer*, September 1922	Sylvaphone the new CWS Gramophone	3	3	0	(up to £65)
Iron	*The Ideal Home*, November 1923	"Umadis" Self-Heating Iron		6	0	
Wireless	*The Pound in Your Pocket 1870–1970*, 1925	Three Valve Set Wireless	7	15	0	
Headphones		BTH Headphones	1	1	0	
Boiler	*The Ideal Home*, September 1926	Steel Kokette Boiler	10	10	0	
		Glow Worm Junior	8	10	0	
		Thermostove Combination Boiler and Oven	13	15	0	(upwards)
Fire		Magnet Electric Fire	1	11	0	
		Belling Electric Fire	7	0	0	(upwards)
Heater		Magnet Pedestal Heater	1	1	0	
Iron		Electric Iron		17	6	
		Magnet Iron 4lb. size		16	0	
Kettle		Magnet Electric Kettle	1	6	0	
Toaster		Magnet Electric Toaster	1	6	6	
Cleaner		"Central" Electric Vacuum Cleaner	13	0	0	
		"Siemens" Electric Suction Cleaner	12	12	0	
Lamp	*Affleck & Brown*, Manchester 1929	Jacobean Style Electric Table Lamp		12	11	(sale price)
Cleaner	*Harrods Ltd*, London 1929	The "Whirlwind" Suction Sweeper	4	19	6	
		"Brivac" Hand Operated Vacuum Cleaner	5	5	0	
		"Goblin" Electric Cleaner	10	10	0	
Washstand		Portable Washstand	3	9	9	
Refrigerator		Mode V-5 Frigidaire	49	10	0	
Cooker		Valor Junior Oil Stove	1	8	0	
Iron		Flat Iron		1	3	(up to 3/6)
Mangle		"Acme Major" Combined Table and Mangle	7	2	0	
Gramophone		Oak Console Cabinet; Plays two 12in. records	14	10	0	

Continued

3.4.3 Prices, Selected *continued*

Item	Source	Description	Price £	s.	d.
Gramophone *contd.*		Mahogany Console Cabinet; Plays three 12in. records	27 10		0
		New Columbia Portable Junior Model	3 10		0
Wireless		Pye 4-Valve Receiver	19 15		0
		Burndept Screened Grid 4-Valve	29 6		0
Baby Equipment					
Pram	*Bradshaws ABC Railway Guide*, 1925	"Roma" Baby Car	2 10		0 (upwards)
Clothing and Footwear:					
Children's					
Vests	*P. Steinmann & Co*, London 1919	Wool Vests		1	6 (up to 5/0)
Petticoats		Flannel Petticoats		5	9 (up to 16/9)
Frocks		Cotton Frocks		11	6 (up to 120/0)
Shoes		Shoes		3	9 (up to 15/6)
Spencers		Knitted Spencers		5	0 (up to 8/9)
Layette No.1		Comprising:			
		4 Infant Woollen Shirts		9	0
		6 Infant Nightgowns	1	14	6
		4 Day Flannels	1	11	0
		2 Monthly Gowns	1	1	0
		2 Robes	1	13	0
		3 dozen Turkish Diapers	1	9	3
		3 pairs Wool Boots		4	6
		1 Head Square		5	9
		1 Head Square Embroidered		8	9
		3 Petticoats		14	3
Coat	*Debenham & Freebody*, London 1919	Coat 2–3 years	1	15	6
		Coat 5 years	2	0	0
Frock		Frock 2–3 years		18	9
		Frock 5 years	1	1	9
Boots	*Affleck & Brown*, Manchester 1920	Box Calf Boots		16	9
Suit	*Producer*, July 1923	Boy's Flannel Suit		12	6 (upwards)
Coat	*Affleck & Brown*, Manchester 1923	Girl's Coat	1	9	9
Slippers		Children's Warm Slippers		1	11
Sweater		Children's Warm Fleecy Jumper		4	11
Dress		Girl's Navy Serge School Dress	1	9	9 (up to 33/9)
Suit	*Affleck & Brown*, Manchester 1925	Boy's Chilprufe Suit		15	0 (up to 18/0)
Tunic		Girl's Gym Tunic in Navy Serge		12	11 (size 24")
Suit	*Good Style Clothing*, 1927	Boy's Lovat Tweed Suit	1	1	0 (up to 26/0)
Coat		Summer coat	1	14	6 (up to 42/0)
Nightdress	*Affleck & Brown*, Manchester, 1929	Child's Nightie		7	3 (up to 12/3)
Men's					
Shirt	*Affleck & Brown*, Manchester, 1920	Gent's Union Wool Shirt		8	11
Pyjamas		Gent's Union Flannel Pyjamas	1	0	0 (up to 23/6)
Boots		Gent's Glacé Kid Boots	1	12	0
	Producer, September 1922	Gent's Reliable Footwear: CWS Standard Boot		16	6

Continued

3.4.3 Prices, Selected *continued*

Item	Source	Description	£	s.	d.
Suit	*Producer*, July 1923	Special Men's Suits	1	19	6 (upwards)
	Producer, February 1924	Men's Suits	2	10	0
Shoes	*Producer*, April 1924	Men's Shoes	1	1	0
Suit	*Austin Reed*, 1925	Harris Tweed Sports Suit	6	16	6
Shirt	*Affleck & Brown*, Manchester, 1925	Gent's Union Wool Shirt		7	6
Boots		Gent's Glacé Kid Boots		10	6
Raincoat	*Good Style Clothing*, 1927	Fine Egyptian Colston Lightweight Raincoat	1	4	0
		Navy Cashmere Trenchcoat		19	0
Suit		Hardwearing Tweed Suit	1	11	6
Trousers		Flannel Trousers		9	0
Boots	*Affleck & Brown*, Manchester 1929	Box Calf Boots	1	8	9
Ladies					
Coat	*Debenham & Freebody*, London 1919	Country and Street Coats	3	18	6 (up to 89/6)
Blouse		Dainty Blouse	1	1	9
Dress		Inexpensive Frock	5	18	6
Nightdress		Ladies Nightie	1	9	6
Boots		Ladies Calf Leather Boots	1	18	0
Shoes		Ladies Glacé Kid Shoes	1	18	0
Sweater	*Affleck & Brown*, Manchester 1920	Model Crepe Jumper with Fringe	2	9	11
Blouse		Crepe Corona Blouse		19	11
Coat		Wool Coat		17	11
Suit		Suit in Navy and Black Serge	3	19	9
Skirt	*Producer*, April 1922	Wool Skirt		8	11
Corsets		Long Stay Corsets		5	6 (up to 7/6)
Suit		Wool Suit	2	10	0
Skirt	*Producer*, June 1922	Wool Skirt		8	11
Shoes	*Producer*, July 1923	Black Glacé Shoe	1	0	0
		Box Calf Gibson Patent Cap		16	6
		Glacé Gibson Patent Cap		12	6
Coat	*Affleck & Brown*, Manchester, 1923	Wool Coat	1	19	9
Dress		Wool Dress	1	5	0
Stockings		Black Silk Hose		12	6
Boots		Glacé Kid Boot		12	6
Suit	*Tatler*, February 1925	Knitted Suit for Springwear	4	4	0
Shoes	*C & J Clark Ltd*, 1925	Promenade Suede Calf Two Bar Straps	1	0	6
		Sylvia Dress Shoe in Glacé Kid		11	0 (up to 11/6)
Dressing Gown	*Affleck & Brown*, Manchester, 1925	Quilted Dressing Gown	1	4	6
Cardigan		Fine Quality Fleecy Wool Cardigan		13	11
Suit		Ready for Wear Plain Tailored Suit	4	4	0
Shoes		Glacé Kid Walking Shoe		12	9
		Welted Walking Shoe	1	1	9
Nightdress	*Affleck & Brown*, Manchester, 1929	Viyella Nightie		17	11
Stockings		Pure Silk Hose		4	11
Shoes		Dark Brown Glacé Kid Shoes	1	1	9

Continued

3.4.3 Prices, Selected *continued*

Item	Source	Description	Price		
			£	s.	d.
Food Products					
Tinned Fruits	*Producer*, December 1920	First Quality Apricots		2	4 (per tin)
		First Quality Pears		3	3 (per tin)
		Fourth Quality Apricots		1	4 (per tin)
Bacon	*J Sainsbury Archives*, 1920	Unsmoked Back Bacon		2	11 (per lb.)
Butter		Loose Butter		3	1 (per lb.)
Cheese		Cheddar Cheese		1	6 (per lb.)
Biscuits		McVities Digestive		1	0 (½ lb.)
Breakfast Cereal		Shredded Wheat		1	0½ (12's)
Cordial		Kia-Ora Squash		2	6 (20oz.)
Soup		Heinz Tomato Soup		1	1 (15oz. tin)
Tea		Red Label Tea		2	8
Condensed Milk	*Scottish CWS Ltd.*, July 1921	Nestlé Sweetened Condensed Full Cream Milk		1	3½ (½ lb. tin)
		Ideal Unsweetened Concentrated Full Cream Milk		0	11½
		Pure Thick Cream		1	2½
Sugar	*Producer*, May 1923	Tate & Lyle Sugar			7 (lb.)
Cheese	*J Sainsbury Archives*, 1923	Cheddar Cheese		1	6 (lb.)
Tea		Red Label Tea		2	4 (lb.)
Fish	*Producer*, November 1923	Kippers			8 (lb.)
		Whiting			9 (lb.)
Cream	*The Ideal Home*, November 1923	Devonshire Clotted Cream by Post		3	9 (lb.) post free
Cake	*The Pound in Your Pocket 1870–1970*, 1925	Lyons Swiss Roll		1	0
Confectionery		Cadburys Fruit and Nut		1	1 (½ lb.)
Spices	*Scottish CWS Ltd.*, January 1926	Caraway, Finest Ground			9 (per lb.)
		Cloves, Ground		1	11 (lb.)
		Mace, Ground		4	10 (lb.)
		Pie Spice, Special			6 (lb.)
		Ginger, Whole Finest Jamaica		1	6 (lb.)
		Cloves, Whole Finest Penang		3	2 (lb.)
Custard	*The Ideal Home*, September 1926	Birds Custard		1	3½ (tin)
Beans	*Harrods Ltd*, London 1929	Heinz Baked Beans		1	3 (15oz. tin)
Beef Cubes		Oxo Cubes			6 (6 cubes)
Biscuits (per lb.)		Huntley & Palmers Abernethy Thin		1	5
		Crawfords Butter Puffs		1	4
		Huntley & Palmers Mixed Chocolate		2	4
		McVities Digestive		1	6
		Jacobs Water Biscuits		1	2
		Huntley & Palmers Wheatmeal		1	6
Marmalade		Hartleys			8 (jar)
		Silver Shred			7½ (jar)
Macaroni		Quaker Milkaroni			9½ (packet)
Mayonnaise		Heinz		1	0 (bottle)
Cordial		Kia-Ora		1	1 (bottle)
Tinned Fruits		Peaches		1	4 (lb. tin)

Continued

3.4.3 Prices, Selected *continued*

Item	Source	Description	Price £	s.	d.
Tinned Fruit *contd.*		Pears		1	4 (lb. tin)
Terrines		Bloc de Foie Gras Entier Doyen's		14	0 (tin)
Furniture					
Bed	*Affleck & Brown*, Manchester, 1923	Oak Fumed Bedstead with Wire Mattress	3	3	6
Suite	*The Ideal Home*, November 1923	Morton Real Hide Suite	28	7	0
Carpets	*Bradshaws ABC Railway Guide*, 1925	Wool Axminster Carpets 2 x 2½ yds.	2	9	6
Floor Covering	*The Ideal Home*, September 1926	Oak Parquet		5	6 (sq.yd.)
Suite		Three Piece Chesterfield Suite	28	7	0
Cabinet	*Affleck & Brown*, Manchester 1929	Bow Front Mahogany Dwarf Cabinet	10	0	0 (sale price)
Bench		Solid Oak Monks Bench	6	10	0 (sale price)
Sideboard		Solid Oak Sideboard		12	5
Table		Figured Oak Gate Leg Table	5	10	0
Chair		Upholstered Spring Back Chair	2	7	6
Bed		Solid Oak Bedstead 3ft. wide and 6ft. 6in. long	2	2	6
Mattresses		Hair Mattresses	2	7	6 (upwards)
Wardrobe		Oak Panelled Fitted Wardrobe 3ft 6in. wide,	1	12	6
Mirror		Solid Oak Cheval Mirror	2	12	6 (sale price)
Bed		4ft. 6in. Oak Panel Bedstead	5	15	0
Table		Antique Oak Bedside Table	1	12	0
Heat and Light					
Coal	*The Pound in Your Pocket 1870–1970*, 1925	Coal per ton	1	9	6
Electricity		Electricity per unit			2
Gas		Gas per therm			8
Firelighters	*Producer*, March 1923	Eight Firelighters			2
Hotel Rates					
Shaftesbury Hotel, London	*Bradshaws ABC Railway Guide*, 1920	Rate per Night		7	0
West Central Hotel, Southampton Row, London	*Bradshaws ABC Railway Guide*, 1925	Bedroom Service and Breakfast		8	6 (upwards)
Central Hotel, Tottenham Court Road, London		Bedroom Service and Breakfast		7	0
Arlington Hotel, Brighton		Bed, Breakfast and Bath		9	0
Kensington Palace Hotel, London	*The Pound in Your Pocket 1870–1970*, 1925	Double Room		12	0 (per night)
Household Goods					
Bedding	*Producer*, November 1921	Blankets	1	5	6 (upwards)
	Producer, January 1922	Flannelette Sheeting		1	3 (yard)
	Producer, November 1925	Hemstitched Plain Hercules Sheets		15	3 (up to 24/11 per pair)
		Hemstitched Pillow Cases		3	2 (pair)

Continued

3.4.3 Prices, Selected *continued*

Item	Source	Description	Price £	s.	d.
Bedding *contd.*	*Affleck & Brown*, Manchester, 1925	Bedspreads		16	6 (up to 21/6 for double)
		White Flannelette		1	3½ (yd.)
		Twill Wincyette		1	3½ (yd.)
	Producer, March 1926	Pillow Cases			8½ each
		Bolsters		1	6 (up to 1/11)
		Single Bed Ticks		6	6
		Full Size Bed Ticks		7	6
		Bleached Twill Sheets		11	6
		White Flannelette Blankets		7	11 (up to 12/6)
Towels		Turkish Towels			7½ (up to 1/11½)
		Russia Crash Towelling			10½
Table Linen		Bordered Table Cloth		3	11
		Serviettes			7½
Cleaning Materials	*The Ideal Home*, September 1926	Johnsons Liquid Wax		7	6 (quart)
		Johnsons Weighted Floor Polishing Brush		15	6
		Harpic Lavatory Cleanser			6½ (up to 1/9)
		Mansion Polish			6 (tin)
	Harrods Ltd., 1929	Parazone Bleach		1	6 (bottle)
		Marbalette Marble Cleaner		1	0 (bottle)
		Borax Household Treasure			6 (packet)
Cutlery	*Affleck & Brown*, Manchester, 1929	Stainless Steel Dinner Knives		14	11 (six)
		Pastry Forks in Nickel Silver		9	11 (six)
		Afternoon Tea Spoons in Nickel Silver		8	6 (six)
Tableware		One Dish and Six Plates		6	9
		One Fruit Dish and Six Fruit Plates		10	6
		"Rosol" Tea and Coffee Set	1	8	6
Cutlery Box		Oak Cutlery Box		8	9 (sale price)
Wine Rack	*Harrods Ltd*, London 1929	Safety Wood Block Wine Bins		11	0 (3 dozen)
Pastry Table		Plain Wood Frame, Enamelled White Porcelain Top	1	10	0 (up to 36/3)
Vegetable Rack		Hygienic Vegetable Rack		18	6 (3 tiers, 4 bins)
Houses					
House	*The Pound in Your Pocket 1870–1970*, 1924	5 Bedroom House, Clarence Rd, Dulwich	2,000	0	0
Freehold Site	*Bradshaws ABC Railway Guide*, 1925	Kinmel Bay, Rhyl, N. Wales	25	0	0 (ready for building)
House	*The Pound in Your Pocket 1870–1970*, 1925	3 Bedroom House, Welwyn Garden City	975	0	0
		4 Bedroom Custom Built House, Guildford	1,399	0	0
		4 Bedroom Cottage, Oxley	1,400	0	0
	The Ideal Home, September, 1926	Cedars Estate, Rickmansworth	1,400	0	0
		Martin Houses, Warminster Rd, Norwood	1,250	0	0

Continued

3.4.3 Prices, Selected *continued*

Item	Source	Description	Price £	s.	d.
		10 to 12½ miles			5
		12½ to 15 miles			6
		15 to 20 miles			8
Parcel Postage Rates	*Post Office Archives*,1920	2 lb. weight			9
		5 lb.		1	0
		11 lb.		1	6
	Post Office Archives, 1923	2 lb.			6
		5 lb.			9
		11 lb.		1	3
Insurance	*Bradshaws ABC Railway Guide*, 1925	Railway Accident Policy: Lancashire and General		5	0 (per £100)

Sewing Equipment and Supplies

Item	Source	Description	Price £	s.	d.
Scissors	*Affleck & Brown*, Manchester, 1923	Cutting Out Shears		1	0
		High Class Scissors			10½
Machine		"Avenue" Sewing Machine	2	10	0
Fabrics (per yard)	*Affleck & Brown*, Manchester, 1925	Aynbee Gingham			10½
		Cotton Crêpe			11
		All Wool Delaines		2	11
		Dress Casement Cloth			11½
		Crêpe Flannel		3	6
Linings		Printed Coat Lining		1	6 (up to 2/6)
		Printed French Foulard		2	3
Fabrics	*Affleck & Brown*, Manchester, 1929	Madapollam			9½
		Check Crêpe		1	0
		Kimono Crêpe			10½
Linings		Satin Hygrade		2	2
		Artificial Silk		1	8
		Satinette		1	3
Machine	*Harrods Ltd*, London 1929	"Jones" 3 Drawer Sewing Machine	11	11	0

Sports and Hobbies

Item	Source	Description	Price £	s.	d.
Sports Equipment	*Tatler*, February 25, 1925	Wooden Golf Clubs		15	6
		Wooden Golf Balls		13	6 (up to 30/0 doz.)
	Harrods Ltd., London 1929	College Lawn Tennis Racket 9–11½ oz.		17	6
		Split Cone Trout Rod	6	0	0
		Canadian Canoe 14ft.	17	10	0
Photographic Equipment	*Producer*, April 1926	Bush Folding Camera with Improvements	2	7	6 (sale price)
	People's Year Book, 1927	Cine-Kodak	16	0	0
	Harrods Ltd, London 1929	All-Distance Pocket Ensign Camera	1	17	6
		Box Tengor Camera	1	1	0
		Miroflex Folding Reflex Camera	39	12	6
		Ensign Speed Film Reflex for Roll Films	10	10	0

Tobacco Products

Item	Source	Description	Price £	s.	d.
Cigarettes	*Scottish CWS Ltd.*, July 1921	Virginia Special Straight Cut		15	0 (per lb. in ¼lb. boxes)

Continued

3.4.3 Prices, Selected *continued*

Item	Source	Description	Price		
			£	s.	d.
Cigarettes *contd.*		Turkish No 1	1	0	0 (per lb. in ¼ lb. boxes)
Cigars		Statesman Dukes, 50's	2	16	6 (per 100)
		Merielettes		14	6 (per 100)
Snuff (lb. tins)		Morton's Mixture		9	6
		London Brown		8	3
Cigarettes	*The Pound in Your Pocket 1870–1970*, 1925	Players No 3			10 (for 8)
	Scottish CWS Ltd., January 1926	Straight Cut Virginia Cigarettes: Cork Tipped	1	19	4 (per 1000, in packs of 10's)
Cigars	*Harrods Ltd.*, London 1929	La Bella Otero: Half a Corona	5	16	0 (per 100)
		Henry Clay: Fernandos	3	10	0 (50)
		Castaneda: General Prim	7	10	0 (25)
Transport and Vehicles					
Rail Fares	*Bradshaws ABC Railway Guide*, 1920	Manchester to London Return	1	10	11 (up to 49/0)
		Manchester to London Single		15	5½ (up to 24/6)
Motor Bike	*Producer*, March 1921	Federation Motor Cycle 2¾ h.p. J.A.P. Engine	80	4	0
Vehicle	*Producer*, April 1921	Dennis Char-A-Banc 2–2½ ton Chassis	850	0	0 (sale price)
	Producer, February 1922	Dennis 25–30cwt. Delivery Van	550	0	0
Bicycle	*Producer*, November 1923	Adult Bicycle	5	19	6
Vehicle	*Producer*, 1924	Dennis Commercial Vehicle 20–25 Chassis	295	0	0
	Bystander, March 11, 1925	11.9 2 Seater Morris Cowley	175	0	0
		14–28 h.p. Morris Oxford Models with 4 Wheel Brake	260	0	0 (upwards)
	The Pound in Your Pocket 1870–1970, 1925	Rolls Royce Silver Ghost	1,850	0	0 (chassis)
Air Fare	*British Imperial Airways*, 1925	London to Paris	21	0	0 (single)
Rail Fares	*Bradshaws ABC Railway Guide*, 1925	Manchester to London Return	2	6	4 (up to 77/2)
		Manchester to London Single	1	3	2 (up to 38/7)
Vehicle	*The Ideal Home*, September 1926	Armstrong Siddeley 14 h.p. "Cotswold" 5 Seater	330	0	0
Motor Bike	*Harrods Ltd.*, London 1929	Triumph 277 SV		36	0
		BSA 174 2 Stroke	26	5	0
Travel					
Tours	*Travellers Gazette*, July 1920	Weekend Tour to the Battlefields	6	10	0 (via Hull & Zeebrugge)
		Week's Tour to the Battlefields	16	12	6 (via Hull & Zeebrugge)
Holiday		Fortnight in Ostend with Hotel Accommodation	11	5	6
		7 Day Tour to Paris from London	13	13	0 (inc. travel and accommodation)
		10 Day Tour of Interlaken	7	5	0 (Full Board)
Excursion	*Producer*, May 1924	Day Trip to London from North Shields	1	17	6 (travel, meals & exhibition ticket)
Cruise	*The Pound in Your Pocket 1870–1970*, 1925	Holidays Afloat the Norfolk Broads	4	0	0 (week)
Punt Hire		Punt down the Thames		12	0 (day)

Continued

3.4.3 Prices, Selected *continued*

Item	Source	Description	Price		
			£	s.	d.
Cruise	*Bystander*, February 25, 1925	12 Day Cruises to Norway from London	15	15	0
		10 Day Cruise to Norway from Leith	13	13	0
Miscellany					
Pesticide	*The Ideal Home*, November 1923	"Blatis" Union Cockroach Paste		1	6 (up to 5/0 in tins)
Name Plates		House Name Plates in Copper, Bronze and Brass		7	6 (upwards)
Dress		Fancy Leathers in 15 Colours			9 (sq. ft.)
Office Equipment	*Producer*, November 1923	Remington Typewriter	26	0	0
	Bradshaws ABC Railway Guide, 1925	Portable Underwood Typewriter	12	12	0
		Foote's Standard Duplicator	3	15	0
Poultry	*Producer*, March 1925	Day Old Chicks and Sitting Eggs		18	0 (12 No. 1 Eggs)
		Chicks	1	7	0 (12)
Holiday Guide	*Producer*, April 1926	Wheatsheaf Holiday Guide: 232 pages of useful information			3 (copy)

3.5 Finance and Economic Data

3.5.1 Finance, Personal

	1919	1920	1921	1922	1923	1924	1925	1926	1927	1928	1929
	s. d.	s. d.	s. d.	s. d.	s. d.	s. d.	s. d.	s. d.	s. d.	s. d.	s. d.
Income Tax Rates[1]	6 0	6 0	6 0	6 0	5 0	4 6	4 6	4 0	4 0	4 0	4 0
Old Age Pension	5 0	5 0	5 0	5 0	5 0	5 0	5 0	5 0	5 0	5 0	5 0
Base Interest Rates in percent[2]	6%	7%	7%	5%	3%	4%	4%	5%	5%	5%	5½%

Mitchell, B.R. *British Historical Statistics*, Cambridge University Press, 1988; CWS Year Book; Bank of England.

[1]Rates apply to years ended 5th April. [2]Rates apply to January of each year.

3.5.2 Financial Markets

3.5.2a Highest Closing Price of UK Major Stocks

	1919	1920	1921	1922	1923	1924	1925	1926	1927	1928	1929
Barclays Bank	$7^{11}/_{16}$	$7^{5}/_{16}$	$6^{13}/_{16}$	8	$8^{11}/_{32}$	$8^{1}/_{2}$	$8^{3}/_{8}$	$8^{9}/_{32}$	$8^{7}/_{32}$	$8^{5}/_{16}$	$8^{15}/_{32}$
Boots the Chemist	39/0	39/3		36/1½	44/6	45/6	45/0	45/3	45/0	47/6	48/6
Burmah Oil	$19^{11}/_{16}$	$22^{3}/_{8}$	$8^{3}/_{16}$	$6^{7}/_{32}$	$5^{25}/_{32}$	$5^{9}/_{16}$	$5^{27}/_{32}$	$7^{3}/_{32}$	$7^{15}/_{32}$	$5^{3}/_{8}$	$9^{7}/_{7}$
Courtaulds	$15^{3}/_{8}$	$9^{7}/_{8}$	41/9	63/6	74/4½	69/9	$7^{23}/_{32}$	$7^{11}/_{32}$	8	$9^{1}/_{8}$	$5^{9}/_{32}$
Guinness	395	358¾	440	474⅜	395	501	793	774	580	525	97/0
Lever Brothers	20/4½	19/4½	18/6	21/3	24/0	22/4½	22/4½	21/1½	21/8¼	23/10½	23/9
Reckitt and Sons	48/3	46/6	41/9	61/9	77/6	77/7½	93/9	93/0	91/3	96/3	87/6
Schweppes	23/6	20/1½	20/6	24/7½	24/6	24/9	25/0	24/3	24/0	24/1½	24/3
Viyella	10½	4	$2^{17}/_{32}$	69/6	70/6	66/10½	68/9	64/3	68/9	78/0	73/3
Whitbread	58½	50	51½	63	64	65	64	66	67	71	72

Mathieson, F.C. and Sons, *Stock Exchanges Ten Year Record of Prices and Dividends*.

Fractions are quoted as parts of £1=32.

3.5.2b Commodities

	Best Coal (price per ton)		Raw Cotton (per lb.)	Gold (average market price)	Sugar (annual average world price)	Wheat (per imperial quarter)[4]		Wool (average import value)
	s.	d.	old pence (d.)	£ per troy oz.	£ sterling per metric ton	s.	d.	pence per lb.
1919	45	4	19.65	4.504	29.856[1]	72	11	22.3
1920	32	0	23.14	5.603	64.632	80	10	24.1[3]
1921	32	3	9.40	5.352	24.443	71	6	13.1
1922	34	5	12.10	4.685	15.256	47	10	12.8
1923	32	5	15.25	4.512	25.344	9	10	15.2
1924	27	6	16.26	4.684	21.407	11	6	22.1
1925	29	8	12.64	4.274	12.549	12	2	23.7
1926	30	4[2]	9.40	4.247	12.057	12	3	18.5
1927	23	1	12.10	4.247	13.533	11	6	17.5
1928	21	5	10.92	4.247	11.401	10	0	18.6
1929	23	5	10.26	4.248	8.858	9	10	17.6

Mitchell, B.R. *British Historical Statistics*, Cambridge University Press, 1988; World Gold Council; Czarnikow Sugar.

Original source, Sauerbeck, A. *Prices of Commodities and the Precious Metals, Journal of the Statistical Society*. [1]Sugar controlled by Royal Commission on Sugar Supply. [2]Prices for January–April only. [3]Prior to 1920 the import value of wool includes noils. [4]From 1923 in hundredweight (cwt.).

3.5.2c Foreign Exchange Rates

	Berlin Reichsmarks per £1	Paris Francs per £1	New York Dollars per £1
1919	226.98	31.75	4.402
1920	404.59	52.47	3.661
1921	8,155.85	51.89	3.846
1922	n/a	54.60	4.427
1923	18.90	75.64	4.574
1924	20.28	85.24	4.417
1925	20.41	102.54	4.829
1926	20.46	152.38	4.858
1927	20.39	123.85	4.861
1928	20.39	124.10	4,866
1929	20.40	124.02	4.857

Mitchell, B.R. *British Historical Statistics*, Cambridge University Press, 1988.

3.5.3 Balance of Payments and GNP

3.5.3a Balance of Payments

	Merchan-dise Exports	Merchan-dise Imports	Overall Visible Balance	Exports of Services	Imports of Services	Property Income from Abroad	Property Income Paid Abroad	Balance of Current Transfers	Overall Invisible Balance	Overall Current Balance
	£m	£m	£m	£m	£m	£m	£m	£m	£m	£m
1919	990	1,460	-470	480	220	230	65	n/a	+425	-45
1920	1,585	1,761	-176	464	224	295	41	-1	+493	+317
1921	874	1,022	-148	292	172	222	44	+43	+341	+193
1922	888	951	-63	225	150	237	60	+12	+264	+201
1923	914	1,011	-97	247	146	240	64	+3	+280	+183
1924	958	1,172	-214	242	152	261	65	+6	+292	+78
1925	943	1,208	-265	215	149	295	63	+19	+317	+52
1926	794	1,140	-346	223	152	300	63	+20	+328	-18
1927	845	1,115	-270	245	142	302	63	+26	+368	+98
1928	858	1,095	-237	234	140	304	64	+27	+361	+124
1929	854	1,117	-26	242	152	307	64	+26	+359	+96

Mitchell, B.R. *British Historical Statistics*, Cambridge University Press, 1988.

Original source, Feinstein, C.H. *National Income, Expenditure and Output in the UK 1855-1965*, Cambridge, 1972.

3.5.3b GNP at Factor Cost and Its Component Incomes at Current Prices

	Income from Employ-ment	Income from Self Employ-ment	Gross Trading Profits of Compa-nies	Gross Trading Surplus of Public Enter-prises	Rent	Stock Apprecia-tion	Gross Domestic Product	Net Property Income from Abroad	Gross National Product	Capital Consump-tion	National Income
	£m	£m	£m	£m	£m	£m	£m	£m	£m	£m	£m
1919	3,076	662		36	259	200	4,858	165	5,023	357	4,676
1920	3,525	752	621	20	284	-200	5,384	254	5,638	414	5,224
1921	2,835	618	343	25	252	-350	4,423	178	4,601	352	4,249
1922	2,411	626	437	44	270	-62	3,850	177	4,027	314	3,713
1923	2,318	614	456	44	267	45	3,654	176	3,830	288	3,542
1924	2,376	633	477	40	278	40	3,764	196	3,960	283	3,677
1925	2,419	652	468	42	290	-139	4,010	232	4,242	283	3,959
1926	2,336	642	420	40	299	-56	3,793	237	4,030	283	3,747
1927	2,505	653	478	48	311	-28	4,023	239	4,262	279	3,983
1928	2,497	670	474	51	330	-18	4,040	240	4,280	284	3,996
1929	2,545	668	485	52	347	-80	4,177	243	4,420	293	4,127

Mitchell, B.R. *British Historical Statistics*, Cambridge University Press, 1988.

Original source, Feinstein, C.H. *National Income, Expenditure and Output of the UK, 1855-1965*, Cambridge, 1972.

3.6 Miscellaneous

3.6.1 Cooperative Hairdressing Prices

	s.	d.
Ladies		
Singeing		6
Long hair cutting and singeing	1	0
Bobbing (first time)	1	6
Bobbing (trim)	1	0
Shingling (first time)	1	6
Shingling (trim)	1	0
Waving	1	6
Hair massage (vibro)	1	0
Hair treatment (electric)	2	0
Course of six treatments	10	6
Shampooing	1	0
Mud pack	1	6
Brightening	4	6
Face massage (vibro)	1	0
Manicure	1	6
Children		
Cutting	1	0
Trimming		9
Shampooing		9

Producer, April, 1926, p. 313.

Taken from the charge list of the Droylsden Society's ladies and children's hairdressing saloon.

3.6.2 Motor Tyre Prices

Size of motor tyres	£	s.	£	s.[1]	Percent %
760 x 90	5	8	4	13	14
815 x 105	7	0	6	4	11½
815 x 120	9	8	8	5	12½
30 x 3½	4	19	4	12	7½

Producer, May, 1926, p. 224.

[1]On April 19, there was a reduction in the price of pneumatic tyres.

3.6.3 Wage Earners' Savings, 1928

Savings Institutions	Estimate of savers	£m
Post Office Savings Bank Deposits	two thirds	192
Trustee Savings Bank	two thirds	54
Other Savings Banks	two thirds	54
Post Office Government Stock	one third	63
Trustee Savings Bank Government Stock	one third	13
Trustee Savings Bank, Special Investments	one third	13
Industrial and Provident Societies		20
Cooperative Banks		140
Friendly Societies		100
Building Societies' Share Capital and Deposits	one third	85
Building Societies' Borrowers Interest	one third	66
Trade Union Funds		10
Industrial Assurance Funds		216
National Savings Certificates	one fourth	120
Total		1,146

The People's Year Book, 1931, p. 266.

– Four –
1930-1938

Years of Expansion

PRIME MINISTERS
J. Ramsay MacDonald (Coalition), August 1931–June 1935
Stanley Baldwin (Coalition), June 1935–May 1937
Neville Chamberlain (Coalition), May 1937–May 1940

CHANCELLORS OF THE EXCHEQUER
P. Snowden, June 1929–November 1931
N. Chamberlain, November 1931–May 1937
Sir J. Simon, May 1937–May 1940

The General Election of 1929 saw the beginning of the second period of office for a Labour Government, albeit with the Liberals holding the balance of power. More than ever the crucial problem that faced the new Government was that of unemployment. The single minded tackling of this problem was undermined by two principal factors. Firstly, internal political dissent in the Labour and Conservative parties left both in disarray. Secondly, and of far greater importance, was the deepening world economic crisis.

The Wall Street financial crisis came at the end of October 1929, but the British economic situation did not start to become desperate until early 1931. Severe doubt about the health of the British economy led to gold reserves pouring out of the country. MacDonald's Labour Government was forced into drastic economies by the terms placed on a massive loan by the banking community. This precipitated a large reduction in unemployment benefits. This was unacceptable to several key members of the Government who subsequently resigned. The Labour Government fell from power and was replaced, also under MacDonald's leadership, by a 'National Coalition'. This government was dominated by Conservatives, and it was a Conservative set of solutions, primarily protection (through import duties), that were adopted.

By 1933 economic recovery was beginning and it continued until 1935. Unemployment fell from its peak of nearly three million in the winter of 1932–3 to below two million in July 1935. The index of production, from a base line of 100 in 1929, fell to 84 in 1931 but rose again to 93 in 1933, and to 110 in 1935. While imports were maintained, exports declined. This resulted in depressed areas in which industry was dependent on export trade. The cost-of-living fell, and those

in continuous employment were, in general, better off. The burden of recovery was carried by the unemployed, and by foreign producers whose goods Britain imported more cheaply than ever before. Favourable terms of trade probably did more to maintain the standard of living than any deliberate measures of the Government.

One of the most important factors in industrial recovery was the building boom, which included domestic houses and commercial/industrial building. Financed mainly through the help of building societies and local authorities, the new houses were cheap enough to effect a real rise in the standard of living. The rehousing of the British people was one of the most encouraging aspects of an otherwise rather bleak social scene.

On the political level, the mid-1930s was marked by a strong pacifist movement. The mainstream political parties were fatally divided about strategy towards the growing militarism of Germany, Italy and Japan. Inconsistencies and political weakness led to serious delays in recognizing this threat and to inappropriate rearmament policies. Military initiatives by the Germans in the Rhineland, Italy in North Africa, and Japan in China seemed only to further the British Government's paralysis. The Spanish Civil War also had a profound effect on British public opinion. At the end of 1936, the nation was gripped by the personal and constitutional crisis of the King, Edward VIII (the affair with Wallace Simpson).

In May 1937, after the Kings's abdication, Baldwin resigned as Prime Minister to be replaced by another conservative, Neville Chamberlain. The new Prime Minister attempted to negotiate with the German Chancellor, Adolf Hitler, and the notion of 'appeasement' became popular linguistic currency.

The decade began with the formation of one National Government in the face of an economic crisis and ended with the formation of a second in the face of military crisis. During the intervening years, the economic crisis had, in large measure, receded as the military crisis grew. Within so brief a time span, the people of Britain experienced deep economic depression and widespread distress, prolonged crises and intense anxieties, fumbling leadership and moments of national humiliation. Yet the 'devil's decade' was also a period of considerable prosperity and creative activity.

4.1 Historical Snapshots

4.1 Historical Snapshots

1930	Perspex invented in the UK.
	Car firms Rover, Lanchester and Standard merge.
	A draft highway code is issued.
1931	The Youth Hostelling Association (YHA) is formed.
	Malcolm Campbell sets a new world land speed record of 245 miles per hour in the USA.
	Traffic lights are introduced in Britain.
1932	The BBC makes its first transmission from Broadcasting House.
	Instant coffee is first sold in UK.
1933	Nearly 3 million workers are out of work – one in four of the total British labour force.
	The Trades Union Congress (TUC) calls for a boycott of Germany to protest against Hitler.
1934	Fred Perry becomes the first Briton to win the US Open Tennis Championship since 1903.
	First commercially produced synthetic detergent is made by ICI.
	Introduction of a drum-scanner facsimile telegraph.
	The *Daily Express* becomes the first daily newspaper to top 2 million sales.
1935	Glass eye reflectors, known as "Cats Eyes" and invented by Percy Shaw, are used on British roads.
1936	King George V dies.
	A treaty with Egypt gives Britain use of the Suez Canal for 20 years.
	Crystal Palace burns down.

	The economist John Maynard Keynes publishes a theory on how to combat the recession.
	Unilever becomes the UK's largest employer with 60,000 employees.
	Edward VIII abdicates.
1937	George VI is crowned.
	Factory Act cuts maximum working hours for young people and women to between 44 and 48 hours per week.
	The Dandy is published for the first time.
	Billy Butlin opens his first holiday camp.
	Frank Whittle develops the first jet engine.
	Ferdinand Porsche introduces prototype of the Volkswagen Beetle in Germany.
	Lazlo Biro patents the ball point pen in Hungary.
1938	All school children are issued with gas masks.
	Neville Chamberlain pledges Britain to defend France and Belgium.
	The *Queen Elizabeth*, the world's largest liner, is launched.
	£200,000 is spent on air raid shelters.
	The USA-owned Gallup Opinion Polls forms a company in the UK.
	A 90 mph Jaguar costing £385 is the star of the motor show.
	The BBC makes its first television broadcast from Alexandra Palace.

Chronicle of Britain, J.L. International Publishing, 1992; Williams, T.I. *Invention and Discovery in the 20th Century,* Harrap, 1990.

4.2 Earnings and Employment

4.2.1 Earnings, Standard Tables

4.2.1a Incomes and Wages

	1930	1931	1932	1933	1934	1935	1936	1937	1938
Solicitor						£1,238 (a)			
General Practitioner						£1,094 (a)			
Teacher		£480 (a)				£480 (a)			
Clerical Worker						£192 (a)			
Train Driver	72 to 90s.	69s. 5d.	69s. 5d.	69s. 5d.	69s. 0d.	70s. 2d.	71s. 1d.	72s. 0d.	72s. 0d.
Coal Miner		45 2				44 8			
Fitter and Turner	59s. 1d.	59 1	59 1	59 1	59 1	60 9	64 1	67 2	67 2
Bricklayer	70 7	69 1	67 3	65 5	65 6	67 5	69 4	71 1	73 1
Labourer	52 7	51 10	50 2	49 2	49 4	50 6	52 2	53 3	55 1
Compositor	73 10	73 10	73 10	73 10	73 10	73 10	73 10	73 10	73 10
Farm Worker	31 7½	31 3	30 9	30 9	31 5½	32 0	32 9	34 2	34 8
Baker	63 5	62 1	61 9	61 7	61 7	62 0	62 1	62 7	63 4
Textile Worker (weaver)	32 6	30 9				35 6	31 5	36 6	

British Labour Statistics, HMSO, 1971; Bowley, A.L. *Wages and Incomes in the UK since 1860*, Cambridge University Press, 1937; Routh, G. *Occupation and Pay in Great Britain, 1906-1979*, Macmillan Press, 1980.

Blank space denotes no available data. Wages are weekly unless otherwise stated. (a) – annual.

4.2.1b Average Weekly Earnings

	Males		Females	
	1931	1935	1931	1935
	s.	s.	s.	s.
Bricks, Pottery and Glass	51.7	52.5	22.4	23.9
Metals	53.8	58.8	25.6	26.9
Textiles	48.0	49.2	26.9	27.5
Clothing	53.6	54.3	26.9	27.8
Food, Drink and Tobacco	57.5	56.6	28.0	26.6
Paper and Printing	71.8	75.4	28.3	28.1
Total Building	57.2	55.9	27.4	28.1
Total Miscellaneous	61.6	60.4	26.0	26.8
Local Government	52.7	52.7	26.2	28.0
Railway Works	64.0	68.4	0	0
Average Full-Time Earnings	57.3	56.6	28.0	27.2

Bowley, A.L. *Wages and Income in the UK since 1860*, Cambridge University Press, 1937.

Original source, *Ministry of Labour Gazette*. These Industry Groups are prior to the 1948 Standard Industrial Classification (SIC).

4.2.2 Regional Earnings by Selected Occupation

		London		Manchester		Newcastle		Leeds		Glasgow	
		s.	d.	s.	d.	s.	d.	s.	d.	s.	d.
Bricklayer (hourly)	1930	1	8½	1	7	1	7	1	7	1	8
	1938	1	9	1	7½	1	7½	1	7½	1	8½
Bricklayer's Labourer (hourly)	1930	1	3½	1	2¼	1	2¼	1	2¼	1	2¾
	1938	1	3½	1	2¾	1	2¾	1	2¾	1	3
Compositor (weekly)	1930	89	0	77	6½	74	6	74	6	77	6
	1938	89	0	77	6	74	6	74	6	77	6
Fitter and Turner (weekly)	1930	62	11	58	0	n/a		n/a		58	1½
	1938	70	11	66	0	n/a		n/a		66	1½
Labourer (weekly)	1930	45	3½	40	0	n/a		n/a		42	11¼
	1938	53	3½	49	0	n/a		n/a		50	11¼

British Labour Statistics, 1886–1968, HMSO, 1971.

4.2.3 Incomes, Miscellaneous

4.2.3a Regional Wages in Principal Industries, 1931

	London		Glasgow		Birmingham		Liverpool		Manchester		Bedford		Carlisle		Worcester		Norwich	
	s.	d.	s.	d.	s.	d.	s.	d.	s.	d.	s.	d.	s.	d.	s.	d.	s.	d.
Fitters and Turners	62	11	58	1	58	0	58	0	58	0	57	0	57	0	55	0	55	0
Ironmoulders	62	11	64	10½	60	0	64	6	62	6	58	0	58	6	57	6	54	0
Engine Shop Labourers	45	3½	42	4½	42	0	42	0	41	0	40	5					40	6
Electricians (Wiremen)	81	4	70	6	69	6	69	6	69	6	64	6	64	6	59	8	64	6
Vehicle Builders (skilled)	68	6	72	6	66	6	66	6	66	6	62	7	62	7	62	7	66	6
Shipwrights	66	6	62	3			63	0										
Shipyard Labourers	51	6	43	3			48	0	44	0								
Flour Mill (First Roller Men)	73	0			73	0	73	0	73	0	64	6			68	0	70	6
Flour Mill (Labourers)	57	0			57	0	57	0	57	0	48	6			52	0	54	6
Cabinet Makers	73	6	71	8	65	10	73	7	67	8								
Upholsterers			71	8	65	10	71	7	67	8								
Compositors	89	0	77	6	74	6	77	6	77	6	65	6	68	6	65	6	65	6
Bookbinders	80	0	77	6	74	6	77	6	77	6			68	6	65	6	65	6
Printers' Assistants			53	6	55	6	57	6	57	6	49	6	51	6	49	6	49	6
Building Craftsmen	69	8	67	10	67	0	69	7	66	0	58	7	66	0	62	3	62	3
Building Labourers	52	3	49	6	51	0	52	3	50	0	44	0	50	0	47	1	47	1
Tram Drivers (maximum)	73	0	62	0	64	6	62	6	61	6							55	6
Tram Conductors (maximum)	73	0	62	0	61	0	60	0	59	0							52	0
Local Authorities: General Yard Labourers	56	11	52	3	50	7	49	4	49	4	44	0	50	8			52	6

The People's Year Book, 1936, p. 110.

Wages are weekly. Blank space denotes no data available.

4.2.3b Coal Miners' Earnings per Shift

	Durham		UK	
	s.	d.	s.	d.
1930	8	0¾	9	3½
1931	8	0¼	9	2¼
1932	8	1	9	2
1933	8	0½	9	1½
1934	8	0½	9	1¾
1935	8	0½	9	3¼
1936	8	7	10	0¼
1937	9	1	10	8
1938	9	8¼	11	2¼

Garside, W.R. *The Durham Miners 1919–1960*, 1971.

Original source, *Reports of HM Inspectors of Mines, 1920–1938*.

4.2.3c Regional Earnings of Weavers

District	Weavers engaged solely on artificial silk						Weavers engaged solely on cotton						Weavers engaged on both cotton and silk					
	1936			1937			1936			1937			1936			1937		
	£	s.	d.	£	s.	d.	£	s.	d.	£	s.	d.	£	s.	d.	£	s.	d.
Colne	2	0	2	2	5	8	1	14	2	1	19	5	1	15	5	2	3	6
Nelson	1	18	2	2	5	1	1	14	9	2	1	1	1	17	1	2	1	0
Skipton	1	14	3	1	18	1	1	11	1	1	14	2	1	12	5	2	1	0
Preston	1	11	3	1	19	11	1	7	0	1	13	8½	1	7	11	1	16	8

A History of the Lancashire Cotton Industry and the Amalgamated Weavers Association, Amalgamated Weavers Association, 1969.

The figures are for average actual weekly earnings.

4.2.3d North British Locomotive Company Wages

	Average wages per man per week	
	s.	d.
1930	51	8¼
1931	45	4
1932	45	9
1933	46	1½
1934	50	6
1935	49	5¼
1936	54	0¾
1937	54	9¼
1938	61	6½

Business History, Vol.XX, No.2, July, 1978, p. 231.

Taken from *North British Locomotive Company Papers*, in Mitchell Library, Glasgow.

4.2.3e Wages for John Brown and Co., Shipbuilders

Year	Average Number of Men per Week	Average Pay Bill £ s. d.	Average Weekly Wages per Man £ s. d.
1930	5,085	13,430 15 1	2 12 10
1931	3,556	9,480 13 7	2 13 4
1932	422	1,279 4 7	3 0 7
1933	675	1,847 10 5	2 14 9
1934	3,758	10,366 13 9	2 15 2
1935	5,381	14,504 8 4	2 13 11
1936	5,617	16,172 2 3	2 17 7
1937	6,198	18,645 2 1	3 0 2
1938	8,075	25,657 5 4	3 3 7

Business History, Vol. XIX, No.2, July, 1977, p. 204.

Compiled from *Abstract Wage Books, John Brown & Co., Clydebank, 1914–1938.*

4.2.4 Employment

4.2.4a Unemployment[1]

July	Males Number	Males Percent	Females Number	Females Percent	Total Number	Total Percent
1930	1,519,474	17.4	550,614	16.5	2,070,088	17.1
1931	2,127,615	23.8	678,860	19.5	2,806,475	22.6
1932	2,415,819	26.3	505,125	14.1	2,920,944	22.9
1933	2,122,540	22.8	385,233	11.0	2,507,773	19.6
1934	1,791,584	19.2	367,661	10.4	2,162,245	16.8
1935	1,658,523	17.6	333,338	9.5	1,991,861	15.4
1936	1,366,651	14.3	292,963	8.3	1,659,614	12.7
1937	1,117,386	11.5	268,246	7.4	1,385,632	10.4
1938	1,381,513	13.9	437,565	11.7	1,819,078	13.3

The People's Year Book, 1942, p. 79.

[1]Persons 16–64 years, insured under the General Scheme.

4.2.4b Employment by Region

	1930	1931	1932	1933	1934	1935	1936	1937	1938
	000's	000's	000's	000's	000's	000's	000's	000's	000's
London	2,256	2,347	2,366	2,399	2,437	2,466	2,750[1]	2,855	2,896
South East	930	973	996	1,012	1,037	1,074	938[1]	1,052[2]	1,077
South West	864	895	908	913	918	929	960	940[2]	963
Midlands	1,847	1,893	1,892	1,910	1,928	1,952	2,008	2,053[2]	2,090
North East	2,021	2,073	2,085	2,084	2,081	2,075	1,396[1]	1,428[2]	1,443
North							778[1]	785	799
North West	2,182	2,223	2,194	2,188	2,165	2,157	2,080[1]	2,122	2,143
Scotland	1,308	1,350	1,340	1,346	1,352	1,356	1,376	1,398	1,418
Wales	592	606	619	621	622	618	611	610	617
Great Britain	12,000	12,360	12,400	12,473	12,540	12,627	12,897	13,243	13,448
Northern Ireland	266	270	265	263	268	276	287	295	297
UK	12,266	12,630	12,665	12,736	12,808	12,903	13,184	13,538	13,745

British Labour Statistics, 1886–1968, HMSO, 1971.

Figures are for the mid-year for those insured under the General Scheme and aged between 16 and 64. [1]In August 1936, Northern region was formed. London region was also enlarged to cover the city of London and hence South Eastern region became smaller. [2]In August 1937, the South Eastern region was enlarged. Some districts were also transferred from Midlands region to the North East region. Original sources, *Gazette* and *22nd Abstract of Labour Statistics*.

4.3 Consumer Expenditure

4.3.1 Consumer Expenditure, Standard Table

	Food	Alcoholic Drink	Tobacco	Housing	Fuel and Light	Clothing	Durable House-hold Goods	Motor Cars and Motor Cycles	Other Goods	Other Services	Total Con-sumer Expendi-ture
	£m	£m	£m	£m	£m	£m	£m	£m	£m	£m	£m
1930	1,163	301	140	375	162	418	133	34	396	822	3,932
1931	1,093	282	140	382	162	395	133	27	385	810	3,805
1932	1,042	264	139	386	157	364	136	36	370	809	3,683
1933	1,006	258	142	394	158	366	136	30	384	820	3,696
1934	1,027	262	146	402	161	371	151	38	407	839	3,802
1935	1,054	273	153	416	164	388	160	44	424	861	3,935
1936	1,082	283	161	431	176	402	169	47	440	893	4,080
1937	1,136	297	169	443	185	426	178	49	483	930	4,289
1938	1,157	294	176	455	188	438	174	43	498	965	4,392

Mitchell, B.R. *British Historical Statistics*, Cambridge University Press, 1988.

Original source, Feinstein, C.H. *National Income, Expenditure and Output of the UK, 1855-1965*, Cambridge, 1972.

4.4 Prices

4.4.1 Food Prices

4.4.1a Food Basket

Article (per lb. unless otherwise stated)	1933		1938	
	s.	d.	s.	d.
Beef, home-killed:				
Ribs	1	2	1	2½
Thin flank		7½		7¾
Beef, chilled or frozen:				
Ribs		9		9¾
Thin flank		4½		5
Mutton, home killed:				
Legs	1	2½	1	3¾
Breast		7½		7¾
Mutton, frozen:				
Legs		9¼		10½
Breast		3¾		4¼
Bacon, streaky		11½	1	3¼
Flour (per 7lb.)	1	0¼	1	3¼
Bread (per 4lb.)		7½		9
Tea	1	9¼	2	3½
Sugar granulated		2¼		2½
Milk (per quart)		5¾		6¾
Butter:				
Fresh	1	2¼	1	4¾
Salt	1	0½	1	3½
Cheese		9¼		10¾
Margarine		6¼		6½
Eggs, fresh, each		1½		1¾
Potatoes (per 7lb.)		5½		6¾

British Labour Statistics, 1886–1968, HMSO, 1971.

The table was compiled from information supplied for the "Cost of Living Index" by over 5,000 retailers in approximately 500 towns.

4.4.1b Standard of Living in Sheffield

	Price per lb.		Total Cost
	s.	d.	d.
Bread (5.25lb.)		1¾	9.19
Flour (2.06lb.)		1¼	2.58
Rolled Oats (0.83lb.)		3	2.49
Rice (0.3lb.)		3	0.90
Dried Peas (1lb.)		3½	3.50
Biscuits (0.69lb.)		7	4.83
Bacon (0.26lb.)		7	1.82
Butter (0.11lb.)	1	2	1.54
Margarine (0.35lb.)		6	2.10
Fresh Milk (2.01pts.)		3	6.03
Condensed Milk (0.33lb.)		3½	1.10
Cheese (0.183lb.)		8	1.46
Sugar (1.28lb.)		2½	3.20
Fresh egg, one		1¼	1.25
Beef (0.98lb.)		7	6.86
Mutton (0.5lb.)		8	4.00
Beef Sausage (0.9lb.)		7	6.30
Lard (0.224lb.)		6½	1.46
Tea (0.15lb.)		10	1.50
Potatoes (3.4lb.)		1	3.40
Carrots (1lb.)		1½	1.50
Cabbage (1lb.)		1½	1.50

Wilsher, P. *The Pound in Your Pocket 1870–1970*, Cassell and Company Ltd., 1970.

A basic standard diet calculated at the prices ruling in the city in November and December, 1931, to provide the minimum physiological needs of an adult male engaged in medium–heavy manual work.

4.4.2 Prices, General Articles

	1930		1931		1932		1933		1934		1935		1936		1937		1938	
	s.	d.	s.	d.	s.	d.	s.	d.	s.	d.	s.	d.	s.	d.	s.	d.	s.	d.
Aspirin (100)							1	6										
Beer (1 pint)		5		7		7		7		7		7		7		7		8
Cadbury's Milk Chocolate (½ lb. bar)	1	0	1	1	1	1½	1	2	1	1	1	5	2	0	1	11	2	1
Cheddar Cheese (1 lb.)	1	4									1	0						
Colmans Mustard (1 lb.)	2	10													2	1¾		
Colmans Starch (tin)		1														1		
Daily Mail		1		1		1		1		1		1		1		1		1
Guinness Extra Stout (1 pint)		10										10						
Inland Letter Post		1½		1½		1½		1½		1½		1½		1½		1½		1½
Pears Transparent Soap			1	0							1	2						
Petrol (1 gallon)			1	4½			1	7½										
Red Label Tea (1 lb.)	2	0									1	4						
Swan Vestas Matches		1½																
The Times		4		4		4		4		4		4		4		4		4

The Boots Company; British Library; Burmah Castrol; Cadburys Ltd; Colmans of Norwich; Guinness Brewing GB; Royal Mail; Sainsbury's Archives; Scotch Whisky Association and Unilever Historical Archives.

Blank space denotes no prices available.

4.4.3 Prices, Selected

Item	Source	Description	Price £	s.	d.	
Alcoholic Drink						
Spirits	*The Tatler*, February 18, 1925	Gloags Grouse Brand Whisky in Casks	18	0	0	(5 gallon cask)
		Gloags Whisky		12	6	(bottle)
Vermouth	*The Ideal Home*, June 1938	Martini Sweet		4	6	(litre)
		Martini Dry		5	6	(litre)
Appliances: Domestic and Electrical						
Lamp	*Affleck & Brown Ltd.*, Manchester, 1932	Electric Table or Reading Lamp		15	11	
	Affleck & Brown Ltd., Manchester, 1933	Standard Lamp		16	11	
Cooker	*Homes and Gardens*, January 1935	Briffo Clean Coal Cooker	38	0	0	
Refrigerator	*Homes and Gardens*, June 1935	Electrolux Air Cooled Refrigerator	19	10	0	
Cleaner	*Homes and Gardens*, April 1936	"Electrix" Dust Flow	5	19	6	
		Vactrix Electric Vacuum Cleaner	6	12	6	
		Bissells Silver Sweeper	1	4	0	
Cooker		Courtier Cooker	11	0	0	
		Interoven Stove	6	15	0	
		Flavel Cooker "Babette"	6	12	6	
		Flavel Cooker "Kabmeat"	12	7	6	
		Esse-Minor Burning Anthracite	45	0	0	
Boiler		Beeston Domestic Boiler	2	15	0	
Fires		Elliott Brick Fireplaces	4	15	0	
		"Wellog" Dogs and Firebars		12	6	(up to 20in.)
		Cosy Cotswold Stone Fires	7	12	6	
Refrigerator		"Zeros" Refrigerator Model ZR1	26	5	0	
Gramophone	*Baxendales & Co. Ltd.*, Manchester, 1936	Portable Gramophone	2	9	6	
Heating Stoves		Artistic Portable Gas Fire	1	10	0	(up to 35/0)
		"Wormo" Oil Heated Portable Radiator	7	17	6	
		"Beatrice" Mottled Enamelled Two Burner Oil Heater		8	6	
Baby Equipment						
Nappies	*Affleck & Brown Ltd.*, Manchester, 1933	Terry Towelling Nappies		7	11	(dozen)
Cot		Baby's Cot with Plycene Mattress	1	12	0	
	Baxendales & Co. Ltd., Manchester, 1936	Baby's Cot 4ft. 6in. x 2ft. 6in.	2	9	6	
Bath		Baby's Bath	2	2	0	
Clothing and Footwear:						
Children's						
Shoes	*C & J Clark Ltd.*, 1930	Child's Buda Bar, White Dyeing Satin		8	0	(up to 9/0)
Dyeing		White Satin Shoes (can be dyed to match)		1	6	(allow 2 days)
Suit	*Affleck & Brown*, Manchester, 1933	Girl's All Wool Scotch Knit Jumper		9	11	(28")
		Child's Sleeping Suit		2	9	(24")
Nightdress		Infant's Wincyette Nightgown		1	9	
Coat	*Affleck & Brown Ltd.*, Manchester, 1936	Girl's Coat and Hat Set of Heavy Frieze	1	13	6	

Continued

4.4.3 Prices, Selected *continued*

Item	Source	Description	Price £	s.	d.
Men's					
Shirt	*Affleck & Brown*, Manchester, 1933	Men's Oxford Shirts		6	11
		Quality Union Flannel Shirts		7	11
Nightwear		Wool Dressing Gown		13	6
		Cotton Poplin Pyjamas		5	11
Women's					
Dress	*Coulsons Stocktaking Sale*, London, 1930	Celofleck Dress	3	3	0
		Crêpe Dress	6	6	0
		Floral Print on a Natural Background	3	9	6
Shoes	*C & J Clark Ltd.*, 1930	Tor Promenade: Medusa Bar	1	11	6
		Acton Bar Brown Crocodile	1	8	0
		Wessex Dress Shoe: Napoli Bar		12	3
		Buda Bar White Dyeing Satin		10	6
Hosiery	*The Tatler*, February 18, 1931	Aristoc Pure Silk Stockings		4	11 (up to 12/6)
Frock	*Affleck & Brown*, Manchester, 1933	Useful Day Frock in Fine Wool Material		14	6
Coat		Leather Coat	2	19	6
Knitwear		Fancy Knit All Wool Double Breasted Cardigan		5	0
Shoes		Patent Leather Shoes		12	11
Nightwear		Wincyette Pyjamas		4	11
Shirt		Ladies Youthful Shirt with Artistic Bow		9	11
Dress	*Guleries Lafayette*, c.1930	Charming Fancy Woollen Material Dress	2	15	0
Coat		Black Cloth Coat cut on the new Paris Line	5	5	0
Frock	*Affleck & Brown*, Manchester, 1936	Exquisite Dinner Frock in Softest Lamé	7	7	0
Coat		Coat Tailored for a Soft Bouclé	3	3	0
Hat		Bowler Hat with Adaptable Brim and Crushed Crown		12	9
Shoes		Brown Calf Oxford Shoe	1	1	9
Hosiery		Pure Silk Stockings		3	11½
Blouse		Crisply Tailored Blouse in Suede Crêpe		14	11
Nightwear		Lace Trimmed Nightgown		5	11
Corsetry		Gossard Corset		18	0
Hat	*Kendals Spring Book*, Manchester, 1938	Soft Felt Hat	3	1	6
Suit		Two Piece Wool Suit	10	10	0
Frock		Tailored Frock	1	19	6
Coat		Bouclé Ladies Coat	8	8	0
Waistcoat		Ladies Waistcoat	1	19	6
Hosiery		Silk Stockings		8	11
Dress	*Affleck & Brown Ltd.*, Manchester, 1938	White Net Evening Dress	6	6	0
Corsetry		Gossard Front Lacing Corsette	1	4	6
Food Products					
Bacon	*J Sainsbury Archives*, 1930	Unsmoked Back Bacon		1	6 (per lb.)

Continued

4.4.3 Prices, Selected *continued*

Item	Source	Description	Price £	s.	d.
Butter		Loose Butter		1	8 (per lb.)
Cheese		Cheddar Cheese		1	4 (per lb.)
Eggs		6 Medium Sized Eggs			6
Breakfast Cereal		Shredded Wheat		1	0½ (12's)
Squash		Kia-Ora Orange Squash		2	0 (20oz. bottle)
Soup		Heinz Tomato Soup			9 (15oz. tin)
Biscuits		McVities Digestive Biscuits		1	0 (½ lb.)
Bacon	*J Sainsbury Archives*, 1935	Unsmoked Back Bacon		1	0 (per lb.)
Butter		Loose Butter		1	3 (per lb.)
Cheese		Cheddar Cheese		1	0 (per lb.)
Eggs		6 Medium Size Eggs		1	0
Breakfast Cereal		Shredded Wheat			8 (12's)
Squash		Kia-Ora Orange Squash		2	0 (20oz. bottle)
Soup		Heinz Tomato Soup			7½ (15oz. tin)
Biscuits		McVities Digestive Biscuits			7½ (½ lb.)
Milk	*The People's Year Book*, 1936	Pint of Milk			3½
Bread		4lb. Loaf			8½
Cocoa		Lutona Cocoa		1	7 (per lb.)
Spices (per lb.)	*Scottish CWS Ltd.*, Glasgow, 1936	Caraway			9
		Cardamom		3	9
		Cloves		1	6
		Ginger No 1		1	3
		Mace		3	2
Whole Spices (per lb.)		Cardamom		3	6
		Cinnamon Stick		2	0
		Mace		3	0
Mustard	*Colmans of Norwich*, 1938	Colmans DSF Mustard			2 (tin)
Starch		Colmans Rice Starch			1 (box)
Furniture					
Carpets	*Bradshaws ABC Railway Guide*, 1931	Hamptons Axminster Carpets		10	6 (sq. yd.)
Table	*Affleck & Brown Ltd.*, Manchester, 1932	Mahogany Circular Coffee Table	2	12	6
		Oak Gate Leg Table 5ft. x 3ft. 6in.	5	12	6
Sideboard		Solid Oak Sideboard 4ft. x 6ft. wide	10	19	6
Chair		Fireside Easy Chair	1	17	6
Seating	*Affleck & Brown*, Manchester, 1933	Three Piece Suite in Moquette	26	10	0
		Floor Pouffes in Artificial Silk		14	11
Bureau		Mahogany Bureau with Mahogany Sides	7	7	0
Bedroom		Oak Hall Wardrobe	7	15	0
Carpets		Deep Pile Axminster Carpets 9ft. x 9ft.	6	15	0
		Deep Pile Axminster Carpets 15ft. x 12ft.	14	9	6
Seating	*Homes and Gardens*, April 1936	"Cowley" Chair	7	7	0
		"Cowley" Settee	12	12	0
Bedroom		Reproduction Burr Walnut Bedroom Suite	40	19	0
Flooring		Linovent			10½ (sq. yd.)

Continued

4.4.3 Prices, Selected *continued*

Item	Source	Description	£	s.	d.
Mirror	*Baxendales & Co. Ltd.*, Manchester, 1936	Cheval Frameless Mirror with Bevelled Edge	6	7	6

Garden Equipment and Supplies

Item	Source	Description	£	s.	d.
Fountain	*Homes and Gardens*, April 1936	Gamages Centrifugal Pump and Motor	2	17	6
Mower		Royal Enfield Motor Mower	12	12	0
		Qualcast Motor Mower 16 inches	15	15	0
Heating Stove	*Baxendales & Co. Ltd.*, Manchester, 1936	Oil Heated Greenhouse Apparatus		15	0 (complete)
		Garage Heater on the lines of a Miners Lamp	1	8	0
Furniture		Folding Arm Chair in Canvas		10	6
		"Sylvan" Couch Hammock in Heavy Nile Fabric	13	5	0
		Rustic Seat in Peeled Oak 6ft.	2	2	9
		Rustic Arm Chair	1	7	6
		"Bedford" Steel Frame Shelters	1	7	6 (woven stripe tick)
		Rustic Bird Table	1	17	6
Greenhouse	*The Ideal Home*, June 1938	Crittall Sectional Steel Greenhouse	12	5	0 (upwards)

Heat and Light

Item	Source	Description	£	s.	d.
Electricity	*Eastern Electricity Board*, 1931	Electricity per unit			3
Gas	*North Thames Board*, 1931	Gas per therm			8
Coal	*The People's Year Book*, 1934	Coal per ton	1	3	2½

Hotel Rates

Item	Source	Description	£	s.	d.
Northway Hotel, Euston Sq, London	*Bradshaws ABC Railway Guide*, 1930	Bedroom, Bath, Table d'Hôte, Breakfast		8	0 (up to 8/6)
Marlborough Private Hotel, Rhyl		Terms from	3	3	0
The York, Whitby		Terms from		10	6 a day

Household Goods

Item	Source	Description	£	s.	d.
Towels	*D.H. Evans*, London, 1931	Big Bath Towels		5	11
Bedding		Witney Blankets		14	9
	Selfridges Archives, 1931	Cotton Sheets Single		10	0 (pair)
		Linen Sheets Single		18	9 (pair)
	Affleck & Brown Ltd., Manchester, 1932	Artifical Silk Bedspreads		14	11 (double)
		Artifical Silk Bedspreads		12	9
Cutlery		Case of Electro Plated Fruit Spoons with Server		12	11
		Case of Electro Plated Fish Servers		14	11
Lighting		Candle Shades			10½ each
Towels		Christy's White Turkish Bath Sheets		5	11
	Affleck & Brown Ltd., Manchester, 1933	Christy's White Turkish Bath Sheets		5	11
Bedding		Plain Cotton Sheets 2 x 3 yards		8	6 (pair)
		Hem Stitched Cotton Pillow Cases		1	6½
		Coloured Blankets		7	6 (upwards)
Table Linen		Real Linen Damask Cloths 54in. x 54in.		2	4½
		Irish Linen Cloths 54in. x 54in.		11	9

Continued

4.4.3 Prices, Selected *continued*

Item	Source	Description	Price £	s.	d.
Cleaning Materials	*Homes and Gardens*, April 1936	Goddards Plate Polish			9 (tin)
		Ronuk Floor Polish		2	6 (tin)
	Unilever Archives, 1935	J. Watson & Sons Ltd. "Sparkla"			1d. blocks and 2d. blocks
		J. Watson "Aerdex" (sold to laundries)	1	16	0 (56 lb. bags)
		J. Watson White Laundry Curd (sold to laundries)	1	13	6 (Bar Soaps in 1 cwt. boxes)
Clocks	*Baxendales & Co. Ltd.*, Manchester, 1936	A/C. Electric Mains Grandmother	12	2	0 (oak)
		Figured Walnut Inlaid with Ebony and Rosewood	3	17	6
		Chromium Plated Bezel, Cream Coloured	2	5	0 (walnut)
Pyrex Brand Oven to Table Ware		Casserole Oval Deep		10	6 (3 pint capacity)
		Round Dish and Cover in E.P.N.S. Stand	1	5	0
		Pudding Dish Round		4	6 (3 pint capacity)
		Utility Plates			6 (up to 2/6 each)
		Soup Plate		2	0 (each)
		Pyrex Gift Set		19	0 (set)

Houses

Item	Source	Description	Price £	s.	d.
Detached (all freehold)	*Homes and Gardens*, April 1936	Pound Farm Estate, Esher, "The Woodlands"	1,095	0	0
Semi Detached			895	0	0
Detached		Pound Farm Estate, Esher "Groveway"	2,500	0	0
		Hanger Hill, Ealing, 3 Bed	1,350	0	0
	The Pound in Your Pocket 1870–1970, 1938	Morrell Homes, Bromley, Kent	920	0	0

Jewellery

Item	Source	Description	Price £	s.	d.
Watches	*Bradshaws ABC Railway Guide*, 1930	H. Samuels Solid Gold Bracelet Watches	1	9	6
		H. Samuels Gent's Silver Wrist Watch	1	5	0
Ring		H. Samuels Diamond Ring	1	15	0 (up to 90/0)

Personal Care Items

Item	Source	Description	Price £	s.	d.
Soap	*Unilever Archives*, 1934	Pears Original Transparent Soap			7 (tablet)
		Golden Glory Scented Transparent Soap			8 (tablet)
		Otto of Rose Soap		5	1 (tablet)
		Glycerine Soap			9 (tablet)
		Wash Balls		1	2 (up to 2/8)
		J. Watson Old English Lavender			3 (tablet)
		J. Watson Palm and Olive Oil			3 (tablet)
Shaving Supplies	*Baxendales & Co. Ltd.*, Manchester, 1936	Gillette Safety Razor with 3 blades		2	6
		Shaving Mirror		12	9
Warmer		Bedtime Foot Warmer		2	0
Water Bottle		Hot Water Bottle 3 quart size		2	3
Perfume	*Affleck & Brown Ltd.*, Manchester, 1938	Coty Perfumes		3	9 (up to 10/6)
Chemists	*Homes and Gardens*, January 1936	Mackenzie Anti-Catarrh Medication		1	6

Continued

4.4.3 Prices, Selected *continued*

Item	Source	Description	£	s.	d.
Chemists *cont.*		John Taylor's Oxygen Tooth Powder			6 (up to 3/6)
Publications					
Guides	*Bradshaws ABC Railway Guide*, 1930	Railway Guide			6
	Bradshaws ABC Railway Guide, 1935				6
Magazines	*Homes and Gardens*, April 1936	The Needlewoman			6
Services					
Cinema	*Kinematograph Year Book*, 1930–1938	Grosvenor Picture Palace Manchester Admission Price			6 (up to 1/0)
	The Pound in Your Pocket 1870–1970, 1931	Cinema Price in London			9 (upwards)
Theatre		Charlie Chaplin at Dominion Theatre, London		2	4 (up to 10/0)
Licences	*Post Office Archives*, 1936	Radio		10	0
	DVLA, 1935	Road Tax	4	10	0 (plus 15/0 per h.p. unit)
Telephone Tariffs	*British Telecom Archives*, 1934				
London (10 mile radius from Oxford Circus)		Quarterly Residential Rental	1	6	0
Birmingham, Glasgow, Liverpool, Manchester			1	3	0
London		Quarterly Business Rental		13	0
Birmingham, Glasgow, Liverpool, Manchester			1	10	0
9 am to 2 pm		7½ to 10 miles			3
		10 to 12½ miles			4
		12½ to 15 miles			5
		15 to 20 miles			7
	British Telecom Archives, 1936				
London		Quarterly Residential Rental	1	6	0
Birmingham, Glasgow, Liverpool, Manchester			1	3	0
London		Quarterly Business Rental	1	15	6
Birmingham, Glasgow, Liverpool, Manchester			1	12	6
9am to 2pm (timing with drawn from calls to 15 m.)		15 to 20 miles			7
		20 to 25 miles			9
		25 to 35 miles		1	0
		35 to 50 miles		1	3
Parcel Postage Rates	*Post Office Archives*, 1935	3lb. weight			6
		5lb. weight			8

Continued

4.4.3 Prices, Selected *continued*

Item	Source	Description	Price		
			£	s.	d.
		15lb. weight		1	0
CWS Health Insurance	*The People's Year Book*, 1934	Sickness Benefit		5	0 (per week extra)
		Disablement Benefit		2	6 (per week extra)
		Maternity Benefit		5	0 (extra)
	The People's Year Book, 1937	Sickness Benefit		3	0 (per week extra)
		Disablement Benefit		1	6 (per week extra)
		Maternity Benefit		3	0 (extra)
Banking (accounts opened)	*Bradshaws ABC Railway Guide*, 1930	Manchester and Salford Bank		1	0 (with 2½ % interest)

Sewing Equipment and Supplies

Item	Source	Description	Price		
Fabrics (per yard)	*Affleck & Brown Ltd.*, Manchester, 1933	All Wool Saxony Suiting		4	11
		Flecked Dress Tweed		2	11
		Silk Pile Chiffon Velvet		6	9
		Rich Multi-coloured Embossed Velour		12	9
Machine	*Baxendales & Co. Ltd.*, 1936	Sewing Machine (hand model)	5	12	6
		Drop Head Treadle Machine in Oak	8	15	0
		Drop Head Treadle Machine in Walnut	9	5	0

Sports and Hobbies

Item	Source	Description	Price		
Sports	*Baxendales & Co. Ltd.*, 1936	Boxing Gloves		10	9 (set)
		Ball Bearing Roller Skates		10	6 (pair)
		Solid Champion Ice Skates	2	2	0 (pair)
Hobbies		Pathescope Projector	15	0	0

Tobacco Products

Item	Source	Description	Price		
Cigarettes	*The Tatler*, January 7, 1931	Players Navy Cut Cigarettes			6 (10)
	Scottish CWS Ltd., Glasgow, 1931	Gold Flake Mild			6 (10)
		Sunbeam			2 (5)
		Pearl			4 (10)
Tobacco		Black Roll Tobacco: Thick Black		10	0 (per lb.)
		Brown Roll Tobacco: Bogie Roll		10	1 (per lb.)
Cigarettes	*The People's Year Book*, 1934	CWS Silk Cut			5 (10)
		CWS Lustre		1	0 (36)
	Homes and Gardens, April 1936	Players No 3		1	4 (20)
Smoking Equipment	*Affleck & Brown Ltd.*, Manchester, 1936	Ladies Cigarette Case in Best Quality Lacquer		12	6
	Baxendales & Co. Ltd., Manchester, 1936	Bakelite Ash Tray		2	0
		Dunhill Pipe	1	15	0
		Dunhill Sports Lighter (plain)	1	10	0
		Dunhill Sports Lighter (9 ct. gold engine turned)	17	17	0

Toys

Item	Source	Description	Price		
Trike	*Baxendales & Co. Ltd.*, Manchester, 1936	Joy Trike for 3 to 7 years	3	13	6

Transport and Vehicles

Item	Source	Description	Price		
Rail Fares	*Bradshaws ABC Railway Guide*, 1930	Manchester to London Return	2	6	0 (up to 76/6)
		Manchester to London Single	1	3	0 (up to 38/3)
Bus Fare	*What it Cost the Day Before Yesterday*, 1933	Paddington to Mansion House, London (4 miles)			4

Continued

4.4.3 Prices, Selected *continued*

Item	Source	Description	Price £	s.	d.
Rail Fares	*Bradshaws ABC Railway Guide*, 1935	Manchester to London Return	1	10	8 (up to 46/3)
		Manchester to London Single	1	3	0 (up to 38/3)
		London to Paris Single First Class	4	7	4 (via Folkestone–Boulogne)
		London to Paris Return First Class	7	17	7 (via Folkestone–Boulogne)
		London to Paris Return by the Short Sea Route	8	5	0 (Return)
Vehicles		Popular Ford Saloon Car	115	0	0 (£6 tax)
	Homes and Gardens, July 1935	"De Luxe" Ford Saloon	135	0	0
		Morris 10, Four Door Saloon	172	0	0 (with fixed head)
	Homes and Gardens, April 1936	Vauxhall Light 6 12 h.p. Saloon Car	205	0	0
		Avon Four Door Saloon Car	335	0	0
Bicycle	*Baxendales & Co. Ltd.*, Manchester, 1936	Gent's Beanco Royal Cycle	5	19	6
		Ladies Beanco Royal Cycle	6	6	0
		Juvenile Beanco	4	5	0 (up to 87/6)

Travel

Item	Source	Description	Price £	s.	d.
Cruises	*Bradshaws ABC Railway Guide*, 1930	White Star Line 17 Day Cruises to Mediterranean	36	0	0 (upwards)
		White Star Line 17 Day Cruises to Atlantic Isles	36	0	0 (upwards)
Youth Hostels		Youth Hostelling		1	0 (night, breakfast extra @ 1/0)
Cooks Grand Tours of Europe	*Thomas Cook Archives*, July 1938	Italy by Special Train (15 days)	24	3	0
		Scandinavia by Special Train (15 days)	30	11	0
		Motor Coach Tour: French Cathedrals (15 days)	23	0	0
Open Air Holidays		Walking, Cycling, Canoeing with Linguist Leaders	6	6	0 (up to 189/0)

Miscellany

Item	Source	Description	Price £	s.	d.
Window Leather	*Affleck & Brown Ltd.*, Manchester, 1933	Chamois Leather 21in. x 22in.		2	0
Lamp	*Baxendales & Co. Ltd.*, Manchester, 1936	Fog Lamp	1	2	6
Mascot		Bulldog Mascot for Car		17	6
Jacks		Garage Jacks for Small Cars	1	2	6
Batteries		Batteries			3 (each)
Writing Equipment		Swan Minor Fountain Pen		10	6
		Leverless Swan with 18 ct. Gold Band	1	10	0
		Swan Ink		1	0 (5 oz. glass bottle)
		Corona Special Portable Typewriter	9	9	0
Office Equipment		"Velos" Perpetual Desk Calendar		1	0
		"Velos" Moistener		2	0 (large)
		Single Ink Stand in Marbelite		2	6

4.5 Finance and Economic Data

4.5.1 Finance, Personal

	1930	1931	1932	1933	1934	1935	1936	1937	1938
	s. d.	s. d.	s. d.	s. d.	s. d.	s. d.	s. d.	s. d.	s. d.
Income Tax Rates[1]	4 0	4 6	5 0	5 0	4 6	4 6	4 9	4 9	5 0
Old Age Pension	5 0	5 0	5 0	5 0	5 0	5 0	10 0	10 0	10 0
Base Interest Rates in percent [2]	5%	3%	6%	2%	2%	2%	2%	2%	2%

Mitchell, B.R. *British Historical Statistics*, Cambridge University Press, 1988; CWS Year Book; Bank of England.

[1]The rates apply to years ended 5th April. [2]The rates apply to January of each year.

4.5.2 Financial Markets

4.5.2a Highest Closing Price of UK Major Stocks

	1930	1931	1932	1933	1934	1935	1936	1937	1938
Barclays Bank	8^{7}/16	8½	10¼	10^{9}/32	11^{1}/16	11⅝	11¾	11^{9}/32	10^{31}/32
Boots the Chemist	47/6	48/9	53/6	55/0	64/6	67/0	65/0	65/0	65/0
Burmah Oil	95/7½	73/1½	70/11¼	91/3	5^{19}/32	85/7½	5^{7}/16	6^{11}/16	6^{9}/32
Courtaulds	57/2¼	46/0	38/1½	45/3	56/6	60/9	61/0	58/4½	48/3
Guinness	5½	5½	89/0	5^{5}/16	6^{15}/32	7⅝	8^{1}/16	7^{5}/32	6¼
ICI[1]	29/0	21/3	25/9	32/5¼	39/3	38/7½	44/3	42/0	35/3
Marks and Spencer	6^{11}/32	9/7¾	5^{15}/16	9⅞	12^{7}/16				
Reckitt and Sons	81/10½	79/4½	95/0	5½	5⅞	5^{29}/32	6^{1}/10	5^{25}/32	5^{15}/32
Schweppes	23/6	24/7½	29/3	29/9	31/6	32/3	31/11½	31/11¼	31/3
Unilever[2]	24/9	24/6	30/0	30/1½	34/0	33/1½	34/7½	34/1½	32/3
Viyella	67/0	55/6	48/0	63/6	68/0	68/7½	67/0¾	55/1½	42/0
Whitbread	74½	79½	91	102½	105½	107½	110	110	105

Mathieson, F.C. and Sons, *Stock Exchanges Ten Year Record of Prices and Dividends*.

Fractions are quoted as parts of £1=32. Blank space denotes no available data. [1]Imperial Chemical Industries. [2]From 1937 known as Unilever Ltd.

4.5.2b Commodities

	Best Coal (price per ton)		Raw Cotton (price per lb.)	Gold (average market)	Sugar (annual average world price)	Wheat (per imperial quarter)		Wool (average import value)	
	s.	d.	old pence (d.)	£ per troy oz.	£ sterling per metric ton	s.	d.	pence per lb.	
1930	24	9	7.49	4.25	6.480	8	0	13	0
1931	24	8	5.90	4.627	6.152[1]	5	9	9	3
1932	23	5	5.24	5.903	5.659	5	11	8	5
1933	22	8	5.54	6.244	5.167	5	4	9	0
1934	20	3	6.68	6.883	4.675	4	10	11	3
1935	20	3	6.71	7.105	4.593	5	2	9	9
1936	23	1	6.70	7.015	4.675	7	2	11	5
1937	24	6	6.43	7.037	6.234	9	4	15	2
1938	25	8	4.93	7.128	5.413	6	9	11	2

Mitchell, B.R. *British Historical Statistics*, Cambridge University Press, 1988; World Gold Council; Czarnikow Sugar.

Original source, Sauerbeck, A. *Prices of Commodities and the Precious Metals, Journal of the Statistical Society.* [1]Prior to suspension of Gold Standard.

4.5.2c Foreign Exchange Rates

	Berlin Reichsmarks per £1	Paris Francs per £1	New York Dollars per £1
1930	20.38	123.88	4.862
1931[1]	20.52	124.06	4.859
1932	14.74	89.19	3.504
1933	13.98	84.59	4.218
1934	12.80	76.94	5.041
1935	12.18	74.27	4.903
1936	12.33	82.97	4.971
1937	12.29	124.61	4.944
1938	12.17	170.65	4.890

Mitchell, B.R. *British Historical Statistics*, Cambridge University Press, 1988.

[1]The figure is for the period prior to UK leaving the gold standard in September.

4.5.3 Balance of Payments and GNP

4.5.3a Balance of Payments

	Merchandise Exports	Merchandise Imports	Overall Visible Balance	Exports of Services	Imports of Services	Property Income from Abroad	Property Income Paid Abroad	Balance of Current Transfers	Overall Invisible Balance	Overall Current Balance
	£m	£m	£	£m	£m	£m	£m	£m	£m	£m
1930	670	953	-283	214	147	277	62	+37	+319	+36
1931	464	786	-322	168	140	211	48	+28	+219	-103
1932	425	641	-216	153	123	175	48	+8	+165	-51
1933	427	619	-192	146	120	183	29	+4	+184	-8
1934	463	683	-220	145	116	195	28	+2	+198	-22
1935	541	724	-183	149	124	212	31	n/a	+206	+23
1936	523	784	-261	174	135	229	34	n/a	+234	-27
1937	614	950	-336	229	144	242	37	-1	+289	-47
1938	564	849	-285	193	152	229	37	-3	+230	-55

Mitchell, B.R. *British Historical Statistics*, Cambridge University Press, 1988.

Original source, Feinstein, C.H. *National Income, Expenditure and Output of the UK, 1855-1965*, Cambridge, 1972.

4.5.3b GNP at Factor Cost and Its Component Incomes at Current Prices

	Income from Employment	Income from Self Employment	Gross Trading Profits of Companies	Gross Trading Surplus of Public Enterprises	Rent	Stock Appreciation	Gross Domestic Product	Net Property Income from Abroad	Gross National Product	Capital Consumption	National Income
	£m	£m	£m	£m	£m	£m	£m	£m	£m	£m	£m
1930	2,485	616	411	54	362	-213	4,141	215	4,356	291	4,065
1931	2,382	552	360	55	373	-63	3,785	163	3,948	290	3,658
1932	2,357	548	321	59	387	-34	3,706	127	3,833	283	3,550
1933	2,402	590	380	62	390	45	3,779	154	3,933	283	3,650
1934	2,507	596	464	67	396	5	4,025	167	4,192	282	3,910
1935	2,597	629	514	68	413	26	4,195	181	4,376	298	4,078
1936	2,744	663	627	69	425	98	4,430	195	4,625	317	4,308
1937	2,908	631	717	71	448	67	4,708	205	4,913	357	4,556
1938	2,989	611	687	72	460	109	4,932	192	5,124	370	4,754

Mitchell, B.R. *British Historical Statistics*, Cambridge University Press, 1988.

Original source, Feinstein, C.H. *National Income, Expenditure and Output of the UK, 1855-1965*, Cambridge, 1972.

4.6 Miscellaneous

4.6.1 Post Office Savings Bank

	Number of accounts	Received from depositors	Amounts due to depositors	Average due to each depositor		
		£	£	£	s.	d.
1930	9,855,817	76,120,000	290,235,000	29	7	4
1932	9,482,532	90,347,000	305,712,000	32	3	0
1933	9,030,309	92,756,000	326,654,000	36	1	3
1934	9,322,828	104,153,000	354,831,000	37	19	1
1935	9,702,295	116,218,000	390,331,000	40	2	7
1936	10,148,794	128,156,000	432,366,000	42	10	1
1937	10,632,000	136,015,000	470,495,000	44	3	2

The People's Year Book, 1942, p. 100.

4.6.2 Trustee Savings Bank

	Number of active accounts		Received from Depositors	Due to Depositors
	Ordinary	Special	£	£
1930	2,345,379	237,634	53,433,000	133,196,000
1932	1,983,004	290,410	59,645,000	154,744,000
1933	2,024,067	304,517	68,000,000	171,408,000
1934	2,076,791	312,056	64,175,000	181,900,000
1935	2,142,676	313,850	64,506,000	197,400,000
1936	2,221,688	316,164	68,100,000	212,156,000
1937	2,320,095	321,250	72,499,000	224,692,000

The People's Year Book, 1942, p. 101.

See Chapters 2 and 11 for financial summary of World War I and the 1990's.

– Five –
1939–1945

Waging World War

PRIME MINISTERS
Winston Churchill (Coalition) May 1940–23rd May 1945
Winston Churchill (Conservative) 23rd May 1945–July 1945

CHANCELLORS OF THE EXCHEQUER
Sir K. Wood, May 1940–September 1943
Sir J. Anderson, September 1943–July 1945

Britain entered a second world war against Germany on 3rd September 1939. Events in Manchuria, Abyssinia and Spain had shown just what brutalities might be expected. Overall 300,000 British combatants were killed, while the civilian population sustained losses of 60,000. The Merchant Navy lost 30,000 men. The theory and practice of total war was developed to a much fuller extent than in 1914–18. Provision for military conscription was made before the outbreak of war, and by its end five million men were in uniform. Science was of crucial importance to the war through the development of the radar, sophisticated armaments and aeroplanes, and, eventually, of atomic power.

When Winston Churchill assumed leadership of Britain and the Commonwealth in May 1940 the spirit of the 1930s died, most visibly and audibly, in the great House of Commons debate of 8th May, which resulted in Neville Chamberlain's resignation. If the saying 'cometh the hour, cometh the man' ever had a meaning, it applied to Churchill. His pugnacious self-confidence, energy, creativity, and ambition had often been out of place in his long political career up to 1940. The crisis facing Britain and the rest of the world was the stage on which he could use his talents to the full. Churchill drew strength from the breadth of the coalition which left him with no regular opposition in Parliament or in the country.

If anything had been learned from the conduct of the 1914–18 war, it was that central, clear direction of the war effort and national unity were vital ingredients to success. The enormous programme of direction and expansion of labour overseen by Churchill led to some remarkable achievements. The agricultural labour force stood at 711,000 in 1939; by 1945 it had expanded to 887,000. In 1939 the engineering and chemical industries together employed 3.1 million; in 1945 they employed 5.2 million. At the same time the armed forces expanded from 480,000 in 1939 to 5.1 million in 1945. The role of women in the workforce was a major factor here, and this in turn contributed to the social revolution that followed the eventual end to hostilities.

The severities and sacrifices of war time had important effects on national spirit and outlook. Morale, in the services and among civilians as a whole, was always high. Whether in conscription for the services or in voluntary organizations (such as the Home Guard), the majority of ordinary citizens contributed essential services willingly. Taxes were high, rationing often severe, dislocation of life by evacuation or air raids widespread. In mid-1941, the weekly ration of certain basic foods amounted to no more than what in a comfortable pre-war household would have constituted a single helping: a shilling's worth of meat (half a pound), one ounce of cheese, four ounces of bacon or ham, eight ounces of sugar, two ounces of tea, eight ounces of fats (including not more than two ounces of butter), and two ounces of jam or marmalade.

One of the most important social consequences of the war was that it made the trade unions, in Churchill's memorable phrase, 'an estate of the realm'. This occurred as a result of the need to enlist the wholehearted support of the trade union movement in the country's war effort. Trade union leader Ernest Bevin became Minister of Labour in Churchill's War Coalition. The organized labour movement was decisive in the election of a Labour Government in 1945.

The experience of evacuation, mutual aid in air-raids, great collective sacrifice and service, and stringent rationing and controls all helped to strengthen a tide of egalitarian feeling which had been present in British society even before the war. The dream was to create a better society in which everyone could have the basic necessities of life, and where the opportunity to work and live in a decent environment would be open to all citizens. It was in the spirit of this mood that the 1942 Beveridge Report was well received, and that the welfare state was eventually established. The need for change also led to the rejection of Churchill's Conservative Government in 1945, and the formation of the reform orientated Labour Government.

5.1 Historical Snapshots

5.1 Historical Snapshots

1939	Outbreak of World War II.
	Children evacuated from major cities.
	First British troops sent to France.
1940	Food, Clothing and Petrol rationing introduced.
	Two million men between 20 and 27 are conscripted.
	Winston Churchill becomes new Prime Minister.
	Royal Air Force (RAF) claims victory after the Battle of Britain.
1941	Doctors complete the first effective treatment using penicillin.
	Igor Sikorsky constructs the first helicopter in USA.
	ICI begins commercial production of polythene.
	Radar developed for allied bombers.
	Britain declares war on Japan.
	Women are called up to meet wartime labour shortages.
1942	Coal, gas, and electricity are rationed.
	Britain and the Soviet Union sign a pact to fight Germany.
	Development of the synthetic polyester fibre terylene.
	First launch of the V2 rocket designed by Braun in Germany.
	Skirts get shorter as material gets scarce.
	Welfare proposed by Sir William Beveridge for everyone from 'cradle to grave'.
1944	D-Day sees the biggest seaborne invasion of Normandy.
	Income tax is collected by a new Pay As You Earn (PAYE) scheme.
	A series of green belts and ring roads are proposed.
1945	Adolf Hitler commits suicide in Germany.
	World War II ends in victory for the USA and British Allies.
	It becomes illegal to dismiss married women teachers.

Chronicle of Britain, J.L. International Publishing, 1992; Williams, T.I. *Invention and Discovery in the 20th Century*, Harrap, 1990.

5.2 Earnings and Employment

5.2.1 Earnings, Standard Tables

5.2.1a Incomes and Wages

	1939	1940	1941	1942	1943	1944	1945
General Practitioner		£1,094 (a)					
Police Constable							£273 (a)
Teacher		£480 (a)					£555 (a)
Coal Miner	59s. 6d.	68s. 8d.	80s. 0d.	93s. 2d.	100s. 0d.	109s. 4d.	112s. 8d.
Fitter and Turner	113 0	135 0	133 0	155 0			
Bricklayer		80 7					
Compositor		57 1					106 6
Farm Worker	39 5½	48 5	57 10	60 0	63 11	67 10½	72 2
Textile Worker (weaver)		51 6	49 2			65 2	77 11

British Labour Statistics 1886–1968, HMSO, 1971; Routh, G. *Occupation and Pay in Great Britain, 1906–1979*, Macmillan Press, 1980, Garside, W.R. *Durham Miners 1919–1960*, 1971; *A History of the Lancashire Cotton Industry*, 1969.

Blank space denotes no available data. Earnings are weekly unless otherwise stated. (a) – annual.

5.2.1b Average Weekly Earnings

	Bricks, Pottery and Glass	Total Metals	Textiles	Clothing	Food, Drink and Tobacco	Paper and Printing	Building	Government Industrial Establish-ments	Transport	All Industries
	£	£	£	£	£	£	£	£	£	£
Males										
1940	3.89	5.12	3.79	3.63	3.82	4.20	4.25	5.30	4.26	4.45
1941	4.43	5.61	4.08	4.24	4.37	4.85	4.85	5.54	4.61	4.97
1942	4.83	6.40	4.52	4.63	4.65	5.28	5.10	6.10	4.95	5.57
1943	5.21	6.91	4.58	4.99	5.08	5.63	5.42	6.61	5.21	6.06
1944	5.40	6.95	5.09	5.33	5.33	6.03	5.40	6.93	5.71	6.22
1945	5.55	6.65	5.23	5.61	5.52	6.15	5.57	6.35	5.74	6.07
Females										
1940	1.65	2.19	2.02	1.87	1.77	1.76	n/a	2.65	2.18	1.95
1941	1.93	2.40	2.10	2.11	2.01	1.98	n/a	2.70	2.98	2.20
1942	2.22	3.03	2.42	2.45	2.30	2.25	2.58	3.34	3.37	2.71
1943	2.47	3.49	2.65	2.58	2.54	2.56	3.07	4.05	3.57	3.11
1944	2.53	3.55	2.78	2.74	2.70	2.69	3.10	4.26	3.95	3.21
1945	2.59	3.45	2.91	2.83	2.83	2.73	3.02	4.05	4.08	3.16

British Labour Statistics, 1886–1968, HMSO, 1971.

These Industry Groups are prior to the 1948 Standard Industrial Classification (SIC).

5.2.2 Regional Earnings by Selected Occupation

		London s. d.	Manchester s. d.	Newcastle s. d.	Leeds s. d.	Glasgow s. d.
Bricklayer (hourly)	1945	2 0	2 1	2 1	2 1	2 2½
Bricklayer's Labourer (hourly)	1945	1 8¾	1 7¾	1 7¾	1 7¾	1 8½
Compositor (weekly)	1945	106 6	95 0	93 6	93 6	95 0
Fitter and Turner (weekly)	1945	100 11	96 0	n/a	n/a	96 1½
Labourer (weekly)	1945	83 3½	80 0	n/a	n/a	80 11¼

British Labour Statistics, 1886–1968, HMSO, 1971.

Original source, *Time Rates of Wages and Hours of Labour*.

5.2.3 Incomes, Miscellaneous

5.2.3a Average Wages in Principal Industries

Industry	Men s. d.	Youths & Boys s. d.	Women s. d.	Girls s. d.	All s. d.
Metal Engineering and Shipbuilding:					
Pig Iron (Blast Furnaces)	98 1	40 11			93 10
Iron Puddling, Steel Smelting, Rolling etc.	106 2	42 3			96 10
Engineering:					
General Engineering and					
Engineers Iron and Steel Founding	97 11	35 6	47 7	27 4	85 4
Electrical Engineering	106 6	38 0	47 6	27 3	72 5
Marine Engineering	101 4	35 9			84 0
Constructional Engineering	95 8	33 5			82 8
Motor Vehicles, Cycles and Aircraft:					
Manufacture and Repair	114 11	40 0	50 2	36 5	106 5
Shipbuilding and Repair	103 3	28 6			90 8
All	100 3	36 4	43 11	25 8	85 1
Textile Industries:					
Cotton	74 6	37 9	44 1	29 5	51 6
Woollen and Worsted	75 6	33 5	40 2	27 4	50 5
All	75 10	32 6	39 9	24 3	48 10
Clothing	72 10	28 3	36 5	20 0	40 2
Food, Drink and Tobacco	76 8	32 11	35 10	21 2	53 8
Woodworking	77 5	29 0	38 11	19 11	61 5
Paper and Printing	83 10	27 9	35 4	19 0	57 1
Building and Contracting	84 0	37 1			80 7

The People's Year Book, 1940, p. 184.

Wages are weekly for the week ending 30 July 1940. Original source, Ministry of Labour.

5.2.3b Wages During the War

	Men		Youths & Boys		Women		Girls		All Workers	
	s.	d.	s.	d.	s.	d.	s.	d.	s.	d.
October, 1938	69	0	26	1	32	6	18	8	53	3
January, 1943	113	0	41	1	58	6	32	1	87	11
July, 1943	121	3	47	2	62	2	33	10	93	7

The People's Year Book, 1945, p. 104.

Original source, Ministry of Labour Survey, 1944.

5.2.4 Employment

5.2.4a Unemployment

	Wholly Unemployed			Temporarily Stopped			
	Men	Women	Boys and Girls	Men	Women	Boys and Girls	All
	000's	000's	000's	000's	000's	000's	000's
September 1930	661	292	99	116	102	10	1,331
December	764	325	82	89	50	4	1,362
March 1940	628	273	64	69	37	3	1,121
June	382	226	40	39	40	3	767
September	318	227	68	98	79	8	830
December	248	244	50	82	54	5	705
March 1941	160	165	39	41	52	3	458
June	110	102	31	18	28	2	302
September	88	79	30	8	15	1	230

The People's Year Book, 1941, p. 72.

5.2.4b Employment by Region

	1939	1945
	000's	000's
London and South Eastern	3,760	2,861
Eastern	750	676
Southern	642	619
South Western	751	698
Midland	1,527	1,378
North Midland	1,084	956
East and West Ridings	1,457	1,241
Northern	951	899
North Western	2,376	2,009
Scotland	1,677	1,463
Wales	696	678
Great Britain	15,671	13,478
Special schemes for banking and insurance[1]	199	162
Total in Great Britain	15,870	13,640
Northern Ireland (including special schemes)	353	360
Total insured employees in the UK	16,223	14,000

British Labour Statistics, 1886-1968, HMSO, 1971.

Figures are for the mid-year for those insured under the General Scheme and for males between the ages of 14 and 64, and females between 14 and 59. [1]No regional analysis is available for any year between 1923 and 1947 for those persons insured under the special scheme for the banking and insurance industries. Original source, *Gazette*.

5.3 Consumer Expenditure

5.3.1 Consumer Expenditure, Standard Table

	Food	Alcoholic Drink	Tobacco	Housing	Fuel and Light	Clothing	Motor Cars and Motor Cycles	Other Goods	Other Services	Total Consumer Expenditure
	£m	£m	£m	£m	£m	£m	£m	£m	£m	£m
1939	1,216	311	204	513	199	461	37	636	928	
1940	1,244	378	260	528	222	501	5	735	961	
1941	1,288	468	317	531	237	460	1	763	1,051	
1942	1,334	550	414	536	238	498	1	772	1,106	
1943	1,267	634	491	553	233	441		776	1,153	
1944	1,348	678	507	575	240	511		796	1,210	
1945	1,398	705	562	616	259	535	2	921	1,347	

Mitchell, B.R. *British Historical Statistics*, Cambridge University Press, 1988.

Original source, Feinstein, C.H. *National Income, Expenditure and Output of the UK, 1855-1965*, Cambridge, 1972. Blank space denotes no available data. Durable Household Goods – no data available during war.

5.4 Prices

5.4.2 Prices, General Articles

	1939		1940		1941		1942		1943		1944		1945	
	s.	d.	s.	d.	s.	d.	s.	d.	s.	d.	s.	d.	s.	d.
Aspirin (100)	2	3												
Beer (1 pint)		8		9		10	1	0	1	1	1	1	1	1
Cheddar Cheese (1 lb.)			1	2										
Daily Mail		1		1		1		1		1		1		1
Guinness Extra Stout (1 pint)		10		11										11
Inland Letter Post		2½		2½		2½		2½		2½		2½		2½
Pears Transparent Soap	1	3												
Petrol (1 gallon)	1	8											1	11½
Red Label Tea (1 lb.)			2	8										
Scotch Whisky (standard bottle)	14	3	16	0	17	6	23	0	25	9				
Swan Vestas Matches				3										
The Times		2		2		2		2		2		2		

The Boots Company; British Library; Burmah Castrol; Cadbury's Ltd; Colmans of Norwich; Guinness Brewing GB; Royal Mail; Sainsbury's Archives; The Scotch Whisky Association and Unilever Historical Archives.

Blank space denotes no available prices.

5.4.3 Prices, Selected

Item	Source	Description	Price		
			£	s.	d.
Alcoholic Drink					
Spirits	*Ideal Home*, June 1939	Gordons Gin		12	6
Beer	*Brewers' Society*, 1939	Pint Draught Bitter			8
Appliances: Domestic and Electrical					
Carpet Sweeper	*People's Year Book*, 1939	"Society" Carpet Sweepers	1	1	0 (up to 32/6)
Kettle	*The Ideal Home*, June 1939	Swan Brand Electric Kettle	1	4	0 (upwards)
Washer		Stowaway Electric Washing Machine	4	10	0
Kettle	*Peter Robinson's Wartime Shopping*, c.1940	Automatic Aluminium Electric Kettle	1	7	6 (3 pint capacity)
Iron		Pre-Selective Heat Control Electric Iron		17	6
Fire		Portable Electric Fire		18	6
Lamp		Utility Lamp for Desk Table		18	6
Toaster		Chromium Plated Electric Toaster		19	3
Water Filter	*Ideal Home*, September 1941	"Berkefeld" Drip Filter	1	1	6
		"Berkefeld" De-Chlorinator Pump Filter	4	4	0
Clothing and Footwear:					
Children's					
Coat	*Peter Robinson's Wartime Shopping*, c.1940	Girl's Strong Trench Coat	1	6	0
Nightwear		Girl's Ceylon Flannel Pyjamas		15	9
Suit		Girl's Siren Suit	1	9	6 (up to 29/6)
		Boy's Duraflon Suit		12	6
		Boy's Double Breasted Coat	2	2	0
Knitting Wool		Wool for Children's Wear 3 and 4 ply			7 (oz.)
		Pure Silk and Wool for Baby Clothes			9½ (per ½ oz. skein)
		Artificial Silk Crepe for Baby Dresses and Coats		1	6 (per 2oz. skein)
		Children's and Babies Wear, 3 and 4 ply fingering			8 (oz.)
Men's					
Shirt		Sports Shirt		11	6
		Poplin Shirt		10	6
Nightwear		Dressing Gown	1	15	6
Knitting Wool		Service Wool Suitable for Men's Socks			6½ (per oz.)
		Wool Suitable for Men's Pullovers			6½ (per oz.)
		Very Soft Thick Wool in Plain Shades			7 (per oz.)
Women's					
Coat		Tweed Swagger Coat	1	10	0
		Angora Coat with Pleated Front and Back	6	6	0
Dress		Angora Woollen Dress	2	9	6
		Ladies Emergency Dress in Cosiest Wool	1	15	9
Suit		Excellent Ladies Siren Suit in Cosiest Woollen	2	9	6

Continued

5.4.3 Prices, Selected *continued*

Item	Source	Description	£	s.	d.	
Trousers		Land Girls Tailored Cotton Cord Breeches		17	6	
		Pull on Slacks	1	3	6	
Knitwear		Twin Set in Lambswool and Angora		12	9	(short sleeved)
				15	9	(long sleeved)
Hosiery		Robina Silk Stockings		3	3	
Underwear		Peach Satin Brassiere		5	11	
Knitting Wool		Pure Silk and Wool			9½	(½ oz. skein)
		Bedjacket Wool			8½	(oz. ball)
Ready to Wear Uniforms for the Services		Boiler Suit for Ambulance Driver/First Aid Worker	1	13	9	(khaki drill)
British Red Cross Society		Regulation Dress		12	6	
		Greatcoat in Velour or Proofed Serge	2	19	6	
		Shoes (black)	1	5	9	
		Stockings (black)		2	11	
Womens Royal Naval Society (WRNS)		Suit in Navy Blue Cloth	9	9	0	
		Shirts (white with two polo collars)		15	9	
		Shoes without toecaps	1	5	9	
		Ties (silk barathea)		4	11	
		Gloves (tancape with one button)		10	6	
Shoes	*C.J. Clark Ltd.*, 1940	Shelburne Gusset Brown Snake Calf		16	3	
		Banchory Lace "Craftsewn" Crêpe Rubber Soles		13	0	
		Babbacombe Lace Corrugated Crêpe Rubber Soles		13	3	
Coat	*Fortnum & Masons*, London, 1941	Déreta Coat	4	3	11	(+15 coupons)[1]
		Camel Haired Coat	17	17	0	(+18 coupons)
		Made to Measure Coat and Skirt	42	0	0	
Jacket		Cotton Wind Jacket	2	7	0	
Suit		Jaeger Suit	4	17	4	(+18 coupons)
Trousers		Tweed Trousers	1	7	10	(+8 coupons)
Dress		Spectator Dress	3	2	10	(+12 coupons)
Nightwear		Silk Nightie with Lace Trim	14	8	0	
Suit	*Woollands of Knightsbridge*, 1943	Angora Two Piece Suit	7	7	0	
Knitwear		Lisle Jumper		15	0	
		Cashmere Jumper	1	9	6	
Shirt		Smart Shirt in Fine Wool	1	9	6	
Skirt		Skirt in Fine Wool Material	2	5	0	
Dress		Tailored Lightweight Woollen Dress	5	5	0	
Hosiery		Artificial Silk Hose (lined wool)		4	9	
		Silk Stockings		14	9	(pair)
Skirt	*Debenham & Freebody*, London, 1943	Tailored Skirt of Scotch Tweed	3	10	9	(+6 coupons)
		Grey Flannel Skirt	2	19	6	(+6 coupons)
Suit		Jersey Suit	6	4	6	(+14 coupons)
Dress		Maternity Dress	7	9	2	(+7 coupons)
Knitwear		Cashmere Twin Set	1	17	3	(jumper)

Continued

5.4.3 Prices, Selected *continued*

Item	Source	Description	£	s.	d.
Suit *cont.*			2	10	6 (golfer)
Coat	*Debenham & Freebody*, London, 1944	Useful Well Cut Cardigan Coat	4	11	5 (+5 coupons)
Dress		Popular Shirt-Waist Dress in Wool Jersey	6	5	7 (+11 coupons)
		Coupon Saver Dress	9	9	0 (+11 coupons)
Frock		Cotton Washing Frock	2	8	11 (+7 coupons)
		Pure Linen Washing Frock	4	18	11 (+7 coupons)
Shirt		Popular Crepon Neat Practical Shirt	2	9	11 (+4 coupons)
Skirt		Popular Skirt for Country and Sports	4	4	0 (+6 coupons)

Food Products

Item	Source	Description	£	s.	d.
Bacon	*J Sainsbury Archives*, 1940	Unsmoked Back Bacon		1	6 (per lb.)
Butter		Loose Butter		1	3 (per lb.)
Cheese		Cheddar Cheese		1	2 (per lb.)
Eggs		Six Medium Size			7½
Tea		Red Label Tea		2	8 (per lb.)
Breakfast Cereal		Shredded Wheat			8 (12's)
Spices (per lb.)	*Scottish CWS Ltd.*, January 1941	Cardamom		6	3
		Cinnamon No. 1		2	0
		Cloves		1	6
		Mace		4	0
Whole Spices (per lb.)		Cardamom Seed		6	0
		Cinnamon Stick		2	0
		Cloves, Penang		4	0
		Pepper, Black			7
Butter	*J Sainsbury Archives*, 1945	Loose Butter		1	2 (per lb.)
Eggs		Six Medium Size		1	2
Bread	*People's Year Book*, 1945	4lb. Loaf			8½

Furniture

Item	Source	Description	£	s.	d.
Old World Furniture at Pre-War Bargains	*Ideal Home and Gardening*, September 1941				
Cupboard		3ft. Bow Walnut Corner Cupboard	8	8	0 (was 12 gns.)
Bookcase		3ft. 6in. Mahogany Bureau Bookcase	30	0	0 (was £45)
Wardrobe		5ft. 6in. Mahogany Adams Wardrobe	35	0	0 (was £55)
Bedstead		Pair 3ft. 6in. Hepplewhite 4 Posters with Mattress	50	0	0 pair (was £90)

Gardening Equipment and Supplies

Item	Source	Description	£	s.	d.
Fencing	*The Ideal Home*, September 1941	Wattle Fencing 72ft. x 3ft.	1	17	6
Garden Plans		Ideal Home Book of Garden Plans		2	6

Heat and Light

Item	Source	Description	£	s.	d.
Electricity	*Eastern Electricity*, 1941	Electricity per Unit			3
Gas	*British Gas North Thames*, 1941	Gas per Therm			9
Coal	*What it Cost the Day Before Yesterday*	Coal per Ton	1	14	0

Hotel Rates

Item	Source	Description	£	s.	d.
Kingsley Hotel, London	*The Ideal Home*, June 1939	Bed and Breakfast		9	6 (night)
Shaftesbury Hotel, London	*Bradshaws ABC Railway Guide*, 1940	Bedroom Bath and Breakfast		7	6 (night)

Continued

5.4.3 Prices, Selected *continued*

Item	Source	Description	Price £	s.	d.
Kingsley Hotel, London	*Bradshaws ABC Railway Guide*, 1945	Bedroom Bath and Breakfast		10	6 (night)
Norfolk Hotel, Strand, London		Single Bed and Breakfast from		13	6
Royal Hotel, Glasgow		Bedroom Bath and Breakfast		12	0 (inclusive)
Victoria Hotel, Buttemere, Lake District		Full Board	5	5	0 (per week)

Household Goods

Item	Source	Description	Price £	s.	d.
Bedding	*Peter Robinson's Wartime Shopping*, c.1940	Government Unbleached Sheeting 70in. wide		1	9 (yard)
		Utility Down Quilt: Double Bed	1	5	0
		Warm Sleeping Bags	2	5	0
Towels		Christy's Turkish Bath Mats		4	6
Food Storage		Vacuum Food Jar		8	6
Tableware		Pyrex Casserole		15	0 (3 pint capacity)
Napkins		Paper Serviettes		1	0 (100)
				8	6 (1000)
Gifts		Hand Decorated Biscuit Tin		4	6
Food Preservation Equipment	*The Ideal Home and Gardening*, September 1941	New Snap Vacuum Closure to fit Standard Jam Jars		2	6 (per carton)
Cleaning Materials		Town Talk Liquid Silver Polish			8 (up to 2/6 bottle)
		Kleenoff Oven Cleaner			10 (large tin)
	Unilever Archives, 1941	D.&W. Gibbs Ltd. Magic Self Washer			6½
		D.& W. Gibbs Ltd. Magic Carbolic			5
Bedding	*Woolands of Knightsbridge*, London 1943	Linen Sheets, single	4	10	0 (pair)
		Linen Cambric Pillow Cases		17	6 (each)

Houses

Item	Source	Description	Price £	s.	d.
Rural Homes: Brick or Timber Framed	*The Ideal Home*, June 1939	The "Quebec" 6 Roomed Timber Framed Bungalow	365	0	0 (ready for occupation)
		The "Halstead" 7 Roomed House with Garage	995	0	0 (ready for occupation)
House Purchase by Life Assurance		Half Yearly Interest at 4½ % Gross	13	10	0
On the Loan of £600 over 20 years		Less Income Tax of 4s.6d. in the £	10	9	3
		Half Yearly Premium on 20 year Endowment Assurance	12	15	0
		Saving of Income Tax at 2s.3d. in the £	11	6	4
		Total net half yearly cost	21	15	7

Jewellery

Item	Source	Description	Price £	s.	d.
Bracelet	*Peter Robinsons Wartime Shopping*, c.1940	Sterling Silver Identity Bracelet		3	6

Personal Care Items

Item	Source	Description	Price £	s.	d.
Denture Repair	*Bradshaws ABC Railway Guide*, 1940	Victoria Denture Repair Hospital, Manchester		3	6 (per tooth)
Water Bottle	*Peter Robinsons Wartime Shopping*, c.1940	Hot Water Bottle		2	6
First Aid		First Aid Set		2	9
Toilet Preparations		Cold Cream		3	6 (1lb. pot)

Continued

5.4.3 Prices, Selected *continued*

Item	Source	Description	£	s.	d.
Chemists	*The Ideal Home*, September 1941	Optrex Eye Lotion		2	3 (with eye bath)
		Sanatogen Nerve Tonic Food	1	2	3 (jar)
Publications					
Books	*The Ideal Home*, June 1939	Colour and Interior Decoration by Basil Ionides		10	6
Guides	*Bradshaws ABC Railway Guide*, 1941	Railway Guide			9
Magazines	*The Ideal Home*, September 1941	Ideal Home Magazine		1	0
Books		Ideal Home Book of Plans		3	0 (post free)
Guides	*Bradshaws ABC Railway Guide*, 1945	Railway Guide		1	0
Magazines	*The Ideal Home*, September 1941	Housewife's Guide to Making and Mending			3
Services					
Cinema	*Kinematographic Year Book*, 1939–40	Grosvenor Picture Palace, Manchester			6 (up to 1/0)
	Kinematographic Year Book, 1941–1942	Odeon Theatre, Manchester			9 (up to 3/6)
	Kinematographic Year Book, 1943			1	6 (up to 4/0)
	Kinematographic Year Book, 1945			1	9 (up to 4/6)
Licence	*Post Office Archives*, 1941	Radio Licence	1	0	0
	DVLA, 1940	Road Tax not exceeding 6 h.p.	7	10	0
		For each additional h.p. unit	1	5	0
Telephone Tariffs	*British Telecom Archives*, May 1943	Quarterly Accounting suspended			
Midnight to 6.30 pm and 9.30 pm to Midnight		15 to 20 miles			10
		20 to 25 miles		1	2
		25 to 35 miles		1	6
		35 to 50 miles		1	10
Parcel Postage Rates	*Post Office Archives*, 1940	3lb. weight			7
		5lb. weight			9
		15lb. weight		1	1
Insurance, London and Lancashire Insurance Co.	*The Ideal Home*, June 1939	Buildings Insurance		2	3 (per £100)
		Contents Insurance		5	0 (per £100)
		Accident Policy	4	0	0 (premium per annum)
Taxi Service	*Bradshaws ABC Railway Guide*, 1940	Supercabs Long Distance			6 (per mile for 4 persons)
Sports and Hobbies					
Indoor Sports	*Peter Robinson Wartime Shopping*, c.1940	Table Tennis Set for Four Players		6	6
		Double Sided Cork Faced Dartboard, Wire Numbers		6	0
Games		Bezique Set		3	6
		Perchance Set		4	0
Tobacco Products					
Cigarettes	*Ideal Home*, June 1939	Players No. 3		1	5 (20)
	Woman's Outlook, February 15, 1941	CWS Silk Cut Cigarettes Plain or Cork Tipped		1	7 (25)
	Scottish CWS Ltd., January 1941	Shipmate Navy Cut			9 (10)
		Gold Flake Mild			6 (10)

Continued

5.4.3 Prices, Selected *continued*

Item	Source	Description	Price		
			£	s.	d.
Toys					
Childrens Toys	*Peter Robinson Wartime Shopping,* c.1940	Jig Saw Puzzle		2	9
		Buccaneer for 2–6 Players		7	6 (up to 10/6)
		Pikastyk		2	6
Transport and Vehicles					
Vehicle	*The Ideal Home,* June 1939	10 h.p. Hillman Minor 4 Door Saloon de Luxe	175	0	0
Rail Fares	*Bradshaws ABC Railway Guide,* 1940	Manchester to London Return	1	15	6 (up to 53/3)
		Manchester to London Single	1	6	7 (up to 44/2)
Sailings		Steamers from Liverpool to Belfast Return	1	11	2 (weekdays)
		Steamers from Liverpool to Belfast Single		15	1 (weekdays)
Vehicle	*Complete Catalogue of Austin Cars since 1945*	Austin Eight, 27 b.h.p. 4 Door Saloon	326	0	0 (when introduced)
		Austin Sixteen 58 b.h.p. 4 Door Saloon Estate	569	0	0 (when introduced)
Rail Fares	*Bradshaws ABC Railway Guide,* 1945	Manchester to London Return	1	17	8 (up to 56/6)
		Manchester to London Single	1	8	2 (up to 46/10)
Bus Fare	*What it Cost the Day Before Yesterday*	Paddington to Mansion House, London (4 miles)			4
Miscellany					
Ladder	*The Ideal Home,* June 1939	Gravity Loft Ladder	4	10	0
Eating Out	*Bradshaws ABC Railway Guide,* 1940	Table d'Hôte Lunch at Shaftesbury Hotel, London		2	0
		Table d'Hôte Dinner at Shaftesbury Hotel, London		3	0
Wellington Boots	*Peter Robinson Wartime Shopping,* c.1940	Rubber Wellington Boots		7	11
Torch		Pocket Torch		1	9
Clock		Alarm Clock		5	0 (up to 8/6)
Stationery		Langham Air Mail Stationery		3	3 (120 sheets notepaper)
				3	6 (100 envelopes)
		Officers Writers Pack in Soft Leather Portfolio		15	0
Gas Mask Containers		Satchel Design Gas Mask Container and Handbag		5	11
		Shaped Gas Mask Case of Strong Proofed Leatherette		3	6

5.5 Finance and Economic Data

5.5.1 Finance, Personal

	1939		1940		1941		1942		1943		1944		1945	
	s.	d.	s.	d.	s.	d.	s.	d.	s.	d.	s.	d.	s.	d.
Income Tax Rates[1]	5	6	7	0	8	6	10	0	10	0	10	0	10	0
Old Age Pension	10	0	10	0	10	0	10	0	10	0	10	0	10	0
Base Interest Rates in percent[2]	4%		4%		4%		4%		4%		4%		4%	

Mitchell, B.R. *British Historical Statistics*, Cambridge University Press, 1988; CWS Year Book; Bank of England.

[1]The rates apply to years ended 5th April. [2]The rates apply to January of each year.

5.5.2 Financial Markets

5.5.2a Highest Closing Price of UK Major Stocks

	1939	1940	1941	1942	1943	1944	1945
Barclays Bank	10⅜	10½	11	57/9	57/3	58/9	58/3
Boots the Chemist	63/0	57/6	56/3	57/6		62/6	61/0
Burmah Oil	88/1½	73/6	68/9	60/0	87/6	91/3	93/5¼
Courtaulds	38/3	39/10½	36/9	45/9	56/6	60/7½	59/3
Guinness	5¹¹⁄₁₆	83/0	97/1½	5⁵⁄₁₆	6⁹⁄₃₂	6¹⁵⁄₁₆	7¹³⁄₁₆
ICI[1]	32/7½	33/7½	33/7½	37/0	39/10½	41/0	42/0
Marks and Spencer						71/0	77/3
Reckitt and Sons	5⁵⁄₁₆	5⁷⁄₁₆	5	5¼	5²⁵⁄₃₂	6⅛	6¹⁄₁₆
Schweppes	30/0	29/0	28/9	31/0	32/6	31/10½	32/6
Unilever	29/7½	30/4½	30/10½	32/9	34/1½	47/0	53/9
Viyella	39/0	38/7½	39/0	13/6	50/0	55/0	54/9
Whitbread & Co.	99¾	101½	101	107	109	108½	111½

Mathieson, F.C. and Sons, *Stock Exchanges Ten Year Record of Prices and Dividends*.

Fractions are quoted as parts of £1=32. Blank space denotes no data. [1]Imperial Chemical Industries.

5.5.2b Commodities

	Best Coal (price per ton)		Raw Cotton (per lb.)	Gold (average market)	Sugar (annual average world price)	Wheat (per ton)		Wool (average import value)
	s.	d.	old pence (d.)	£ per troy oz.	£ sterling per metric ton	s.	d.	pence per lb.
1939	25	4	5.95	8.40[1]	6.890[2]	5	0	10.3
1940	28	1	8.10	8.40	9.596[2]	10	0	14.5
1941	30	10	9.14	8.40	11.893	14	8	15.3
1942	32	6	8.83	8.40	18.455	15	11	15.7
1943	34	11	7.83	8.40	18.455	16	3	16.6
1944	38	10	11.32	8.40	18.455	14	11	16.7
1945	42	8	12.75	8.61	20.423	14	5	16.8

Mitchell, B.R. *British Historical Statistics*, Cambridge University Press, 1988; World Gold Council; Czarnikow Sugar.

Original source, Sauerbeck, A. *Prices of Commodities and the Precious Metals, Journal of the Statistical Society.* [1] January/August, 1939. [2] There was virtually no free world price. [3] The official Bank of England buying price for gold was fixed at this figure on 5th September, 1939 and remained at the same level throughout the war.

5.5.2c Foreign Exchange Rates

	Berlin Reichsmarks per £1[1]	Paris Francs per £1[1]	New York Dollars per £1
1939		176.65	4.46
1940		176.62	4.03
1941			4.03
1942			4.03
1943			4.03
1944			4.03
1945		203.89	4.03

Mitchell, B.R. *British Historical Statistics*, Cambridge University Press, 1988.

[1] No dealings during the war.

5.5.3 Balance of Payments and GNP

5.5.3a Balance of Payments

	Merchandise Exports	Merchandise Imports	Overall Visible Balance	Exports of Services	Imports of Services	Property Income from Abroad	Property Income Paid Abroad	Balance of Current Transfers	Overall Invisible Balance	Overall Current Balance
	£m	£m	£m	£m	£m	£m	£m	£m	£m	£m
1939	500	800	-300	200	300	250[2]	90[3]	-10	+50	-250
1940	400	1,000	-600	200	550	260[2]	100[3]	-10	-200	-800
1941[1]	400	1,100	-700	200	450	270[2]	130[3]	-10	-120	-820
1942[1]	300	800	-500	300	550	270[2]	170[3]	-10	-160	-660
1943[1]	240	800	-560	500	700	280[2]	190[3]	-10	-120	-680
1944[1]	270	900	-630	700	800	290[2]	210[3]	-10	-30	-660
1945[1]	450	700	-250	350	1,000	310[2]	230[3]	-50	-620	-870

Mitchell, B.R. *British Historical Statistics*, Cambridge University Press, 1988.

Original source, Feinstein, C.H. *National Income, Expenditure and Output of the UK, 1855–1965*, Cambridge, 1972. [1]Cash transactions only. Lend-lease and reciprocal aid. [2]Including UK taxes paid by non-residents. [3]Including foreign taxes paid by UK residents.

5.5.3b GNP at Factor Cost and Its Component Incomes at Current Prices

	Income from Employment	Income from Self Employment	Gross Trading Profits of Companies	Gross Trading Surplus of Public Enterprises	Rent	Stock Appreciation	Gross Domestic Product	Net Property Income from Abroad	Gross National Product	Capital Consumption	National Income
	£m	£m	£m	£m	£m	£m	£m	£m	£m	£m	£m
1939	3,215	696	865	76	480	200	5,132	160	5,292	390	4,907
1940	3,843	791	1,109	77	485	500	5,805	160	5,965	440	5,530
1941	4,535	892	1,238	90	475	150	7,080	140	7,220	500	6,720
1942	5,042	949	1,377	136	475	100	7,879	100	7,979	530	7,449
1943	5,472	977	1,405	149	495	50	8,448	90	8,538	620	7,918
1944	5,751	991	1,388	134	470	50	8,684	80	8,764	650	8,114
1945	5,889	1,074	1,350	119	405	50	8,787	80	8,867	640	8,227

Mitchell, B.R. *British Historical Statistics*, Cambridge University Press, 1988.

Original source, Feinstein, C.H. *National Income, Expenditure and Output of the UK, 1855–1965*, Cambridge, 1972.

5.6 Miscellaneous

5.6.1 Civilian Consumption of Principal Foodstuffs

		Per head per week	
	Unit	1934–1938 average	1943
Butter	ounces	7.63	2.34
Margarine	ounces	2.77	5.26
Cheese	ounces	2.71	3.63
Fresh Eggs	number	3.26	1.45
Dried Eggs	ounces	0.02	0.80
Liquid Milk	pints	3.25	4.32
Dried Milk	ounces	0.49	1.29
Fresh Meat	ounces	30.40	22.18
Bacon and Ham	ounces	8.40	5.78
Canned Meat	ounces	0.89	2.43
Fresh Fish	ounces	6.52	4.56
Canned Fish	ounces	1.11	0.95
Tea	ounces	2.86	2.22
Sugar	ounces	30.58	20.0
Flour	pounds	3.75	4.43
Potatoes	pounds	3.40	5.25
Fresh Fruit	ounces	27.17	12.00
Other Fruit and Juices	ounces	8.22	5.35

The People's Year Book, 1945, p. 103.

5.6.2 Quantities of Rationed Commodities Allowed to Ordinary Householders

Commodity	Date of Introduction and Changes in Rationing	Quantity
Sugar	January 8, 1940	12 ozs.
	May 27, 1940	8 ozs.
Meat	March 11, 1940	1s. 10d. worth
	September 30, 1940	2s. 2d. worth
Tea	July 6, 1940	2 ozs.
Bacon or Ham	January 8, 1940	4 ozs. (3½ ozs. if cooked)
	January 25, 1940	8 ozs. (7ozs. if cooked)
	June 10, 1940	4 ozs. (3½ ozs. if cooked)
Butter	January 8, 1940	4 ozs.
	March 25, 1940	8 ozs.
	June 3, 1940	4 ozs.
Butter and Margarine (combined ration)	September 2, 1940	6 ozs. (including butter up to 4 ozs. only)
	September 30, 1940	6 ozs. (including butter up to 2 ozs. only)
Cooking Fats	July 22, 1940	2 ozs. (margarine may be taken if desired)

The People's Year Book, 1940, p. 179.

5.6.3 Interim War Budgets, 1940

Features of the Budget on April 23, 1940

Income Tax	Unchanged at 7s. 6d. in the £
Surtax	To be levied on incomes over £1,500
Postage	Letters 2½ d., postcards 2d. No change for letters to the Forces.
Telegrams	Increase of 3d.
Telephones	Rates increased by 15%; private services 25%
Tobacco	Increase of 3d. an ounce
Beer	Increase of 1d. a pint
Whisky	Increase of 1s. 9d. a bottle
Matches	Penny box of 50 to cost 1½ d.
Purchase Tax	Amount not fixed. To be levied between wholesaler and retailer (food, fuel and goods taxed exempt)

Features of the Budget on July 23, 1940

Income Tax	Increased by 1s. to 8s. 6d. in the £; rate on the first £165 increased from 3s. 9d. to 5s.
Surtax	Graded increases to yield another £11 million
Estate Duty	Additional 10% on estates above £10,000
Beer	1d. a pint increase
Tobacco	1½ d. an ounce increase
Wines	Increase of 2s. a gallon (light); 4s. a gallon (heavy)
Entertainments	Increases to produce another £4 million
Merchant Sales Tax	New plan for tax of 33½ % on wholesale value of luxuries

The People's Year Book, 1940, p. 123+.

– Six –
1945–1949

'From the Cradle to the Grave'

PRIME MINISTER
C.R. Attlee (Labour), July 1945–March 1950

CHANCELLORS OF THE EXCHEQUER
Hugh Dalton, July 1945–November 1947
Sir Stafford Cripps, November 1947–October 1950

The end of the war heralded the disintegration of the Coalition Government headed by Winston Churchill. The subsequent June 6 election brought a Labour Government, under Clement Attlee, into power.

Labour's optimistic 'Let us Face the Future' manifesto captured the mood of post-war Britain. Instead of the mass unemployment and class-consciousness of the 1930s, the Labour Government propagated a social and economic programme favouring a new more egalitarian society, in which people could be taken care of 'from the Cradle to the Grave'.

Economically, the nationalization of industry and full employment were Attlee's major concerns. In 1946, civil aviation, coal, cable and wireless, and the Bank of England were brought under public sector control; electricity and railways followed in 1947; gas in 1948; and iron and steel in 1949. Despite the rapid and major changes in Britain's economy, only 20 per cent of industry was nationalized during this period, employing approximately 2.5 million people.

Between 1946–51, Britain experienced above average rates of growth in production in certain sectors. Gas, electricity, and water rose by 36 per cent; transport and commerce by 23 per cent; and other manufacturing by 55.7 per cent; while steel production by the end of the 1940s was 60 per cent higher than its pre-war level.

Labour's social reforms were also impressive. Through a series of revolutionizing acts Labour laid the foundation of the Welfare State. The National Insurance Act (1946) developed ideas introduced in the Beveridge Report of 1942; the National Health Service Act proposed a system which would provide medical care for all through state-funded hospitals; and the Housing Acts of 1946 and 1949 promoted the construction of council houses (from 1945–51 approximately 1 million houses were built).

Against this background of social reform, post-war Britain was suffering from a severe 'dollar gap', which had existed in the 1930s but increased drastically during the war. This eventually led to the establishment of the Organization for European Economic Cooperation (OEEC) which administered US financial aid to Europe. The force of British exports and the maintenance of full employment gradually helped to stabilize the economy – however, the pound was devalued in 1949, and fell from four dollars and three cents to two dollars and eighty cents. Similarly, Dalton and Cripps's restrictive financial policies which used high direct taxation, full employment, and a policy of austerity as tools to aid economic recovery worked well. The 1947 Supplies and Services Bill, although highly unpopular, rationed main foodstuffs, including potatoes and bread for the first time. Prices were rigidly controlled and wages increased at a slower rate than pre-war levels.

By the end of the 1940s the Balance of Payments problem seemed to be stabilizing, exports had risen from 1946 by approximately 11.9 per cent, industrial production had increased by 5.75 per cent, and total output had increased by 2.3 per cent per annum. Despite this Labour's popularity was declining – and the election of February 1950 returned them to power by a small majority.

Internationally, Britain's Empire was crumbling. In 1947 India achieved independence and the new country of Pakistan was created. Ceylon and Burma also detached themselves from the Empire in the same year. In Africa the separatist movement started to grow in importance. In general, the time when Britain had influenced international affairs had long passed, instead the US and USSR became the most important political and economic forces in world affairs.

From 1945–49, Britain experienced a period of great change. Aided by Labour's egalitarian policies, the nation began to recover from the social and financial mayhem caused by World War II. Instead of looking back to mass unemployment, recession, and social inequality, Britain began to look forward with great optimism to a more stable, less class-conscious society.

6.1 Historical Snapshots

6.1 Historical Snapshots

1946	Test flights begin at Heathrow.
	Bananas available at Covent Garden for the first time since the war.
	Student grants introduced for university/college education.
	Bolton football tragedy. 33 die as barriers collapse at cup tie.
1947	Meat rations are reduced.
	Child allowance is introduced.
	First vinylite record disc released in USA.
	Introduction of the printed circuit board by J. R. Sargrove.
	First atomic reactor starts up in Harwell.
	School leaving age is raised to 15.
	Labour nationalizes the coal industry.
	Princess Elizabeth and Prince Phillip of Greece (the Duke of Edinburgh) marry.
1948	A new General Certificate of Education (GCE) is announced for England and Wales.
	Electricity Industry is nationalized.
	Footwear rationing ends.
	Prince Charles (the Prince of Wales) is born.
	National Health Service (NHS) aims to offer free medical care for all.
1949	Footballers accept proposal for a maximum wage of £12 a week.
	Sterling is devalued from $4.03 to $2.80.
	Lake District becomes a national park.
	Gas Industry is nationalized.
	Britain's first launderette opens.
	Chocolate and sweet rationing ends.
	Legal Aid Act helps people to obtain legal advice.
	The world's first passenger jet airliner makes its maiden flight.
	Invention of the transistor by scientists at the Bell Telephone Co. in the USA.
	First atomic bomb test in the USSR.

Chronicle of Britain, J.L. International Publishing, 1992; Williams, T.I. *Invention and Discovery in the 20th Century*, Harrap, 1990; Galsworthy, M. *Encyclopaedia of Association Football*.

6.2 Earnings and Employment

6.2.1 Earnings, Standard Tables

6.2.1a Incomes and Wages

	1946	1947	1948	1949
Police Constable		£273 (a)		£330 (a)
Teacher[1]			£615 (a)	
Nurse[2]				£350 (a)
Train Driver		126s. 6d.	138s. 0d.	138s. 0d.
Coal Miner		100 0	115 0	115 0
Fitter and Turner		106 7¼	106 7¼	111 7¼
Bricklayer		115 6	126 6	130 2
Labourer		92 7	101 9	104 6
Compositor		125 0	140 0	140 0
Farm Worker	72s. 2d.	80 0	90 0	94 0
Baker		101 0	105 0	106 0
Textile Worker (weaver)	84 7	82 6	87 6	87 6

British Labour Statistics 1886–1968, HMSO, 1971; Routh, G. *Occupation and Pay in Great Britain 1906–1979*, Macmillan Press, 1980; Royal College of Nursing.

Blank space denotes no available data. Wages are weekly unless otherwise stated. [1]Secondary school teacher with a degree. [2]The rate applies to a male staff nurse in a General Hospital after three years of service. (a) – annual.

6.2.1b Average Weekly Earnings

	Bricks, Pottery and Glass	Total Metals	Textiles	Clothing	Food, Drink and Tobacco	Paper and Printing	Building and Wood-working	Govern-ment Industrial Establish-ments	Transport	All Industries
	£	£	£	£	£	£	£	£	£	£
Males										
1946	6.00	6.64	5.50	5.81	5.63	6.33	5.53	5.83	5.76	6.04
1947	6.50	7.01	5.96	6.11	6.06	6.86	5.85	6.03	6.18	6.40
1948	6.74	7.20	6.33	6.38	6.20	7.19	6.40	6.26	6.60	6.70
Females										
1946	2.90	3.53	3.18	3.26	3.00	3.03	3.07	3.77	4.22	3.25
1947	3.32	3.68	3.40	3.53	3.25	3.34	3.33	3.89	4.44	3.47
1948	3.48	3.76	3.70	3.68	3.40	3.61	3.39	3.98	4.88	3.65

British Labour Statistics, 1886–1968, HMSO, 1971

6.2.3 Incomes, Miscellaneous

6.2.3a Coal Miners' Earnings per Shift

	Durham		UK	
	s.	d.	s.	d.
1947	27	2	27	8
1948	31	9	31	9
1949	32	7	32	11

Garside, W.R. *The Durham Miners 1919–1960*, 1971.

Original source, *National Coal Board, Annual Reports, 1947–56*.

6.2.4 Employment

6.2.4a Unemployment by Region

	Males and Females	Males	Females
	000's	000's	000's
United Kingdom	338.0	249.9	88.1
Great Britain	308.0	228.0	80.0
England	209.4	153.8	55.6
South East	71.7	51.3	20.4
East Anglia	6.3	4.3	2.0
South West	15.7	11.3	4.4
West Midlands	12.2	9.3	2.9
East Midlands	5.2	3.5	1.7
Yorkshire and Humberside	17.1	13.1	4.0
North West	48.9	36.4	12.5
North	32.2	24.5	7.7
Wales	36.4	26.5	10.0
Scotland	62.1	47.7	14.4
Northern Ireland	30.0	21.9	8.1

British Labour Statistics, 1886–1968, HMSO, 1971.

Figures are averaged over 12 months for those registered as unemployed in 1949.

6.2.4b Employment by Region

	1946	1947	1948[1]	1949
	000's	000's	000's	000's
London and South Eastern	3,358	3,492		
Eastern	758	781		
Southern	681	697		
South Western	774	784		
Midland	1,454	1,500		
North Midland	1,050	1,065		
East and West Ridings	1,386	1,399		
Northern	994	1,001		
North Western	2,229	2,268		
Scotland	1,615	1,658		
Wales	727	731		
Great Britain	15,026	15,376	20,270	20,320
Special schemes for banking and insurance	174	174		
Total insured employees in Great Britain	15,200	15,550		
Northern Ireland (including special schemes)	374	382		
Total insured employees in the UK	15,572	15,930	20,732	20,782

British Labour Statistics, 1886–1968, HMSO, 1971.

Figures are for the mid-year for those entitled to insurance. Males aged between 14 and 64 and females between 14 and 39. [1]Data for the regions for 1948 and 1949 is not available in the same format. Original source, *Gazette*.

6.3 Consumer Expenditure

6.3.1 Consumer Expenditure, Standard Table

	Food	Alcoholic Drink	Tobacco	Housing	Fuel and Light	Clothing	Durable House-hold Goods	Motor Cars and Motor Cycles	Other Goods	Other Services	Total Consumer Expen-diture
	£m	£m	£m	£m	£m	£m	£m	£m	£m	£m	£m
1946	1,580	696	602	692	280	638	197	36	743	1,581	7,273
1947	1,826	726	689	757	300	736	269	49	841	1,667	8,028
1948	1,975	802	764	787	327	902	310	48	854	1,724	8,609
1949	2,148	755	753	801	335	1,013	360	61	927	1,716	8,969

Mitchell, B.R. *British Historical Statistics*, Cambridge University Press, 1988.

Original source, Feinstein, C.H. *National Income, Expenditure and Output in the UK 1855-1965*, Cambridge, 1972.

6.4 Prices

6.4.1 Food Prices

6.4.1a Food Basket

Article (per lb. unless otherwise stated)	d.		d.
Beef, home-killed:		Cabbage	7.6
Sirloin (without bone)	20.0	Cauliflower	n/a
Silverside (without bone)	18.0	Sprouts	n/a
Back ribs (with bone)	14.2	Carrots	n/a
Fore ribs (with bone)	n/a	Onions	3.8
Brisket (with bone)	18.0	Apples:	
Rump steak	n/a	Cooking	8.1
Lamb, home-killed:		Dessert	n/a
Loin (with bone)	20.0	Oranges	8.0
Breast	8.2	Bananas	11.0
Shoulder (with bone)	17.0	Bread:	
Leg (with bone)	n/a	White, per 1¾ lb. loaf	4.5
Lamb, imported:		White, per 1¾ lb. wrapped	n/a
Loin (with bone)	17.0	White, per 14oz. loaf	2.7
Breast	4.2	Flour, self raising 3lb.	10.9
Shoulder (with bone)	15.0	Bacon:	
Leg (with bone)	n/a	Back, smoked	22.3
Pork, home-killed:		Streaky, smoked	17.4
Leg	18.0	Milk, ordinary, per pint	4.5
Belly	16.0	Butter:	
Loin (with bone)	n/a	New Zealand	16.0
Ox liver	14.0	Danish	n/a
Sausages:		Margarine	9.0
Pork	14.5	Lard	n/a
Beef	12.8	Cheese, cheddar type	10.0
Corned Beef	20.0	Eggs:	
Cod fillets	14.5	Large, per dozen	20.7
Haddock, fresh, whole	9.0	Standard, per dozen	20.7
Haddock, smoked, whole	14.0	Medium, per dozen	20.7
Plaice, whole	14.5	Sugar, granulated, per 2lb.	6.0
Herrings	6.5	Tea, per ¼ lb:	
Kippers	9.5	Higher priced	9.0
Potatoes	1.2	Medium priced	9.0
Tomatoes	25.7	Lower priced	9.0

British Labour Statistics, 1886–1968, HMSO, 1971.

The table was compiled from information supplied by some 1,000 retailers in 200 towns for the Retail Price Index. Average of prices.

6.4.1b Rowntree's Subsistence Diet, 1949

	Price per lb.		Cost			Price per lb.		Cost	
	s.	d.	s.	d.		s.	d.	s.	d.
2½ lb. Breast of Mutton		8	1	8	2lb. Oatmeal		6	1	0
2lb. Minced Beef	1	4	2	8	1lb. Jam	1	2	1	2
1½ lb. Shin of Beef	1	6	2	3	1lb. Treacle		10		10
1lb. Liver	1	6	1	6	¼ lb. Cocoa		8½		8½
1lb. Beef Sausages	1	3	1	3	10ozs. Rice		9		5½
1¼ lb. Bacon	1	11	2	4¾	¼ lb. Sago		9		2¼
10ozs. Cheese	1	2		8¾	2ozs. Barley		9		1
14 pts. Milk		5	5	10	½ lb. Peas		10½		5¼
1½ lb. Herrings		8	1	0	6lb. Swedes		2½	1	3
1lb. Kippers	1	0	1	0	4½ lb. Onions		5	1	10½
3lb. 2ozs. Sugar		5	1	3½	4lb. Apples		5	1	8
14lb. Potatoes	(9lb.) 1	0	1	6½	1 Egg		3½		3½
13½ Loaves (23½lb.)		5½	6	2¼	Extra Vegetables and Fruit			1	6
2½ lb. Margarine		10	2	1	½ lb. Tea	3	4	1	8
10ozs. Cooking Fat	1	0		7½	Salt, Oxo cubes				9
1¼ lb. Flour	(3lb. bag) 9½			4	**Total**			47	4

Wilsher, P. *The Pound in Your Pocket 1870–1970*, Cassell and Company Ltd, 1970.

Taken from Seebohm Rowntree's third survey of York in 1950.

6.4.2 Prices, General Articles

	1946		1947		1948		1949	
	s.	d.	s.	d.	s.	d.	s.	d.
Beer (1 pint)	1	1	1	4				
Cadbury's Milk Chocolate (½ lb. bar)			1	5	1	8	1	9
Daily Mail		1				1		1
Guinness Extra Stout (1 pint)		11						
Inland Letter Post								3
Mars Bar[1]								5
Pears Transparent Soap				8½				
Petrol (1 gallon)							2s–2s	3d.
Scotch Whisky (standard bottle)			31	0	33	4		
Swan Vestas Matches								4
The Times		3		3		3		3

The Boots Company; British Library; Burmah Castrol; Cadbury's Ltd; Colmans of Norwich; Guinness Brewing GB; Rowntrees; Royal Mail; Sainsbury's Archives; The Scotch Whisky Association and Unilever Historical Archives.

Blank space denotes no prices available. [1]Mars Bar went on sale in 1949.

6.4.3 Prices, Selected

Item	Source	Description	Price £	s.	d.
Alcoholic Drink					
Fortified Wines	*Binns Department Stores*, 1949	Dry Fly Sherry	1	0	0 (bottle)
Appliances: Domestic and Electrical					
Radio	*Debenham & Freebody*, London, 1946	Ever Ready All Dry Portable Radio	8	0	0 (complete with battery)
Receiver	*Ever Ready Brochure*	Portable Battery Receiver All Dry type "K"	13	0	0
Gramophone	*Manchester Guardian*, April 22, 1949	HMV Radiogram Model 1608	112	17	9
	Producer, August 1949	Defiant Model RGSH 849	108	13	9
Radio		Defiant Model MSH 450	20	15	9
Television		Defiant TR947 9in. Set	62	0	8
	The Pound in Your Pocket 1870–1970, 1949	Black and White 9in. Set	36	15	0
Radio		Portable Radios from	15	15	6
Vacuum Cleaner		GEC Vacuum Cleaner	14	14	0
Clothing and Footwear:					
Children's					
Skirts	*Debenham & Freebody*, London, 1946	Wool Stockinette Skirts	1	5	9 (up to 28/9 + 4 coupons)
Infants Suit		Knitted Breechette Suit		10	6 (+5 coupons)
		Breechette Set with a Design in Fancy Stitch		10	6 (+5 coupons)
Pram Set		Babies Finely Knitted Pram Set		10	6 (+5 coupons)
Hosiery		Oddments in Children's Socks		1	0 (+1 coupon)
Shoes	*Debenham & Freebody*, London, 1949	Children's Shoes in Brown Calf Lace or Bar		7	6 (sale price)
		Children's Brown Sandals, Waterproof Leather Soles		16	6
		Many Oddments to Clear		18	0 (up to 23/0)
Men's					
Ties	*Debenham & Freebody*, London, 1946	Hand Made Silk Ties	1	3	9
Jackets	*Selfridges Archives*, 1949	All Wool Tweed Jackets	3	10	0
	Manchester Guardian, February 24, 1949	Lewis's Sports Jacket in Harris Tweed	5	15	0
Shirts	*The Pound in Your Pocket 1870–1970*, 1949	Summit Cotton Shirts from	1	18	6
Coats		C & A's Bargain Cloth Coats	4	9	11
Women's					
Dress	*Debenham & Freebody*, London, July 1946	Angora Wool Jersey Dress	8	0	0 (+11 coupons)
Suit		Tailored Tweed Coats and Skirts	15	15	0 (+18 coupons)
Nightwear		Nightdress in Heavy Quality Rayon Satin	3	9	6 (+6 coupons)
		Shirt Style Nightie in Artificial Spun Material	3	0	0 (+6 coupons)
Underwear		Combinations in Pure Wool		14	0 (+2 coupons)
		Woollen Vests		8	6 (+3 coupons)
		Pure Silk and Locknit Panties		5	0 (+2 coupons)
Hats		Halo Beret Cleverly Expressed in Cloth		19	11
		Youthful Cap		15	11

Continued

6.4.3 Prices, Selected *continued*

Item	Source	Description	Price £	s.	d.
Cape	*Debenham & Freebody*, London, 1946	Pure French Hand Knitted Angora Cape	12	6	8 (+3 coupons)
Nightwear		Rayon Georgette Nightie	4	11	1 (+6 coupons)
Frock	*Debenham & Freebody*, London, 1947	Flowered Frock	15	1	11 (+7 coupons)
Suit		Ensemble on Classic Lines in a Two Tone Print	23	3	0 (+12 coupons)
Knitwear	*Debenham & Freebody*, London, 1947	Cardigan Suit	13	16	0 (+12 coupons)
		Jersey Suit	17	11	0 (+14 coupons)
		New Length Cardigan	4	3	2 (+6 coupons)
Dress	*Debenham & Freebody*, London, 1949	Woollen Dresses in Several Styles	2	6	5 (up to 63/3)
		Washing Frocks in Several Colours	1	0	0 (7 now 3½ coupons)
Evening Gowns		Evening Gowns reduced to	4	11	4
Suits		Washing Jumper Suits reduced to	4	0	0 (10 now 5 coupons)
Shoes		Grey Lizard and Black Calf Lace Shoe	5	0	0
		Navy Blue Lizard Sandal	3	0	0
Bags		Durable Ostrich Grained Leather	3	12	6
Umbrella		French Rayon Chubby Umbrellas	2	9	6
Shoes	*Binns Department Stores*, 1949	Python Shoes	6	6	3
Gown	*Daily Mail*, February 10, 1949	The "New Look" – A Dior Copy	30	0	0
Food Products					
Milk	*Milk Marketing Board*, 1949	Pint of Milk			5
Confectionery	*Mars*, 1949	Mars Bar			5
Meat (per lb.)	*Rowntree's Post War Subsistence Diet*, 1949	Minced Beef		1	4
		Sausage		1	3
		Liver		1	6
		Bacon		1	11
Cheese		Cheddar Cheese		1	2
Beverages		Tea		3	4
Vegetables		Potatoes		1	0 (9lbs.)
		Onions			5 (lb.)
		Swedes			2½ (lb.)
Fresh Fruit		Apples			5 (lb.)
Furniture					
Utility Furniture from Goodalla	*Manchester Guardian*, April 22, 1949	Bedroom Suite in Australian Walnut	96	0	0
		Quilted Mahogany and Sycamore Bedroom Suite	90	13	4
		Figured Walnut Dining Suite	48	11	4
		Reproduction Walnut Dining Suite	54	10	0
Heat and Light					
Electricity	*Eastern Electricity Board*, 1946	Electricity per Year	1	0	0 (+1d. per unit)
Gas	*British Gas North Thames*, 1946	Gas per Therm		1	3
Coal	*What it Cost the Day Before Yesterday Book*	Coal per Ton	3	12	0
Household Goods					
Bedding	*Debenham & Freebody*, London, 1946	Hand Embroidered Irish Pillow Cases	2	12	6 (pair)
		Superior Irish Cotton Sheets Single	8	8	0 (pair)
Gifts		Chintz Tea Cosy	2	12	6

Continued

6.4.3 Prices, Selected *continued*

Item	Source	Description	Price £	s.	d.
Gifts *cont.*		Metal Waste Paper Tub	2	9	0
		Housekeeping Purse in Strong Hide	1	2	0
		Multi Coloured Felt Mules	1	5	3 (+7 coupons)
		Spirit Flask Chromium Plated	1	12	6
		Leather Photo Frames		12	9 (up to 122/6)
Houses					
Semi Detached House	*What it cost the Day Before Yesterday Book*	3 Bedroom Semi Detched House in South England	2,200	0	0
Terraced House	*Local Estate Agents*, 1949	2 Bedroom House in the North with Outside Toilet	450	0	0
Jewellery					
Necklace	*Debenham & Freebody*, London, 1946	Attractive Red Stone Bead Necklets	1	1	0 (sale price)
Personal Care Items					
Perfumes	*Debenham & Freebody*, London, 1946	Perfume by Goya		10	9
		"La Jocanda" and "Xanadu" by Fragrance	2	12	6
Powder		Talcum Powder suitable as an After Shave for Men		2	0
Brush		Nylon Bristle Hair Brush	1	17	6
Clothes Hanger		Thickly Padded Hanger		5	9
Shaving Preparations		Shaving Set	4	18	11
	Unilever Archives, 1947	Pears "Jif" Shaving Stick			7½ wrapped
		Erasmic Shaving Stick Refill		1	0
		Coroshave Brushless Shaving Cream		1	10½ (in jars)
Soaps		Pears Embassy Opaque Soap			8½
Toilet Preparations		Icilma Foundation Vanishing Cream		2	2 (jar)
		Icilma Cold Cream		2	2 (jars)
		Icilma Face Powder		2	2
		Icilma Wet Shampoos			4
		Icilma Skin Tonic		2	0 (bottle)
		Corofix Non-greasy Hair Dressing		2	9 (bottle)
Publications					
Magazines	*Producer*, August 1946	Annual Subscription for the "Producer"		3	6 (post free)
		Subscription for a dozen copies		1	9
Services					
Cinema	*Kinematographic Year Book*, 1947–1949	Odeon Theatre, Park Royal, London, Admission Price		1	0 (up to 2/9)
	Kinematographic Year Book, 1947–1949	Odeon Theatre, Manchester, Admission Price		1	9 (up to 4/6)
Licence	*Post Office Archives*, 1946	Radio	1	0	0
		Television, Black and White	2	0	0
	DVLA, 1947	Road Tax First Registered on or after 1.1.47	1	0	0
		Subject at the same minimum 6 h.p. scale	7	10	0

Continued

6.4.3 Prices, Selected *continued*

Item	Source	Description	£	s.	d.
Telephone Tariffs	*British Telecom Archives*, 1946				
Midnight to 6.30 and 9.30 pm to Midnight		15 to 20 miles			10
		20 to 25 miles		1	2
		25 to 35 miles		1	6
		35 to 75 miles		1	10
Parcel Postage Rates	*Post Office Archives*, 1947	3lb. weight			9
		5lb. weight		1	0
		15lb. weight		1	4
Tobacco Products					
Smoking Equipment	*Debenham & Freebody*, London, 1946	Cigarette Case of Superior Quality Chromium Plate	1	1	9
Cigarettes	*The Pound in Your Pocket 1870–1970*, 1949	Players Navy Cut		3	6 (20)
		Wills Three Castles		3	10 (20)
		Woodbines		2	9 (20)
Transport and Vehicles					
Air Fares	*Reed Travel Group*, June 1948	London to Paris	8	0	0
		London to New York	86	17	0
Rail Fares	*Bradshaws ABC Railway Guide*, July 1948	Manchester to London Return	1	17	8 (up to 50/6)
		Manchester to London Single	1	8	2 (up to 46/10)
Bus Fares	*Manchester Corporation Transport Dept.*, 1949	Manchester to Wythenshawe (8.2 miles)		1	0 (return)
Air Fares	*The Tatler*, April 20, 1949	London to Dublin Return by Aer Lingus	11	0	0
		Liverpool to Dublin by Aer Lingus	6	6	0
Vehicles	*Complete Catalogue of Austin Cars since 1945*	Austin Twelve, 42 b.h.p. 4 Door Saloon Estate	531	0	0 (price when introduced)
		A 90 Atlantic 88 b.h.p. 2 Door Sports Saloon	1,017	0	0
		A 120 Princess, 135 b.h.p. 4 Door Saloon	1,917	0	0
	The Pound in Your Pocket 1870–1970, 1949	Rover "75"	1,016	0	0
		Morris Oxford	546	7	3
Travel					
Tours	*Producer*, August 1946	CWS 10 Day Tours to Switzerland	19	0	0 (inclusive)
	The Pound in Your Pocket 1870–1970, 1949	15 Day Coach Tour to the Dolomites and Venice	61	19	0
Miscellany					
Travelware	*Debenham & Freebody*, London 1946	Lightweight Canvas Travel Case 20 ins.	4	14	3
	Debenham & Freebody, London, 1949	Lightweight Semi-Stiffened Case	3	3	3
		Hide Travel Bag with Slide Opening	8	17	6
		School Satchels in Pig-Grain Hide	1	5	0
		Red Fibre School Trunk	8	17	6
Stationery		Leather Writing Case with Folding Flap		17	6
	The Pound in Your Pocket 1870–1970, 1949	Ball Point Pens		4	6 (up to 13/9)
		Refills		1	10

6.4.4 Prices, Miscellaneous

6.4.4a Woman's Clothing Budget

	Per Year		
	£	s.	d.
Dress at £2 2s. 0d. once every 3 years		14	0
Coat and skirt (second hand)		12	6
Odd skirt (second hand)		2	6
Overcoat at £6 6s. 0d. once every 3 years	2	2	6
Raincoat (second hand)		12	6
Jumper		3	6
Hat at 17s. 6d. once in 3 years		5	10
Shoes at £1 10s. 0d. once in 2 years		15	0
Stockings, 12 pairs a year at 3s.	1	16	0
Under slip		7	6
Vest, 2 a year at 5s. 6d.		11	0
Knickers, 4 pairs a year at 6s. 6d.	1	6	0
Corset	1	1	0
Nightdress, one in 2 years at £1 10s. 0d.		15	0
Apron, 3 a year at 4s.		12	0
Wool for gloves		2	0
Handkerchiefs, 2 a year at 1s.		2	0
Shoes repaired every 3 months at 10s. 6d.	2	2	0
Total	14	2	4

Wilsher, P. *The Pound in Your Pocket 1870–1970*, Cassell and Company Ltd., 1970.

This is how one thirty-eight-year-old mother-of-three children managed to keep her spending down to the minimum.

6.5 Finance and Economic Data

6.5.1 Finance, Personal

	1946		1947		1948		1949	
	s.	d.	s.	d.	s.	d.	s.	d.
Income Tax Rates[1]	10	0	9	0	9	0	9	0
Old Age Pension:								
Married	41	0	41	0	41	0	41	0
Single	26	0	26	0	26	0	26	0
Child Benefit[2] for second child	5	0						
Unemployment Benefit[3]:								
Personal Benefit					26	0		
					(higher rate)			
Base Interest Rates[4] in percent	4%		4%		4%		4%	

Mitchell, B.R. *British Historical Statistics*, Cambridge University Press, 1988; Bank of England; Department of Social Security.

[1]The rates apply to years ended the 5th April. [2]Family allowance was introduced in 1946. It was replaced by child benefit in 1977. [3]Unemployment benefit was introduced in 1948. [4]The rates apply to January of each year. There was no change in the interest rate between 1940 and 1950.

6.5.2 Financial Markets

6.5.2a Highest Closing Price of UK Major Stocks

	1946	1947	1948	1949
Barclays Bank	69/6	68/4½	59/0	57/7
Boots the Chemist	65/0	67/6	67/6	66/3
Burmah Oil	80/0	5¹/₁₆	83/1½	73/9
Courtaulds	58/9	58/6	46/1½	38/9
Guinness	8⁵/₁₆	17²/₈	7²⁷/₃₂	7¹/₁₆
Imperial Chemical Industries (ICI)	49/0	53/6	53/0	49/4½
Marks and Spencer	85/6	93/0	75/9	75/3
Reckitt and Sons	6¹⁵/₁₆	6²⁹/₃₂	6³/₃₂	5³/₁₆
Schweppes	35/2½	36/10½	35/0	33/3¾
Unilever	59/0	58/9	56/4½	51/6
Viyella	70/10½	79/6	73/3	62/1½
Whitbread & Co.	131¾	132	24/0	23/6

Mathieson, F.C. and Sons, *Stock Exchanges Ten Year Record of Prices and Dividends*.

Fractions are quoted as parts of £1=32. Blank space denotes no data available.

6.5.2b Commodities

	Best Coal (price per ton)		Raw Cotton (per lb.)	Gold (average market)	Sugar (annual average world price)	Wheat (per ton)		Wool (average import value)
	s.	d.	old pence (d.)	£ per troy oz.	£ sterling per metric ton	s.	d.	pence per lb.
1946	45	2	14.87	8.613	26.492	14	10	19.0
1947	48	2	21.21	8.613	30.840	16	9	23.2
1948	54	9	23.23	8.613	27.067	21	0	30.7
1949	54	9	24.85	8.613	35.843	23	3	37.4

Mitchell, B.R. *British Historical Statistics*, Cambridge University Press, 1988; World Gold Council; Czarnikow Sugar.

Original source, Sauerbeck, A. *Prices of Commodities and the Precious Metals, Journal of the Statistical Society.*

6.5.2c Foreign Exchange Rates

	Berlin Reichsmarks per £1[1]	Paris Francs per £1	New York Dollars per £1
1946		480.00	4.03
1947		480.00	4.03
1948		879.00	3.68
1949		1,053.06	2.80

Mitchell, B.R. *British Historical Statistics*, Cambridge University Press, 1988.

Blank space denotes no available data. [1]Dealings with Germany still not resumed.

6.5.3 Balance of Payments and GNP

6.5.3a Balance of Payments

	Merchan-dise Exports	Merchan-dise Imports	Overall Visible Balance	Exports of Services	Imports of Services	Property Income from Abroad	Property Income Paid Abroad	Balance of Current Transfers	Overall Invisible Balance	Overall Current Balance
	£m	£m	£m	£m	£m	£m	£m	£m	£m	£m
1946	960	1,063	-103	470	762	198	113	+244	+37	-66
1947	1,180	1,541	-361	472	687	261	111	+204	+139	-222
1948	1,639	1,790	-151	557	644	360	125	+263	+411	+260
1949	1,863	2,000	-137	632	697	351	128	+171	+329	+192

Mitchell, B.R. *British Historical Statistics*, Cambridge University Press, 1988.

Original source, Feinstein, C.H. *National Income, Expenditure and Output in the UK, 1855-1965*, Cambridge, 1972.

6.5.3b GNP at Factor Cost and Its Component Incomes at Current Prices

	Income from Employ-ment	Income from Self Employ-ment	Gross Trading Profits of Comp-anies	Gross Trading Surplus of Public Enter-prises	Rent	Stock Apprecia-tion	Gross Domestic Product	Net Property Income from Abroad	Gross National Product	Capital Consump-tion	National Income
	£m	£m	£m	£m	£m	£m	£m	£m	£m	£m	£m
1946	5,758	1,126	1,476	106	429	125	8,770	85	8,855	690	8,165
1947	6,227	1,210	1,604	155	472	450	9,308	150	9,458	770	8,688
1948	6,785	1,305	1,793	220	456	325	10,234	235	10,469	848	9,621
1949	7,246	1,363	1,843	258	475	200	10,985	219	11,204	893	10,311

Mitchell, B.R. *British Historical Statistics*, Cambridge University Press, 1988.

Original source, Feinstein, C.H. *National Income, Expenditure and Output of the UK, 1855-1965*, Cambridge, 1972.

6.6 Miscellaneous

6.6.1 Manchester City Transport Bus Fares

Number of Stages	Distance in Miles	1940 d.	1946 d.	1949 d.
1	.53	1	1	1½
2	1.05	1	1	1½
3	1.58	1½	2	2
4	2.11	2	2	2½
5	2.64	2½	3	3
6	3.17	3	3	3
7	3.69	3½	4	4
8	4.22	4	4	4
9	4.75	4½	5	5
10	5.28	5	5	5
11	5.81	5½	6	5
12	6.33	6	6	6
13	6.85	6½	7	6
14	7.39	7	7	6
15	7.92	7½	8	7
16	8.45	8	8	7
17	8.98	8½	9	7
18	9.51	9	9	8
19	10.04	9½	9	8
20	10.57	10	10	8

Manchester City Transport Statement, September 23, 1969.

– Seven –
1950–1959

Recovery and Crisis

PRIME MINISTERS
Clement Attlee (Labour), March 1950–October 1951
Sir Winston Churchill (Conservative), October 1951–April 1955
Sir Anthony Eden (Conservative), April 1955–January 1957
Harold Macmillan (Conservative), January 1957–October 1963

CHANCELLORS OF THE EXCHEQUER
Sir S. Cripps, November 1947–October 1950
Hugh Gaitskell, October 1950–October 1951
R.A. Butler, October 1951–December 1955
H. Macmillan, December 1955–January 1957
P. Thorneycroft, January 1957–January 1958
D. Heathcoat Amory, January 1958–July 1960

By the end of the 1940s Britain appeared to be experiencing recovery. Despite this Labour popularity was in decline, and in 1951, the Conservative Party, under Winston Churchill, returned to power.

The early years of the 1950s were overshadowed by death and illness among the nation's leaders. In 1952, George VI died, and was succeeded by his young daughter, Elizabeth II. Churchill himself had a serious stroke in 1953, and Anthony Eden, who became acting Prime Minister, also became ill in 1953. Finally, in 1955, Churchill retired, leaving his protegé, Eden, to take his place as Prime Minister.

The Britain Eden inherited was in good shape, economically and financially. Unemployment was low, the Balance of Payments was stable, and housing, the bane of the Labour administration, was finally under control, due to the effective policies of Harold Macmillan, Minister of Housing, 1951–54.

Eden promoted private property ownership and partnership in industry (between management and workers). This fitted in well with the progressively more democratic stance that society was taking. Since 1947, Britain's middle-range income group had been the fastest growing. The lower-middle class and the high-earning working class groups had risen from 75 per cent in 1947 to 81 per cent of the total, in 1955.

Saving and investment was also rising – and the building and rearmament programmes (the latter triggered by the Korean War, 1950–53) had led to a boom.

However, in the international arena, Britain was suffering. In 1956, British troops were sent to prevent a Mau uprising in Kenya. This was quickly overshadowed by the Suez Crisis with Egypt. Both Britain and the USA had offered Egypt substantial funding to build the Aswan High Dam, however, the USA quickly withdrew its offer, and Britain followed. Consequently, Egypt announced the nationalization of the Suez Canal Company, a move that breached several international agreements. The ensuing crisis divided the British government, and caused several ministers to resign. Finally Eden himself resigned in January 1957, and Macmillan was asked to form a new Government.

Towards the end of the 1950s Conservative support began to wane, in part because of the Suez Crisis, in part because of policies that tried to promote expansion while reducing inflation. The 'credit squeeze' of 1959 proved one such highly unpopular policy.

For the most part the 1950s was the period of the 'affluent' society which had become used to full employment, mass consumption, economic growth, and rich rewards. Mass consumerism made Macmillan's promises that society had 'never had it so good' and the self-orienting 'I'm alright Jack' more attractive than ever before. Gone was the interest in the Welfare State, and a more egalitarian society seen in the 1940s – self interest and wealth were motivating forces. As the rich became richer, minority groups, such as the elderly and the sick, suffered. It seemed that the competitive British society of the 1950s no longer had room for its waifs and strays.

7.1 Historical Snapshots

7.1 Historical Snapshots

1950	Rover produces the first gas-turbine car.
	Petrol goes up to 3s. a gallon, its highest price since 1920.
	Ford launches its Consul and Zephyr range in UK.
	J. Sainsbury's first self-service store opens in Croydon.
	First pocket transistor radio marketed by Sony in Japan.
1953	Footballers accept proposal for a maximum wage of £15 per week.
	USSR explodes its first hydrogen bomb.
1954	London Gold Market opens up for the first time since 1939. Gold is priced at $35 an ounce.
	British Petroleum Company is formed.
1955	Rootes Motors take over Singer Motors.
	Women teachers and civil servants win equal pay.
	Cardiff becomes capital of Wales.
1956	First provincial ITV station starts broadcasting in the Midlands.
	First premium bonds go on sale.
	Opening of Calder Hall, the world's largest nuclear power station.
	Bell Telephone Co. in the USA develops a videophone.
	Fortran, the first computer programming language, is developed in USA.
	Remington-Rand Univac is the first electronic computer to be available commercially.
1957	Vauxhall introduces new Cresta and Velox models.
	1958, Footballers accept proposal for a maximum wage of £20 per week.
	BMC unveils its new sports car, the Austin Healey Sprite.
1959	First commercial Xerox copier is introduced.
	House of Fraser launches counter bid for Harrods.
	Barclays becomes the first British bank to order a computer for branch accounts.
	Rolls Royce launches its new £8,905 Phantom V.
	The bank rate is cut to 5 per cent.
	Vauxhall launches its new Victor saloon which gives 40 miles per gallon.
	Flashing direction indicator lights become legal on motor vehicles in Britain.

Chronicle of Britain, J.L. International Publishing, 1992; Williams, T.I. *Invention and Discovery in the 20th Century*, Harrap, 1990; Galsworthy, M. *Encyclopaedia of Association Football*.

7.2 Earnings and Employment

7.2.1 Earnings, Standard Tables

7.2.1a Incomes and Wages

	1950		1951		1952		1953		1954		1955		1956		1957		1958		1959	
Solicitor											£2,086 (a)									
Police Constable			£400 (a)						£445 (a)		£475 (a)				£490 (a)		£510 (a)			
Teacher[1]			£766 (a)		£806 (a)				£891 (a)				£1,275 (a)						£1,465 (a)	
Nurse[2]					£394 (a)				£420 (a)				£455 (a)		£478 (a)				£540 (a)	
Clerical Worker											£523 (a)									
Train Driver	138s.	0d.	149s.	0d.	161s.	6d.	168s.	6d.	178s.	6d.	195s.	0d.	212s.	0d.	222s.	6d.	222s.	6d.	229s.	0d.
Coal Miner	115	0	127	0	140	6	146	6	155	0	166	0	180	6	190	0	190	0	197	6
Fitter and Turner	111	7¼	122	7¼	133	7¼	140	11¼	140	11¼	160	6	173	0	173	0	184	0	191	4
Bricklayer	132	0	143	0	154	0	161	4	165	0	172	4	185	2	198	0	207	2	214	6
Labourer	92	7	101	9	104	6	110	0	122	10	133	10	141	2	144	10	152	2	161	4
Compositor	140	0	155	0	170	0	179	0	181	0	186	0	188	0	223	0	230	0	233	0
Farm Worker	94	0	94	0	108	0	113	0	120	0	127	0	135	0	141	0	150	0	156	0
Baker	107	4	111	2	120	9	128	5	134	2	143	9	155	3	155	3	166	9	174	5
Textile Worker	95	0	102	6	108	6	115	0	119	0	124	0	1300		136	6	143	6	148	6

British Labour Statistics 1886-1968, HMSO, 1971; Rowley, G. *Occupation and Pay in Great Britain 1906–1979*, Macmillan Press, 1980; Royal College of Nursing.

Income is weekly, unless stated otherwise. (a) – annual. Blank space denotes no data available. [1]Rates for secondary school teacher with degree. [2]Male Staff Nurse rates in a General Hospital after three years service.

7.2.1b Average Weekly Earnings

	Non-Metaliferous Mining[1] Products	Ship-building and Marine Engineering	Textiles	Clothing	Food, Drink and Tobacco	Paper and Printing[2]	Building and Contracting[3]	Public Administration	Transport and Communication	All Industries
	£	£	£	£	£	£	£	£	£	£
Males										
1950	7.72		7.34	7.33	6.95	8.25	7.25	5.88	7.01	7.52
1951	8.66		8.14	7.58	7.73	9.37	8.05	6.60	7.86	8.30
1952	9.17		8.57	8.30	8.17	9.82	8.73	7.05	8.35	8.93
1953	9.80		9.23	8.75	8.62	10.66	9.18	7.37	8.73	9.46
1954	10.49		9.84	9.21	9.28	11.38	9.93	7.87	9.45	10.22
1955	11.38		10.38	9.84	10.11	12.35	10.78	8.55	10.58	11.15
1956	12.05		10.94	10.64	10.91	13.69	11.73	9.19	11.37	11.90
1957	12.49		11.54	11.02	11.60	14.18	12.05	9.67	12.11	12.58
1958	12.91		11.62	11.38	12.02	14.82	12.46	10.03	12.35	12.83
1959[4]	13.60	13.37	12.40	11.80	12.42	16.13	12.96	10.33	13.09	13.54
Females										
1950	3.97		4.25	4.14	3.87	3.98	3.76	3.75	5.13	4.12
1951	4.32		4.78	4.26	4.27	4.64	4.05	4.13	5.93	4.49
1952	4.59		4.91	4.63	4.54	4.97	4.33	4.43	6.44	4.81
1953	4.85		5.32	4.93	4.75	5.29	4.54	4.69	6.58	5.12
1954	5.13		5.60	5.17	4.99	5.48	4.78	4.93	7.04	5.41
1955	5.45		5.82	5.51	5.45	5.78	5.21	5.41	7.75	5.77
1956	5.73		6.15	5.91	5.83	6.50	5.65	5.87	8.38	6.16
1957	6.07		6.50	6.15	6.14	6.64	5.93	6.18	9.31	6.49
1958	6.26		6.57	6.33	6.43	7.01	6.09	6.49	9.15	6.70
1959[4]	6.59	7.33	6.96	6.67	6.60	7.53	6.14	6.64	9.48	7.03

British Labour Statistics, 1886–1968, HMSO, 1971.

Industry Groups according to the 1948 Standard Industrial Classification (SIC). [1]Described as bricks, pottery, glass and cement from 1959. [2]Described as paper, printing and publishing from 1959. [3]Described as construction from 1959. [4]There were minor changes in coverage due to the new SIC in 1959. Blank space denotes no data available.

7.2.2 Regional Earnings by Selected Occupation

		London		Manchester		Newcastle		Leeds		Glasgow	
		s.	d.	s.	d.	s.	d.	s.	d.	s.	d.
Bricklayer (hourly)	1950	3	0	2	10½	2	10½	2	10½	2	10½
	1955	4	1½	4	0	4	0	4	0	4	0
Bricklayer's Labourer (hourly)	1950	2	5	2	3¾	2	3¾	2	3¾	2	3¾
	1955	3	7	3	5½	3	5½	3	5½	3	5½
Compositor (weekly)	1950	150	0	131	0	131	0	131	0	131	0
	1955	186	0	174	0	174	6	174	6	174	6
Fitter and Turner (weekly)	1950	111	7¼	107	0	n/a		n/a		107	1½
	1955	160	5½	155	10	n/a		n/a		155	11½
Labourer (weekly)	1950	95	1¼	92	1¼	n/a		n/a		92	4½
	1955	135	11½	132	11¼	n/a		n/a		133	2½

British Labour Statistics 1886–1968, HMSO, 1971.

7.2.3 Incomes, Miscellaneous

7.2.3a Coal Miners' Earnings per Shift

	Durham		UK	
	s.	d.	s.	d.
1950	33	4	34	0
1951	36	8	37	3
1952	40	10	41	5
1953	42	9	43	5
1954	44	10	48	7
1955	48	2	52	11
1956	52	10	57	2

Garside, W.R. *The Durham Miners, 1919–1960*, 1971.

Original source, *National Coal Board, Annual Reports, 1947–56.*

7.2.4 Employment

7.2.4a Unemployment by Region

	1950 000's	1951 000's	1952 000's	1953 000's	1954 000's	1955 000's	1956 000's	1957 000's	1958 000's	1959 000's
Males and Females										
UK	341.1	281.4	462.5	380.0	317.8	264.5	287.1	347.2	500.9	512.1
Great Britain	314.2	252.9	414.2	342.0	284.8	232.2	257.0	312.5	457.4	475.2
England	215.1	174.5	318.3	250.1	202.5	163.8	185.3	231.4	340.0	344.0
South East	74.3	60.8	86.7	82.6	68.3	50.9	58.7	74.8	97.7	94.4
East Anglia	7.3	5.3	7.5	7.1	7.1	5.6	6.4	9.1	11.6	10.2
South West	16.5	13.2	17.3	18.4	16.7	13.5	14.9	21.2	26.8	26.1
West Midlands	9.9	8.5	18.0	21.3	12.3	10.2	23.0	27.0	33.8	31.5
East Midlands	5.6	5.4	12.3	6.8	6.4	5.8	6.9	10.8	19.7	18.6
Yorkshire/Humberside	19.2	18.0	36.6	23.7	19.1	14.8	15.7	19.6	38.5	38.2
North West	47.3	35.8	107.3	60.6	44.2	40.8	40.0	47.3	80.8	82.1
North	34.8	27.5	32.6	29.4	28.3	22.3	19.7	21.6	31.1	43.1
Wales	34.4	25.0	26.6	27.8	22.9	17.3	19.5	24.8	36.3	36.3
Scotland	64.7	53.4	69.3	64.1	59.5	51.1	52.2	56.3	81.1	94.9
Northern Ireland	26.9	28.5	48.3	38.0	33.0	32.3	30.1	34.7	43.5	36.9
Males										
UK	241.1	182.3	254.7	245.5	208.2	169.5	191.0	241.9	351.5	369.6
Great Britain	220.1	161.5	227.9	218.2	184.4	146.7	168.8	216.6	321.4	343.8
England	148.3	108.3	169.8	158.4	131.2	102.7	122.3	162.2	239.3	249.4
South East	50.5	38.2	54.9	54.7	45.6	33.9	39.9	53.8	71.5	70.7
East Anglia	4.7	3.2	4.7	4.8	5.0	4.0	4.8	7.0	9.0	8.0
South West	11.1	8.0	10.2	11.6	10.6	8.5	9.7	15.0	19.4	18.7
West Midlands	7.0	5.1	9.8	13.3	7.6	6.4	15.4	17.8	23.9	21.9
East Midlands	3.5	2.6	5.0	4.2	3.8	3.3	4.3	7.4	14.0	13.4
Yorkshire/Humberside	13.9	11.2	18.6	15.4	12.8	9.7	10.6	14.2	27.3	28.5
North West	32.5	21.7	47.7	36.5	28.4	23.1	24.7	31.9	51.7	55.7
North	25.1	18.2	18.8	18.0	17.4	13.8	12.9	15.1	22.5	32.4
Wales	24.1	16.5	16.5	18.8	14.7	10.8	12.6	16.8	25.6	25.4
Scotland	47.8	36.7	41.6	41.0	38.5	33.2	33.8	37.6	56.5	69.1
Northern Ireland	21.0	20.8	26.8	27.3	23.8	22.8	22.2	25.3	30.1	25.8
Females										
UK	100.0	99.1	207.9	134.5	109.6	95.0	96.1	105.3	149.4	142.5
Great Britain	94.1	91.4	186.4	123.8	100.4	85.5	88.2	95.9	136.0	131.4
England	66.8	66.2	148.6	91.7	71.2	61.1	63.0	69.2	100.7	94.6
South East	23.9	22.6	31.8	28.0	22.8	17.0	18.8	21.0	26.1	23.6
East Anglia	2.6	2.1	2.8	2.4	2.1	1.7	1.7	2.1	2.6	2.2
South West	5.4	5.2	7.2	6.8	6.1	4.9	5.2	6.2	7.4	7.4
West Midlands	2.9	3.4	8.2	8.0	4.7	3.8	7.7	9.2	10.0	9.6
East Midlands	2.1	2.8	7.2	2.6	2.6	2.5	2.5	3.4	5.7	5.1
Yorkshire/Humberside	5.3	6.7	18.0	8.4	6.2	5.1	5.1	5.4	11.2	9.7
North West	14.8	14.1	59.6	24.1	15.8	17.7	15.3	15.4	29.2	26.3
North	9.7	9.3	13.8	11.4	10.9	8.5	6.8	6.5	8.7	10.7
Wales	10.3	8.5	10.1	9.0	8.2	6.5	6.9	8.0	10.7	10.9
Scotland	17.0	16.7	27.7	23.1	21.0	17.9	18.4	18.7	24.6	25.8
Northern Ireland	5.9	7.7	21.5	10.7	9.2	9.5	7.9	9.4	13.4	11.1

British Labour Statistics 1886–1968, HMSO, 1971.

Figures are annual averages.

7.2.4b Employment by Region

	1951 000's	1952 000's	1953 000's	1954 000's	1955 000's	1956 000's	1957 000's	1958 000's	1959 000's
Total Males and Females									
UK	20,970	20,916	21,041	21,404	21,702	21,965	22,058	21,884	22,008
Great Britain	20,526	20,489	20,609	20,961	21,258	21,517	21,610	21,450	21,565
England	17,533	17,513	17,603	17,926	18,208	18,445	18,545	18,441	18,540
South East/East Anglia	7,087	7,162	7,225	7,369	7,505	7,633	7,718	7,696	7,779
South West	1,112	1,120	1,126	1,149	1,165	1,178	1,185	1,180	1,206
West Midlands	2,009	2,008	1,996	2,057	2,123	2,136	2,120	2,111	2,132
E Mids/Yorks/Humber	3,192	3,147	3,154	3,197	3,230	3,280	3,280	3,269	3,263
North West	2,917	2,872	2,876	2,923	2,946	2,953	2,954	2,919	2,901
North	1,214	1,207	1,221	1,231	1,237	1,263	1,263	1,269	1,260
Wales	912	912	921	925	932	940	937	923	928
Scotland	2,074	2,057	2,075	2,101	2,107	2,122	2,119	2,077	2,088
Northern Ireland	443	427	433	443	445	448	448	434	443
Males									
UK	13,767	13,772	13,796	13,954	14,086	14,244	14,294	14,220	14,262
Great Britain	13,490	13,499	13,526	13,678	13,810	13,966	14,017	13,948	13,984
England	11,457	11,470	11,484	11,628	11,759	11,907	11,960	11,926	11,967
South East/East Anglia	4,556	4,609	4,633	4,702	4,762	4,841	4,887	4,879	4,925
South West	754	761	764	777	783	791	793	789	806
West Midlands	1,315	1,321	1,313	1,340	1,376	1,385	1,380	1,380	1,393
E Mids/Yorks/Humber	2,140	2,116	2,107	2,124	2,138	2,166	2,179	2,168	2,159
North West	1,825	1,806	1,795	1,813	1,827	1,836	1,838	1,822	1,808
North	867	861	868	874	873	899	887	889	875
Wales	671	670	675	671	671	673	673	662	662
Scotland	1,356	1,353	1,361	1,370	1,372	1,378	1,377	1,354	1,348
Northern Ireland	277	274	270	276	276	278	278	272	278
Females									
UK	7,203	7,144	7,245	7,450	7,616	7,721	7,764	7,664	7,747
Great Britain	7,036	6,990	7,083	7,282	7,448	7,551	7,593	7,502	7,581
England	6,076	6,043	6,119	6,298	6,449	6,539	6,585	6,515	6,572
South East/East Anglia	2,531	2,553	2,592	2,666	2,743	2,793	2,832	2,816	2,854
South West	358	360	362	373	373	383	393	391	399
West Midlands	693	687	684	718	718	747	740	733	739
E Mids/Yorks/Humber	1,053	1,031	1,048	1,073	1,073	1,092	1,122	1,096	1,103
North West	1,092	1,066	1,082	1,110	1,119	1,116	1,115	1,097	1,092
North	348	348	354	358	363	373	377	380	384
Wales	241	242	247	254	261	267	264	261	267
Scotland	719	704	715	729	735	744	742	723	740
Northern Ireland	166	154	163	167	169	170	170	162	166

British Labour Statistics, 1886–1968, HMSO, 1971.

Figures are for each mid-year.

7.3 Consumer Expenditure

7.3.1 Consumer Expenditure, Standard Table

	Food	Alcoholic Drink	Tobacco	Housing	Fuel and Light	Clothing	Durable House-hold Goods	Motor Cars and Motor Cycles	Other Goods	Other Services	Total Consumer Expenditure
	£m	£	£m	£m	£m	£m	£m	£m	£m	£m	£m
1950	2,371	734	766	841	356	1,063	424	64	993	1,760	9,461
1951	2,599	774	800	886	392	1,116	480	74	1,095	1,880	10,215
1952	2,857	779	821	934	424	1,097	462	117	1,145	2,000	10,766
1953	3,156	795	837	1,001	451	1,115	528	186	1,204	2,101	11,475
1954	3,327	794	855	1,056	490	1,205	603	234	1,287	2,198	12,163
1955	3,615	832	880	1,122	528	1,297	624	310	1,443	2,350	13,110
1956	3,820	866	935	1,183	597	1,378	616	268	1,556	2,496	13,821
1957	3,962	906	981	1,276	618	1,439	685	320	1,650	2,648	14,582
1958[1]	4,028	909	1,031	1,434	690	1,458	741	425	1,786	2,716	15,306
1959	4,157	920	1,061	1,533	687	1,525	858	506	1,911	2,855	16,118

Mitchell, B.R. British, Historical Statistics, Cambridge University Press, 1988.

Original source, Feinstein, C.H. *National Income, Expenditure and Output of the UK, 1865-1965,* Cambridge, 1972. [1]From 1958, the definition employed is that used in the 1983 Blue Book.

7.3.2 Regional Household Expenditure

	North	E & W Ridings	North Mids	East	London and South East	South	South West	Wales	Mid-lands	North West	Scot-land	N. Ire-land	UK
	s.	s.	s.	s.	s.	s.	s.	s.	s.	s.	s.	s.	s.
Average weekly house-hold expenditure	223.17	235.48	238.46	232.01	257.56	233.92	220.93	240.50	254.47	243.03	228.52	251.80	240.19
Average weekly expenditure per person	67.83	77.21	74.98	73.87	84.71	72.20	71.28	76.36	74.83	76.66	69.66	65.57	75.49
Average weekly expenditure on housing	18.03	18.64	19.37	21.58	27.93	22.39	21.47	18.68	19.46	21.70	16.32	15.53	21.22

British Labour Statistics, 1886-1968, HMSO, 1971.

Original sources, *Report of an enquiry into Household Expenditure in 1953-1954,* and the *Gazette,* March 1965.

7.4 Prices

7.4.1 Food Prices

7.4.1a Food Basket

Article (per lb. unless otherwise stated)	1952 d.	1957 d.		1952 d.	1957 d.
Beef, home-killed:			Tomatoes	18.5	18.7
Sirloin (without bone)	30.2	49.5	Cabbage	3.5	4.3
Silverside (without bone)	29.8	50.8	Cauliflower	8.3	11.2
Back ribs (with bone)	22.6	38.6	Sprouts	8.7	8.0
Brisket (with bone)	14.2	25.2	Carrots	4.3	4.4
Rump steak	n/a	62.5	Onions	7.0	7.4
Lamb, home-killed:			Apples:		
Loin (with bone)	28.0	45.9	Cooking	6.0	9.0
Breast	13.1	17.7	Dessert	n/a	14.2
Shoulder (with bone)	28.0	41.3	Oranges	8.9	10.1
Leg (with bone)	n/a	47.8	Bananas	12.0	13.6
Lamb, imported:			Bread:		
Loin (with bone)	24.1	37.9	White, per 1¾lb.	6.0	7.5
Breast	10.0	12.6	White, per 1¾lb. wrapped and sliced	n/a	n/a
Shoulder (with bone)	25.8	35.3	White, per 14oz. loaf	3.5	4.3
Leg (with bone)	n/a	42.2	Flour, self raising, 3lb.	14.5	19.8
Pork, home-killed:			Bacon:		
Leg	28.0	43.9	Back, smoked	45.1	46.7
Belly	23.8	31.2	Streaky, smoked	34.8	39.4
Loin (with bone)	n/a	45.9	Milk, ordinary, per pint	6.0	7.0
Ox Liver	22.0	39.7	Butter:		
Sausages:			New Zealand	30.0	49.5
Pork	26.0	33.4	Danish	n/a	55.9
Beef	18.5	23.8	Margarine	14.0	20.0
Corned Beef	28.0	50.5	Lard	n/a	18.3
Roasting Chicken:			Cheese, cheddar type	23.9	35.8
Frozen	n/a	n/a	Eggs:		
Fresh or chilled	n/a	n/a	Large, per dozen	n/a	51.3
Cod Fillets	23.3	23.6	Standard, per dozen	63.6	45.5
Haddock, fresh, whole	20.2	18.8	Medium, per dozen	n/a	41.2
Haddock, smoked, whole	26.1	27.0	Sugar, granulated, per 2lb.	12.0	16.1
Plaice, whole	28.2	27.7	Tea, per ¼ lb.:		
Herrings	11.0	11.4	Higher priced	11.3	20.5
Kippers	16.8	16.7	Medium priced	11.3	20.5
Potatoes	1.9	3.1	Lower priced	11.3	20.5

British Labour Statistics, 1886–1968, HMSO, 1971.

The table was compiled from information supplied by some 1,000 retailers in 200 towns for the Retail Price Index.

7.4.2 Prices, General Articles

	1950		1951		1952		1953		1954		1955		1956		1957		1958		1959	
	s.	d.	s.	d.	s.	d.	s.	d.	s.	d.	s.	d.	s.	d.	s.	d.	s.	d.	s.	d.
Aspirin (100)	1	0			1	3														
Average House Price[1]													£2,280		£2,330		£2,390		£2,410	
Beer (1 pint)			1	3¼	1	3¼	1	3¼	1	3¼	1	3¼	1	3½	1	4	1	4½	1	2½
Cadbury's Dairy Milk Chocolate (½ lb.)	1	9	2	3	2	3	2	4	2	4	2	4	2	0	2	0	2	3	2	4
Cheddar Cheese (1 lb.)	1	2									1	8								
Colmans Starch (4 ozs.)						9														
Daily Mail		1		1		1		1		1		1		1		2½		2½		2½
Guinness Extra Stout (1 pint)		11									1	3								
Inland Letter Post		2½		2½		2½		2½		2½		2½		2½		3		3		3
Mars Bar		5		5		6		6		6		6		6		6		6		6
Pears Transparent Soap						10½														
Petrol (1 gallon)	3	0	3	1½	4	2¾	4	5¼			4	6	4	7½	6	1½	4	8	4	8
Red Label Tea (1 lb.)	3	8							6	0										
Swan Vestas Matches		4																		
The Times		3		3		4		4		4		4		4		4		4		4

The Boots Company; British Library; Burmah Castrol; Cadbury's Ltd; Colmans of Norwich; Guinness Brewing GB; Halifax Building Society; Rowntrees; Royal Mail; Sainsbury's Archives; The Scotch Whisky Association and Unilever Historical Archives.

Blank space denotes no prices available. [1]The average house price is for a new house at mortgage approval stage.

7.4.3 Prices, Selected

Item	Source	Description	Price		
			£	s.	d.
Alcoholic Drink					
Fortified Wines	*Ideal Home*, December 1955	Dry Fly Sherry	1	0	0 (bottle)
Spirits		Haig's Gold Label Scotch Whisky	1	16	0 (bottle)
Appliances: Domestic and Electrical					
Lighting	*Derry's*, London, 1950	Floor Standard	5	10	6
Iron		Hoover Steam Iron	4	15	0
Kettle		Aluminium Kettle	3	9	11
Cleaner	*Ideal Home*, February 1951	GEC Electric Cleaner	14	14	0
Cooker	*Army & Navy Stores*, 1953	Portable Gas Oven		14	9
	Ideal Home, October 1954	GEC Ovenmaster Electric Cooker	37	12	6
		Courtier Stove	4	17	6
Boiler		Glow Worm Aristocrat	22	0	0
Drier		English Electric Tumble Drier	7	0	0
Cleaner		Electrolux Home Cleaner	28	13	6
Refrigerator		Electrolux Silent Refrigerator	54	18	0
Washing Machine		Servis Superheat Model	81	16	3
		Goblin Washing Machine	26	5	0
Boiler	*The Ideal Home*, December 1955	Torwood Domestic Hot Water Boiler	15	5	4
		Perkins Diesel Fuel Domestic Boiler	45	0	0
		Tayco Domestic Boiler	25	0	0
Clock		Smiths Electric Clock "Lynside"	6	5	3
Coffee Maker		Espresso Coffee Maker	4	10	0
Cooker		Rayburn Cooker and Water Heater	55	0	0
		Esse Century Solid Fuel Cooker	118	2	6
Fire		Ferranti Electric Fire Model F5164	5	8	7
		Berry's Magicoal Electric Fire	13	2	10
Heater		Morris Doorvec Space Heater	8	19	6
Iron		Kenwood Steam Iron	5	7	6
		Tilleys Paraffin Pressure Iron	4	9	6
Mixer		Kenwood Electric Mixer	28	7	6
Refrigerator		Coldrator C133	69	3	0
Washing Machine		Ada Coronation Electric Washing Machine	48	13	0
		Servis Superheat	81	16	3
Wringer		Fleetway Cabinet Wringer	8	3	9
Television	*Radio Times*, August 23, 1957	Murphy Black and White 17in. Television	72	19	6
Radiogram	*Oxendales*, Manchester, 1959	Dansette Radiogram	31	10	0
Cleaner		Goblin Wizard de Luxe	19	8	6
		Hoover Dustette	8	19	6
Fire		One Bar Electric Fire	2	6	3
Spin Dryer		Hoover Spinarinse	35	12	6
Baby Equipment					
Pram	*SKL Ltd.*, London, 1954	Baby Cariage	17	13	4
		Baby Lido Car	3	9	8
Pram Accessories		Pram Canopy	1	13	9

Continued

7.4.3 Prices, Selected *continued*

Item	Source	Description	Price		
			£	s.	d.
Pram Accesories *cont.*		White All Wool Pram Set	1	11	4
Clothing and Footwear:					
Children's					
Knitwear	*Affleck & Brown*, Manchester, 1950	Toddlers Utility Cardigan		14	10
Frock		Child's Frock "Robia Voile" 20 ins.	1	16	9
		Cotton Dress and Knicker Set 22 ins.	2	18	9
Suit		Two Piece Romper in Super Poplin 16 ins.	2	3	6
		"Dayella" Two Piece Sleeping Suit 26 ins.		15	8
Boots	*Affleck & Brown*, Manchester, 1953	"Skelter" Warm Lined Boot in Black and Brown Suede	1	1	9
Coat		Girl's Duffle Coat in Plain or Plaid Material	9	17	6
Dress		Chilprufe Dress and Knicker Set 16 ins.	2	3	0
Suit		Buster Suit "Alec" 16 ins.	2	2	0
Shirts		Boy's "Clydella Shirts		19	6 (up to 34/6)
Nightwear		Boy's Pyjamas in Ceylon Flannel	1	19	11
Blazer	*SKL Ltd.*, London 1954	Green Flannel Blended Woollen Blazer	1	3	5 (up to 31/6)
Raincoat		Raincoat in Navy Fleece Backed Mackintosh	1	17	6 (up to 47/6)
Shirt		Khaki Drill Shirt		7	8 (up to 10/2)
		Rayon and Cotton Interlock Sportshirt		9	6 (up to 11/11)
Suit		Lovat Rayon Blended Two Piece suit	2	16	6 (up to 63/5)
		Rayon Crêpe Buster Rompers 16 ins.		12	0
Blouse		Printed Cotton Haircord Girl's Blouse		8	3 (up to 8/8)
Coat		Navy and White Diagonal Tweed Coat	3	7	0
Frock		Candystripe Frock	1	5	5
Skirt		Flannel Grey Wool Skirt		18	2 (up to 20/10)
Swimwear		Junior Miss Swimsuit	1	3	9
		Spun Rayon Swimsuit	1	1	1
		Black Art Satin Swimsuit	1	11	7
Knitwear		Sky Rayon Plush Twin Set	1	10	7
Nightwear		Wincyette Nightdress		8	9 (up to 10/3)
		Wincyette Pyjamas		13	7 (up to 18/7)
Shoes		Infant's Shoes in Calf Leather		15	11 (up to 19/6)
		Black Patent Cromwell Buckle Ankle Strap size 2–5		7	4
Coat	*Jays Ltd.*, London and Leeds, 1956	All Wool Bouclé Tweed Coat	4	19	9 (up to 108/9)
		All Wool Velour Duffle Coat	3	7	9 (up to 103/9)
		Union Gaberdine Raincoat	3	19	9 (up to 99/9)
Dress		Party Frock in Fine Check Rayon Taffeta	1	17	9 (up to 41/9)
Nightwear		Girl's Wincyette Pyjamas		12	6 (up to 18/6)

Continued

7.4.3 Prices, Selected *continued*

Item	Source	Description	Price £	s.	d.
Shoes		Teenage Ballerina Shoes in Black Suede	1	19	11
		Leather Gibson Shoes	1	2	9
School Uniform		Girl's Regulation Gym Blouse "Trutex"		18	11 (up to 24/11)
		Trutex Gym Slip in Wool Serge	2	10	6 (up to 69/6)
Coat	*Jays Ltd.*, London and Leeds, 1959	All Wool Velour Coat	4	10	0
Dress		Girl's Iced Cotton Dress	1	9	11
Jeans		Child's ¾ Length Jeans	1	9	11
Men's					
Hosiery	*Army & Navy Stores*, 1953	Wolsey Cardinal Pure Wool Socks		6	6 (pair)
		Viyella Short Ankle Socks		5	6 (pair)
Shirts		Super Oxford Sports Shirts	1	7	6
		Old England Tafatex Shirts	1	5	0
		Plusmore Shirt with One Spare Collar and Cuffs	2	4	6
Nightwear	*Affleck & Brown*, Manchester, 1953	Jaeger All Wool Tafetta Pyjamas	6	6	0
		Jaeger All Wool Dressing Gown	6	16	6
Coat	*SKL Ltd.*, London 1954	Gaberdine Raincoat	5	1	0
Jacket		Lovat Tweed Single Breasted Sports Jacket	3	16	6
Shirts		Men's Cotton Shirt		14	8 (up to 22/2)
Suit		Lovat Rayon Blended Suit	6	10	5
		Lovat Blended Woollen Suit	5	13	11
Trousers		Grey Blended Wool Sports Trousers	1	6	6
Shoes		Brown Calf Leather Ghillie Brogue	2	5	0
Suit	*Picture Post*, 1954	Drape Suit Worn by "Teddy" Boys	20	0	0
Blazer	*Selfridges Ltd.*, London, 1959	All Wool Blazers	8	8	0
Coats		Selfridge All Wool Showerproof Coat	9	9	0
		Three Quarter Smart Overcoat in Camel	16	16	0
Jackets		Dunlop Golf Jacket	6	6	0
		Handwoven Harris Tweed Sports Jacket	6	10	0
		Real Suede Jacket	10	15	0
Suits		"Sumrie" Ready to Wear Lounge Suit	26	5	0
		Tropical Suit in Moygashel Cloth	9	19	6
		Three Piece "Maenson" Suit	19	19	0
Trousers		Casual Wool Sports Trousers	4	4	0
		"Steegan" Lightweights in Terylene	5	19	6
Waistcoats		Smart Fancy Waistcoats from	3	3	0
Women's					
Cape	*Affleck & Brown*, Manchester, 1950	Luxurious Dyed Blue Fox Cape	2	17	7
Coat		"Crayson" Stroller Coat	22	1	0
		"Dannimac" Wool Gaberdine Coat	14	16	7
Dress		Utility Wool Dress	6	4	0

Continued

7.4.3 Prices, Selected *continued*

Item	Source	Description	Price £	s.	d.
Dress *cont.*		Afternoon Dress in Check Twill Rayon	11	17	11
		Sun Frock in Pique with Halter Neckline	3	13	10
Hat		Edna Wallace Cap in Black Satin	6	17	0
Shoes		Bally Court Shoe in Baby Calf	5	9	11
		Maxi Coolie Sandal by "Joyce"	2	5	6
Underwear		Morley Fancy Wool Cami Knickers		16	11
		Wolsey All Wool Opera Top Vests		6	11
		Court Royal Step In Girdle	1	7	0
		Court Royal Brassiere		4	10
Dress	*Alice Edwards*, 1950	"Ecco" in Drip Dry Minimum Iron Poplin	4	19	6
		"Amalfi" Carefree Drip Dry Cotton	4	4	0
		"Palermo" in Satin Cotton	4	14	6
		Round the Clock Dress in Self Flecked Pure Wool	6	12	6
Hosiery	*Derrys*, 1950	Rayon Hose		6	4
		Lisle Hose		6	5
Coat	*Affleck & Brown*, Manchester, 1953	Dannimac Double Sheen Raincoat	4	12	6
Hosiery		Kayser Bondor Fashioned Silk and Rayon Stockings		7	6
		Excelle Mercerised Superfine Lisle Stockings		7	11
		Bear Brand Superfine Pure Silk Stockings		9	11
Nightwear		Chilprufe All Wool Nighties	5	0	0
Overalls		Durable Spun Rayon Overall	1	12	0
		Coolie Smock, Sleeveless Style		17	11
		Frilled Waist Apron		6	11
Underwear		Jaeger Vest and Panties	1	9	6
Boots		Clarks "Igloo" Sheepskin Boots	2	19	9
Shoes		"Siesta" Bally Swiss Shoe	6	10	0
		"Clarendon" by Clarks	3	9	9
Coat	*Marshall & Snelgrove*, Manchester, 1956	Budget Coats in Novelty Tweed	16	0	0
Suit		Budget Suits in Worsted Flannel	15	15	0
Knitwear		Dalkeith Raglan Sleeve Golfer by Pringle	3	7	6
Wedding Dress		Bridal Gown, Moulded Bodice in Chantilly Lace	18	18	0
Coat	*Jays Ltd.*, London and Leeds, 1956	Heavyweight Velour Coat	19	8	6
		Wool and Camel Haircoat	7	19	9
Dress		Wool Bouclé Two Piece Dress	5	19	6
		Pebble Tweed Button Through Dress	3	9	6
Knitwear		Twin Set in Classical Style	2	12	6
Nightwear		Flowered Wincyette Nightie	1	1	0 (up to 23/9)
Skirts		Tweed Look Full Gored Skirt	4	19	6
		Fine Worsted Repp Pencil Slim Skirt	2	9	9

Continued

7.4.3 Price, Selected *continued*

Item	Source	Description	Price £ s. d.
Suit		Classic Suit in Worsted	12 1 6
Trousers		Tapered Slacks	3 9 6
Underwear		Taffeta Half Slip with Net Frills	3 19 11
		Nylon Slip	1 15 11
		Gossard Bra	7 11 (up to 9/11)
Shoes		Calf Court Shoe with Leather Bow	2 19 11
		Lotus Hand Fashioned Shoes	3 19 9
Coat	*Jays Ltd.*, London and Leeds, 1959	Alexon Wool and Worsted Coat	11 11 0
Dress		Linzi Dress in Slub Rayon and Linen	3 19 6
		Shirtwaister Dress in Cotton Poplin	4 9 11
		Dress and Jacket	4 19 6
Nightwear		Baby Doll Pyjamas	1 9 11
Skirt		Circular Skirt in Pleated Tricel and Viscose	2 9 11
Swimwear		Slix Rayon Batiste Swimsuit	2 19 11
Underwear		Tailored Slip in 40 Denier Nylon	1 19 11
		Floating Action Bra	1 2 0
Shoes		Walking Shoe in Glove Soft Leather	2 19 11
Food Products			
Bacon	*J Sainsbury*, 1950	Unsmoked Back Bacon	2 7 (per lb.)
Butter		Loose Butter	1 6
Cheese		Cheddar Cheese	1 2 (per lb.)
Eggs		Medium Size, 6	6½
Tea		Red Label Tea	3 8 (per lb.)
Beverages	*Ideal Home*, February 1951	Nescafé	9 0 (lb. tin)
		Ovaltine	2 6 (4oz. tin)
Starch	*Colmans of Norwich*, 1952	Colmans Rice Crystal Starch	1 6 (8oz.)
Bacon	*J Sainsbury*, 1955	Unsmoked Back Bacon	3 0 (per lb.)
Breakfast Cereal		Shredded Wheat	1 0 (12's)
Butter		Loose Butter	3 6 (per lb.)
Cheese		Cheddar Cheese	1 8 (per lb.)
Eggs		Medium Size, 6	1 6
Soup		Heinz Tomato Soup	1 3 (15½ oz.)
Squash		Kia-Ora Squash	3 0 (20 oz.)
Beverages	*Ideal Home*, December 1955	Cadbury's Cup Chocolate	2 6 (½ lb.)
Biscuits		Cadbury's Chocolate Biscuits	1 11 (½ lb.)
		Huntley & Palmer's biscuits	1 3 (½ lb.)
Confectionery		"Lindt" Mountain Rose	12 6 (lb.)
Preserves		Tiptree Marmalade	1 11 (lb. jar)
Confectionery	*Radio Times*, July 19, 1957	Fry's Milk Chocolate with Golden Honeycomb Crisp	6 (2 oz.)
Furniture			
Bed	*Derrys*, 1950	De Luxe Spring Interior Divan 2ft. 6in. x 6ft. 3in.	15 15 0
Chairs	*Jenners*, Edinburgh, 1954	Dining Chairs	10 2 6
Drawers		Four Drawer chest in Burr, Walnut or Mahogany	20 15 0

Continued

7.4.3 Prices, Selected *continued*

Item	Source	Description	£	s.	d.
Settee		Three Piece Lounge Suite	104	10	0
		Two Piece Lounge Suite	95	10	6
Sideboard		Sideboard in Walnut or Mahogany	64	12	6
Table		Pedestal Table 6ft. x 3ft.	53	15	0
		Writing Table	47	10	6
Flooring	*Ideal Home*, December 1955	Linovent Floor Covering		2	0 (sq. yd.)
Bells		Friedland Big Ben Door Bell		16	6
Bed	*Oxendales*, Manchester, 1959	Vono Divan Bed with Mattress Single	15	0	0
		Two Tier Bunk	14	14	0
Bookcase		Bookcase in Medium Oak Shade	6	5	0
Bureau		Writing Bureau in Seasoned timber	8	5	0
Chair		Fireside Chair in Uncut Moquette	9	19	6
Settee		Two Seater Settee with Matching Chairs	16	19	11
Table		Gate Leg Table	9	9	0

Garden Equipment and Supplies

Item	Source	Description	£	s.	d.
Watering Can	*Army & Navy Stores*, 1953	Galvanised Watering Can		16	6
Fountain	*Ideal Home*, October 1959	Illuminated Fountains with Changeable Nozzles from	6	0	0
Gates		7ft. Double Iron Gates from	5	9	6
Lawn Mower		"Atco" 14in. Petrol Mower	37	0	0

Heat and Light

Item	Source	Description	£	s.	d.
Electricity	*Eastern Electricity Board*, 1951	Electricity per unit	1	14	11 per year (+ 1d. per unit)
Gas	*North Thames Board*	Gas per therm		1	7
Coal	*What it Cost the Day Before Yesterday Book*	Coal per ton	7	13	2

Hotel Rates

Item	Source	Description	£	s.	d.
Imperial Hotel, London	*Bradshaws ABC Railway Guide*, 1950	Supper, Bed and Breakfast		17	6 (night)
Bonnington Hotel, London		Dinner, Bed and Breakfast		16	6 (single)
Grey Walls Hotel, Windermere, Lake District		Full Board	6	6	0 (up to 7 gns. inclusive)
Hotel Craig-holme, Edinburgh		Full Board	5	5	0 (inclusive of all meals)
Imperial Hotel, London	*Bradshaws ABC Railway Guide*, 1955	Bed and Breakfast Double	2	3	0
Cockburn Hotel, Edinburgh		Bed and Breakfast from	1	1	0

Household Goods

Item	Source	Description	£	s.	d.
Cutlery EPNS Spoons and Forks (per 6)	*Derry's*, London, 1950	Table Spoons and Forks	2	2	0
		Dessert Spoons and Forks	1	12	6
		Soup Spoons	1	12	0
		Tea Spoons		15	6
Table Lamp		Table Lamp and Shade	1	5	0
Tea Pot		Hotel Patterned Tea Pot	3	13	0

Continued

7.4.3 Prices, Selected *continued*

Item	Source	Description	Price £	s.	d.
Tea Set		18 Piece Tea Set in Wedgewood		12	6
Bedding	*Army & Navy Stores*, 1953	All Wool Blankets from	2	9	6 each
		Cellular Blankets from	2	11	0 each
		All Wool Witney Blankets from	2	9	6 each
		Linen Sheets from	9	7	6 (pair)
		Plain Housewife Pillow Cases from		12	6 each
Cutlery		Case of 6 Stainless Steel Tea Knives	2	5	0
		Polished Wood Canteen for 6 persons	17	5	0
		Silver Spoon and Fork with Coronation Hallmark	4	0	0
		Set of 6 Teaspoons with Coronation Hallmark	4	0	0
Food Storage		Glass Store Dishes		11	6 (set of 3)
		Family Meat Safe	2	17	0
		Egg Carrier and Container		4	9
		Thermos Flask		8	6 (pint)
Coffee Pot		Extra Large Coffee Pot	1	1	0
Tableware		Dandy China Lined Porringers		18	0 (½ pint)
Ironing Table		Folding Ironing Table	1	9	9
Wash Bowl		Unbreakable Wash Bowl		19	6
Household Linen		Tea Cloths	2	15	0 (dozen)
Towels		Turkish Towels from		3	3 (up to 52/0)
Clock		Swiss Ebosal Alarm Clock	1	8	0
Table		Bed Table with Folding Legs	2	5	0
Bedding	*Ideal Home*, October 1954	Dunlopillo Pillow	2	9	6
	Jenners, 1954	"Lan-Air-Cel" Cellular Blankets from	3	19	6 each
Kitchenware		Salad Bowl in Selected Walnut	3	12	0
		Hors d'Oeuvres Tray	5	5	0
Household Linen		Egyptian Cotton and Rayon Tablecloths	3	7	6
Towels		Thistletex Coloured Bath Towels from	1	8	6
Bedding	*Ideal Home*, December 1955	Dormy Blankets from	2	9	6 each
Kitchenware		Vitreous Enamel Salter Kitchen Scales		18	9
Bedding	*Jays Ltd.*, London and Leeds, 1959	Horrockses Coloured Sheets and Pillow Cases from	3	2	6 (set)
Towels		Christy Towels from		11	3
Houses					
Semi Detached	*Household Receipt*, 1952	Three Bed Semi Detached with Gardens in Stretford	1,400	0	0
Terraced	*Household Receipt*, 1955	Two Bed Terraced in Rochdale	500	0	0
New House	*Halifax Building Society*, 1957	New House at Mortgage Completion Stage	2,330	0	0 (average price)
	Halifax Building Society, 1958		2,390	0	0
Cape Built Detached Houses	*Household Receipt*, 1959	Four Bed Detached in Holmes Chapel, Cheshire	3,950	0	0 (without central heating)

Continued

7.4.3 Prices, Selected *continued*

Item	Source	Description	Price £	s.	d.
Jewellery					
Necklace	*Derry's*, London, 1950	Glamorous Pearls 16in. Single Row		8	9
	Affleck & Brown, Manchester, 1952	3 Row Imitation Pearl Necklace	3	5	0
		Imitation Pearl Necklace with Paste Inset	2	9	6
	Jenners, 1954	Rhinestone Necklace	4	18	6
Watch	*Ideal Home*, December 1955	Omega 850/B Watch in 18 ct. Gold	83	0	0
	Army & Navy Stores, 1953	Ladies Timex Watch	4	7	9
		Ingersoll Popular Watch	2	12	6
Bracelet	*Oxendales*, Manchester, 1959	9 ct. Gold Charm Bracelet	5	2	6
Chain		9 ct. Gold Cross and Chain	2	1	3
Personal Care Items					
Perfumes	*Derry's*, London, 1950	"Obelisque" by Miss Dior	1	1	0
		"Baccarat" by Miss Dior	1	7	0
Cosmetics	*Unilever Archives*, 1952	Poem Cleansing Cold Cream		3	6 (jar)
		Poem Face Powder		3	6
		Poem Lipstick		5	6
		Poem Tinted Foundation Cream		3	6 (large jar)
Shaving Preparation		Erasmic Shaving Stick		2	0 (holder)
				1	3 (refill)
		Shavallo Lather Cream		2	9 (jar)
Soap		Pears Transparent Soap			10½
		Pears Embassy Soap			9
Toilet Preparations		Pears Gloria Shampoo		1	6 (bottle)
		Pears Baby Powder		2	11 (large)
		Solidox Toothpaste		1	4 (tube)
		Icilma Foundation Vanishing Cream		2	9 (large jar)
Cosmetics	*Affleck & Brown*, Manchester, 1952	Coty Talcum Powder in Muguet du Bris Perfume		4	10 (bottle)
		Silk Tone Foundation		9	9 (up to 18/9)
Perfume		Lavender Water		16	6 (bottle)
		Coty Toilet Water in Muguet du Bris Perfume	1	1	0
Cosmetics	*Army & Navy Stores*, 1953	Yardley Feather Foundation		5	10 (bottle)
Perfume		4711 Eau-de-Cologne		3	10 (bottle)
		Lavender Water		16	6 (bottle)
Brushes		Men's Wood Back Hair Brush	1	17	9
Shaving Equipment		Shaving Mirror		16	6
		Pocket Razor Set	1	1	3
Chemists	*Ideal Home*, October 1954	Anadin Tablets from		1	9
Perfume		Yardleys Lavender Water		6	0 (up to 37/4)
Toilet Preparations		Mornay Talcum Powder		3	4½ (3 oz. tin)
		Mornay Bath Salts		3	1½ (box of 6)
		Gordon Moore's Dental Creme		1	7
Hair Dryer	*Ideal Home*, December 1955	Hawkins Hair Dryer	5	8	2
Chemists	*Which*, 1957	Unbranded Aspirin from Boots			4 (25 tablets)

Continued

7.4.3 Prices, Selected *continued*

Item	Source	Description	Price £	s.	d.
Prescription Charges					
	Department of Health, June 1, 1952	Prescription Charges Introduced per Form			5
Prescription Charges *cont.*	*Department of Health*, December 1, 1956	Charge Changed to per Item			5
Publications					
Book	*The Pound in Your Pocket 1870–1970*, 1957	*Little Women* (standard edition)		10	6
	Household Receipt, 1954	*Nineteen Eighty Four*, G. Orwell, Penguin		3	6
		Lord of the Flies, W. Golding, Penguin		2	6
Comics	*The Pound in Your Pocket 1870–1970*, 1957	Eagle			4½
		Girl			4½
Magazine	*Jenners*, Edinburgh, 1955	Woman's Own			6
		Woman's Realm			6
	Ideal Home, 1959	Ideal Home		1	6
Services					
Cinema	*Kinematographic Year Book*, 1950–1951	Odeon Theatre, Manchester, Admission Price		1	3 (up to 2/3)
		Odeon Theatre, Liverpool, Admission Price		1	10 (up to 4/7)
		Odeon Theatre, London, Admission Price		1	3 (up to 2/10)
	Kinematographic Year Book, 1953–1955	Odeon Theatre, Manchester, Admission Price		2	3 (up to 5/0)
	Kinematographic Year Book, 1953–1959	Grosvenor Picture Palace, Admission Price		1	0 (up to 1/6)
	Kinematographic Year Book, 1955–1956	Odeon Theatre, Manchester, Admission Price		2	3 (up to 5/0)
	Kinematographic Year Book, 1957–1959			2	6 (up to 5/6)
Licences	*Post Office Archives*, 1956	Radio	1	0	0
		Black and White Television	4	0	0
	DVLA, 1953	Road Tax	12	10	0
Telephone Tariffs	*British Telecom Archives*, January 1956				
London (10 mile radius from Oxford Circus)		Quarterly Business Rental	3	0	0
Birmingham, Glasgow, Liverpool, Manchester			2	17	6
London		Quarterly Residential Rental	2	10	0
Birmingham, Glasgow, Liverpool, Manchester			2	7	6
Untimed Calls		Up to 5 miles			2
		5 to 7½ miles			4
		7½ to 12½ miles			6

Continued

7.4.3 Prices, Selected *continued*

Item	Source	Description	Price £ s. d.
Untimed Calls *cont.*		12½ to 15 miles	8
Timed Trunk Calls (6 pm to 10.30 pm)		15 to 20 miles	8 (3 mins plus 2d. for each add. minute)
STD Tariff introduced for Pay-on-Answer Coin Boxes	*British Telecom Archives*, September 1959	Monday to Saturday 6am to 6pm & Sunday 6 to 2 pm	2 (for 3 minutes)
Dialled Trunk Calls		Up to 35 miles	3 (for 30 seconds)
		35 to 50 miles	3 (for 20 seconds)
		Over 50 miles	3 (for 12 seconds)
Parcel Postage Rates	*Post Office Archives*, 1952	2 lb. weight	11
		5 lb. weight	1 5
		15 lb. weight	1 0
	Post Office Archives, 1956	2lb. weight	1 3
		5 lb. weight	1 11
		15 lb. weight	1 9
	Post Office Archives, 1957	2 lb. weight	1 6
		5 lb. weight	2 3
		15 lb. weight	3 6
Babysitting Service	*The Pound in Your Pocket 1870–1970*, 1957	Mayfair Babysitting Agency Charges	3 6 (per hour)

Sewing Equipment and Supplies

Item	Source	Description	Price £ s. d.
Haberdashery	*Affleck & Brown*, Manchester, 1950	7in. Cutting Shears	9 0
		Brass Pins	2 2 (¼ lb. box)
		Shoulder Pads	1 5 (pair)
		Dress Shields	1 6 (pair)
Fabrics (per square yard)	*Derry's*, London, 1950	Cream Spun Silk	19 11
		All Wool Suiting and Dress Fabrics from	15 0
	Affleck & Brown, Manchester, 1953	Novelty Woollen Dress Fabrics	16 11
		Swiss Brocades	16 11 (up to 35/9)
		Woollen Dress Weight Fabric	1 5 6
		"Marastex" Lightweight Twill Wincey	6 11
Tartan Fabrics 54 to 56in. wide	*Jenners*, 1954	"Glen Mar" like Glen Urquhart with Green Overcheck	2 5 6
		"Gairloch" in a Dog Tooth Check	2 5 6
		"Auchentroig" Double Overcheck in Brown and Lemon	2 9 6
		"Shepherd" Classic Black and White Tweed	2 5 6
Machine	*Ideal Home*, December 1955	Hand Knitting Machine	24 0 0
Knitting Wool	*Derry's*, London, 1956	3-ply Botany Knitting Wool	1 4 (oz.)
		4-ply Clerical Sock Wool	1 0 (oz.)
Fabrics (per square yard)	*Oxendales*, 1959	Seerloop Dyed Cotton Fabric	5 11
		Check Gingham	2 11
		Spun Rayon	12 11

Continued

7.4.3 Prices, Selected *continued*

Item	Source	Description	Price		
			£	s.	d.
Fabrics (per sq. yd.) *cont.*		Blended Wool Blazer Cloth		8	9
		Sailcloth "Gay and Tough"		7	11
Machine		Jones Sewing Machine, Hand	25	12	6
		Jones Sewing Machine, Electric	33	0	8
	Household Receipt, 1959	"Alfa" Electric Zig Zag Machine	59	0	0

Sports and Hobbies

Item	Source	Description	Price		
Sporting Clothes	*Affleck & Brown*, Manchester, 1953	Tailored Jodhpurs in Cavalry Twill	5	11	0
Camping Goods	*Army & Navy Stores*, 1953	Picnic Boiling Set		17	6
Sporting Equipment		"Harrow" Cricket Bats, Full Size	3	10	0 (1st. Grade)
			2	11	6 (3rd. grade)
		"Special Crown" Cricket Balls	1	17	6
		"Club Make" Cricket Balls	1	12	0
		Batting Gloves from	1	4	6
		"Nicols" Pinsplitten Golf Clubs	3	2	0 (iron)
			3	11	6 (wood)
		"Gradidge" Bobby Locke Golf Clubs	3	0	6 (iron)
			3	14	6 (wood)
		Dunlop 65 Balls	2	0	0 (doz.)
		Warwick Golf Balls	1	8	6 (doz.)
		Slazenger Tennis Racket	7	0	0
		Dunlop Mazply Tennis Racket	5	4	5
		Dunlop Tennis Balls	1	17	0 (doz.)
		Lightweight 2 Seater Folding Canoe	33	0	0
Photographic Equipment		Kodak Brownie Box Model C	1	19	9
		Roll of Film		3	0
Sporting Clothes	*SKL Ltd.*, London, 1954	White Duck Cricket Boot	1	13	9
	Jenners, 1954	Olympic Jodhpurs with Buckskin Strapping	6	0	0
		Olympic Jodhpur Boots	3	15	0
Sporting Equipment	*Oxendales*, 1959	7-ply Laminate Tennis Racket	1	7	0
Photographic Equipment		"Mastra V.35" Camera (with 5 year guarantee)	13	14	11

Tobacco Products

Item	Source	Description	Price		
Cigars	*Army & Navy Stores*, 1953	"La Corona" 5in. Havana Cigars	7	15	0 (box of 25)
Cigarettes	*Scottish CWS Ltd.*, c.1950	Gold Flake, Mild		2	4 (boxes of 50)
		Pearl		1	7½ (boxes of 50)
Tobacco		Thick Black Roll Tobacco		9	6 (per lb.)
		Dundalk Brown Roll Tobacco		9	7 (per lb.)
		Special Chewing Roll		9	6 (per lb.)

Toys

Item	Source	Description	Price		
Toys	*Jenners Xmas Catalogue*, Edinburgh, 1955	Junior Typewriter	1	10	6
		Pull Along Truck with 24 Coloured Wood Bricks		13	6
		Precision Made Sewing Machine for the Older Girl	2	0	6
		"Noddy" Cuddly Soft Doll with Moving Eyes	1	0	0

Continued

7.4.3 Prices, Selected *continued*

Item	Source	Description	Price £	s.	d.
Toys *cont.*		"Noddy" Wipe off Cards		6	0
		Vacuum Cleaner for the Youngest Housewife	2	0	6
Game		"Highway Hazard" Road Game for All Children		19	6
Transport and Vehicles					
Air Fares	*Reed Travel Group*, 1950	London to Paris	8	0	0
		London to New York	125	0	0
Rail Fares	*Bradshaws ABC Railway Guide*, 1950	Manchester to London Return	2	10	0 (up to 75/0)
		Manchester to London Single	1	17	8 (up to 62/3)
Bicycle	*Army & Navy Stores*, 1953	Raleigh Model 11 3-Speed	17	5	2
Motor Cycle		Vespa Runabout	125	1	3
Rail Fares	*Bradshaws ABC Railway Guide*, 1954	Manchester to London Return	1	6	10 (up to 40/3)
Vehicle	*Ideal Home*, October 1954	A 30 Austin Seven, 2-Door Model	335	0	0
		A 30 Austin Seven, 4-Door Model	355	0	0
Air Fares	*Reed Travel Group*, 1955	London to Paris, 1st. Class	9	9	0
		London to Paris, Tourist Class	7	16	0
		London to New York, 1st. Class	142	18	0
		London to New York, Tourist Class	103	12	0
Rail Fares	*Bradshaws ABC Railway Guide*, 1955	Manchester to London Return	1	8	11 (up to 43/5)
Bus Fares	*What it Cost the Day Before Yesterday Book*	Paddington to Mansion House, London (4 miles)			3 (average, 4 changes)
Vehicle	*Complete Catalogue of Austin Cars since 1945*	A 50 Cambridge 50 b.h.p., 2-Door Saloon	678	0	0 (price when introduced)
		Austin Healey Sprite Mark 1, 43 bhp, Open 2-Seater	669	0	0
Travel					
Round the World Tour	*Thomas Cook Archives*, 1950	140 Day Tour	400	0	0
Ideal Escorted Tours to Switzerland		15 Day Tours from	70	7	0
Holiday		8 Days in Bellagio, Lake Como	29	15	0
		15 Days Holiday at Belgian Coastal Resorts from	27	16	0
		10 Days at Hotel Montreux in Switzerland from	36	8	6
Miscellany					
Handkerchiefs	*Affleck & Brown*, Manchester, 1950	Four Pure Linen Handkerchiefs	1	7	1
Leather Goods	*Derry's*, 1950	Crocodile Effect Handbag	1	9	6
	Affleck & Brown, Manchester, 1952	Rayon Lined Handbag with Two Handles	2	2	0
		Doeskin Gloves with Bangle Cuff		16	9
Spectacles	*Army & Navy Stores*, 1953	Sun Glasses	2	5	0
Stationery		Orchid Efficiency Pencil		7	0
		Steel Constructed Home File	4	1	4
Wellingtons	*SKL Ltd.*, 1954	Black Wellingtons from		12	11 (up to 14/7)

7.4.4 Prices, Miscellaneous

7.4.4a William Whiteley's[1] Christmas Gift List 1957

	£	s.	d.		£	s.	d.
TV Chair	10	10	0	Record Player	13	17	6
Electric Blanket	10	17	6	Crystal Tankard	2	3	6
Pyrex Casseroles (3)	1	8	6	Crystal Ashtray	1	8	9
Linen Table Mats	1	5	0	Long-sleeve Pullover	3	3	0
Woollen Cape	2	19	6	Pure Silk Square	1	7	6
Lady's Umbrella	3	2	6	Non-iron shirt	1	19	6
Perfume Spray	3	9	6	Driving Gloves	1	15	6
Electric Razor	10	17	6	6'×40" Rug	4	17	6
Travel Clock	5	10	0	Work Box	6	12	6
Electric ¼" Drill	6	12	6	Evening Stole	6	15	0
Lady's Toilet Case	3	19	6	Delft Biscuit Barrel	1	0	6
Photo Flash Outfit	3	5	1	Brocade Evening Bag	1	5	0
Dress Studs	1	19	11	Four Lace Hankies	1	3	6
Man's Toilet Set	2	17	6	Walnut TV Table	1	9	6
Brief Case	3	15	0	Crystal Brandy Glasses	5	17	0
Velvet Housecoat	8	4	6	Man's Umbrella	4	9	6
Portable Radio	12	1	6	Man's Dressing Gown	4	9	6
Lady's Evening Gloves	1	19	11	Pen and Pencil Set	8	3	4
Desk Compendium	1	7	6	Tropical Fish Tank	4	4	0
Record Cabinet	10	10	0	Pigskin Wallet	1	19	11
Ironide Suitcase	10	5	0	Brown Suede Slippers	2	2	11
Cashmere Cardigan	10	17	6	Adjustable Desk Lamp	1	9	6

Wilsher, P. *The Pound in Your Pocket 1870–1970*, Cassell and Company Ltd, 1970.

[1] William Whiteley General Store in Bayswater, London.

7.4.4b Cost of Driving, 1947 and 1957

	1947			1957		
	£	s.	d.	£	s.	d.
12 horse-power car (Austin)	597	0	0	820	0	0
Road Tax	10	0	0	12	10	0
Insurance (comprehensive, London)	15	10	6	34	0	0
Petrol (gallon)		1	11½		4	11½
Battery (12 volt)	9	10	7	10	18	0
Labour Charges (per hour)		10	0		15	0
Tyres (each)	3	4	0	6	8	6

Wilsher, P. *The Pound in Your Pocket 1870–1970*, Cassell and Company Ltd, 1970.

See Chapter 11, Table 11.4.4a. for the 1993 prices.

7.5 Finance and Economic Data

7.5.1 Finance, Personal

	1950 s. d.	1951 s. d.	1952 s. d.	1953 s. d.	1954 s. d.	1955 s. d.	1956 s. d.	1957 s. d.	1958 s. d.	1959 s. d.
Income Tax Rates[1]	9 0	9 0	9 6	9 6	9 0	9 0	8 6	8 6	8 6	8 6
Retirement Pension:										
Married	41 0	50 0		54 0		65 0	65 0		80 0	
Single	26 0	30 0		32 6		40 0	40 0		50 0	
Child Benefit:										
Second				8 0		8 0	8 0		8 0	
Third and Subsequent				8 0		8 0	10 0		10 0	
Unemployment Benefit: Men, Single Women and Widows				32 6		40 0	40 0		50 0	
Base Interest Rates in percent[2]	4%	2½%	4%	4%	3½%	3½%	4½%	5½%	7%	4%

Mitchell, B.R. *British Historical Statistics*, Cambridge University Press, 1988; Bank of England; Department of Social Security.

Blank space denotes no data available. [1]The rates apply to years ended 5th April. [2]The rates apply to January of each year.

7.5.2 Financial Markets

7.5.2a Highest Closing Price of UK Major Stocks

	1950	1951	1952	1953	1954	1955	1956	1957	1958	1959
Barclays Bank	53/6	52/0	44/9	46/6	51/9	58/10½	50/4½	49/0	114/6	88/0
Boots the Chemist	64/4½	63/0	53/6	20/9	21/6	21/4½	18/6	18/9	24/6	21/9
Burmah Oil	68/8¼	71/3	70/0	60/4½	6⁹/₃₂	9¹¹/₃₂	5⅞	11⅞	119/4½	87/3
Courtaulds	41/6	54/7½	46/3	51/4½	55/0	55/6	44/3	43/9	37/9	34/9
Guinness	6¹³/₁₆	7¹¹/₁₆	62/7	33/7½	43/3	49/3	45/10	48/6	44/9	57/0
ICI[1]	44/3	54/10½	47/4½	54/4½	75/9	61/6	49/10½	49/6	46/6	38/0
Marks and Spencer	83/3	5⅛	86/3	76/0	5¼	91/0	81/0	71/1½	57/3	55/9
Reckitt and Colman[2]	5¼	5⁷/₁₆	94/0	5³/₃₂	43/9	46/1½	44/6	44/3	50/9	68/3
Schweppes	30/9¾	29/6	25/0	26/3	27/6	28/6	23/6	17½	21/10½	20/0
Unilever	44/6	58/1½	49/7½	58/0	5⅜	5¹/₃₂	83/0	82/6	114/6	88/0
Viyella	60/1½	70/0	52/9	50/3	63/0	29/6	25/10½	25/7½	28/0	24/1½
Whitbread & Co.	22/3	20/7½	17/10½	19/3	19/9	19/3	16/3	75/0	87/3	111/0

Mathieson, F.C. and Sons, *Stock Exchanges Ten Year Record of Prices and Dividends*.

Fractions are quoted as parts of £1=32. [1]Imperial Chemical Industries. [2]Reckitt and Colman from 1954.

7.5.2b Commodities

	Best Coal (price per ton)		Raw Cotton (per lb.)	Gold (average market)	Sugar (annual average world price)	Wheat (per ton)		Wool (average import value)
	s.	d.	old pence (d.)	£ per troy oz.	£ sterling per metric ton	s.	d.	pence per lb.
1950	53	0	36.15	12.400	42.240	25	10	63.2
1951	58	6	46.01	12.400	51.673	28	8	113.2
1952	64	11	38.92	12.400	38.550	29	7	59.0
1953	69	6	31.83	12.400	30.512	31	2	66.6
1954	62	6	32.72	12.469	29.199	28	3	64.8
1955	66	4	31.70	12.547	31.496	22	11	58.9
1956	74	3	26.95	12.514	34.285	25	6	57.6
1957	79	9	25.35	12.510	46.229	21	7	67.1
1958	82	10	24.21	12.490	30.876	21	9	48.8
1959	81	7	21.49	12.493	26.872	21	0	46.9

Mitchell, B.R. *British Historical Statistics*, Cambridge University Press, 1988; World Gold Council; Czarnikow Sugar.

Original source, Sauerbeck, A. *Prices of Commodities and the Precious Metals, Journal of the Statistical Society.*

7.5.2c Foreign Exchange Rates

	Frankfurt Deutschmarks per £1[1]	Paris Francs per £1	New York Dollars per £1
1950		980.00	2.80
1951		979.74	2.79
1952		981.48	2.81
1953	11.70	982.76	2.81
1954	11.73	981.64	2.79
1955	11.74	978.10	2.80
1956	11.71	982.74	2.79
1957	11.73	1,060.24	2.81
1958	11.72	1,177.56	2.81
1959	11.74	13.77[2]	2.81

Mitchell, B.R. *British Historical Statistics*, Cambridge University Press, 1988.

Blank space denotes no available data. [1]Frankfurt from 1953. [2]New francs.

7.5.3 Balance of Payments and GNP

7.5.3a Balance of Payments

	Merchan-dise Exports	Merchan-dise Imports	Overall Visible Balance	Exports of Services	Imports of Services	Property Income from Abroad	Property Income Paid Abroad	Balance of Current Transfers	Overall Visible Balance	Overall Current Balance
	£m	£m	£m	£m	£m	£m	£m	£m	£m	£m
1950	2,261	2,312	-51	734	764	558	162	+158	+524	+473
1951	2,735	3,424	-689	913	907	553	211	+50	+398	+182
1952	2,769	3,048	-279	991	885	500	248	+119	+477	+198
1953	2,683	2,927	-244	1,004	908	495	266	+81	+506	+262
1954	2,785	2,989	-204	1,052	972	540	290	-8	+322	+117
1955	3,073	3,386	-313	1,104	1,095	517	343	-24	+159	-155
1956	3,377	3,324	+53	1,221	1,230	571	342	-65	+155	+208
1957	3,509	3,538	-29	1,327	1,240	583	334	-74	+262	+233
1958	3,406	3,377	+29	1,304	1,206	682	389	-60	+331	+360
1959	3,527	3,642	-115	1,329	1,243	658	396	-51	+293	+172

Mitchell, B.R. *British Historical Statistics*, Cambridge University Press, 1988.

Original source, Feinstein, C.H. *National Income, Expenditure and Output in the UK, 1855-1965*, Cambridge, 1972.

7.5.3b GNP at Factor Cost and Its Component Incomes at Current Prices

	Income from Employ-ment	Income from Self Employ-ment	Gross Trading Profits of Comp-anies	Gross Trading Surplus of Public Enter-prises	Rent	Stock Apprecia-tion	Gross Domestic Product	Net Property Income from Abroad	Gross National Product	Capital Consump-tion	National Income
	£m	£m	£m	£m	£m	£m	£m	£m	£m	£m	£m
1950	7,627	1,402	2,126	335	551	650	11,391	396	11,787	964	10,823
1951	8,501	1,438	2,483	381	564	750	12,617	342	12,959	1,129	11,830
1952	9,107	1,490	2,180	322	611	-50	13,760	252	14,010	1,283	13,729
1953	9,634	1,538	2,313	388	685	-75	14,633	229	14,862	1,333	13,529
1954	10,284	1,577	2,576	466	751	75	15,579	250	15,829	1,392	14,437
1955	11,244	1,660	2,886	431	822	196	16,847	174	17,021	1,517	15,504
1956	12,267	1,713	2,928	472	881	208	18,053	229	18,828	1,657	16,625
1957	12,963	1,773	3,075	458	937	187	19,019	249	19,268	1,781	17,487
1958	13,470	1,783	2,983	501	1,085	-5	19,827	293	20,120	1,888	18,232
1959	14,107	1,885	3,317	560	1,164	98	20,935	262	21,197	1,947	19,250

Mitchell, B.R. *British Historical Statistics*, Cambridge University Press, 1988.

Original source, Feinstein, C.H. *National Income, Expenditure and Output in the UK, 1855-1965*, Cambridge, 1972.

– Eight –
1960–1969

Affluence and Decadence

PRIME MINISTERS
Harold Macmillan (Conservative), October 1959–October 1963
Lord A. Douglas-Home (Conservative), October 1963–October 1964
Harold Wilson (Labour), October 1964–June 1970

CHANCELLORS OF THE EXCHEQUER
S. Lloyd, July 1960–July 1962
R. Maudling, July 1962–October 1964
J. Callaghan, October 1964–November 1967
R. Jenkins, November 1967–June 1970

The changes that occurred in Britain during the 1960s can to some extent be seen as the effect of international influence on the nation.

Britain's population at the beginning of the Sixties exceeded the 50 million mark. A high level of immigration from Commonwealth countries, including the West Indies, India, and Pakistan, had added significantly to the population. From 1952–61, West Indian immigration reached 50,000 per annum. This was controlled to some degree by the much criticized Commonwealth Immigration Act (1962) which restricted immigration to people who had a guaranteed job or a special skill to give to the economy. This act was seen unofficially as introducing the 'colour bar'.

The population was enjoying a higher standard of living than it had done in many years, and while mortality rates were decreasing, birth rates were increasing. However, following the increase in immigration, there had been a rise in neo-fascist activity, and some politicians feared that if unemployment or inflation increased the minority foreign groups might be blamed.

In fact Britain's Balance of Payments was again suffering. Strong competition from abroad had reduced its export market drastically. Rapid economic growth and moderately stable prices were now replaced by a period of much slower growth and rising prices which exacerbated the Balance of Payments problem further.

Macmillan's position also started to disintegrate. Firstly, the French President de Gaulle blocked Britain's entry into the European Common Market (EEC), and then political scandal rocked the Conservative Party. The Profumo Affair, which involved the Secretary of State for War, John Profumo, and a prostitute who was linked with an attaché to the Soviet Embassy, brought demands for Macmillan's resignation. In the end ill health forced the Prime Minister to stand down in October 1963. He was succeeded by Sir Alec Douglas-Home, the former Foreign Secretary.

Douglas-Home did not enjoy much public support. His aristocratic background alienated the working class; he did not come across well on television (this was the beginning of the political manipulation of the media); and his party was divided. His cabinet was, however, responsible for bringing down both inflation and unemployment, and for helping to promote Britain's export industry. Despite this in the general election held in 1964, Labour won, and Harold Wilson became Prime Minister.

The Labour Government tried to learn from the Conservative mistakes which from necessity had used a restrictive-expansionary Stop-Go economic policy. Labour tried to evolve an effective and realistic policy which would lead to economic growth.

Devaluation seemed to be the best way to set the economy back on course, but the Wilson administration was unwilling to do this. Instead it embarked on a series of unpopular policies including the Selective Employment Tax which imposed a pay-roll tax on workers in the service sector.

GDP did, however, rise by 7.7 per cent between 1967–70, but private consumption only increased by 5.4 per cent and public consumption by less than 1 per cent. Exports rose by 27 per cent compared with a 17 per cent increase in imports. By 1970 the Balance of Payments surplus was over £735 million on the current account – the Wilson administration bequeathed its successors one of the highest Balance of Payments surpluses this century. Among its successes, however, was its development of regional policy and its use of investment grants to improve Britain's infra-structure. It also increased public spending in education, health, and social security.

Against this political and economic background Britain's population was enjoying the benefits of greater sexual and intellectual freedom. Influenced by events taking place across the world in the USA, a cultural explosion took place in music, and the arts. For Britain the 1960s was a period of great change and social and economic development.

8.1 Historical Snapshots

8.1 Historical Snapshots

1960	BBC wants second TV Channel.
	A new £1 note goes into circulation.
	Olympics held in Rome.
	First heart pacemaker is developed.
	1961, World's largest computer is installed in Harwell to aid atomic research and weather forecasting.
	Abolition of the footballers' maximum wage.
	The *News Chronicle* merges with the *Daily Mail*.
	Britain formally applies for membership of the European Economic Market.
	Government agrees to the principle of currency decimalization.
1962	Share values fall by £1000 million,, the biggest slump since 1929.
	France and Britain sign an agreement to build Concorde, the first supersonic passenger aircraft.
1963	First Women's Charter adopted by the Trades Union Congress (TUC).
1964	Britain and France agree to build Channel Tunnel.
	First word processor introduced by IBM in the USA and Europe.
1966	Barclays Bank introduces Barclaycard, the first British credit card.
1967	Decimal Currency Bill is published.
	Barclays Bank introduces Britain's first cash dispensing machine.
	British Steel Corporation is formed.
	Invention of Dolby noise reduction system.
1968	National Provincial Bank and the Westminster Bank announce a merger as Britain's biggest bank.
	Rolls Royce wins a £150 million order for RB2-11 engines from Lockheed.
	The first decimal coins come into circulation for 5 new pence and 10 new pence.
	Barclays Bank merges with Martins Bank.
	Two-tier postal system introduced.
1969	Ford unveils a new sports saloon, the Capri.
	1,600 female workers at Ford win equal pay with their male colleagues.
	ITV makes its first colour transmissions.
	The seven-sided 50 new pence coin comes into circulation.
	Labour MP Robert Maxwell launches a £26 million bid for the News of the World Organisation.
	On the 20th July 1969, Neil Armstrong, the American astronaut, is the first person to set foot on the moon.
	Concorde supersonic airliner makes its maiden flight from Toulouse.
	Handley Page, the oldest aircraft manufacturer in Britain, falls into receivership.

Chronicle of Britain, J.L. International Publishing, 1992; Williams, T.I. *Invention and Discovery in the 20th Century*, Harrap, 1990; Galsworthy, M. *Encyclopaedia of Association Football*.

8.2 Earnings and Employment

8.2.1 Earnings, Standard Tables

8.2.1a Incomes and Wages

	1960	1961	1962	1963	1964	1965	1966	1967	1968	1969
General Practitioner	£2,425 (a)	£2,425 (a)	£2,425 (a)	£2,765 (a)	£2,765 (a)	£2,775 (a)	£3,700 (a)	£3,700 (a)	£3,775 (a)	£4,000 (a)
Police Constable	£600 (a)		£620 (a)	£635 (a)	£700 (a)			£765 (a)		
Teacher[1]		£1,690 (a)			£1,780 (a)		£1,970 (a)		£2,085 (a)	
Nurse[2]	£567 (a)		£ 608 (a)	£660 (a)	£680 (a)		£790 (a)		£878 (a)	
Clerical Worker	£682 (a)									
Train Driver	266s. 0d.	266s. 0d.	274s. 0d.	290s. 0d.	307s. 0d.	334s. 0d.	345s. 0d.	357s. 0d.	369s. 0d.	397s. 4d.
Coal Miner	197 6	211 0	211 0	227 6	227 6	237 0	253 0	265 0	277 6	292 6
Fitter and Turner	191 4	199 10	199 10	205 10	216 4	221 4	236 8	246 8	257 8	300 0
Labourer								187 4	217 4	240 0
Bricklayer				343 0	343 0	345 4	365 9	381 5	413 5	
Labourer					307 6	341 8	353 7	375 11	405 0	
Compositor	244 0	247 0	266 0	275 2	286 8	297 0	323 6	323 6	339 6	353 6
Farm Worker	166 8½	172 7	181 9	189 1	198 10½	202 0	210 0	216 0	231 0	248 0
Baker	174 5	183 1	183 1	194 1	194 1	203 0	208 4	208 4	208 8	221 8
Textile Worker (weaver)	155 0	155 0	165 0	171 0	177 0	187 0	197 0	197 0	216 0	224 4

British Labour Statistics 1886-1968, HMSO, 1971; Routh, G. *Occupation and Pay in Great Britain, 1906-1979*, Macmillan Press, 1980; British Medical Association; Royal College of Nursing.

Income is weekly unless otherwise stated. (a) – annual. Blank space denotes no available data. [1]Assistant Master in secondary school. [2]Staff Nurse rates in a General Hospital after three years of service.

8.2.1b Average Weekly Earnings

	Bricks Pottery and Glass	Ship-building and Marine Engineer-ing	Textiles	Clothing	Food, Tobacco and Drink	Paper, Printing and Publishing	Construc-tion	Public Adminis-tration	Transport and Communi-cation	All Industries
	£	£	£	£	£	£	£	£	£	£
Males										
1960	14.62	14.39	13.32	12.99	13.57	16.95	13.95	10.88	14.33	14.50
1961	15.62	15.22	13.97	13.60	14.49	17.87	15.25	11.73	14.96	15.34
1962	16.18	15.43	14.43	14.09	15.06	18.66	16.10	12.25	15.25	15.86
1963	17.21	16.18	15.36	14.85	15.91	19.50	16.63	12.88	16.61	16.75
1964	18.60	17.84	16.37	15.79	17.13	21.19	18.20	13.93	17.66	18.11
1965	20.03	19.79	17.86	17.23	18.68	22.83	19.77	15.03	19.77	19.59
1966	20.86	21.29	18.53	17.79	19.73	23.85	20.56	15.64	20.88	20.30
1967	21.94	21.88	19.56	18.76	20.84	24.76	21.68	16.76	21.66	21.38
1968	23.38	23.93	21.33	20.27	22.10	26.95	22.87	17.47	24.20	23.00
1969[1]	24.90	26.13	22.85	21.44	24.14	29.12	24.43	18.46	25.92	24.80
Females										
1960	6.93	7.50	7.40	7.16	7.12	7.67	6.64	7.48	10.36	7.42
1961	7.27	7.69	7.63	7.42	7.47	8.12	7.12	8.06	10.92	7.73
1962	7.61	7.83	7.85	7.76	7.79	8.52	7.54	8.22	11.15	8.04
1963	8.00	8.18	8.33	8.08	8.23	8.82	7.82	8.82	11.57	8.41
1964	8.54	8.63	8.83	8.69	8.70	9.37	8.06	9.34	12.43	8.95
1965	9.25	10.00	9.46	9.36	9.38	10.15	8.42	9.66	13.55	9.60
1966	9.74	10.22	9.94	9.88	9.81	10.73	8.95	10.12	14.00	10.07
1967	10.27	10.46	10.35	10.16	10.23	10.95	9.87	10.48	14.54	10.56
1968	10.85	10.75	11.17	10.98	10.95	11.69	10.05	11.22	15.59	11.30
1969[1]	11.90	11.50	11.88	11.51	11.93	12.57	11.39	11.86	16.87	12.10

British Labour Statistics, 1886–1968, HMSO, 1971.

Industry groups according to the 1958 Standard Industrial Classification. [1]There were minor changes in coverage on the adoption of the new Standard Industrial Classification.

8.2.2. Regional Earnings by Selected Occupation

		London		Manchester		Newcastle		Leeds		Glasgow	
		s.	d.	s.	d.	s.	d.	s.	d.	s.	d.
Bricklayer (hourly)	1960	5	1	4	11½	4	11½	4	11½	4	11½
	1965	8	7	6	5½	6	5½	6	5½	6	6½
	1968	7	10	7	8½	7	8½	7	8½	7	8½
Bricklayer's Labourer (hourly)	1960	4	5½	4	4	4	4	4	4	4	4
	1965	5	8½	5	7	5	7	5	7	5	8½
	1968	6	8½	6	7	6	7	6	7	6	7
Compositor (weekly)	1960	244	0	228	9	228	0	228	9	228	9
	1965	297	0	281	0	281	0	281	0	281	0
	1968	339	0	323	0	323	0	323	6	323	6
Fitter and Turner (weekly)	1960	191	3½	186	8	n/a		n/a		186	9½
	1965	216	3½	211	8	n/a		n/a		211	9½
	1968	257	8	257	8	n/a		n/a		257	8
Labourer (weekly)	1960	160	5½	157	5¼	n/a		n/a		157	8½
	1965	182	5½	179	5½	n/a		n/a		179	8½
	1968	217	4	217	4	n/a		n/a		217	4

British Labour Statistics 1886–1968, HMSO, 1971.

8.2.4 Employment

8.2.4a Unemployment by Region

	1960 000's	1961 000's	1962 000's	1963 000's	1964 000's	1965 000's	1966 000's	1967 000's	1968 000's	1969 000's
Males and Females										
UK	392.8	376.8	499.9	612.3	413.4	359.7	390.9	599.1	601.3	597.1
Great Britain	360.4	340.7	463.2	573.2	380.6	328.8	359.7	559.5	564.1	559.3
England	255.8	247.4	349.4	432.4	274.6	237.4	266.8	434.6	442.0	437.9
South East	73.2	75.0	98.3	118.6	77.2	69.5	80.1	131.9	130.5	124.9
East Anglia	8.0	7.4	9.8	12.8	8.7	7.9	8.8	12.7	12.3	12.5
South West	20.6	17.8	22.5	27.9	20.5	20.9	24.5	33.8	33.5	35.8
West Midlands	21.4	31.4	40.5	46.9	21.6	20.4	31.7	57.8	51.8	46.2
East Midlands	13.1	13.0	17.9	24.7	13.6	13.3	15.9	26.0	26.9	28.1
Yorkshire/Humberside	24.5	21.0	34.3	42.5	26.4	22.8	25.4	44.4	52.9	53.6
North West	57.8	49.3	76.8	93.6	62.5	48.4	45.5	74.9	72.7	73.3
North	37.2	32.4	49.3	65.4	44.0	34.3	35.1	53.1	61.4	63.5
Wales	26.0	24.9	30.7	36.0	25.7	25.9	29.4	40.3	39.2	40.2
Scotland	78.7	68.4	83.1	104.8	80.3	65.5	63.5	84.6	82.9	81.2
Northern Ireland	32.4	36.1	36.7	39.0	32.8	30.9	31.2	39.6	37.2	37.8
Males										
UK	283.9	275.4	370.3	468.3	309.7	272.7	307.8	478.7	501.5	505.1
Great Britain	259.8	249.6	344.9	440.1	286.2	250.3	285.1	451.2	473.7	475.9
England	185.3	183.1	261.7	335.8	210.1	184.4	215.6	357.0	377.4	377.6
South East	54.3	56.2	75.0	94.6	60.7	55.4	66.4	112.0	112.5	108.5
East Anglia	6.3	5.7	7.6	10.1	6.8	6.2	7.2	10.4	10.4	10.7
South West	14.6	12.7	16.6	21.4	15.3	16.0	19.3	27.0	27.4	29.6
West Midlands	15.0	23.7	30.8	37.2	16.1	15.7	26.2	47.9	44.3	39.7
East Midlands	9.5	9.5	13.2	19.3	10.5	10.4	12.8	21.0	23.1	24.5
Yorkshire/Humberside	17.7	15.4	26.3	33.1	20.0	17.4	20.2	36.7	45.7	46.6
North West	40.1	35.5	53.9	68.5	46.9	36.6	35.2	58.3	61.4	63.2
North	27.9	24.4	38.5	51.5	33.8	26.7	28.3	43.7	52.5	54.8
Wales	17.7	17.7	22.4	26.9	18.6	18.9	22.4	31.0	31.6	33.2
Scotland	56.8	48.7	60.8	77.4	57.4	47.0	47.1	63.2	64.8	65.2
Northern Ireland	24.1	25.8	25.4	28.2	23.6	22.4	22.7	27.5	27.7	29.2
Females										
UK	108.9	101.4	129.6	143.9	103.6	87.0	83.1	120.4	99.9	92.0
Great Britain	100.6	91.1	118.3	133.1	94.4	78.5	74.6	108.3	90.4	83.4
England	70.5	64.3	87.7	96.6	64.4	53.0	51.2	77.6	64.6	60.3
South East	18.9	18.8	23.4	24.0	16.5	14.1	13.7	19.9	18.0	16.4
East Anglia	1.7	1.7	2.3	2.7	1.9	1.7	1.6	2.3	1.9	1.8
South West	6.0	5.1	5.9	6.5	5.2	4.9	5.2	6.7	6.1	6.2
West Midlands	6.4	7.7	9.6	9.7	5.5	4.7	5.5	10.0	7.5	6.5
East Midlands	3.6	3.5	4.7	5.3	3.1	2.9	3.0	5.0	3.8	3.7
Yorkshire /Humberside	6.8	5.6	8.1	9.5	6.4	5.4	5.2	7.7	7.1	7.0
North West	17.7	13.8	22.9	25.0	15.6	11.8	10.3	16.6	11.3	10.0
North	9.4	8.0	10.8	13.9	10.2	7.5	6.8	9.5	8.9	8.7
Wales	8.3	7.2	8.3	9.1	7.1	6.9	7.0	9.3	7.6	7.0
Scotland	21.8	19.6	22.3	27.4	22.9	18.5	16.4	21.4	18.1	16.1
Northern Ireland	8.3	10.3	11.3	10.8	9.2	8.7	8.5	12.2	9.5	8.6

British Labour Statistics Year Book, 1969, HMSO, 1971.

Figures are annual averages.

8.2.4b Employment by Region

	1960 000's	1961 000's	1962 000's	1963 000's	1964[1] 000's	1965 000's	1966 000's	1967 000's	1968 000's
Total Males and Females									
UK	22,491	22,825	23,026	23,061	23,357	23,622	23,783	23,305	23,125
Great Britain	22,036	22,373	22,572	22,603	22,892	23,147	23,301	22,828	22,645
England	18,974	19,291	19,471	19,527	19,772	20,011	20,162	19,764	19,600
South East						7,962	8,013	7,881	7,856
East Anglia	7,984	8,149	8,281	8,343	8,420	597	609	606	607
South West	1,230	1,262	1,277	1,296	1,318	1,326	1,339	1,315	1,312
West Midlands	2,217	2,236	2,262	2,265	2,311	2,346	2,375	2,300	2,271
East Midlands	3,332	3,387	3,416	3,425	3,468	1,413	1,426	1,424	1,398
Yorkshire/Humberside						2,081	2,094	2,034	2,002
North West	2,941	2,976	2,959	2,939	2,979	2,984	2,999	2,926	2,899
North	1,270	1,281	1,276	1,261	1,277	1,301	1,309	1,279	1,255
Wales	948	957	958	962	977	985	986	952	950
Scotland	2,105	2,116	2,134	2,102	2,133	2,139	2,143	2,100	2,086
Northern Ireland	455	452	454	459	465	475	482	477	480
Males									
UK	14,483	14,661	14,762	14,772	14,899	15,015	14,999	14,651	14,445
Great Britain	14,199	14,379	14,480	14,486	14,611	14,722	14,704	14,358	14,151
England	12,173	12,346	12,466	12,477	12,583	12,701	12,699	12,407	12,235
South East						4,974	4,948	4,846	4,821
East Anglia	5,026	5,132	5,206	5,241	5,276	389	398	395	394
South West	815	834	836	847	858	859	860	842	835
West Midlands	1,441	1,445	1,461	1,464	1,484	1,509	1,524	1,472	1,443
East Midlands	2,188	2,211	2,233	2,239	2,263	918	916	912	892
Yorkshire/Humberside						1,344	1,343	1,302	1,270
North West	1,828	1,847	1,841	1,834	1,849	1,843	1,845	1,801	1,774
North	875	877	869	850	854	865	863	837	807
Wales	669	672	668	669	672	670	664	640	629
Scotland	1,349	1,351	1,358	1,331	1,346	1,342	1,332	1,302	1,279
Northern Ireland	284	282	283	288	288	293	295	294	294
Females									
UK	8,008	8,164	8,264	8,289	8,458	8,606	8,784	8,653	8,680
Great Britain	7,837	7,994	8,093	8,116	8,281	8,425	8,597	8,470	8,494
England	6,801	6,945	7,026	7,051	7,188	7,311	7,463	7,357	7,366
South East						2,989	3,065	3,035	3,035
East Anglia	2,957	3,017	3,075	3,100	3,145	208	210	210	214
South West	415	429	441	448	460	468	478	473	477
West Midlands	776	790	800	801	826	837	850	828	828
East Midlands	1,144	1,176	1,183	1,186	1,206	496	510	511	506
Yorkshire/Humberside						737	750	732	732
North West	1,113	1,130	1,118	1,105	1,129	1,140	1,154	1,125	1,125
North	395	404	407	410	422	436	445	443	448
Wales	278	284	289	292	305	316	322	312	320
Scotland	757	764	775	771	786	797	810	798	807
Northern Ireland	171	170	171	173	177	181	187	183	185

British Labour Statistics 1886–1968, HMSO, 1971.

Figures are for each mid-year. [1]A new method of calculating regional employment estimates was introduced for the June 1965 estimates and from 1965 to 1968. All the estimates shown in this table are on a comparable basis.

8.3 Consumer Expenditure

8.3.1 Consumer Expenditure, Standard Table

	Food	Alcoholic Drink	Tobacco	Housing	Fuel and Light	Clothing	Durable House-hold Goods	Motor Cars and Motor Cycles	Other Goods	Other Services	Total Consumer Expen-diture
	£m	£m	£m	£m	£m	£m	£m	£m	£m	£m	£m
1960	4,225	963	1,140	1,643	752	1,664	832	568	2,061	3,011	16,939
1961	4,366	1,075	1,217	1,758	795	1,729	851	500	2,246	3,215	17,841
1962	4,560	1,162	1,242	1,935	910	1,771	881	538	2,396	3,436	18,930
1963	4,689	1,232	1,286	2,151	1,010	1,873	945	640	2,546	3,635	20,137
1964	4,889	1,390	1,343	2,338	1,001	1,971	1,008	733	2,811	3,857	21,501
1965	5,059	1,499	1,428	2,616	1,087	2,099	1,052	707	3,094	4,101	22,933
1966	5,297	1,626	1,504	2,860	1,160	2,154	1,046	703	3,360	4,382	24,330
1967	5,485	1,739	1,512	3,088	1,208	2,219	1.110	777	3,619	4,636	25,529
1968	5,696	1,870	1,578	3,397	1,341	2,375	1,242	875	4,092	4,997	27,528
1969	6,019	2,029	1,694	3,679	1,430	2,505	1,254	809	4,403	5,400	29,233

Mitchell, B.R. *British Historical Statistics*, Cambridge University Press, 1988.

Original source, Feinstein, C.H. *National Income, Expenditure and Output of the UK, 1855–1965*, Cambridge, 1972. Thereafter, *CSO Economic Trends Annual Supplement* and *CSO National Income and Expenditure*.

8.3.2 Regional Household Expenditure

	North	Yorks and Humber	North West	East Mids	West Mids	East Anglia	South East	Greater London	Rest of S East	South West	Wales	Scot-land	N. Ire-land	UK
	s.	s.	s.	s.	s.	s.	s.	s.	s.	s.	s.	s.	s.	s.
Average weekly household income:														
1962–63	367.10	412.97	414.87	408.35	488.58		462.67	481.08	44198	420.00	37329	397.21		426.54
1964–66	422.31	432.40	478.80	497.50	548.60	468.46	564.10	582.61	543.09	463.76	454.44	477.37		503.38
1967–68	532.55	510.90	555.17	564.37	613.61	567.21	653.41	683.32	630.80	557.28	522.50	554.46	493.07	582.30
Average weekly income per person:														
1962–63	118.88	138.10	136.54	128.60	159.05		162.83	173.12	151.75	143.46	124.63	120.28		140.99
1964–66	136.58	163.08	158.04	161.90	178.26	157.93	195.35	206.54	183.65	155.72	150.17	148.27		166.86
1967–68	176.73	176.39	186.29	188.49	202.95	200.50	225.34	245.43	211.17	186.91	173.51	178.33	139.05	195.48
Average weekly household expenditure:														
1962–63	322.80	341.78	353.62	349.77	414.79		393.25	416.65	366.61	372.76	330.83	356.88		367.32
1964–66	372.93	374.91	406.46	408.13	454.27	387.57	465.82	492.43	439.66	382.96	332.53	416.62		420.21
1967–68	436.04	419.35	473.24	451.01	437.67	457.94	535.50	560.01	517.00	474.83	452.76	467.92	469.09	482.55
Average weekly expenditure per person:														
1962–63	104.39	114.29	116.38	110.16	135.03		138.40	149.86	125.88	127.32	110.46	108.07		121.40
1964–66	120.61	126.73	134.14	132.79	147.61	130.66	161.29	174.57	148.68	128.59	126.41	129.40		139.29
1967–68	144.70	144.78	158.80	150.63	161.30	161.88	184.68	201.14	173.08	159.26	150.35	150.49	132.29	161.99
Average weekly expenditure on housing:														
1962–63	31.37	30.42	33.21	31.34	43.25		48.87	52.76	44.34	36.23	30.41	30.08		37.50
1964–66	38.42	39.83	45.24	40.22	44.47	37.49	64.13	71.38	56.78	45.27	42.41	35.16		47.96
1967–68	46.13	44.46	52.58	49.59	57.53	56.47	76.61	85.28	70.05	65.69	49.77	43.64	36.71	58.50

British Labour Statistics 1868-1968, HMSO, 1971.

Original sources, *Family Expenditure Surveys 1962-1968* and the *Gazette*, March 1965 and March 1967. Blank space denotes no available data. Based on standard regions as constituted at January, 1966.

8.4 Prices

8.4.1 Food Prices

8.4.1a Food Basket

Article (per lb unless otherwise stated)	1960 d.	1961 d.	1962 d.	1963 d.	1964 d.	1965 d.	1966 d.	1967 d.	1968 d.	1969 d.
White Wheat Bread (1¾lb.)	11.5	12.7	12.9	13.3	13.9	14.8	15.6	16.8		
Wrapped and Sliced (1¾lb.)									19.1	20.0
Unwrapped and Sliced (1¾lb.)									18.5	19.4
Other Bread[1] (14oz.)	8.6	9.5	10.2	10.4	10.8	11.1	11.3	11.9	13.1	13.5
Flour (wheat) white, self raising (3lb.)									23.2	23.1
Flour (wheat) white (3lb.)	21.4	21.0	21.1	21.3	22.6	21.9	21.9	22.6		
Rice, whole grain, polished	11.1	11.1	11.7	11.9	12.2	12.5	12.8	13.6	18.4	19.5
Beef, home-killed, first quality:										
Sirloin (without bone)	65.0	62.3	66.3	68.1	81.1	85.7	83.7	82.1	92.5	103.0
Brisket (with bone)	26.9	24.5	26.2	27.4	31.6	33.9	34.0	30.6	38.9	40.9
Pork, home-killed:										
Leg (foot off)	51.0	49.9	46.6	50.1	51.5	49.5	57.0	55.8	60.5	62.7
Loin (with bone)	56.8	56.1	54.1	58.9	60.1	59.3	67.2	68.7	71.8	74.6
Mutton, home-killed, first quality:										
Leg (with bone)	42.3	41.0	43.9	39.1	44.4	45.5	48.8			
Ham, cooked, sliced (without bone)	97.4	95.8	94.1	97.4	102.2	103.1	112.2	113.1	116.3	123.5
Bacon:										
Back, smoked	58.7	50.9	58.8	63.5	61.0	60.7	69.8	68.1	70.7	76.9
Streaky, smoked									44.5	48.1
Streaky, thick smoked	34.7	29.6	32.7	37.2	34.9	32.3	41.7	41.9		
Fish fresh cod fillets									42.9	45.3
Fish fresh cod cuts	33.0	34.2	35.0	36.4	37.8	40.1	41.4	43.5		
Margarine (½lb.)	10.2	10.6	10.6	10.6	11.0	12.3	12.3	10.2		
Lard	16.1	16.5	16.0	15.4	16.1	17.0	17.7	16.7	15.1	17.2
Milk (pint)	8.0	8.0	8.5	8.5	9.0	9.5	9.5	10.0	10.5	11.0
Butter	38.9	33.9	40.8	45.9	46.4	44.1	43.4	43.8	42.8	42.9
Cheese	33.8	33.9	34.7	35.9	38.9	40.3	41.2	41.4	41.7	42.4
Eggs, fresh, home produced, first quality:										
Weight, not less than 2³⁄₁₆oz. (one)	5.9	5.0	4.4	5.1	3.7	4.9	4.4	4.1	4.1	4.7
Potatoes[2]	19.1	24.7	3.4	3.8	3.7	3.7	4.5	4.5	3.8	4.7
Cabbage, green	4.2	5.0	4.3	4.9	7.0	5.1	6.8	7.0	7.2	7.5
Onions, ripe	5.7	6.1	6.8	6.6	6.7	7.3	8.0	7.6	8.3	8.8
Apples, eating	11.4	18.8	12.9	12.9	13.4	14.7	17.6	21.4	20.3	17.2
Oranges	11.3	14.5	13.2	13.1	14.1	14.2	15.1	14.8	15.9	17.1
Prunes (dried)	27.4	28.9	28.4	28.3	28.6	28.3	28.8	29.4	32.3	33.7
Sugar, white granulated (2lb.)	16.1	15.7	16.0	21.5	19.3	16.9	16.7	17.1	16.9	17.
Coffee, pure roasted	86.0	86.0	86.0	86.0	94.0	98.0	95.0	99.5	115.5	115.0
Tea	78.7	77.9	76.5	76.3	75.9	75.5	76.2	75.7		
Cocoa (not sweetened) proprietary brands in tins	27.0	27.0	27.0	27.0	27.0	27.0	25.0	27.0	27.0	29.0
Salt, cooking (1½lb.)	7.0	6.5	7.0	7.0	6.7	7.0	7.0	7.0	8.0	8.0

Central Statistical Office.

Average retail prices collected by the Department of Employment in 200 areas in the UK. [1]Bread baked from a proprietary brand of brown flour. [2]1960 and 1961 potatoes 7lbs. 1962 to 1969 potatoes 1lb.

8.4.2 Prices, General Articles

	1960		1961		1962		1963		1964		1965		1966		1967		1968		1969	
	s.	d.	s.	d.	s.	d.	s.	d.	s.	d.	s.	d.	s.	d.	s.	d.	s.	d.	s.	d.
Aspirin (100)											1	0								
Average House Price	£2,530		£2,770		£2,950		£3,160		£3,460		£3,820		£4,100		£4,340		£4,640		£4,880	
Beer (1 pint)			1	2½	1	5	1	5½	1	7	1	9	1	9	1	10	1	10	1	11½
Cadbury's Milk Chocolate (½ lb.)	2	4	2	3	2	3	2	3	2	3	2	5								
Cheddar Cheese (1 lb.)	2	0									3	8							3	6
Colmans Mustard (1 lb.)			5	0½	5	10			6	0							6	3		
Colmans Starch (4 ozs.)				9																
Daily Mail		2½		2½		2½		2½		2½		2½		2½		2½		2½		2½
Guinness Extra Stout (1 pint)	1	6									2	1								
Inland Letter Post[1]		3		3		3		3		3		3		4		4		5		5
Mars Bar		6		6		6		7		7		7		7		7		8		8
Mini Car[2]	£495	19	£495	19	£526	5	£447	13	£469	16	£469	16	£478	0	£508	15	£561	2		
Pears Transparent Soap																	1	2½	1	9½
Petrol (1 gallon)	4	8	4	10½			4	9	4	9½	5	2	5	7	5	4½	5	10½	6	3½
Red Label Tea (1 lb.)	6	4									8	0								
Scotch Whisky (standard bottle)	37	6	41	6			41	6	44	6	48	6	51	11			54	5	58	6
Swan Vestas Matches		4		4		5		5		5		5		5		5		5		5
The Times		6		6		6		6												

Autocar; The Boots Company; British Library; Burmah Castrol; Cadbury's Ltd; Colmans of Norwich; Guinness Brewing GB; Halifax Building Society; Rowntrees; Royal Mail; Sainsbury's Archives; The Scotch Whisky Association and Unilever Historical Archives.

Blank space denotes no available data. [1]In 1968 a two-tier letter service was introduced. The prices referred to in this and other tables are for first class stamps. [2]The costs are for the basic Mini, including car and purchase tax. The cost in 1989 was £4,554 and in 1993, the cost was approximately £6,000.

8.4.3 Prices, Selected

Item	Source	Description	Price £	s.	d.
Alcoholic Drink					
Fortified Wine	*Ideal Home*, March 1960	Dry Fly Sherry	18	0	(bottle)
Beer	*Which*, 1960	Whitbread Draught Bitter		8½	(½ pint)
		Ansells Draught Mild		6½	(½ pint)
		Charrington Draught Bitter		9½	(½ pint)
Appliances: Domestic and Electrical					
Boiler	*Ideal Home*, March 1960	Valor Oil Fired Boiler	65	0	0
Cooker		Creda Mercury Four	51	9	0
		Belling Electric Cooker	51	0	0
		Autocraft Gas Cooker	68	5	0
Cleaner		Metroluk Carpet Sweeper	3	13	10
Drier		Burco Tumbleair Warm Air Drier	49	13	7
Heater		Sadia Water Heater UDB20	34	13	2
Kitchen		Beautiful Dream Kitchen	49	18	6
Refrigerator		AEG Frigomat	111	9	0
		Sigma Luxury Model	66	3	0
Sink		Wrighton Single Drainer Sink Unit	27	15	0
Spin Dryer		AEG Spin Dryer	24	3	0
Washing Machine		AEG Lavalux	87	3	0
Boiler	*Oxendales*, Manchester, 1960	Five Gallon Electric Boiler	4	17	6
Cleaner		Hoover Constellation	18	0	0
		Cylinder Vacuum Cleaner	11	13	6
		Ewbank Sprite	3	1	6
Iron		Hoover Steam/Dry Iron	4	12	1
Kettle		Bescol Electric Kettle	3	10	3
Spin Dryer		Hoover Spinarinse	35	12	6
Washing Machine		Hoover Washing Machine	45	10	0 (with heater)
Radio		Transistor Portable Set	23	12	6
		Piccadilly Pocket Radio	16	16	0
Record Player		Dansette Major Record Player	18	7	6
Cleaner	*Which*, 1960	Morphy Richards VBA	24	4	3
		Hoover de Luxe 652	36	0	0
Dishwashers		Colston	89	5	0
		Westinghouse	180	14	6
Electric Light Bulb		Osram Single Coil		1	5
Television		Alba T656	65	2	0
		Ferguson 506T	66	3	0
		Pye V310S	68	5	0
Washing Machines		Bendix De Luxe	99	15	0
		Acme Twin Tub	85	3	3
Coffee Makers	*Which*, 1964	Swan 4475	2	0	0
		Pyrex de Luxe Vacuum	3	2	1

Continued

8.4.3 Prices, Selected *continued*

Item	Source	Description	Price £	s.	d.
Electric Blankets		Philips EA1210	5	10	0
		Dreamland	6	12	0
Food Mixers		Braun Multiquirl	15	17	0
		Kenwood Chefette	11	16	0
Refrigerators		Beekay TI355	49	7	0
		Electrolux S56	56	14	0
Television		Ferguson 3619	75	12	0
		Decca DR101	90	6	0
Cleaner	*Ideal Home*, October 1965	Hotpoint Vacuum Cleaner	25	4	0
Cooker		Leisure 76 De Luxe Gas Oven Unit	46	16	6
Food Mixer		Kenwood Chef	29	8	0
Heater		Hotpoint Fan Heater	8	17	6
Kettle		Hotpoint Electric Kettle	5	5	0
Washing Machine		Bendix Washer	115	10	0
Stereo Music Systems		Truvox TSA100 Transistorised Integrated Amplifier	51	9	3
		Thorens TD135 Turntable with BTD Pickup Arm	62	9	11
		Wharfedale W3 Speakers	79	0	0 (pair)
		Leak F.M. Variable Tuner	31	14	6
Washing Machine	*Homes and Gardens*, October 1966	Bendix L7 Auto Combustion Washer/Dryer	159	18	0
Stereogram		Grundig Stereogram	93	9	0
Freezers	*Which*, 1967	Lec F120	62	5	4
		Prestcold FF621	95	0	0
Irons		Hoover Steam Iron	5	2	6
		Sunbeam Ironmaster Dry	3	18	3
Toasters		AEG	7	12	1
		Sunbeam XT50A	7	19	11
Washing Machines		Bendix de Luxe LA	117	5	6
		Hoovermatic de Luxe	84	0	0
		Burco Twin Tub	67	3	5
Cleaner	*Which*, 1968	Hoover Junior 1334	31	8	3
		Electrolux 80	29	17	6
Dishwashers		Colston Classic	130	9	11
		Westinghouse	236	14	0
Food Mixers		Kenwood Chefette	12	12	0
		Moulinex Major BT2A	6	15	6
Refrigerators		Beekay TI355	34	2	6
		Electrolux S56	49	12	0
Stereo Radio Tuners		Philips GH927	42	6	1
		Quad FM Stereo	50	0	0
		Trio TK-350E	56	0	0
Stereo Systems		Ferguson	81	11	0
		Philipsa	63	0	8
Televisions		Alba Colourstar	351	8	5

Continued

8.4.3 Prices, Selected *continued*

Item	Source	Description	Price		
			£	s.	d.
Televisions *cont.*		Pye CT70	330	0	0
Sink	*Ideal Home*, March 1969	Leisure Sink	48	12	0
Dishwasher		Colston Classic Dishwasher	133	1	4
Cookers (Electric)	*Which*, 1969	Belling Super 60	69	17	6
		Creda Cavalier Four	49	0	0
		Tricity Marquis	72	15	0
Cookers (Gas)		Cannon Super de Luxe	82	7	8
		Newhome Caravel	53	6	8
		Parkinson Cowan	71	18	7
Kettles		Swan Royal Two Pint	5	15	5
		Russell Hobbs Three Pint	7	17	2
		Swan Sovereign	7	2	0
Stereo Systems		Dansette Hi-Fi Regina	41	13	5
		Boots Stereo	30	9	0
Tumble Dryers		Burco Tumbleair D3	59	13	2
		Hoover 3020	65	5	2
		Westinghouse DTX-552	174	18	0
Washing Machines		Bendix de Luxe LS	132	12	5
		English Electric Liberator	120	15	0

Baby Equipment

Item	Source	Description	Price		
Mattress	*Oxendales*, Manchester, 1960	Cot Mattress with Spring Interior	3	9	11
Nappies		Terry Towelling Nappies	1	8	6 (dozen)
Push Chair	*Oxendales*, Manchester, 1960	Handy Stroller Chair	2	18	6
Pram Accessory		Pram Canopies	1	2	6
Sleeping Cot		Waterproof Luxicot	1	15	7
High Prams	*Which*, 1964	Silver Cross Arcadia	24	9	6
		Swallow Kimberley Classic	28	19	6
Low Prams		Leeway Diana	14	19	6
		Queen of the Road (CWS) Blandford 640	17	11	6
Foldaway Prams		Pedigree Eliza F	17	10	0
		Shuresta Cumfifolda Elite	16	19	6

Clothing and Footwear:
Children's (Girl's)

Item	Source	Description	Price		
Coat	*Oxendales*, Manchester, 1960	Fleecy Textured Coat	4	19	0 (up to 105/0)
		Double Breasted Teenage Coat	5	19	6
		Two Coats for	3	5	6
		Girl's Stroller in Woollen Tweed	4	8	0 (up to 105/0)
Blouse		Blouse in Terylene		16	6 (up to 17/6)
Blazer		Striped Blazer in Rayon Sailcloth	1	3	6 (up to 26/9)
Dress		Teenage Dress in Nylon Organdie	4	4	0 (up to 96/6)
		Toddlers Dress in Nylon Organdie	2	7	6 (up to 53/0)
		Tootals Cotton Frock	1	13	6 (up to 36/0)
		Nautical Design Frock	1	3	6 (up to 27/0)
Skirt		Skirt in Sailcloth	1	5	3 (up to 28/9)
Suit		Buster Romper Suit		18	9

Continued

8.4.3 Prices, Selected *continued*

Item	Source	Description	Price £	s.	d.
Suit *cont.*		Teenager's Two Piece in Fine Woollen Tweed	5	9	6
		Girl's Two Piece Suit	3 12	0 (up to 91/6)	
Swimwear		Swimsuit with Skirt for Teenagers	1	5	6
		Gingham Play Overalls		5	6 (up to 6/3)
Trousers		Popular Trews in Woven Rayon	1	7	6 (up to 31/6)
		Teenagers Slacks in Cotton Gaberdine	1	6	6 (up to 27/6)
		Tartan Rayon Trews		10	0 (up to 13/0)
Babywear		Matinee Coat in Spun Rayon	1	0	6 (up to 21/9)
		All Wool Shawl	1	2	6

Children's (Boy's)

Item	Source	Description	Price £	s.	d.
Shirts	*Oxendales*, Manchester, 1960	Sports Shirts in Knitted Cotton		7	9 (up to 10/3)
		Grey School Shirts in Wincyette		12	6 (up to 15/0)
Suits		Nylon Reinforced Suit	2	11	6 (up to 65/0)
Blazer		Single Breasted Blazer	3	2	6
Jacket		Hacking Sports Jacket	2	19	6 (up to 67/6)
Shoes (Boys and Girls)		Infants Leather Shoes		18	11
		Toddlers Dress Shoe in White Buckskin		19	6
		Girl's Casual Shoe	1	6	6
		Teenager's Dainty Shoes	1	8	11
Coat	*Affleck & Brown*, Manchester, 1963	Wool Tweed Coat by Alexon Young Set	7	7	0
Dress		Tricel Dress with Crisp Pleats	3	9	11
Suit		Two Piece Suit in French Grey Wool	5	12	0
Knitwear		High-Necked Jumper in Ban-Lon Nylon		14	3 (up to 21/0)

Men's

Item	Source	Description	Price £	s.	d.
Blazer	*Oxendales*, Manchester, 1960	Single Breasted Blazer in All Wool Barathea	6	5	0
Hosiery		Wool/Nylon Socks		7	9 (pair)
		Cashmere Socks		5	11 (pair)
Jackets		Gaberdine Bush Jackets	2	6	6
		Suedette Casual Jackets	4	12	6
		Harris Tweed Hacking Jackets	5	19	6
Knitwear		Shawl Collar Cardigan in Wool	2	5	9
		All Wool Pullover	2	7	6
		Cashmere Weight Pullover	1	10	0
		Bri-Lon Slipover	1	19	6
Nightwear		Tootal Dressing Gowns	4	9	6
		Striped Cotton Pyjamas	1	1	11
Shirts		Shirts in White Poplin	1	7	6
		Banded Shirts in Oxford Material without Collars	1	1	0
		Hard Wearing Drill Shirts	1	9	6
Suits		Terylene Hacking Style Suits	9	19	6
		Terylene Worsted Suits	10	10	0

Continued

8.4.3 Prices, Selected *continued*

Item	Source	Description	Price £	s.	d.
Suits *cont.*		Made to Measure Suit in Superfine Worsted	15	0	0
Trousers		Sports Trousers	4	15	0
Underwear		Cotton Interlock Vests		6	11 (up to 12/0)
		Cotton Interlock Pants		9	6 (up to 13/6)
Waistcoat		Jersey Weave Waistcoat	1	19	11
Workwear		Boiler Suit	1	19	6
		Drill Jeans	1	4	6
		Navy Merton Trousers	1	3	6
		Leatherette Bush Jackets	1	12	11 (up to 35/6)
		Donkey Jackets	1	8	0 (up to 38/9)
		Heavy Duty Wellingtons	2	7	9
Shoes		High Grade Oxford Shoes	3	3	9
		"John White" Shoe in Brown Leather	2	14	9
		Smart Mock-Brogue Style in Leather	2	17	6
	Producer, September 1963	Sleek Step in with Elastic Gusset	2	16	11
		Almond Toe Style with Porthole Punching Relief	2	9	11
		Two Eyelet Slim Toe Style	1	17	11
Underwear	*Which*, 1964	Wolsey Plain Ribbed Briefs		7	6
		Wolsey Plain Ribbed Vest		7	6
		St. Michael Interlock Briefs		5	6
		St. Michael Interlock Vest		4	11
		Keynote Interlock Briefs		4	6
		Keynote Interlock Vest		4	6
Women's					
Coat	*Oxendales*, Manchester, 1960	Floral Cotton Duster Coat	3	19	11
		Sailcoth Cotton Coat	3	19	11
		Raincoat in Cotton Poplin	6	6	0
		Telemac Raincoat in Spun Rayon	5	19	11
Dress		Crisp Cotton Shirtwaister	2	17	6
		Crisp Courtaulds Tested Viscose Rayon Summer Frock	2	18	9
		Blended Wool Pinafore Frock	1	9	11
Hosiery		Wolsey "Gaystep" Nylons		6	11
		Vel Crêpe 30 Denier Stockings		10	11
		Seamless Mesh 15 Denier Nylons		5	0
Knitwear		Unlined Cardigan Jacket in All Wool Velour	2	19	11
Nightwear		Candlewick Dressing Gown	3	5	0
		Drip Dry Cotton Nightie	1	6	3
		Drip Dry Cotton Pyjama Suit	1	14	6
Skirt		Skirt in Marshall Hushama Cotton	1	9	11
		Pleated Skirts in All Wool Check Tweed	2	19	9
		Skirt in Drip Dry Tricel Rayon	1	15	9
Suit		¾ Loose Back Suit in Blended Wool	7	19	11

Continued

8.4.3 Prices, Selected *continued*

Item	Source	Description	£	s.	d.
Suit *cont.*		All Wool Velour Suit	7	10	6
		Double Jersey Knit Suit	9	9	0
Swimwear		Glazed Cotton Swimsuit	1	5	0
Trousers		Sailforised Denims with Pockets Front and Back	1	5	0
		Cavalry Twill Trousers	2	9	11
Underwear		Gossards Banlon Corselette	2	5	9
		Lightly Boned Nylon Belt		8	11
		Cambric Bra		6	11
		Gossard "perma lift" Bra	1	6	9
		Gossard "silskin" Bra		7	6
		Rubber Corsets	2	2	6
		Two Way Stretch Roll On		8	9
		Cotton Interlock Vests		5	3 (up to 6/0)
		Underslip and Panties in 30 Denier Nylon	1	7	0 (up to 30/0)
Dress	*Sunday Times Magazine*, 1962	"Mary Quant" Dress	27	0	0
	Producer, August 1963	Smartly Sophisticated Satin Dress	4	4	0
		Dress with Gold Belt and Chain Fastening (5ft. 2in.)	4	4	0
		Dress with Attractively Draped Cowl Neckline	4	10	0
Coat	*Affleck & Brown*, Manchester, 1963	Canadian Fur Lined Suede Coat	33	12	0
		Washable Bri-Nylon Raincoat	3	5	0
Dress		Eastex Dress in Perma Pleated Tricel	8	8	0
Hat		Off the Face Hat in Stitched Fur Felt	2	19	11
Jacket		Finger Tip Length Sheepskin Jacket	30	9	0
		Dannimac Jacket in Double Wool	10	10	0
Suit		Casual Outfit by Dereta in Two Tone Wool	5	5	0
Handbag		Handbag in Ostrich Grain Patent Leather	5	15	0
Coat	*Woollands of Knightsbridge*, London, 1965	Dereta Coat in Shetland Tweed	17	6	6
Dress		Susan Small Skinny Topped Flaring Dress	18	10	0
		Frank Usher After Six Dress in Crêpe	13	0	0
		Polly Peck Well Brought Up Dress in Wool	7	17	0
		Frederick Starke Young Aristocrat Evening Dress	18	0	0
Suit		Classic Blazer Suit in Jaska Jersey	19	5	0
Shoes	*C & J Clark Ltd.*, 1965	Elsa Black Calf with Torlite Soles	3	9	11
		Shandi Hickory Soft Side with Rubber Soles	1	19	11
		Liz in Black Calf/Patent with Torlite Soles	2	19	11
		Micki in Black Suede/Patent with Torlite Soles	2	19	11
Dress	*Tricosa*, 1966	Crêpe Fabrina Dress	19	19	0

Continued

8.4.3 Prices, Selected *continued*

Item	Source	Description	£	s.	d.
Suit		Three Piece Suit in Tennis Tweed	43	2	0
		Coat and Skirt in Mohair Bouclé	55	13	0
Dress	*Marshall & Snelgrove*, Manchester, 1967	Crochet Bri-Nylon Dress by Dobett	14	14	0
		Terylene Dress	10	19	6
Suit		Crimplene Suit by Glaser	11	11	0
		Wosley Bri-Nylon V-Neck Sweater and Skirt	6	6	0
Blouse	*Biba*, London, 1969	Huntsman Blouse in Creamy White Satin	3	3	0
Cap		Baker Boy Needlecord Cap	1	7	6
Coat		Riding Mac with a Military Look	8	8	0
		Reefer Coat with Brass Buttons in Linen Like Rayon	6	19	6
Dress		All Wool Pinafore Dress	2	19	6
		Lean Tunic Dress with Wide Collar in Jersey	4	19	6
		Slinky Hooded Dress in Silk Jersey	3	15	6
		Moss Crepe Dress with Billowing Sleeves	4	4	0
Trousers		Reefer Trousers with Brass Button in Linen Rayon	2	19	6

Food Products

Item	Source	Description	£	s.	d.
Bacon	*J Sainsbury*, 1960	Unsmoked Back Bacon		4	0 (per lb.)
Breakfast Cereal		Shredded Wheat		1	3 (12's)
Butter		Best Butter		2	8
Biscuits		McVities Digestive			11½ (½ lb.)
Cheese		Cheddar Cheese		2	0 (per lb.)
Eggs		Six Medium Size		1	6
Soup		Heinz Tomato Soup		1	3 (15½ oz. tin)
Tea		Red Label Tea		6	4 (per lb.)
Baby Foods	*Colmans of Norwich*, February 1962	Robinson's Patent Barley		1	7½ (½ lb.)
		Robinson's Patent Groats		1	4 (½ lb.)
		High Protein Cereal		2	0 (packet)
		Robsweet		1	9 (tin)
Mustard		Ready Mixed Mild Mustard		1	3 (jar)
		French Mustard			8½ (tube)
Semolina		Colman's Semolina		1	2½ (1 lb.)
Oats		Three Bear Oats		1	10½ (1½ lb.)
Lemon Juice		Jif Lemons		1	0 (2 fl.oz.)
Soft Drinks		Lemon Barley Crystals		1	3 (4 oz.)
		Lemon Barley		3	3 (20 fl. oz.)
		Orange Barley		3	3 (20 fl. oz.)
		Orange Squash		2	6 (26 fl. oz.)
		Soft Drink Miniatures in Various Flavours			6
Confectionery	*Cadbury's Ltd.*, July 1962	Milk Brazil		3	3 (½ lb. blocks)
		Cadbury's Milk Fruit and Nut		2	8 (½ lb. block)
		Bournville		1	2 (¼ lb. block)

Continued

8.4.3 Prices, Selected *continued*

Item	Source	Description	£	s.	d.
Confectionery *contd.*		Milk Tray Block			7 (small block)
	Cadbury's Ltd., January 1964	Milk Brazil		3	4 (½ lb. block)
		Milk Fruit and Nut		2	11 (½ lb. block)
		Bournville		1	3 (¼ lb. block)
		Coffee Filled Block			6 (small block)
Mustard	*Colmans of Norwich*, December 1964	Double Superfine Mustard		6	0 (lb.)
				1	1 (2 oz.)
Jam	*Ideal Home*, October 1965	Tiptree Jam		2	9 (12 oz. jar)
Bacon	*J Sainsbury*, 1965	Unsmoked Back Bacon		4	6 (lb.)
Breakfast Cereal		Shredded Wheat		1	5½ (12's)
Cheese		Cheddar Cheese		3	8 (lb.)
Soup		Heinz Tomato Soup		1	2 (15½ oz. tin)
Tea		Red Label Tea		8	0 (lb.)
Mustard	*Colmans of Norwich*, January 1968	Double Superfine Mustard		6	3 (lb.)
				1	2 (2 oz.)
		Ready Mixed English Mustard		2	5 (6 oz. jar)
		French Mustard in Decorated Opal Jar		2	11 (7½ oz. jar)
Bacon	*J Sainsbury*, 1969	Middle Unsmoked Bacon		5	6 (lb.)
Beans		JS Beans			6½ (15 oz. tin)
Beefburgers		Beefburgers		3	3 (4's)
Breakfast Cereal		Kellogg's Corn Flakes		2	3 (500 g.)
Butter		Best Butter		5	11 (lb.)
Cheese		Cheddar Cheese		3	6 (lb.)
Chicken		3 lb. Roasting Chicken		9	9
Coffee		JS Instant Coffee Refill		2	0
Jam		Strawberry Jam		2	0 (lb.)
Sugar		Sugar		1	5½ (2 lb.)
Tea		Loose Red Label Tea		2	6 (½ lb.)
Tinned Fruit		JS Peach Slices		1	9 (14½ oz.)
Tomato Sauce		Heinz Tomato Ketchup		2	5 (20 oz.)
Cheese (per lb.)	*Which*, 1969	Caerphilly		3	10
		Lancashire		4	4
		Stilton		6	6
		English Farmhouse Cheddar		4	6
Furniture					
Bed	*Ideal Home*, March 1960	Myers Vogue Divan Single	18	17	0
		Myers Vogue Divan Double	27	10	0
Bookcase		4ft. Bookcase	19	11	6
Dining Furniture		G-Plan Large Extending Table	26	15	0
		G-Plan Chairs	6	10	0 (each)
		G-Plan Long Low Sideboard	39	10	0
		Nathan Drop Leaf Table and Four Chairs	61	19	0
Floorcovering		Deep Pile Carpet	1	4	0 (sq. yd.)
Seating		Minty Lizard Settee	32	0	0
		Minty Lizard Chair	21	15	0

Continued

8.4.3 Prices, Selected *continued*

Item	Source	Description	Price £	s.	d.
Seating *cont.*		Minty Lizard Footstool	5	10	0
Bed	*Oxendales*, Manchester, 1960	Nulux Spring Interior Mattress Single	10	10	0
		Vono Divan Bed with Mattress Single	15	10	0
Dining		Drop Leaf Kitchen Table in Formica	9	5	0
		Dining Chair in Medium Oak	2	17	6 (each)
		Seasoned Timber Gate Leg Table	9	9	0
Floorcovering		Feltbase Floorcoverings		5	11 (2 yds. wide)
		Printed Cork Linoleum		16	2 (2 yds. wide)
		Inlaid Moire Linoleum		19	0 (2 yds. wide)
		Traditional Tartan Axminster Rugs 63in. x 52in.	2	12	11
		Jute Velvet Pile Rugs 54in.x 27in.		19	11
		Spool Axminster Broadloom Carpeting	6	10	10 (3 yds. wide)
Lounge		TV Trolley in Selected Timber	2	19	6
		Record Cabinet and Table	5	19	11
Seating		Rocking Chair	11	19	6
		Easy Chair with Latex Cushion	10	19	9
		Two Seater Settee to Match Chair	16	19	11
Floorcovering	*Ideal Home*, October 1965	Scotsway Luxurious Wall to Wall Carpeting		8	9 (18in. wide)
		7 Star Deep Pile Carpet		7	0 (sq. yd.)
		Rylton Wilton Carpet	1	19	0 (sq. yd.)
Planter		Chelsea De Luxe Planter and Room Divider	7	15	6
		Chelsea Corner Planter	4	12	6
Seating		Miss Muffet Pouffes and Tuffets from	1	6	6
Mattress		Spring Interior Nursery Mattress	2	15	0
Garden Equipment and Supplies (inc. Garages)					
Fencing	*Ideal Home*, March 1960	Garden Panels 7ft. x 9ft.	1	8	0
Garage		Ideal Concrete Garage from	43	0	0
Gates		7ft. Opening Cotswold Gates	8	19	6 (pair)
Greenhouse		Crittall Rustless Greenhouse 6ft. 3in. sq.	25	0	0
Planters		Large Shrub Tubs	4	15	6
Tools		Power Sure Grip Weeder	1	17	6
Barrow	*Oxendales*, Manchester, 1960	Lightweight Wheelbarrow	3	17	6
Chair		Deck Chair in Good Quality Canvas	1	7	6
Hose		Hose on Reel	2	5	0
Mower		Super Panther Roller Mower	8	12	6
		Suffolk Swift Mower	6	10	6
Swing		Outdoor Swing	4	19	6
Tools		Set of 5 Garden Tools	1	5	0
		Gardening Spade in Sheffield Steel	1	5	6
		Gardening Fork in Sheffield Steel	1	5	6
Watering Can		Plastic Watering Can		18	9

Continued

8.4.3 Prices, Selected *continued*

Item	Source	Description	Price		
			£	s.	d.
Mowers	*Which*, 1960	Qualcast E1 Hand Driven Mower	5	11	3
		J.P.Maxees Roller	16	9	5
		Qualcast Powered Panther Power Driven	25	14	6
	Which, 1964	J.P.Maxees Roller	37	10	0
Flower Bulbs	*The Observer Weekend Review*, 1964	Peacock's Mixed Tulip Bulbs		3	6 (dozen)
Garage	*Ideal Home*, October 1965	Marley Concrete Garages from	26	0	0
		Batley Up and Over Doors	12	5	0
Gates		7ft .Opening Iron Double Gates from	5	9	6
Greenhouse		Crittall Rustless Greenhouse from	23	2	0
Outdoor Lighting		Raydyot Reproduction Coach Lamps from	5	5	0
Mowers	*Which*, 1969	Atco 14in. Petrol Mower	37	0	0
		Suffolk Super Punch	29	19	6
		Qualcast Super Panther 12in. Electric	23	19	6
Tools		Bulldog 5605AM Spade	2	11	0
		Jenks and Cattell 210/PD	1	10	6
		Spearwell 1000	7	18	6

Heat and Light

Item	Source	Description	Price		
Electricity	*Eastern Electricity*	Electricity per unit	1	11	6 (per year and 1d. per unit)
Gas	*British Gas North Thames*,	Gas per therm		2	2 (+ 9/6 a quarter)
Coal	*Digest of UK Energy Statistics*,	Coal per ton	15	0	0

Hotel Rates

Item	Source	Description	Price		
Belgravia Hotel, London	*Bradshaws ABC Railway Guide*, 1960	Single Bed and Breakfast	1	5	0 (up to 32/6 daily)
Kenilworth Hotel, Glasgow		Bed, Bath and Breakfast	1	7	6 (night)

Household Goods

Item	Source	Description	Price		
Cleaning Detergent	*Ideal Home*, March 1960	Squeezy Washing Liquid		2	0 (bottle)
		1001 Cleaner		2	6 (bottle)
Linen Bin		Linen Bin/Stool	2	8	6
Toilet Seat		Belvedere Toilet Seat	3	1	6
Kitchen Equipment		Salter Kitchen Balance	3	8	8
Drinks Equipment		Sparklets Syphons	4	16	0
Cleaning Detergents	*Which*, 1960	Stardrops			10½ (19.6 fl. oz.)
		Handy Andy		2	3 (14 fl. oz.)
Bedding	*Oxendales*, Manchester, 1960	Striped Cotton Quilt Single	1	8	6
		Striped Cotton Quilt Double	1	16	6
		Feather Filled Quilt Single	2	17	6
		Feather Filled Quilt Double	3	9	6
		Terylene Pillows	2	2	6 (each)
		Latex Foam Pillows	1	19	6
		Candlewick Bedspread Single	5	5	0
		Candlewick Bedspread Double	6	0	0

Continued

8.4.3 Prices, Selected *continued*

Item	Source	Description	Price £	s.	d.
Bedding *cont.*		Popular Quality White Cotton Sheets from	2	3	6 (pair)
Cookware		Three Aluminium Saucepans	1	8	6
		Milk Pan		12	2
		Aluminium Chip Pan		19	3
		Vitreous Enamel Mincer	1	5	9
		Non-Stick Frying Pan	1	6	3
Kitchen Equipment		Bread Crock in Moulded Plastic	1	0	3
		Plastic Vegetable Rack	1	10	9
		Seven Kitchen Utensils	1	5	0 (complete)
Table Linen		Irish Damask Cloth 52in. x 52in.		12	0
		Irish Damask Napkins		8	6 (each)
Tableware		21 Piece Tea Set	2	2	0
		8 Piece Harlequin Tea Set	1	11	4
		Pyrex Dinner Set	6	6	0
		Pyrex Heated Casserole	1	15	0
Towels		Harlequin Towels 21in. x 42in.		10	0 (pair)
Ironing Table		Beldray All Steel Ironing Table	3	18	3
Chimney Cleaning		Chimney Cleaning Set	2	12	6
Terry Towels	*Which*, 1964	Christy Mayfair 22in. x 43in.		14	6
		Dorma Allegro 20in. x 43in.		7	11
		Woolworth 320 20in. x 37in.		3	6
		Zorbit DW148 22in. x 44in.		7	6
Cutlery	*Ideal Home*, October 1965	Prestige Three Piece Cutlery Set	1	7	6
Cleaning Detergent	*Which*, 1967	Fairy Liquid		3	2 (19½ fl. oz.)
		1001 Sparkle		1	6 (20 fl. oz.)
Washing Powder		Daz Powder		3	2 (26½ oz.)
		Tide Powder		3	2 (26½ oz.)
Tableware	*Ideal Home*, March 1969	18 Piece Bone China Tea Set	3	0	1
Houses					
Crouch Built Homes	*Ideal Home*, March 1960	Maisonette in Hinchley Wood, Surrey	3,050	0	0 (upwards)
		Detached Houses in Hinchley Wood, Surrey	4,095	0	0 (upwards)
		Semi Detached Houses in Herefordshire	2,195	0	0
		Semi Detached Houses in Gloucestershire	2,285	0	0
Jewellery					
Watch	*Oxendales*, Manchester, 1960	Timex Cocktail Watch	2	15	0
		Avia 9 ct. Gold Watch	11	10	0
Personal Care Items					
Dryer	*Oxendales*, Manchester, 1960	Pifco Hair Dryer	3	14	6
Scales		Salter Bathroom Scales	3	15	6
Chemists	*Which*, 1960	Vick Formula 44		3	6
		Venos Cough Mixture		2	6 (up to 4/0)
Tissues		Kleenex for Men		1	0

Continued

8.4.3 Prices, Selected *continued*

Item	Source	Description	£	s.	d.
Tissues *cont.*		Boots		1	3
		Scotties Economy		2	9
Hairdressers	*Affleck & Brown*, Manchester, 1963	Shampoo and Set		8	6
		Cut		4	0
		Perm from	2	2	0
Beauty Treatment		Manicure		5	0
Curlers	*Which*, 1967	Carmen 18 Rollers	16	5	6
		Babyliss Tongs	6	6	0
		Pifco Vanity Curl	2	0	0
Dryers		Braun	8	10	0
		Pifco Hi-Speed	4	16	0
		Philips Hair Dryer	3	16	2
Hair Shampoo		Palmolive Family		4	0 (14½ fl. oz.)
		Sainsbury's Family		2	10 (277 cc.)
Hair Spray		Aqua Net		3	11 (113 g.)
		Silvikrin		4	7 (126 g.)
		Vitapointe		6	11 (175 g.)
Toilet Preparations	*Which*, 1968	Elizabeth Arden Cleansing Cream		13	9 (71 cc.)
		Boots No.7 Cleansing Cream		4	2 (58 cc.)
		Yardley Cleansing Cream		6	5 (84 cc.)
Sunlamp	*Which*, 1969	Hanovia Bahama	21	1	7
		Pifco Supertonic 1025	8	15	10
Toilet Soap		Knights Castile		1	6½ (bar)
		Camay		1	9
		Lux		1	9

Prescription Charges

Item	Source	Description	£	s.	d.
	Department of Health, March 1, 1961	Charge per Item			10
	Department of Health, March 1, 1965	Prescription Charge Abolished			
	Department of Health, June 10, 1968	Charge per Item with Exemptions			12½
	Department of Health, November 1, 1968	Prepayment Certificates (PPC)	1	10	0 (for 6 months)
			2	15	0 (for 12 months)

Publications

Item	Source	Description	£	s.	d.
Guide	*Bradshaws ABC Railway Guide*, 1960	Bradshaws Air Guide		7	6 (monthly)
Book	*The Observer Weekend Review*, January 5, 1964	*Snowball*, B. Brophy, Secker & Warburg		16	0
		The Palace, C. Simon, Cape	1	1	0
		Merrie England, P. Johnson, McGibbon & Kee		16	0 (hardback)
		Custom House, F. King, Panther		5	0
Magazine	*Manchester Central Library*, c.1960's	Woman's Own		1	6

Services

Item	Source	Description	£	s.	d.
Cinema	*Kinematographic Year Book*, 1961–1965	Odeon Theatre, Manchester, Admission Price		2	9 (up to 6/0)

Continued

8.4.3 Prices, Selected *continued*

Item	Source	Description	Price £	s.	d.
Cinema *cont.*	*Kinematographic Year Book*, 1961–1965	Grosvenor Cinema, Manchester, Admission Price		1	3 (up to 1/9)
	Kinematographic Year Book, 1962	Odeon Theatre, Manchester, Admission Price		3	6 (up to 6/6)
	Kinematographic Year Book, 1966–1968	Grosvenor Cinema, Admission Price		1	6 (up to 2/0)
	Kinematographic Year Book, 1969	Manchester Film Theatre		5	0 (up to 10/0)
Licence	*Post Office Archives*, 1965–1969	Radio	1	10	4
	Post Office Archives, 1965–1968	Black and White Television	5	0	0
	Post Office Archives, 1968	Colour Television	10	0	0
	Post Office Archives, 1969	Black and White Television	6	0	0
		Colour Television	11	0	0
	DVLA, 1961	Road Tax	15	0	0 (12 months)
	DVLA, 1965		17	10	0 (12 months)
	DVLA, 1968		25	0	0 (12 months)
Telephone Tariffs	*British Telecom Archives*, 1961				
Exchange Line Rentals		Exclusive Business Quarterly Rental	4	0	0
		Exclusive Residential Quarterly Rental	3	10	0
Trunk Call Charges	*British Telecom Archives*, 1963				
Calls made via Operator		Up to 35 miles			9
		35 to 50 miles		2	0
		50 to 75 miles		3	0
		75 to 125 miles		3	6
		Over 125 miles		4	0
Revised Quarterly Rental	*British Telecom Archives*, 1968	Exclusive Residential Exchange Line	4	0	0
		Shared Service	3	10	0
Trunk Calls from STD Exchanges (standard Mon–Fri)		Up to 35 miles			2 (for 24 seconds)
		35 to 50 miles			2 (for 12 seconds)
		Over 50 miles			2 (for 8 seconds)
Coin Boxes		Up to 35 miles			6 (for 48 seconds)
		35 to 50 miles			6 (for 24 seconds)
		Over 50 miles			6 (for 16 seconds)
Parcel Postage Rates	*Post Office Archives*, 1963	2 lb. weight		2	0
		5 lb. weight		2	9
		10 lb. weight		4	0
Ordinary Rate	*Post Office Archives*, 1966	2 lb. weight		3	0
		6 lb. weight		4	6
		10 lb. weight		6	0
Ordinary Parcels	*Post Office Archives*, 1968	2 lb. weight		3	0
		6 lb. weight		4	6
		10 lb. weight		6	0

Sewing Equipment and Supplies

Machine	*Ideal Home*, March 1960	Cresta 5 Star Sewing Machine	48	18	0

Continued

8.4.3 Prices, Selected *continued*

Item	Source	Description	£	s.	d.
Machine *cont.*		Dependable Electric Sewing Machine	29	14	6
Fabrics (per yard)	*Oxendales*, Manchester, 1960	Lingerie Spun Rayon		2	6
		Seerloop Check		5	11
		Rayon Suiting		9	6
		Rayon Sailcloth		4	6
		Rayon Satin		4	6
		Cotton Cambric		3	3
		Check Gingham		3	6
		Rayon Serge		8	11
		Grey Flannel		9	6
		Bridal/Evening Brocade		6	11
Machine		Jones Sewing Machine Hand Model	25	12	6
		Jones Sewing Machine Electric Model	33	0	8
	Which, 1967	Bernina 700	69	6	0
		Pfaff 91	67	0	0
		Viking 19	75	11	0
Knitting Machine		Brother 551	40	19	0
		Busch EM180	41	0	0
		Familia Super	28	17	6

Sports and Hobbies

Item	Source	Description	£	s.	d.
Photographic Equipment	*Oxendales*, Manchester, 1960	Coronet Consul Box Camera	1	17	6
Sportswear	*Which*, 1964	Adams Riding Hat	3	7	6
		Charles Owen Riding Hat	3	5	0
		Rowes of Bond Street Riding Hat	4	4	0
Sports Equipment	*Which*, 1967	Davies PW2 Roller Skates from Woolworths	1	2	6
		Raleigh Sunbeam Roller Skates	1	10	6
		Milbro S33	2	7	11
Photographic Equipment		Kodak Brownie 127	1	19	9
		Boots Beiretta 11	8	11	6
	Which, 1969	Ashai Pentax SLA	79	19	6
		Practica Nova 1	47	19	6

Tobacco Products

Item	Source	Description	£	s.	d.
Cigarettes	*Ideal Home*, March 1960	Craven A Tipped Cigarettes		3	11 (20)
	Scottish CWS Ltd., 1961	Rocky Mount		3	6 (20)
		Gold Flake Medium		4	1 (20)
		Shipmate Navy Cut		2	0½ (10)
Cigars		Savana 25's	12	10	0 (100)
Whiffs		Henri Winterman's Scooters		6	0 (10)
		Henri Winterman's Senoritas		3	6 (5)
Snuff		London Brown	2	15	0 (lb.)
Tobacco		Thick and Bogie Black Roll		4	3 (oz.)
		Revor Plug		4	3½ (per plug)
		Golf Mixture Cut Tobacco		4	10½ (oz.)

Continued

8.4.3 Prices, Selected *continued*

Item	Source	Description	Price		
			£	s.	d.
Tobacco *cont.*		Heath Brown Flake		4	7 (oz.)
		Union Black Cut Cavendish		4	2 (oz.)
Cigarettes	*Scottish CWS Ltd.*, 1966	Rocky Mount Filters		4	7 (20)
		Gold Flake Medium		5	5 (20)
		Shipmate Medium		2	8½ (10)
Cigars		Savana 25's	19	10	0 (100)
Whiffs		Henri Winterman's Scooters		7	11 (10)
		Henri Wintermans Senoritas		4	3 (5)
Snuff		Kendal Brown	3	13	4 (lb.)
Tobacco		Thick and Bogie Black Roll		5	10½ (oz.)
		Revor Plug Sliced		5	11 (oz.)
		Golf Mixture Cut		6	8 (oz.)
		Heath Brown Flake		6	3 (oz.)
		Union Flake Empire Brand		5	10½ (oz.)
Toys					
Soft Toys	*Which*, 1967	Chad Valley Washable Bear	2	8	11
		Lefray Hygienic Toy	1	19	6
		Woolworth's Teddy Bear		10	9
Transport and Vehicles					
Air Fares	*Reed Travel Group*, 1960	London to Paris 1st Class	11	0	1
		London to Paris Economy	9	1	0
		London to New York	178	12	0
	Bradshaws ABC Railway Guide, 1960	Manchester to Bournemouth; Jersey Airlines Int.	5	10	0 (return)
	Bradshaws ABC Railway Guide, 1960	Manchester to Bournemouth; Jersey Airlines Int.	13	11	0 (return)
Bus Fares	*Manchester City Transport*, 1960–1963	1.05 miles			3
Rail Fares	*Bradshaws ABC Railway Guide*, 1960	Manchester to London Return 1st. Class	2	12	0
		Manchester to London Return 2nd. Class	1	18	6
	Bradshaws ABC Railway Guide, 1961	Manchester to London Return 1st. Class	2	17	6
Air Fares	*Reed Travel Group*, 1965	London to Paris 1st. Class	13	15	0
		London to Paris Economy	9	16	2
		London to new York 1st. Class	133	19	0
		London to New York Economy	91	2	0
Bus Fares	*Manchester City Transport*, 1964	1.05 miles			4
	Manchester City Transport, 1965–66	1.05 miles			6
Rail Fares	*Bradshaws ABC Railway Guide*, 1965	Manchester to London Return	5	0	0
Vehicles	*Ideal Home*, March 1960	Triumph Herald Saloon	702	7	6
		Wolseley 1560	660	0	0
	Ideal Home, October 1960	Wolseley 16/60	853	8	9
	Which, 1964	Ford Consul Corsair 4-Door De Luxe	716	10	0
		Hillman Super Minx MK11	743	13	9
		Triumph Vitesse	744	17	11
		Vauxhall Victor Super	687	18	3

Continued

8.4.3 Prices, Selected *continued*

Item	Source	Description	Price £	s.	d.
Bicycles	*Which*, August 1964	Moulton Standard M1 3-Speed	26	9	6
		Moulton Safari M3 4-Speed	43	19	6
Vehicles	*Complete Catalogue of Austin Cars since 1945*	Mini Cooper Mark I, 55 b.h.p., 2-Door Saloon	679	0	0 (price when introduced)
		Mini Mark II, 850 & 1100, 38 b.h.p.	509	0	0 (price when introduced)
	Homes and Gardens, June 1969	Datsun 1600	968	8	4
Travel					
Holidays	*The Observer Weekend Review*, January 5, 1964	15 Days in Hungary, Milbanke Tours Ltd.	59	17	0
		11 Days on the Costa Brava by Globalair	30	9	0
		15 Days in the Sun by Air, Horizon Holidays from	43	0	0
	Thomas Cook Archives, 1965	14 Nights in Majorca from	48	7	0 (all inclusive)
		14 Nights on Costa del Sol	68	19	0
		14 Nights on the Italian Riviera	50	18	0
		14 Nights on the Costa Brava	47	3	0
Miscellany					
Saddle Bag	*Oxendales*, Manchester, 1960	Cycle Saddle Bag in Leather		17	6
Office Equipment		Empire Aristocrat Typewriter	19	19	0
	Ideal Home, October 1965	British Home Office	63	0	0
Blinds		Reliant Venetian Blinds	4	3	0 (per blind)
Lighting		Infra Red Combined Heat and Light Fitting	1	17	6 (post 3/6 extra)
Office Equipment	*Which*, 1968	Boots Model 40 Typewriter	27	6	0
		Imperial Concorde	24	15	0
		Smith Corona	18	19	6

8.5 Finance and Economic Data

8.5.1 Finance, Personal

	1960		1961		1962		1963		1964		1965		1966		1967		1968		1969	
	s.	d.	s.	d.	s.	d.	s.	d.	s.	d.	s.	d.	s.	d.	s.	d.	s.	d.	s.	d.
Income Tax Rates[1]	7	9	7	9	7	9	7	9	7	9	7	9	8	3	8	3	8	3	8	3
Retirement Pension:																				
Married	80	0	92	6	92	6	109	0	109	6	130	0	130	0	146	0	146	0	162	0
Single	50	0	57	6	57	6	67	6	67	6	80	0	80	0	90	0	90	0	100	0
Child Benefit:																				
Second			8	0			8	0	8	0	8	0			8	0	15	0	18	0
Third and Subsequent			10	0			10	0	10	0	10	0			10	0	17	0	20	0
Unemployment Benefit: Men, Single Women and Widows			57	6			67	6	67	6	80	0			90	0	90	0	100	0
Base Interest Rates in percent[2]	5%		5%		6%		4%		4%		7%		6%		6½%		8%		7%	

Mitchell, B.R. *British Historical Statistics*, Cambridge University Press, 1988; Bank of England; Department of Social Security.

Blank space denotes no data available. [1]The rates apply to years ended 5th April. [2]The rates apply to January of each year.

8.5.2 Financial Markets

8.5.2a Closing Price of UK Major Stocks in January

	1960	1961	1962	1963	1964	1965	1966	1967	1968	1969
Barclays Bank	144/0	120/0	55/0	47/3	37/1½	36/9	36/1½	34/1½	45/1½	84/0
Boots the Chemists	32/0	29/9	36/0	35/3	27/6	18/0	18/3	21/3	21/4½	30/4½
Burmah Oil	54/9	59/6	49/6	44/6	69/3	61/10½	56/3	70/6	67/6	125/0
Courtaulds	67/9	59/0	47/6	55/1½	77/9	23/4½	22/9	21/10½	23/0	34/9
Guinness	82/6	72/6	60/6	51/6	23/9	24/3	22/0	19/0	23/6	28/3
ICI[1]	62/6	75/3	81/6	61/6	50/0	49/6	49/1½	45/1½	48/9	74/6
Marks and Spencer	78/3	104/0	106/9	100/6	73/0	48/1½	40/3	40/4½	39/7½	60/7½
Reckitt and Colman	68/3	90/0	99/0	44/9	39/9	36/6	32/1½	35/0	36/6	68/3
Schweppes	34/9	38/3	41/10	38/0	28/10½	16/7½	13/1½	15/3	18/0	26/0
Unilever	144/0	180/0	55/0	47/3	37/1½	36/9	36/1½	34/1½	45/1½	84/0
Viyella[2]	36/4½	60/6	34/6	43/0	24/1½	23/0	15/3½	16/0¾	11/5¼	22/3¾
Whitbread & Co.	137/0	135/6	37/9	42/4½	19/9	19/0	16/7½	15/9	9/3	12/0

Financial Times, 1960–1969.

Fractions quoted as parts of £1=32. [1]Imperial Chemical Industries. [2]1962–1966, Viyella was known as Viyella Investments.

8.5.2b Commodities

	Best Coal (price per ton)		Raw Cotton (per lb.)	Gold (average market price)	Sugar (annual average world price)	Wheat (per ton)		Wool (average import value)
	s.	d.	old pence (d.)	£ per troy oz.	£ sterling per metric ton	s.	d.[1]	pence per lb.
1960	84	5	21.66	12.560	28.030	21	4	50.0
1961	89	9	23.27	12.55	25.279	20	7	48.2
1962	88	9	23.66	12.504	25.572	21	10	47.5
1963	89	11	22.80	12.530	70.571	£1.05[2]		53.4
1964	88	8	22.48	12.566	50.309	1.10		61.2
1965	88	1	22.49	12.584	21.171	1.08		49.6
1966	88	1	21.70	12.588	17.592	1.09		50.6
1967	66[1]			12.822	19.051	1.10		46.2
1968	70			16.378	21.482	1.12		43.5
1969	75			17.199	33.294	1.16		46.0

Mitchell, B.R. *British Historical Statistics*, Cambridge University Press, 1988; World Gold Council; Czarnikow Sugar; Digest of Energy Statistics.

Blank space denotes no data available. Original source, Sauerbeck A. *Prices of Commodities and the Precious Metals, Journal of the Statistical Society*. From 1967, *Annual Statement of Trade Statistics of the UK*. [1]New pence per hundredweight. [2]Price in pounds per hundredweight.

8.5.2c Foreign Exchange Rates

	Frankfurt Deutschmarks per £1	Paris Francs per £1	New York Dollars per £1
1960	11.740	13.770	2.8100
1961	11.256	13.745	2.8023
1962	11.224	13.758	2.8078
1963	11.161	13.721	2.8003
1964	11.099	13.684	2.7927
1965	11.165	13.702	2.7962
1966	11.168	13.723	2.7932
1967	10.971	13.539	2.7563
1968	9.555	11.855	2.3937
1969	9.379	12.424	2.3903

Mitchell, B.R. *British Historical Statistics*, Cambridge University Press, 1988.

8.5.3 Balance of Payments and GNP

8.5.3a Balance of Payments

	Merchandise Exports	Merchandise Imports	Overall Visible Balance	Exports of Services	Imports of Services	Property Income from Abroad	Property Income Paid Abroad	Balance of Current Transfers	Overall Invisible Balance	Overall Current Balance
	£m	£m	£m	£m	£m	£m	£m	£m	£m	£m
1960	3,737	4,138	-401	1,419	1,411	671	438	-68	+528	-228
1961	3,903	4,043	-140	1,488	1,467	676	422	-88	+185	+47
1962	4,003	4,103	-100	1,523	1,505	754	420	-97	+255	+155
1963	4,331	4,450	-119	1,546	1,577	842	444	-123	+244	+125
1964	4,568	5,111	-543	1,633	1,709	900	494	-158	+272	-371
1965	4,913	5,173	-260	1,701	1,799	1,005	557	-168	+182	-79
1966	5,276	5,384	-108	1,890	1,875	979	576	-181	+237	+129
1967	5,241	5,840	-599	2,146	2,015	1,001	601	-216	+315	-284
1968	6,433	7,145	-712	2,547	2,235	1,135	776	-223	+448	-264
1969	7,269	7,478	-209	2,820	2,452	1,376	844	-206	+694	+485

Mitchell, B.R. *British Historical Statistics*, Cambridge University Press, 1988.

Original source, Feinstein, C.H. *National Income, Expenditure and Output of the UK, 1855-1965*, Cambridge, 1972

8.5.3b GNP at Factor Cost and Its Component Incomes at Current Prices

	Income from Employment	Income from Self Employment	Gross Trading Profits of Companies	Gross Trading Surplus of Public Enterprises	Rent	Stock Appreciation	Gross Domestic Product	Net Property Income from Abroad	Gross National Product	Capital Consumption	National Income
	£m	£m	£m	£m	£m	£m	£m	£m	£m	£m	£m
1960	15,174	2,008	3,730	72	1,246	122	22,759	233	22,992	2,047	20,945
1961	16,396	2,314	3,625	747	1,336	171	24,247	254	24,501	2,184	22,317
1962	17,298	2,469	3,581	829	1,449	152	25,474	334	25,808	2,380	23,428
1963	18,190	2,586	4,094	948	1,522	152	27,188	398	27,586	2,615	24,971
1964	19,730	2,729	4,546	1,043	1,668	243	29,473	406	29,879	2,793	27,086
1965	21,310	2,989	4,761	1,117	1,864	291	31,750	448	32,198	3,000	29,198
1966	22,842	3,183	4,618	1,166	2,026	305	33,530	403	33,933	3,247	30,686
1967	23,799	3,338	4,661	1,259	2,204	137	35,124	400	35,524	3,432	32,092
1968	25,455	3,646	5,302	1,514	2,443	583	37,777	359	38,136	3,732	34,404
1969	27,227	3,893	5,731	1,626	2,743	733	40,487	532	41,019	4,078	36,941

Mitchell, B.R. *British Historical Statistics*, Cambridge University Press, 1988.

Original source, Feinstein, C.H. *National Income, Expenditure and Output of the UK, 1855-1965*, Cambridge, 1972. Thereafter *CSO National Income and Expenditure* (later National Accounts) annually.

– Nine –
1970–1979

Years of Change

PRIME MINISTERS
Edward Heath (Conservative), June 1970–February 1974
Harold Wilson (Labour), February 1974–April 1976
Jim Callaghan (Labour), April 1976–May 1979
Margaret Thatcher (Conservative), May 1979–November 1990

CHANCELLORS OF THE EXCHEQUER
I. Macleod, June 1970–July 1970
A. Barber, July 1970–February 1974
D. Healey, February 1974–May 1979

In 1970 unemployment was at its highest level in years, inflation was raging out of control, and economic growth was at its lowest level since 1964. The violence in Northern Ireland had exploded in 1969, and British troops had been placed on the streets of Belfast.

Edward Heath's Conservative Government came to power in June 1970 amid general chaos. One of the first measures adopted to deal with the chronic unemployment was the 'lame-duck' policy of investing public money in redundant industries, such as shipbuilding. While this alleviated the employment situation in the short term, creating jobs in seemingly uncompetitive areas of the economy, it also helped to increase public expenditure by 8 per cent between 1970–72, and subsequently exacerbated the rising level of inflation. Attempts were made to introduce restrictive wage policies to help control inflation. One of the results of these policies was the first coal strike since the 1926 General Strike, and subsequent wage increases for the industry of more than 30 per cent, in comparison to the 7.5 originally proposed by the National Coal Board.

Rapid world commodity prices caused an even worse Balance of Payments crisis than anticipated, and the outbreak of the Yom Kippur War between Israel and the Arab States caused oil prices to quadruple in 1973. Although the Chancellor of the Exchequer tried to deal with the situation with massive reductions in public expenditure and tighter credit restrictions the ensuing Conservative defeat in the General Election of 1974 hardly came as a surprise.

The Wilson administration of 1974–79 did not fare much better.

The Public Sector Borrowing Requirement (PSBR) increased by 75 per cent between 1975–77, and the value of the pound decreased radically which led the Government to go to the International Monetary Fund (IMF) for monetary aid.

Inflation continued to increase at a higher rate than Britain's European competitors, although it fell into single figures (8.2 per cent) in 1978 for the first time in five years. Unemployment, however, reached a peak of 1.6 million in 1977.

Between 1970–79 Britain had four different Prime Ministers and experienced several different types of monetary policy. It suffered from chronic unemployment and high inflation, and lagged behind its export competitors in technology and business practices. Prices doubled and unemployment tripled. The Labour Government lost public support and sympathy, and instead, in the election of 1979, Britain elected its first woman Prime Minister, Margaret Thatcher.

9.1 Historical Snapshots

9.1 Historical Snapshots

1970	Development of the 'floppy disk' computer memory by IBM.
	Boeing 747 jumbo jets enter transatlantic service.
	Rover announces its new all-purpose four-wheel drive Range Rover.
	Equal Pay Act, Matrimonial Proceedings and Property Acts are passed through Parliament.
	Rolls Royce declares itself bankrupt.
	The *Daily Sketch,* Britain's oldest newspaper, closes down.
1971	Decimalization of sterling.
	1d. and 3d. coins cease to be legal tender.
1972	Unemployment rises to above one million.
	House of Commons pass bill to bring Britain into EEC.
1973	Value Added Tax (VAT) introduced.
	Share values fall £2 million as Arab funds are withdrawn from banks.
1975	Equal Opportunities Commission set up.
1976	The Bank of England raises its minimum lending rate from 13 to 15 per cent.
	Building Societies put up mortgage interest rates to 12.25 per cent.
1977	Development of the neutron bomb in USA.
	The Government introduces a bill giving the Prices Commission power to freeze prices.
	British Aerospace is formed to run Britain's nationalized aviation industry.
	Inflation drops to 11 per cent.
	New, smaller £1 notes are introduced.
	Swan Hunter Shipyard loses a £52 million order because fitters cannot agree on overtime.
1979	Margaret Thatcher becomes Britain's first woman Prime Minister.
	Building Societies put the mortgage rate up 3.5 per cent to a record 15 per cent.

Chronicle of Britain, J.L. International Publishing, 1992; Williams, T.I. *Invention and Discovery in the 20th Century*, Harrap, 1990.

9.2 Earnings and Employment

9.2.1 Earnings, Standard Tables

9.2.1a Incomes and Wages

	1970[1]		1971	1972	1973	1974	1975	1976	1977	1978	1979
	s.	d.	£	£	£	£	£	£	£	£	£
Full Time Male											
Solicitor								106.0	118.1	124.4	139.1
General Practitioner						88.9	106.7	139.3	153.2	163.3	178.5
Police Constable				41.0	40.2	48.2	64.1	78.5	80.5	91.0	109.8
Teacher (secondary)				42.1		52.8	73.5	90.3	94.1	102.7	107.4
Nurse				25.2	39.9		53.9	81.3	86.7	87.4	74.3
Train Driver	417	0		30.7	35.5	43.9	64.3	74.5	80.2	86.0	78.2
Coal Miner (face trained)	320	0			36.9	51.3	74.5	80.7	84.9	112.4	126.7
Fitter	325	0		33.4	37.0	50.1	60.5	70.5	73.5	84.4	98.7
Turner	258	6		33.9	35.5	47.4	59.3	67.3	77.5	81.9	
Bricklayer				26.9	40.6	46.5	57.6	65.8	71.5	79.6	90.6
Labourer				27.5		39.7	49.6	57.8	64.1	68.6	
Compositor	373	6		34.6	39.7	49.3	58.6	74.3	79.6	91.0	109.8
Farm Worker	263	0		19.9	22.2	33.0	37.4	46.8	51.6	62.5	66.9
Numerical Clerk				29.4	31.4	40.0	54.1	60.6	66.1	71.8	78.2
Baker	275	0		22.2	40.6						
Textile Worker	242	4		27.4	39.4	42.6	50.5	60.0	70.9	68.8	84.9
Full Time Female											
Solicitor					58.3						
Teacher (secondary)						45.3	63.9	78.8	82.3	90.1	93.7
Nurse				21.2		26.0	42.8	49.7	52.4	54.0	61.7
Farm Worker	197	6									
Numerical Clerk				21.0	21.4	25.9	33.8	41.4	46.7	52.9	58.6
Baker	196	8			36.0						
Textile Worker	185	4		16.9	18.7	22.8	29.1	34.9	39.3	46.9	
Typist				18.5	21.0	23.9	31.9	39.8	43.8	50.1	55.8
Nursery Nurse						21.1	35.4	43.5	47.4	47.9	53.6
Hairdresser					17.4	22.2	31.5	38.0	41.7	46.4	

New Earnings Survey.

All figures are weekly earnings. Blank space denotes no available data. [1]For 1970 earnings are in shillings and pence. From 1971, earnings are in pounds.

9.2.1b Average Weekly Earnings

	Bricks, Pottery, Glass and Cement	Ship-building and Marine Engineering	Textiles	Clothing	Food, Drink and Tobacco	Paper, Printing and Publishing	Building and Contracting	Public Administration	Transport and Communication	All Industries Covered
	£	£	£	£	£	£	£	£	£	£
Males										
1970	28.72	29.59	25.29	24.12	28.00	33.08	26.85	21.60	29.68	28.05
1971	31.95	33.13	28.02	26.00	31.60	36.04	30.11	24.51	33.73	30.93
1972	37.25	34.98	32.05	29.52	35.75	41.21	36.59	26.93	37.97	35.82
1973	42.59	41.60	36.75	33.90	40.24	48.69	41.41	31.32	43.31	40.92
1974	50.40	50.40	43.74	40.37	47.97	54.96	48.75	37.87	52.06	48.63
1975	61.07	67.53	53.65	48.16	60.29	65.17	60.38	49.88	63.81	59.58
1976	68.82	72.09	61.19	53.30	66.81	73.88	65.80	53.97	71.22	66.97
1977	75.15	76.37	65.32	61.61	72.46	82.09	72.91	59.04	76.96	72.89
1978	87.42	88.64	75.96	67.50	83.91	96.79	81.77	67.15	88.03	93.50
1979	102.32	95.46	87.35	80.37	99.79	114.88	94.06	76.92	103.30	96.94
Females										
1970	13.88	14.17	13.40	13.15	14.34	15.51	12.83	15.39	19.30	13.99
1971	15.64	17.23	15.09	14.53	16.65	17.10	13.42	17.57	22.32	15.80
1972	18.32	18.29	17.28	16.60	19.40	19.86	15.20	18.52	24.95	18.30
1973	21.16	24.09	19.89	19.03	22.68	22.79	18.96	23.37	28.84	21.16
1974	27.54	28.01	25.52	24.04	28.75	30.09	23.92	29.18	34.58	27.01
1975	35.20	39.19	31.76	28.70	37.28	38.51	30.45	38.64	44.07	34.19
1976	42.22	46.08	37.93	33.59	43.69	45.20	36.11	43.62	50.23	40.61
1977	45.59	49.55	40.95	38.08	47.51	48.87	39.14	46.41	53.25	44.31
1978	52.12	56.59	46.02	41.94	53.85	55.33	42.97	52.98	63.79	50.03
1979	60.06	61.00	52.44	50.43	62.86	67.15	48.23	57.04	72.38	58.24

Mitchell, B.R. *British Historical Statistics*, Cambridge University Press, 1988.

9.2.2 Regional Earnings

	South East	Greater London	Rest of South East	East Anglia	South West	West Mids	East Mids	Yorks and Humber	North West	North	Eng- land	Wales	Scot- land	UK
	£	£	£	£	£	£	£	£	£	£	£	£	£	£
Full Time Male														
1970	32.6	34.7	30.2	27.0	27.8	30.9	28.0	27.9	29.5	28.5	30.3	28.8	28.3	30.0
1971	35.8	38.0	33.2	30.1	30.9	33.5	30.7	30.6	32.3	30.8	33.2	31.8	31.3	32.9
1972	39.8	42.3	37.1	33.3	34.2	37.1	34.5	34.3	35.7	34.8	36.9	35.8	35.0	36.7
1973	45.1	47.6	42.3	38.5	39.5	42.4	39.2	39.3	40.7	40.1	42.1	40.6	40.4	41.9
1974	51.5	54.9	47.9	44.6	44.9	47.5	44.7	45.1	46.4	46.2	48.0	46.2	46.0	47.7
1975	65.3	69.7	60.6	56.2	56.2	58.4	58.6	58.4	59.1	60.5	60.9	59.0	60.3	60.8
1976	77.0	82.2	71.7	66.4	67.2	68.9	67.3	68.9	70.3	71.4	71.9	69.8	71.6	71.8
1977	84.1	89.4	78.8	72.6	73.4	76.3	74.5	75.4	76.8	77.5	78.8	76.5	78.3	78.6
1978	95.3	101.0	89.4	82.6	82.5	85.7	85.4	86.1	87.1	88.4	89.3	86.1	88.5	89.1
1979	108.5	115.5	101.9	95.9	92.4	98.1	97.1	99.1	99.2	99.7	101.6	97.6	101.2	101.4
Full Time Female														
1970	18.1	19.4	16.4	14.4	15.4	15.7	15.4	14.9	15.5	15.0	16.5	15.9	15.3	16.3
1971	20.1	21.6	18.1	17.0	17.1	17.6	17.1	16.7	17.4	17.2	18.4	17.8	17.4	18.3
1972	22.6	24.3	20.5	19.2	19.3	19.6	19.3	18.9	19.6	19.4	20.7	19.9	19.5	20.5
1973	25.3	27.2	23.1	21.9	21.7	22.2	21.9	21.3	21.9	21.5	23.2	22.4	22.2	23.1
1974	29.7	31.9	27.0	25.0	25.7	26.0	23.6	24.8	25.6	25.5	27.2	25.7	25.7	26.9
1975	41.0	44.3	37.0	34.8	35.7	35.1	34.9	35.6	35.8	36.2	37.7	35.8	35.9	37.4
1976	50.0	53.5	45.9	43.4	44.4	44.8	42.9	43.3	44.4	45.0	46.5	45.5	44.6	46.2
1977	54.9	58.5	50.7	48.4	49.6	49.2	47.2	47.9	49.4	49.6	51.3	50.2	48.9	51.0
1978	61.1	65.3	56.2	53.5	53.6	54.9	52.5	52.9	54.4	54.4	56.7	53.9	54.6	56.4
1979	68.4	73.3	63.3	60.2	60.0	61.4	59.7	59.4	60.5	60.6	63.5	61.4	60.4	63.0

New Earnings Survey.

Earnings are averaged, before tax and include overtime.

9.2.3 Incomes, Miscellaneous

9.2.3a UK Pay: Highest Full Time Male Weekly Earnings, 1979

Occupation	£
Medical Practitioners	178.50
Top Managers: Trading Organisations	171.50
Finance, Insurance, Tax Specialists	162.70
Police Inspectors and above, Fire Service Officers	155.90
Ships' Officers	153.60
University Academic Staff	148.90
Company Secretaries	146.50
Deputies: Coalmining	144.80
Marketing and Sales Managers	144.60
Judges, Barristers and Solicitors	139.10

Labour Research, January, 1980.

Original source, *New Earnings Survey.*

9.2.4 Employment

9.2.4a Unemployment by Region

	1970 000's	1971 000's	1972 000's	1973 000's	1974 000's	1975 000's	1976 000's	1977 000's	1978 000's	1979 000's
Males										
United Kingdom	522.9	665.9	735.6	522.8	523.8	764.8	1,005.6	1,044.8	1,009.5	930.1
North	52.9	62.4	69.0	51.3	50.8	62.9	74.2	79.4	83.7	81.0
Yorkshire and Humberside	38.4	64.8	70.6	48.2	47.1	65.6	85.6	86.1	87.6	82.2
East Midlands	27.4	34.5	36.6	28.4	28.6	43.5	55.4	57.4	56.4	52.5
East Anglia	12.0	16.8	15.7	10.6	11.1	19.2	26.0	27.9	25.7	22.7
South East	110.2	132.5	140.3	98.4	100.4	163.6	236.5	245.4	222.3	192.3
South West	31.3	37.3	39.0	28.6	34.6	59.2	78.1	81.5	75.3	64.9
West Midlands	38.0	56.6	68.4	41.7	n/a	70.8	97.1	93.1	88.0	85.4
North West	68.3	93.9	116.2	87.4	83.7	120.0	147.8	149.6	145.0	134.9
England	390.6	498.9	555.9	391.7	397.8	604.2	800.5	820.7	784.0	715.6
Wales	31.0	36.1	40.7	29.7	32.2	46.9	58.7	60.5	61.6	57.1
Scotland	73.7	99.7	108.4	77.9	70.9	84.6	109.9	122.8	120.1	114.4
Northern Ireland	27.6	31.1	30.5	23.4	22.8	28.9	36.5	40.8	43.8	43.0
Females										
United Kingdom	95.1	126.2	149.9	107.5	107.2	176.4	296.0	357.9	373.4	365.6
North	6.6	11.4	9.3	6.7	7.3	14.7	23.8	29.6	32.6	32.6
Yorkshire and Humberside	7.4	10.3	12.7	8.8	8.6	13.2	24.0	28.8	31.6	32.3
East Midlands	4.4	6.0	6.4	4.4	5.2	9.7	15.6	18.5	19.5	18.5
East Anglia	1.8	2.9	2.9	1.9	2.0	3.8	6.6	8.2	8.4	8.1
South East	16.4	20.3	22.4	15.6	16.7	33.6	63.8	76.0	73.6	65.4
South West	6.4	7.8	8.2	5.8	6.7	13.2	21.7	26.1	27.1	25.6
West Midlands	7.2	9.9	12.8	8.6	n/a	18.1	29.5	34.2	34.5	34.9
North West	9.0	16.0	21.1	15.0	15.1	24.6	40.6	49.5	52.6	52.1
England	63.1	84.5	100.6	70.9	74.0	130.9	225.6	270.8	279.8	269.4
Wales	6.6	8.3	9.3	6.7	7.3	10.5	16.7	20.8	23.2	23.4
Scotland	17.2	24.1	29.1	21.0	17.8	24.7	38.4	49.3	52.0	53.9
Northern Ireland	8.2	9.3	10.9	8.9	8.5	10.3	15.3	17.0	18.4	18.9

Regional Trends, HMSO.

Figures are annual averages. Original source, Department of Employment.

9.2.4b Employment by Region

	1970	1971	1972[1]	1973	1974	1975	1976	1977	1978	1979
	000's	000's	000's	000's	000's	000's	000's	000's	000's	000's
Males										
United Kingdom	14,129	13,835	13,608	13,844	13,671	13,548	13,449	13,363	13,385	13,343
North	801	776	775	791	772	770	760	763	749	761
Yorkshire and Humberside	1,238	1,203	1,187	1,205	1,208	1,199	1,193	1,193	1,187	1,196
East Midlands	872	851	850	868	902	894	885	905	911	904
East Anglia	404	391	391	403	[2]	[2]	[2]	410	412	408
South East	4,675	4,617	4,455	4,453	4,742	4,660	4,621	4,215	4,235	4,224
South West	820	814	837	856	906	898	901	908	915	910
West Midlands	1,423	1,389	1,364	1,390	1,381	1,332	1,319	1,329	1,331	1,318
North West	1,725	1,682	1,636	1,549	1,598	1,566	1,555	1,544	1,541	1,514
England	11,958	11,725	11,494	11,620	11,509	11,319	11,234	11,268	11,281	11,247
Wales	603	603	630	636	621	608	605	608	614	610
Scotland	1,258	1,207	1,194	1,221	1,219	1,219	1,212	1,198	1,200	1,199
Northern Ireland	298	293	288	293	296	n/a	n/a	288	289	288
Females										
United Kingdom	8,761	8,674	8,512	8,893	8,990	9,172	9,172	9,255	9,372	9,527
North	469	466	455	482	485	496	488	493	493	513
Yorkshire and Humberside	738	721	704	737	779	787	786	790	801	805
East Midlands	520	512	512	542	599	597	590	612	624	620
East Anglia	233	229	231	249	[2]	[2]	[2]	270	272	283
South East	3,023	2,999	2,914	3,003	3,323	3,319	3,282	3,012	3,056	3,008
South West	490	493	508	543	605	601	615	635	651	661
West Midlands	836	828	807	852	887	863	856	873	883	882
North West	1,117	1,097	1,063	1,104	1,111	1,104	1,092	1,102	1,109	1,132
England	7,424	7,345	7,194	7,512	7,789	7,767	7,709	7,786	7,889	7,986
Wales	327	327	342	364	380	378	377	390	401	403
Scotland	819	811	795	828	860	855	860	873	867	894
Northern Ireland	189	189	181	187	198	n/a	n/a	206	214	225

Regional Trends, HMSO.

Blank space denotes no data available. Original source, Department of Employment. [1]From 1972 estimates are based on censuses of employment. Prior to this, estimates were based on counts of national insurance cards. [2]Numbers for East Anglia are included with those for the South East.

9.2.4c Occupational Analysis, 1974

Occupation	Males %	Females %
Managerial (general management)	0.9	0.1
Professional and related supported management	4.9	1.0
Literary, artistic and sports	0.6	0.3
Professional and related in science	6.3	0.8
Managerial (excluding general management)	5.2	1.1
Clerical and related	9.7	33.6
Selling	4.4	9.3
Security and protective service	1.8	0.3
Catering, cleaning, hairdressing etc.	3.9	19.9
Farming, fishing and related	1.7	0.3
Materials processing (excluding metals)	3.8	3.0
Making and repairing (excluding metals)	5.8	6.0
Processing, making and repairing and related (metal and electrical)	21.4	2.8
Painting, repetitive assembling, product inspecting, packaging and related	5.0	8.8
Construction, mining and related not identified	5.6	0
Transport, operating, materials moving and storing	12.1	1.0
Miscellaneous	3.5	0.3
Professional and related in education, welfare and health	3.4	11.4
All Occupations	100.0	100.0

Jones, J. *Equal Pay and Equal Opportunities*, Transport and General Workers Union Pamphlet, 1974

9.2.4d Married Women Working

Age	1931%	1971%
20–24	18.5	45.7
25–34	13.2	38.4
35–44	10.1	54.5
45–54	8.5	57.0
55–59	7.0	45.5

Jones, J. *Equal Pay and Equal Opportunities*,
Transport and General Workers Union Pamphlet, 1974.

9.3 Consumer Expenditure

9.3.1 Consumer Expenditure, Standard Table

	Food	Alcoholic Drink	Tobacco	Housing	Fuel and Light	Clothing	Durable House-hold Goods	Motor Cars and Motor Cycles	Other Goods	Other Services	Total Con-sumer Expen-diture
	£m	£m	£m	£m	£m	£m	£m	£m	£m	£m	£m
1970	6,349	2,300	1,720	4,048	1,495	2,753	1,397	997	4,832	5,921	31,778
1971	6,974	2,593	1,791	4,619	1,619	2,990	1,636	1,438	5,408	6,663	35,599
1972	7,412	2,910	1,808	5,279	1,797	3,365	2,069	1,793	6,184	7,599	40,183
1973	8,471	3,423	1,945	6,254	1,897	3,847	2,429	1,799	7,033	8,725	45,759
1974	9,759	3,915	2,238	7,410	2,270	4,474	2,678	1,586	8,600	9,923	52,626
1975	11,961	4,856	2,748	9,221	2,914	5,166	3,232	2,135	10,534	12,252	64,652
1976	13,941	5,759	3,107	10,635	3,590	5,749	3,742	2,654	12,019	14,470	74,850
1977	16,047	6,645	3,632	12,422	4,258	6,527	4,066	3,017	13,960	16,698	85,948
1978	17,927	7,462	3,910	14,020	4,656	7,704	4,849	4,350	15,873	19,252	98,867
1979	20,364	8,847	4,270	16,756	5,340	8,947	6,035	5,686	18,921	22,893	117,071

CSO Economic Trends Annual Supplement and *CSO National Income and Expenditure.*

9.3.2 Regional Household Expenditure

	Housing	Fuel, Light and Power	Food	Alco-holic Drink	Tobacco	Clothing and Foot-wear	Durable House-hold Goods	Trans-port and Vehicles	Other Goods	Services and Miscel-laneous	Total	Average
	£/wk	£/wk	£/wk	£/wk	£/wk	£/wk	£/wk	£/wk	£/wk	£/wk	£/wk	£/wk
UK	3.80	1.82	7.71	1.37	1.33	2.73	1.94	4.09	2.23	2.85	29.85	10.22
North	3.08	1.63	7.23	1.64	1.47	2.57	1.76	3.85	1.90	2.51	27.67	9.55
Yorkshire and Humberside	2.87	1.64	7.21	1.38	1.31	2.30	1.75	3.30	1.94	2.51	26.20	9.13
East Midlands	3.11	1.81	7.43	1.35	1.25	2.52	2.09	3.58	2.14	2.33	27.61	9.36
East Anglia	3.26	1.73	7.41	1.14	1.08	2.21	2.19	4.30	2.42	2.36	28.11	9.57
South East	4.77	1.87	8.04	1.29	1.27	2.92	2.21	4.72	2.57	3.41	33.07	11.68
Greater London	5.19	1.77	8.22	1.45	1.46	3.15	2.28	4.39	2.49	3.41	33.80	12.26
Rest of South East	4.49	1.94	7.91	1.19	1.14	2.76	2.17	4.95	2.62	3.41	32.57	11.30
South West	3.80	1.80	7.22	1.03	1.02	2.36	1.79	4.17	2.07	2.63	27.88	9.80
West Midlands	3.63	1.73	7.91	1.55	1.38	2.91	1.73	4.36	2.27	2.78	30.24	10.05
North West	3.90	1.99	7.79	1.57	1.49	2.67	1.74	3.85	2.15	3.03	30.17	10.11
Wales	3.30	1.77	7.75	1.18	1.33	2.70	2.01	3.56	2.04	2.21	27.85	9.29
Scotland	3.32	1.90	7.81	1.49	1.54	2.88	1.79	3.54	2.04	2.60	28.91	9.66
Northern Ireland	2.75	1.96	7.73	1.01	1.38	3.64	1.52	4.30	1.67	2.35	28.31	8.57

Regional Trends.

Original source, *Family Expenditure Survey* and *Central Statistical Office.*

9.4 Prices

9.4.1 Food Prices

9.4.1a Food Basket

Article (per lb. unless otherwise stated)	1971 p.	1972 p.	1973 p.	1974 p.	1975 p.	1976 p.	1977 p.	1978 p.	1979 p.
White Wheat Bread									
Wrapped and sliced (1¼ lb./800g)	9.5	10.4	11.3	13.9	16.0	19.2	22.1	26.7	30.0
Unwrapped and sliced (1¼ lb./800g)	9.4	10.3	11.4	14.3	16.5	20.4	24.5	28.6	32.3
Other Bread[1] (14oz./400g)	6.4	7.3	8.3	10.4	11.5	14.8	17.2	19.5	21.7
Flour (wheat) white, self raising	11.2	12.1	14.0	19.4	19.6	21.2	31.9	35.6	36.6
Rice, (whole grain, polished)	8.4	8.4	12.3	22.0	19.3	19.1	23.8	26.5	28.1
Beef, home-killed, first quality:									
Sirloin (without bone)	53.2	63.1	78.3	79.2	96.4	133.4	141.4	172.0	206.7
Brisket (with bone)	22.2	27.0	36.3						
Brisket (without bone)				47.1	55.1	76.8	80.7	88.2	101.3
Pork, home-killed:									
Leg (foot off)	30.5	35.3	47.7	49.1	62.0	69.6	73.4	79.9	87.5
Loin (without bone)	35.8	42.9	55.2	61.9	76.3	83.2	89.6	98.9	107.3
Ham, cooked, sliced (without bone)	57.9	61.3	81.0	86.4	103.4	117.4	121.2	131.7	152.4
Bacon:									
Back, smoked	37.2	44.8	63.0	70.6	80.5	91.8	95.9	103.4	115.9
Streaky smoked	22.5	27.9	42.8	47.2	59.8	72.9	74.0	74.7	80.3
Fish, fresh cod fillets	28.5	32.5	45.9	49.1	56.9	74.0	90.1	95.6	107.2
Margarine, standard quality (½ lb./250g)	6.3	6.0	7.1	9.8	11.7	12.0	15.7	14.6	15.9
Lard (1lb./500g)	9.4	8.6	12.7	18.8	19.6	20.5	25.0	24.4	25.6
Milk (pint)	5.5	5.5	5.5	4.5	7.0	9.5	11.5	12.5	15.0
Butter	28.4	24.3	22.4	24.3	33.3	48.9	54.1	66.7	79.7
Cheese	25.8	32.0	32.5	39.3	45.8	51.9	67.2	71.9	86.9
Eggs, fresh, home produced, first quality:									
Weight 63–70g size 2 (dozen)	22.1	22.3	44.2	41.6	42.4	50.7	53.3	54.0	66.2
Potatoes [2]:									
White	1.9	2.2	2.4	3.1	6.7	11.5	4.2	4.1	6.4
Red				3.6	7.2	12.0	4.7	4.7	7.2
Cabbage, green	4.0	4.3	5.6	6.3	9.3	10.0	6.6	8.4	10.1
Onions, ripe	4.0	4.7	5.3	7.0	9.5	14.0	8.8	9.8	12.6
Apples, eating	8.5	12.8	10.6	13.2	13.2	15.0	24.6	17.5	18.2
Oranges	7.7	9.1	10.3	12.0	13.6	15.6	21.8	20.5	21.8
Sugar, white granulated (2lb.)	8.5	8.7	10.2	14.8	22.6				
Sugar, white granulated (1kg)						25.2	26.6	29.6	33.1
Coffee (pure, roasted)	57.7	60.5	62.7	78.5	80.5	145.4	343.6	236.9	221.1
Prunes (dried)	18.0	19.3	27.3	25.9	28.8	37.9	65.3		
Tea:									
Higher priced	43.6	43.2	43.2	45.2	50.8	65.2	135.2	110.2	103.2
Medium priced	34.0	33.6	33.2	36.0	42.0	54.8	116.4	91.2	92.0
Lower priced	32.4	32.0	32.0	33.6	38.0	50.0	110.0	78.8	79.6
Cocoa (not sweetened) proprietary brands in tins	14.4	14.3	14.8	23.0	26.5	35.9	61.1	97.2	104.5
Salt, cooking (packaged)	3.8	4.3							

Central Statistical Office.

Blank space denotes no available prices. Collected by the Department of Employment in 200 areas in the UK. [1]Bread baked from a proprietary brand of brown flour. [2]1971–1973 inclusive not specified white or red.

9.4.2 Prices, General Articles

	1970	1971[1]	1972	1973	1974	1975	1976	1977	1978	1979
	s. d.[1]	p.	p.	p.	p.	p.	p.	p.	p.	p.
Aspirin (100)			12.0						20.0	25.0
Average House Price	£5,180	£5,970	£7,850	£10,690	£11,340	£12,406	£13,442	£14,768	£17,685	£22,728
Beer (1 pint)	2 2	12.0	12.5	15.0	15.0	19.5	23.0	26.5	28.5	34.0
Cadbury's Dairy Milk Chocolate (½ lb.)	3 5					31.0				
Cheddar Cheese (1 lb.)	3 10				30.0	44.0				92.0
Colmans Mustard (1 lb.)		36.0								
Daily Mail	6	2.0	3.0	3.0	4-5	6.0	7.0	8.0	8.0	9.0
Guinness Extra Stout (1 pint)	1 4					25.0				
Inland Letter Post		3.0	3.0	3.5	4.5	8.5	8.5	9.0	9.0	10.0
Mars Bar	9	4.0	4.0	4.0	7.0	7.0	8.0	9.0	10.0	11.0
Pears Transparent Soap						19.0				
Petrol (1 gallon)	6 7	34.0	36.0	37.5	50.0	76.0	77.0	84.0	78.0	80.0
Pocket Money[2]						33.0	36.0	45.0	62.0 T	78.0
Red Label Tea (1 lb.)	5 4					28.0				
Scotch Whisky (standard bottle)	61 6	307.5	317.5	275.0	293.0	350.0	390.0	430.0	445.0	470.0
Swan Vestas Matches		2.0								
The Times	1 0	5.0			6.0	8.0	10.0	12.0	15.0	

The Boots Company; Birds Eye Walls Ltd; British Library; Burmah Castrol; Cadbury's Ltd; Colmans of Norwich; Guinness Brewing GB; Halifax Building Society; Rowntrees; Royal Mail; Sainsburys Archives; The Scotch Whisky Association and Unilever Historical Archives.

Blank space denotes no available data. [1] 1970 prices are in shillings and pence. From 1971 prices are in new pence. [2] The Wall's monitor is based on a Gallup survey and provides trend data on children's income in the UK.

9.4.3 Prices, Selected

Item	Source	Description	Price £ p.
Alcoholic Drink			
Wine	*Reward*, 1972	Wine	58 (70 cl.)
Spirits		Whisky	2.69 (75.7 cl.)
Lager	*Which*, March 1973	Fosters	17 (13 fl.oz.)
		Stella Artois	15 (33 cl.)
		Holsten Export	20 (12 fl.oz.)
		Carling Black Label	9½ (9⅔ fl.oz.)
Fortified Wine	*Which*, December 1979	Cockburns Ruby Port	2.60
Spirits		Bell's Whisky	4.85
		Haig Whisky	4.60
		Teachers Whisky	4.85
		Gordons Gin	4.55
		Smirnoff Vodka	4.55
		Bacardi White Rum	5.20
		Lambs Navy Rum	5.10
		Martell 3 Star Brandy	7.10
		Courvoisier Brandy	7.00
Vermouth		Martini Dry	1.50
Appliances Domestic and Electrical			
Coffee Percolator	*Ideal Home*, January 1970	Russell Hobbs	12.60
Cooker		Creda Split Level Cooker	102.75
		Creda Simplex Cooker Hood	41.25
		Radiation New World 51A Gas Cooker	69.50
Dishwasher		Kenwood Dishwasher	105.20
Food Mixers		Kenwood Kenmix Blender	17.20½
		Braun Hand Food Mixer	16.50
Heating		Servowarm Central Heating	198.00
		Dunsley Central Heating	200.00
		Shell Central Heating	245.00
		Aladdin Oil Heater	12.96½
		Portable Gas Fire by J.Harper	6.24
		Blue Flame 98 Convector Heater	9.45
		Hoover 3kw. Fan Heater	13.00
Iron		Sunbeam Iron	7.39
Kettle		Russell Hobbs Rapide Electric Kettle	7.97½
Toaster		Philips Electric Toaster	9.43
Washing Machine		English Electric Reversomatic	110.25
Cleaners	*Which*, February 1970	Betterwear	2.59
		Bex Bissell Sweepmaster	5.60
		Prestige Ewbank 1300	5.47½
	Which, 1970	Electrolux 160	32.55
		Hotpoint Light and Easy	29.37
Food Mixer		Morphy Richards Easy Mix, Hand Held	10.97½

Continued

9.4.3 Prices, Selected *continued*

Item	Source	Description	Price
			£ p.
Freezers		Hoover 6070R	67.50
		Lec 5120	67.00
		English Electric	90.00
Irons		Hoover 4354	4.87
		Hoover Spray Steam	7.75
		Morphy Richards	7.60
Kettles		Hotpoint Electric Kettle	6.63
		Russell Hobbs Rapide	7.97½
Television		Philips Super 20in. Black and White	72.45
		GEC 2040 Colour	241.50
		Philips 511 Colour	272.00
Washing Machine		Hotpoint Auto 1504	113.00
		Bendix	229.00
Radio and Stereo Equipment		Quad Amplifier 33/303	98.00
		Quad FM Stereo	51.00
		Quad Electrostatic Loudspeakers	132.00
		Wharfedale Melton Loudspeakers	59.00
		Bang & Olufsen	39.90
		Ortofon SL15E Pick up Cartridge	36.64½
		Decca 4RC	16.80
		HMV 2164 Radio	20.85
		Aiwa AR160	11.55
		Blaupunkt Dixie	23.00
		Boots Auto Stereo Record Player	36.75
		Garrard SL 95B Turntable	55.57½
		Thorens TD124	58.81
Cookers	*Which*, 1973	Parkinson Cowan 1100 de Luxe Gas	58.00
		Newhome Corvette de Luxe Gas	55.00
		Creda Autoclean 40013 Electric	136.00
		English Electric Rapide 66	87.00
Food Mixers		Kenwood Chefette Hand Held	16.70
		Moulinex Marvel 118	9.68
		Sunbeam Mixmaster	29.95
Irons		Hoover 4354 Electric Iron	5.14
		Hoover Spray/Steam	8.75
		Morphy Richards	5.24
Radio		Fidelity RAD21	31.75
		HMV 2176	24.00
		Boots Supertone IC	24.35
Spin Dryer		Colston Suparinse	33.99
		Morphy Richards 1011	36.14
Washing Machines		Hotpoint Auto 1504	148.00
		Hoover Automatic	125.00
Cleaners	*Which*, 1975	Hoover Junior	43.23
		AEG Vanyr TK700	49.50
Cookers		Newhome Telstar Gas	140.00

Continued

9.4.3 Prices, Selected *continued*

Item	Source	Description	Price £ p.
Cookers *cont.*		Valor Gourmet Gas	175.00
		Creda Cavalier Electric	96.00
		Creda Autoclean 40014	213.00
Dishwashers		Ariston Aristella Bio	139.00
		Colston Jetstream 303	141.00
Freezers		Electrolux	167.00
		Bosch	196.00
		Philips	130.00
Food Mixers		Kenwood Chefette	19.98
		Moulinex Marvel 118	12.35
		Sunbeam Mixmaster	43.99
Irons		Rowenta	11.99
		AEG DS	13.01
		Peugeot FVA	16.05
Spin Dryer		Colston Suparinse	53.00
		Servis Rinspin	50.00
Toaster		Sunbeam T011	11.50
		AEG AT2E Toaster	12.25
Tumble Dryer		Burco Tumbleair D9	95.00
		Creda Sensomatic	128.00
Cleaners	*Which*, 1977	Hoover Ranger Senior	60.00
		Goblin Vacuum Cleaner	35.00
Washing Machine		Electrolux WH31	170.00
Coffee Makers	*Which*, 1979	Rowenta KG19	23.00
		Melitta Comfert 140	35.00
Cookers		Creda Carefree 40073	185.00
		Belling Compact Fantasia 430FXR	140.00
Microwave Oven		Creda 40131	249.00
		Philips 610D	323.00
Refrigerator		Electrolux RF751	102.00
		Electrolux RP1211	195.00
Stereo Radio Recorder		Aiwa TPR-905K	120.00
		JVC RC-636L	130.00
		Sharp GF-9191E	190.00
Tumble Dryer		Bendix Auto Dryer De Luxe	135.00
		Creda Sensomatic	96.00
Washing Machine		Bosch	390.00
		Electra A3E02	180.00
Baby Equipment			
	Mothercare, 1971	Mothercare Carry Cot and Transporter	8.00 (approx.)
	Mothercare, 1973	Mothercare Push Chair	3.99
Baby Carrier	*Which*, 1974	Karrimor Papoose 111	6.25
		Mothercare Baby Sling	1.45
Prams	*Which*, March 1974	Mothercare 9321 + Chassis 9501	32.00

Continued

9.4.3 Prices, Selected *continued*

Item	Source	Description	Price
			£ p.
Prams *cont.*		Raleigh Traveller	23.50
		Silver Cross Braemar	39.65
		Silver Cross Berkeley	49.75
High Chairs	*Which*, July 1977	Boots Baby Seat	13.15
		Cindico Superseat	17.50
		Littlewoods Luxury	12.00
Terry Nappies	*Which*, March 1978	Boots de Luxe	9.70 (dozen)
		Zorbit Superior	13.00 (dozen)
Disposable Nappies		Mothercare	26 (10)
Clothing and Footwear:			
Children's			
Jeans	*Which*, November 1970	Ladybird 52/66	1.45
		Lee Cooper 7411	1.74
		Lybro Seadogs Girls	2.12½
T Shirts	*Clothkits*, Summer 1979	Child's T Shirts from	2.50
		Child's T Shirt Dress Style	3.35
Shorts		Cotton Shorts from	2.50
Socks		Cotton Socks from	50
Dress	*Household Receipt*, 1979	Ladybird Dress from Woolworths	5.99 (sale price)
Men's			
Shoes	*Which*, May 1973	K New Gatling Leather Uppers/Leather Soles	7.99
		Hush Puppies "Denver"	4.99
		John White New Town Shoes Synthetic Uppers	4.25
Jeans	*Which*, June 1973	Lee Cooper 2330	5.95
		Levi 5020117	4.55
		Keynote Corduroy Jeans	1.99
		St. Michael's Corduroy Jeans	3.99
		Wrangler 11-012	4.55
Hosiery	*Clothkits*, Summer 1979	Men's Cotton Socks from	99
Knitwear	*Simpson*, Piccadilly, London, 1979	Knitted Zip Blouson in Wool/Acrylic	55.00
		Lambswool Slipover	15.50
Shirt		Zip Safari Overshirt	39.00
		Check Shirt	16.50
Suit		Daks Polyester/Wool Mix Suit in Navy Pinstripe	79.00
		Linen Flax/Polyester Suit	67.00
Trousers		Navy Corduroy Trousers	37.00
		Polyester Mix Trousers	19.00
Ready Made Bought Suits	*Which*, September 1979	Aquascutum	150.00
		Hepworths	59.65
		John Collier	39.95
		Marks and Spencer	39.95
Shirt	*Household Receipt*, 1979	Cotton Polyester Shirt from Hepworths	9.95

Continued

9.4.3 Prices, Selected *continued*

Item	Source	Description	Price £ p.
Shirt *cont.*		Ben Sherman Cotton Shirt	9.99
Ladies			
Shoes	*C & J Clark Ltd.*, 1970	Northcott Waxwood Softee Leather Shoe	5.50
		Kimble Waxwood Aniline Calf	4.99
		Bedelia Brown Cape Grain	3.99
		Shandel Nut Brown Gluvside	3.29
		Nettie Brown Mock Crocodile Torlon	2.99
Boots	*Kendals*, Manchester, Autumn 1970	Crocodile Look Boots in Brown Calf	12.60
		Wet Look Boots	10.50
Coat		Shetland Wool Coat	18.00
		Jaeger Military Style Coat	29.50
Dress		Jersey Day Dress by Colin Glascoe	17.50
		Ultra Feminine Cocktail Dress by Jean Varon	21.50
		Frank Usher Evening Gown in Crimplene	26.50
Hat		Racoon Cossack Style Hat	23.00
Hosiery		Christian Dior Tights	1.05
Suit		Suit in Brown Check Wool	19.50
		Three Piece Suit by Colin Glascoe	22.50
Coat	*Kendals*, Manchester, Summer 1971	Shiny Wet Look Raincoat in PVC	15.00
Dress		Sun Dress in Terylene Voile by Peter Barron	10.25
		Gingham Dress by Polly Peck	12.15
		Linen Look Moygashel Dress	4.95
		Sleeveless Dress by Berketex	9.20
Shorts		Clingy Bermuda Shorts	4.95
Suits		Daks Sizzling Safari Suit	18.35
		Daks Tough Guy Trouser Suit	19.90
Swimwear		Slix Bikini	4.75
Leather and Suede Coats	*Wear Leather Fashion Magazine*, 1972	Suede Coat with Inset Sleeves	48.00
		¾ Length Rambler Sheepskin Coat	52.00
		Safari Jacket in Leather	48.00
		Double Breasted Rambler Sheepskin Coat	58.00
		Double Breasted Slimline Leather Coat	52.00
		Double Breasted Leather Coat, Lucra Lamb Collar	75.00
Shoes	*C & J Clark Ltd.*, 1975	Bonito Brown Suede Clippers	10.99
		Rosemary Brown Patent Leather	9.99
		Debra Bronze Metallic Torlon, ½ in. Platform	8.99
		Chartres Brown Leather with Cuban Heel	10.99

Continued

9.4.3 Prices, Selected *continued*

Item	Source	Description	Price £ p.
Dress	*Bernat Klein Design*, Spring/Summer 1978	Sleeveless Cotton Dress Reminiscent of the Twenties	27.00
		Colour Woven Shirtwaister	37.30
Knitwear		Handknitted Mohair Summer Cardigan	23.00
Poncho		Poncho in Random Striped Poncho Cloth	31.40
Shirt		Plain Cotton Shirt	19.70
Skirt		Long Semi-Circular Skirt	26.00
Suit		Spring Suit in Natural Tweed	69.00
Blouse	*Miss Selfridge Magazine No.7*, 1978	Crêpe de Chine Blouses from	9.95
Dress		Indian Cotton Dress	16.95
		Forties Style Dress	19.95
Jackets		Jackets in all Colours from	22.95
Jeans		Straight Leg Jeans	8.95
Knitwear		Knitted Waistcoats	7.95
		Shawls	4.25
		Lacy Knit Jumper	8.95
Skirt		Check Wool Skirts from	12.95
Trousers		Cord Trousers from	17.95
		Flannel Trousers from	13.95
Underwear		Lingerie Sets from	6.00
Jacket	*Clothkits*, Summer 1979	Travelling Jacket	7.25
Knitwear		V Neck Jumper in Acrylic Yarn	5.95
T Shirt		V Neck T Shirt	2.95
Blouse	*Laura Ashley*, 1979	Short Sleeved Romantic Blouse in Cotton Lawn	11.40
		Elegant Long Sleeved Blouse in Swiss Voile	19.65
		Sophisticated Victorian Blouse in Cotton Lawn	20.65
Dress		Short Sleeved Spring Dress in Cotton Lawn	18.90
		Classic Midcalf Smock Style Dress	18.90
Nightwear		Full Length Victorian White Nightie	14.65
Skirt		Three Tiered Gypsy Style Skirt	14.65
Waistcoat		Sleeveless Quilted Waistcoat	13.40
Food Products			
Bacon	*J Sainsbury*, 1970	Unsmoked Back Bacon	34 (lb.)
Biscuits		McVities Digestive	5 (½ lb.)
Breakfast Cereal		Shredded Wheat	9 (12's)
Butter		Best Butter	17½ (lb.)
Cheese		Cheddar Cheese	19 (lb.)
Eggs		Six Medium Size	12½
Soup		Heinz Tomato Soup	6½ (15½ oz.)
Squash		Kia Ora Squash	9 (20 oz.)
Tea		Red Label Tea	26½ (lb.)
Confectionery	*Cadbury Ltd.*, 1970	Cadbury's Dairy Milk King Size	17

Continued

9.4.3 Prices, Selected *continued*

Item	Source	Description	Price £ p.
Confectionery *cont.*		Milk Fruit and Nut	22 (½ lb.)
		Milk Wholenut	23½ (½ lb.)
		Bournville King Size	18
		Golden Crisp	5
		Plain Chocolate for Diabetics	13 (¼ lb.)
Mustard	*Colmans of Norwich*, 1971	Double Superfine	11 (¼ lb.)
		French Mustard	14½ (jar)
Pudding		Semolina	9½ (lb.)
Bacon	*Which*, November 1973	Walls Back Bacon	32 (7½ oz.)
Beans		Heinz Baked Beans	7 (15¾ oz.)
Biscuits		McVities Milk Chocolate Homewheat	11 (8 oz.)
Breakfast Cereal		Kelloggs Cornflakes	10 (12 oz.)
Butter		Anchor Butter	10 (½ lb.)
Coffee		Maxwell House	32 (4 oz.)
Flour		McDougalls Self Raising	14 (3 lb.)
Margarine		Stork	6 (½ lb.)
Peas		Birds Eye	10 (10 oz.)
Salmon		John West Red Salmon	37 (7½ oz.)
Sausages		Walls Pork	14 (½ lb.)
Sugar		Tate & Lyle	9 (2 lb.)
Tea		Typhoo Tea	8 (¼ lb.)
Bacon	*J Sainsbury*, 1974	Middle Unsmoked	84 (lb.)
Beans		JS Beans	11½ (15 oz.)
Beefburgers		Beefburgers	40 (4)
Breakfast Cereal		Kelloggs Cornflakes	17½ (500 g.)
Cheese		Cheddar Cheese	30 (lb.)
Chicken		3 lb. Roasting Chicken	1.54
Coffee		JS Instant Coffee Refill	24½ (4 oz.)
Jam		Strawberry Jam	13½ (lb.)
Sugar		Sugar	10 (2 lb.)
Tea		Loose Red Label	13 (½ lb.)
Tinned Fruit		Peach Slices	19 (14½ oz.)
Tomato Sauce		Heinz Tomato Ketchup	21 (20 oz.)
Bacon	*J Sainsbury*, 1975	Unsmoked Back	76 (lb.)
Biscuits		McVities Digestive	12 (½ lb.)
Breakfast Cereal		Shredded Wheat	16½ (12's)
Butter		Best Butter	28 (lb.)
Cheese		Cheddar Cheese	44 (lb.)
Eggs		Six Medium Size	16
Soup		Heinz Tomato Soup	13½ (15½ oz.)
Squash		Kia Ora Squash	17½ (20 oz.)
Confectionery	*Cadbury Ltd.*, January 27, 1975	Cadbury's Dairy Milk Family Size	31
		Chocolate Buttons	9 (medium pack)
		Milk Fruit and Nut Family Size	37
		Milk Wholenut Family Size	37

Continued

9.4.3 Prices, Selected *continued*

Item	Source	Description	Price
			£ p.
Confectionery *cont.*		Bournville Family Size	35
		Milk Tray Bar	18 (medium pack)
		Peppermint Caramello	9
		Velvet Blend	18
Bacon	*J Sainsbury*, 1979	Middle Unsmoked	95 (lb.)
Beans		JS Beans	23 (15 oz.)
Beefburgers		Beefburgers	72 (4)
Breakfast Cereal		Kelloggs Cornflakes	32½ (500 g.)
Butter		Best Butter	35½ (lb.)
Cheese		Cheddar Cheese	92 (lb.)
Chicken		3 lb. Roasting Chicken	1.26
Coffee		JS Instant Coffee Refill	64 (4 oz.)
Jam		Strawberry Jam	32 (lb.)
Sugar		Sugar	33 (2 lb.)
Tea		Loose Red Label	35 (½ lb.)
Tinned Fruit		Peach Slices	22 (14½ oz.)
Tomato Sauce		Heinz Tomato Ketchup	38 (20 oz.)
Sweeteners	*Which*, February 1979	Boots Saccharin	25 (500)
		Sweetex	49 (500)

Furniture

Item	Source	Description	Price
Bedroom	*Ideal Home*, January 1970	Format Bedroom Furniture from	29.61
Bookcase		Unix Sectional Bookcases by Phoenix from	22.50
Lounge		Lona Sideboard Base Unit	36.75
		Lona Wall Unit from	14.75
		Vivando Living Room Wall Units	15.00 (top cupboard)
			25.00 (bottom cupboard)
Hamlet Solid Pine Furniture		Refectory Tables 5 ft. and 4 ft. from	13.50
		Dining Chairs	5.25 (each)
		Benches	6.50
		Pine Welsh Dresser	34.75
Bedroom	*Ideal Home*, December 1970	Avalon Teak Veneer Bedroom Furniture from	121.75
		Daydream Sofa Bed by Parker & Farr	164.00
Dining		Staples Teak Dining Table 508	29.75
		Staples Teak Chairs	12.00 (each)
		Low Table with Hard Melamine Laminate	8.70
		Red Cloverleaf Fibreglass Table by Lurashell from	20.00
Floorcovering		Kossett Carpets from	3.50 (sq. yard)
		York Wilton All Wool Carpet "Havana"	4.80 (sq. yard)
		Coraire Cortez Cushion Vinyl	1.61 (sq. yard)
Seating		Caroline Suite Sofa 813	78.00
		Seating Unit made up of Modo Base	11.20
		Seating made up of Modo Round	4.50

Continued

9.4.3 Prices, Selected *continued*

Item	Source	Description	Price £ p.
Seating *cont.*		Hi-Back Chair with Cushion on Natural Canvas Frame	18.30
		OMK Slingback Chair with Tubular Steel Frame	15.75
		Gourmet High Back Office Chair from Fibreglass	39.00
Sideboard		Solid Pine with Louvre Door from Skyport Joinery	30.60
Cabinet		Solid Pine Cottage Style Cabinet	12.52½
Wallpaper		Sandersons Wallpaper	95 (roll)
Floorcovering	*Which*, May 1973	Axminster Wool Luxury Domestic	7.25 (sq. yard)
		Wilton Luxury Domestic	5.03 (sq. yard)
		Cord Sisal	1.98 (sq. yard)

Garden Equipment and Supplies inc. Garages

Item	Source	Description	Price £ p.
Bushes	*Ideal Home*, January 1970	Six Golden Rose Bushes	1.47½
Bunker		Concrete Fuel Bunker	1.97½
Garage		Garador Mk 3 Overhead Garage Door	14.50
Mower		Qualcast Hand B1	5.97½
		Suffolk Super Swift Hand	7.75
		Qualcast Rota Mini Electric	11.48½
Paving		Paving Slabs from	25 (each)
Street Lighting		Elegant Victorian Column with Copper Lanterns	27.50 (each)
Tools		Jenks & Cattell Garden Shears	1.20
		Wilkinson's Garden Shears	4.25
Wildbird Food		Bird Food from	45 (up to 740)
		Peanut Kernels from	60 (5 lb.)

Heat and Light

Item	Source	Description	Price £ p.
Electricity	*Eastern Electricity Board*, 1971	Fixed Charge £1.95	88 (unit)
Gas	*British Gas North Thames Board*, 1971	Per Quarter £1.30	13 (therm)
Coal	*Digest of UK Energy Statistics*, 1971	Coal per Ton	16.00
Electricity	*Eastern Electricity Board*, 1974	Fixed Charge £2.21	98 (unit)
Gas	*British Gas North Thames Board*, 1974	Per Quarter £1.46	14¾ (therm)
Coal	*Digest of UK Energy Statistics*, 1974	Coal per Ton	22.00
Electricity	*Eastern Electricity Board*, 1978	Fixed Charge £2.77	2.86 (unit)
Gas	*British Gas North Thames Board*, 1978	22¾ per therm to 52 therms	15½ (therm over 52)
Coal	*Digest of UK Energy Statistics*, 1978	Coal per Ton	48.00

Hotel Rates

Item	Source	Description	Price £ p.
Britannia Hotel, Grosvenor Sq. London	*RAC Guide and Handbook*, 1978	Bed and Breakfast from	29.74
Post House, Bayswater Rd. London		Bed and Breakfast from	16.80
Royal Adelphi, Villiers St. London		Bed and Breakfast from	9.60
Wellington Hotel, Tunbridge Wells		Rates per Person from	7.00

Continued

9.4.3 Prices, Selected *continued*

Item	Source	Description	Price
			£ p.
Hotel Rates *cont.* Beech Hill Hotel, Windermere, Cumbria		Bed and Breakfast from	11.85
Glyn Garth Hotel, Llanbedrog	*Welsh Tourist Board*, 1978	Evening Dinner, Bed and Breakfast from	8.00 (daily)
Craignethan Hotel, Rothesay	*Scottish Tourist Board*, 1979	Weekly Terms from	68.00
Household Goods			
Scourers and Soap Filled Pads	*Which*, May 1970	Ajax Pan Shiners	14 (10)
		Sainsbury's Soap Filled Pads	8½ (10)
		Ajax Cleanser	6 (18 oz.)
		Vim	6½ (18 oz.)
Toilet Preparations	*J Sainsbury*, 1970	Colgate Toothpaste	14½ (standard)
Toilet Rolls		Andrex Toilet Rolls 2's	10
Washing Powder		Bold Washing Powder	14 (large)
Bedding	*Ideal Home*, January 1970	Range of Pillow Cases by Osman	1.04½ (each)
Cookware		Arcopal de Luxe 3 pint Flame Casserole	4.50
		Oblong Roasting Dish	2.92½
		Kitchen Scales by Peter Jones	10.00
		Natural Wood Spaghetti Tongs	34
		Zyliss Household Grater	3.99½
		Olive Stoner by R.Jackson	50
		Jar Opener	27½
		Stainless Steel Milk Saver	24½
		Copy of 17th C. Earthenware Salt Pot	1.75
Table Lamp		Italian Opaque Glass Lamp and Shade from B.H.S.	74½
Tableware		Dartington Glass Carafe and Six Glasses	3.15
		Attractive Pottery Pie Dish	1.37½
Towels		Bath Size Plain and Jacquard Towels from B.H.S.	74½
		Hand Size Plain and Jacquard Towels from B.H.S.	44½
Clock	*Ideal Home*, December 1970	Westclox	3.15
Cutlery		Elkington Six Piece Cutlery Set	6.80
Door Bell		Friedland Bell Chimes	96
Cookware	*Ann Sloan Mail Order Catalogue*, 1972	Paring Knives from	1.50 (each)
Cutlery		Five Piece Solid Stainless Steel Cutlery	60 (set)
Dryer		Multi Purpose Portable Radiator Dryer	1.10
Heater		Multi Purpose Home Space Heater	2.95
Cookware	*Which*, September 1973	Aluminium Saucepan from	85 (up to 3.30)
		Ceramic Saucepan	4.00 (up to 5.50)
		Copper Saucepan	9.00 (up to 10.50)

Continued

9.4.3 Prices, Selected *continued*

Item	Source	Description	Price £ p.
		Stainless Steel Saucepan from	3.30 (up to 8.00)
Tableware		Royal Doulton Larchmont Table Casserole	3.90 (4 pints)
		Wedgewood Greenwood Table Casserole	5.10 (4 pints)
		Le Creuset	3.95 (4½ pints)
		Pyrex Easy Roast	1.12 (3 pints)
Washing Liquids	*Which*, 1973	Palmolive	13½ (17¾ fl. oz.)
		Fairy Liquid	18½ (19½ fl. oz.)
		Super Stardrops	10½ (24 fl. oz.)
Toilet Rolls	*J Sainsbury*, 1975	Andrex Toilet Rolls 2's	22
Kitchenware	*Which*, 1975	Braun Coffee Mill	8.83
		Melitta 75 Coffee Mill	7.37
Bedding	*Which*, November 1978	Coop De Luxe A160 Cotton Flannelette Sheets	10.25 (pair)
Washing Powder	*J Sainsbury*, 1979	Bold Washing Powder	45 (large)
Light Bulb	*Labour Research*, June 1981	Electric Light Bulb	27 (May 1979)
Toilet Rolls		Izal Toilet Roll	21 (May 1979)
Houses			
Detached	*Estate Agents Details*, 1971	Three Bed Dormer Bungalow in Sandbach, Cheshire	5,600.00 (freehold)
Semi-Detached	*Estate Agents Details*, 1975	Two Bed Semi-Detached Bungalow in Cleveland	8,500.00 (freehold)
	Estate Agents Details, 1977	Three Bed Dormer Bungalow in Holmes Chapel	13,950.00 (freehold)
Detached	*Observer*, March 20, 1977	Five Bed House in Harrow on the Hill	49,950.00
		Detached House in Streatham divided into 11 Flats	35,000.00
		Spacious 3 Bed Bungalow in Surrey	30,000.00
Jewellery			
Necklet	*Kendals*, Manchester, 1970	Velvet Choker Necklet	1.70
		Choker Necklet	2.10
Ring	*H.Samuel*, 1971	22 ct. Gold Wedding Ring	12.00
		9 ct. Gold Wedding Ring	6.00
Watch		Timex Watch with Brown Leather Strap	4.75
	Which, August 1972	Seiko Men's Automatic Calendar Watch from	20.95
Musical Instruments			
Piano	*N.J.Tostevin & Son*, 1970	Knight Upright Piano	400.00
		Concert Grand Piano	10,000.00
	Sunday Times, March 20, 1977	Broadwood Modern Baby Grand	550.00 (second hand)
Guitar	*Household Receipt*, 1975	Spanish Guitar	8.95
	Barnes and Mullins, c.1970	Barnes and Mullins Spanish Guitars from	50.00
Piano Tests	*Manchester Music Exchange*, 1979	Specimen Sight-Reading Tests for the Piano	30
Recorder		Wooden Recorder	1.50
Personal Care Items			

Continued

9.4.3 Prices, Selected *continued*

Item	Source	Description	Price
			£ p.
Electrolysis	*Ideal Home*, January 1970	Electronic Pencil to Shift Facial Hair	3.47½ (+ 2½ p. Postage)
Cosmetics	*Which*, 1973	Clinique Lipstick	1.65
		Max Factor Lipstick	95
		Almay Colour Moist Pearl	60
		Boots No.7 Colour Creme	37
		Rimmel Creamy Push Up	15
Shaving Equipment		Remington F2 Battery Shaver	11.35
		Ronson RS 55 Battery	11.99
		Boots 2000	5.40
Toilet Preparations		Supersoft Cream Shampoo	23 (130 g.)
		Vitapointe Lemon	18½ (19½ fl. oz.)
		Sunsilk Herb	26 (24 fl. oz.)
Shaving Preparations	*Which*, April 1977	Gillette Platinum 5 Razor Blades	29
		Wilkinson Sword 5	29
Tissues		Kleenex 100	32
		Scotties 100	29
Toilet Preparations		Camay	15½ (5 oz.)
		Imperial Leather	17 (4½ oz.)
		Shield	12½ (5 oz.)
		Pears Shampoo	33 (130 cc)
		Silvikrin	27 (130 cc)
		Sunsilk	29 (130 cc)
		Colgate Plus Fluoride Toothpaste	25 (50 cc)
		Gibbs SR	27 (50 cc)
		Signal 2	27 (50 cc)
		Arrid Extra Dry Deodorant	46 (190 g.)
		Body Mist	45 (150 g.)
		Sure	46 (150 g.)
		Johnsons Baby Powder	32 (227 g.)
		Yardley	60 (100 g.)
Cosmetics	*Miss Selfridge*, 1978	Lipstick	99
		Nail Colour	65
Toilet Preparations		Cleansing Cream	2.50
		Moisturising Cream	2.50
Chemists	*Labour Research*, June 1981	Aspro (8)	13 (May 1979)
		Optrex	51 (May 1979)
		Sanitary Towels (10's)	39
Hairdryers	*Which*, 1979	Clairol 1200	10.00
		Pifco Jet 2800	5.00
Shaving Equipment		Remington GT3	8.00
		Ronson RS65	10.50
		Boots Sheerline	6.95

Prescription Charges

	Source	Description	Price
	Department of Health, April 1, 1971	PPC increased to £2 for 6 months, £3.50 for 12	20

Continued

9.4.3 Prices, Selected *continued*

Item	Source	Description	Price £ p.
	Department of Health, July 16, 1979	PPC increased to £4.50 for 6 months, £8.00 for 12	45

Publications

Item	Source	Description	Price £ p.
Book	*Ideal Home*, January 1970	Winter Flower Arranging	25
	Penguin, 1971	The Fixer, Bernard Malamud	35
		The Millstone, Margaret Drabble	30
	Observer, March 20, 1977	Staying On by P.Scott, Heinemann	3.90
		Woods and Mirrors by J.Covey, Salamander	3.95
Magazine		Woman's Journal	90
	Manchester Central Library, 1976	Woman's Own	10
	Manchester Central Library, 1977	Woman's Own	12
Yearbook	*Daily Mail Yearbook*, 1977	Daily Mail Yearbook 1977	1.15
Magazine	*Good Housekeeping*, December 1979	Good Housekeeping	45
Book		Vogue Body and Beauty Book, B.Meredith	7.50

Services

Item	Source	Description	Price £ p.
Cinema	*Kinematographic Year Book*, 1970	Manchester Film Theatre Admission Price	30 (up to 60)
	Kinematographic Year Book, 1971		40 (up to 60)
Licence	*Post Office Archives*, February 1, 1971	Radio Licence Fee Abolished	nil
	Post Office Archives	Black and White TV	7.00
		Colour TV	12.00
	Post Office Archives, April 1, 1975	Black and White TV	8.00
		Colour TV	18.00
	Post Office Archives, July 29, 1977	Black and White TV	9.00
		Colour TV	21.00
	Post Office Archives, November 25, 1978	Black and White TV	10.00
		Colour TV	25.00
	Post Office Archives, November 24, 1979	Black and White TV	12.00
		Colour TV	34.00
	DVLA, April 16, 1975	Road Tax	40.00 (12 months)
	DVLA, March 1, 1977		50.00 (12 months)
Telephone Tariffs	*British Telecom*, July 1, 1970		
Revised Quarterly Rental		Business Line (exclusive)	6.00
		Line other than Business	5.00
Local Calls from STD Exchanges	*British Telecom Archives*, February 15, 1971	Monday to Friday 8 am to 6 pm	1 (6 minutes)
		Monday to Friday 6 pm to 8 pm and Sat and Sun	1 (12 minutes)
	British Telecom Archives, April 28, 1975	Monday to Friday 9 am to 1 pm	1.8 (for 2 minutes)
		Monday to Friday 8 am to 9 am and 1 pm to 6 pm	1.8 (for 3 minutes)
		All other times	1.8 (for 8 minutes)
Revised Quarterly Rental	*British Telecom Archives*, May 1, 1975	Business Line (exclusive)	9.75
		Line other than Business	8.25

Continued

9.4.3 Prices, Selected *continued*

Item	Source	Description	Price £ p.
Peak Rate Mon to Fri 9 am to 1 pm	*British Telecom Archives*, January 4, 1977	Local Calls	6 (for 3 minutes)
		Up to 56 km	24
		Over 56 km	60
Telephone Tariffs *cont.* Standard Rate Mon to Fri 8am to 9 am & 1 pm to 6pm		Local Calls	6 (for 3 minutes)
		Up to 56 km	18
		Over 56 km	42
Cheap Rate (all other lines)		Local (from STD Exchanges)	6 (for 9 minutes)
		Up to 56 km	9
		Over 56 km	15
Parcel Postage Rates (Ordinary Parcels)	*Post Office Archives*, March 6, 1972	1½ lb. weight	16
		6 lb. weight	29
		10 lb. weight	37
	Post Office Archives, June 24, 1974	2 lb. weight	22
		6 lb. weight	32
		10 lb. weight	42
	Post Office Archives, June 7, 1976	1 kg. weight	55
		5 kg. weight	1.10
		10 kg. weight	1.60
Finance and Mortgages	*Ideal Home*, January 1970	2nd. Mortgages Repay from	1.77½ (monthly per £100 borrowed)
Conveyancing Fee	*Which*, 1973	Buying a £13,000 house with a £9000 Mortgage	73.75
	Which, 1974		100.00
	Which, 1977		127.50
Dental Treatment	*Which*, 1973	Extraction	47 (up to £1.60)
	Which, 1979		2.20

Sewing Equipment and Supplies

Item	Source	Description	Price £ p.
Machine	*Ideal Home*, December 1970	Singer Touch and Sew	143.95
	Which, 1970	Singer 359	38.67½
		Bernina 708	80.85
		Pfaff 95	80.85
		Jones 821	47.97½
		Cresta	30.45
Fabrics (per metre)	*Kendals*, 1971	Polyester Cotton from	1.25
		Satin Brocade	2.25
		Wool Flannels	2.95
Furnishing Fabrics	*Which*, February 1977	Plain Nets	50 (up to £1.00)
		Patterned Nets	70 (up to £2.50)

Sports Equipment and Hobbies

Item	Source	Description	Price £ p.
Ball	*The Pound in Your Pocket 1870–1970*	Football	2.50
Sports Clothes		Football Boots	6.00
		Football Jersey	1.50
		Football Shorts	75
Hobbies	*Anne Sloan Mail Order Catalogue*, 1972	Galilean Sports Binoculars	1.98
Photographic Equipment	*Which*, 1973	Halina 500	22.90

Continued

9.4.3 Prices, Selected *continued*

Item	Source	Description	Price
			£ p.
		Olympus Trip 35	36.87
		Yashica Electro 35cc	71.42
		Ricoh TLS 401 SLR	135.00
Sports Shoes	*Which*, July 1975	Dunlop Blue Flash	3.80
		Adidas Jonah Barrington Pro	7.99
		Gola Harrier	5.49
		Woolworth 707	1.49
Photographic Equipment	*Which*, 1979	Halina 600 Compact	30.00
		Olympus 35RD	90.00
		Yashica 35MF	70.00
Boat	*Which*, June 1979	Avon Inflatable S100	610.00
		Campari Sea Otter	520.00
		Pirelli Laros 340	835.00
Golf Clubs	*Which*, February 1979	Full set of new clubs from	200.00
Golf Balls		Golf balls from	80

Tobacco Products

Item	Source	Description	Price
Cigarettes (per packet of 20)	*Gallaher Ltd.*, February 19, 1974	Senior Service	27
		Park Drive	21½
		Benson and Hedges King Size Special Filter	30
		Silk Cut Extra Mild	24
	Gallaher Ltd., May 10, 1976	Benson & Hedges King Size Special Filter	47
		Silk Cut Extra Mild	42½
	Gallaher Ltd., January 1, 1978	Benson & Hedges King Size Special Filter	56
		Silk Cut Ultra Mild King Size	55
	Gallaher Ltd., September 17, 1979	Benson & Hedges King Size Special Filter	67
		Silk Cut Ultra Mild King Size	66

Toys

Item	Source	Description	Price
Model Aircraft Kits	*Which*, December 1970	Lockheed Starfighter	21
		McDonnell Phantom	30
		North American Bronco	44
Conjuring Kits	*Which*, 1970	Hamley's Magician's Chest	1.95
		Kay Modern Magic	1.05
		Thomas Salter Magic Set No.2	1.39
Toys	*Which*, December 1976	Lego	6.00
		Tiny Tears Doll	4.50
		Paintbox	75
		Pop a Point Colouring Pencil	30
		Battery Train Set	8.00
		Spinning Top	30

Transport and Vehicles

Item	Source	Description	Price
Air Fares	*Reed Travel Group*, July 1970	London to Paris 1st. Class	17.40
		London to Paris Economy	12.40
		London to New York 1st. Class	156.25

Continued

9.4.3 Prices, Selected *continued*

Item	Source	Description	Price £ p.
	Which, January 1970	London to Dublin Single Tourist Rate	11.90
		Liverpool to Dublin Single Tourist Rate	6.90
Air Fares *contd.*		Manchester to Dublin Single Tourist Rate	8.15
Bus Fares	*What it Cost the Day Before Yesterday Book*, 1	Paddington to Mansion House (4 miles)	7
Rail Fares	*National Railway Museum*, September 1970	Manchester to London Second Class Return	6.40
Vehicle	*Complete Catalogue of Austin Cars since 1945*	Mini Cooper S Mark 111	942.00 (price when introduced)
		Allegro 1100/1.1 49 b.h.p. 2-4 Door Saloon	973.00 (price when introduced)
Air Fares	*Which*, January 1973	London to New York Economy Return	172.00
		London to Tokyo Economy Return	619.00
	Reed Travel Group, June 1975	London to Paris 1st. Class	38.20
		London to Paris Economy	9.85
		London to New York	232.30
Rail Fares	*National Railway Museum*, September 1975	Manchester to London Second Class Return	15.45
Bicycle	*Which*, May 1975	Halfords Apollo Drop Handlebars, 5 Speeds	45.75
		Raleigh Europa Drop Handlebars, 10 Speeds	64.00
		Elswick Hopper Safeway Roadster, 3 Speeds	41.95
		Raleigh Stowaway, Small Wheeler, 3 Speeds	49.50
Vehicle	*Observer*, March 20, 1977	Renault 12 from	2,233.00
	Which, 1978	Ford Escort	2,328.08
Travel			
Steam Railway	*North York Moors Timetable*, 1975	Grosmont to Goathland Second Class Return	50
		Grosmont to Pickering Second Class Return	1.00
Holidays	*Observer*, March 20, 1977	Two Weeks in Corsica by Solmar Travel Ltd. from	84.00
		Round the World Bales Tours in 30 Days	1,454.00
		21 Day Cruises down the Nile with Bales Tours	556.00
		Villa Holidays in Corfu, Minerva Holidays	120.00 (per person per week)
	Sunday Times, March 20, 1977	British Airways to Alicante, Malaga or Nice	52.00 (up to £62)
		Easter in Madrid, Owners Abroad	22.50
Zoo Excursion	*Chester Zoo Leaflet*, 1979	Admission Charges to Chester Zoo	1.00 (adults) 50 (children)
Miscellany			
Ladders	*Ideal Home*, January 1970	Slingsby Loft Ladders from	18.00
Tools		Black and Decker Drill from	4.30

Continued

9.4.3 Prices, Selected *continued*

Item	Source	Description	Price £ p.
		Arcoy Power Plane	21.00
		Goscut Trimming Tool	1.87½
Driving Mat		Minx Driving Mat, Saves Ladies Shoes	1.32½
Wire Baskets		Dipple Dorstor Plastic Coated Wire Baskets	2.37½
Window Locks		Combination Window Locks	49½ (p.+ p.)
Typewriters	*Which*, 1973	Olivetti 300	66.00
		Imperial 220	36.00
		Smith Corona Classic 12	64.00
	Which, 1978	Brother de Luxe 660TR	45.00
		Coronet Super 12	170.00
Music Records	*British Record Industry Yearbook*, 1974	Typical Retail Price of a Single	55
	1975		65
	1976		70
	1977		75
	1978		80
	1979		95

9.5 Finance and Economic Data

9.5.1 Finance, Personal

	1970	1971	1972	1973	1974	1975	1976	1977	1978	1979
	£	£	£	£	£	£	£	£	£	£
Retirement Pension:										
Married	8.20	9.70	10.90	12.50	16.00	21.20[5]	24.50	18.00	31.20	37.30
Single	5.00	6.00	6.75	7.75	10.00	13.30	15.30	17.50	19.50	23.30
Child Benefit:										
First								1.00	3.00	4.00
Second		0.90	0.90	0.90	0.90	1.50	1.50	1.50	3.00	4.00
Third and Subsequent		1.00	1.00	1.00	1.00	1.50	1.50	1.50	3.00	4.00
Unemployment Benefit: Men, Single Women and Widows		6.00	6.75	7.35	8.60	11.10	12.90	14.70	15.75	18.50
Income Tax Rate[1,2]	41.25%	41.25%	38.75%[3]	38.75%	30%	33%	35%	35%	34%	33%
Base Interest Rate[4]	8%	7%	5%	8¾%	12¾%	11¼%	11%	14%	6½%	12½%

Mitchell, B.R. *British Historical Statistics*, Cambridge University Press, 1988; Bank of England; Department of Social Security.

Blank space denotes no data available. [1]From 1969, standard rate was expressed as a percentage. [2]The rate applies to year ended 5th April. [3]Subsequently basic rate. Higher rates are applied to higher income bands. [4]The rate applies to January of each year. [5]From November.

9.5.2 Financial Markets

9.5.2a Closing Price of UK Major Stocks in January

	1970	1971[4]	1972	1973	1974	1975	1976	1977	1978	1979
Barclays Bank	90/0	62/9	64½	460	486	340	325	350	335	360
Boots the Chemists	28/7½	28/3	247	310	320	217	145	148	227	185
Burmah Oil	134/6	85/6	477	488	506	496	100	53	52	82
Cadbury Schweppes[1]	25/3	17/7½	96½	99	74½	59	55½	55	57½	54
Courtaulds	32/3	30/3	150	166	166½	112	154	169	113	117
Guinness	31/4½	31/6	194	181	181	122	142	150	191	165
ICI[2]	73/0	58/0	335	256	294	242	334	402	352	362
Marks and Spencer	57/1½	62/3	331	288	289	226	128	108	155	83
Reckitt and Colman	77/6	55/9	322	350	369	294	341	363	438	452
Unilever	70/0	62/6	355	362	395	336	432	500	548	532
Viyella[3]	17/0¾	11/6¾	64	44½	45½	28	31	36	38	33
Whitbread & Co.	13/1½	11/4½	95	100	100	78½	72	75	95	103

Financial Times, 1970–1979.

For 1970 and 1971 figures, fractions are quoted as parts of £1=32. From 1972 all prices are in new pence. [1]Cadbury's merged with Schweppes in 1969. [2]Imperial Chemical Industries. [3]Viyella was known as Carrington Viyella from 1971. [4]Decimalisation came into force in 1971.

9.5.2b Commodities

	Coal (December retail prices, London)	Gold (average market price)	Sugar (annual average world price)	Wheat (average price)	Wool (average import value)
	new pence per cwt.	£ per troy oz.	£ sterling per metric ton	£ per cwt.	pence per lb.
1970	85	15.01	39.763	1.34	42.0
1971	98	16.67	45.369	1.25	37.6
1972	107	23.39	71.384	1.48	22.1[1]
1973	108	39.58	97.756	2.56	44.3
1974	133	67.83	299.916	3.12	43.0
1975	175	72.34	213.032	2.96	32.7
1976	202	69.34	151.354	3.83	49.2
1977	242	84.56	114.802	4.13	58.3
1978	264	100.65	100.760	4.43	59.0
1979	323	143.54	114.476	4.94	61.6

Mitchell, B.R. *British Historical Statistics*, Cambridge University Press, 1988; Digest of Energy Statistics; World Gold Council; Czarnikow Sugar.

Original source, *Annual Statement of Trade Statistics of the UK*. [1]From 1972, prices in new pence.

9.5.2c Foreign Exchange Rates

	Frankfurt Deutschmarks per £1	Paris Francs per £1	New York Dollars per £1
1970	8.736	13.244	2.396
1971	8.496	13.471	2.446
1972	7.979	12.621	2.503
1973	6.540	10.890	2.453
1974	6.049	11.246	2.340
1975	5.447	9.500	2.220
1976	4.552	8.608	1.805
1977	4.050	8.573	1.746
1978	3.850	8.645	1.920
1979	3.887	9.025	2.123

Mitchell, B.R. *British Historical Statistics*, Cambridge University Press, 1988.

9.5.3 Balance of Payments and GNP

9.5.3a Balance of Payments

	Merchandise Exports	Merchandise Imports	Overall Visible Balance	Exports of Services	Imports of Services	Property Income from Abroad	Property Income Paid Abroad	Balance of Current Transfers	Overall Invisible Balance	Overall Current Balance
	£m	£m	£m	£m	£m	£m	£m	£m	£m	£m
1970	8,150	8,184	-34	3,379	2,963	1,493	898	-182	+829	+795
1971	9,043	8,853	+190	3,884	3,340	1,535	984	-196	+899	+1,089
1972	9,437	10,185	-748	4,204	3,586	1,801	1,209	-272	+939	+191
1973	11,937	14,523	-2,586	5,185	4,501	4,924	3,597	-443	+1,568	-1,018
1974	16,394	21,745	-5,351	6,594	5,645	6,209	4,702	-422	+2,034	-3,317
1975	19,330	22,663	-3,333	7,677	6,341	6,565	5,675	-475	+1,751	-1,582
1976	25,191	29,120	-3,929	10,019	7,774	8,385	6,828	-786	+3,016	-913
1977	31,728	34,012	-2,284	11,625	8,587	8,796	8,550	-1,128	+2,156	-128
1978	35,063	36,605	-1,542	12,440	8,962	11,202	10,375	-1,791	+2,514	+972
1979	40,687	44,136	-3,449	14,336	10,532	17,526	16,338	-2,279	+2,713	-736

Mitchell, B.R. *British Historical Statistics*, Cambridge University Press, 1988.

Original source, *CSO National Income and Expenditure*.

9.5.3b GNP at Factor Cost and Its Component Incomes at Current Prices

	Income from Employment	Income from Self Employment	Gross Trading Profits of Companies	Gross Trading Surplus of Public Enterprises	Rent	Stock Appreciation	Gross Domestic Product	Net Property Income from Abroad	Gross National Product	Capital Consumption	National Income
	£m	£m	£m	£m	£m	£m	£m	£m	£m	£m	£m
1970	30,553	4,191	6,105	1,627	3,126	1,061	44,541	595	45,136	4,613	40,523
1971	33,489	4,890	7,131	1,726	3,495	1,055	49,676	551	50,227	5,325	44,902
1972	37,870	5,866	8,161	1,845	4,009	1,290	56,461	593	57,054	6,138	50,916
1973	43,877	7,505	10,418	2,214	4,666	2,806	65,874	1,327	67,201	7,325	59,876
1974	52,379	8,118	11,457	2,693	6,037	6,109	74,575	1,507	76,082	9,081	67,001
1975	68,494	9,195	11,762	3,210	7,380	5,521	94,520	890	95,410	11,624	83,786
1976	78,005	10,918	14,714	4,636	8,814	6,681	110,406	1,557	111,963	13,990	97,973
1977	86,685	12,156	19,865	5,255	9,926	5,095	128,792	246	129,038	16,547	112,491
1978	98,995	13,813	22,567	5,576	11,282	4,228	148,005	827	148,832	19,260	129,572
1979	115,807	15,998	29,195	5,745	13,449	8,832	171,352	1,188	172,540	22,929	149,611

Mitchell, B.R. *British Historical Statistics*, Cambridge University Press, 1988.

Original source, *CSO National Income and Expenditure*.

– Ten –
1980–1989

Society versus Economy: The Thatcher Years

PRIME MINISTER
Margaret Thatcher (Conservative), May 1979–November 1990

CHANCELLORS OF THE EXCHEQUER
Geoffrey Howe, May 1979–June 1983
Nigel Lawson, June 1983–October 89
John Major, October 1989–November 90

When Margaret Thatcher became Britain's first female Prime Minister in 1979, it signalled the winds of change for the nation – what followed were in essence the hardest and possibly the most successful years for the economy. A 'monetarist' economist, Thatcher appointed Geoffrey Howe to the Exchequer to carry out policies which effectively set unemployment against inflation.

In 1980, unemployment reached 1.3 million for the first time since 1978, and inflation raged at 27.8 per cent. The Thatcher administration employed restrictive policies to decrease public expenditure, most notably by denationalizing several public owned industries and cutting back on social security expenditure. It also promoted private ownership and entrepreneurship. Thatcher's society was a competitive one in which the rich and often the young could become extremely wealthy.

In 1982, after a decline in popularity, and just before a General Election, Thatcher involved Britain in the Falklands War against Argentina from 2 April to 14/15 June 1982, this with the loss of over 1000 lives. The Conservative Party was subsequently re-elected.

As unemployment increased, and inner-city poverty grew rapidly, racial tensions were raised, culminating in several riots in the early 1980s; support for the National Front (the neo-fascist movement) also rose.

The Thatcher administration passed several restrictive laws to limit Trade Union activity – gone were the days when the TUC could grind the nation to a halt with its strike activity. The 1980s also saw a rise in the inequalities between different regions in Britain. The North of England, Scotland, Wales, and parts of Northern Ireland became the poorest areas in Britain, with the highest levels of unemployment.

The Conservative Party promoted new business activity, creating private enterprise grants, and directing large amounts of funding to technical and scientific education in the hope that Britain would once more become a competitive nation.

As the 1980s progressed the Thatcher administration became increasingly unpopular. The proposed dismantling of the Welfare State and the National Health Service provoked much public reaction. However, the Community Charge or 'Poll Tax', a per capita tax introduced firstly in Scotland, and then in the rest of the country, resulted in violent protest and riots. The tax was regressive and fell most heavily on the poor, young, and infirm.

By the end of the 1980s, Britain was divided between the very poor and the very rich. Splits within the Conservative Cabinet over European issues and a crisis in the Government finally resulted in Margaret Thatcher's resignation in 1990.

10.1 Historical Snapshot

10.1 Historical Snapshots

1980	Sixpence pieces cease to be legal tender.
	Budget raises tax allowances and duties on petrol, alcohol and tobacco.
	Unemployment exceeds 1.5 million for the first time since 1978.
	Inflation rises to 21.8 per cent.
	First compact disks (CDs) are produced by Philips in the Netherlands and Sony in Japan.
	Launch of IBM's personal computer in the USA.
	Acquired Immunodeficiency Syndrome (AIDS) diagnosed for the first time in USA.
1981	The stock market suffers the second worst crash in its history.
	British Leyland announces the closure of three plants with the loss of 2,850 jobs.
1982	Murdoch transfers control of *The Times* and *Sunday Times* to News International.
	Mercury receives a licence to operate telephones in competition with British Telecom.
	The 20 pence coin goes into circulation.
1983	The £1 coin comes into circulation.
1984	Robert Maxwell buys the Mirror Newspaper Group for £113.4 million.

	Flotation of 51 per cent of British Telecom shares is launched.
1985	Sir Clive Sinclair, inventor of the C5 electric tricycle, calls in the receiver.
1986	Nuclear reactor explosion at Chernobyl near Kiev in Ukraine.
	Government advocates the privatization of the water industry.
	Austin Rover is renamed the Rover Group.
	Four million people apply for shares in the Trustee Savings Bank (TSB).
	Barclays announces it is disinvesting in South Africa, where it is the biggest bank.
	Four million apply for British Gas Shares.
1987	Ernest Saunders resigns as Guinness Chief Executive over the Department of Trade and Industry (DTI) probe into the Distillers takeover.
	The sterling-dollar exchange rate reaches its highest level in four years - £1=$1.5870.
	Work begins on the Channel Tunnel in UK and France.
1988	World Health Organisation (WHO) estimate HIV-infected cases to be over 120 million, with 120,000 cases of AIDS reported worldwide.

Chronicle of Britain, J.L. International Publishing, 1992; Williams, T.I. *Invention and Discovery in the 20th Century*, Harrap, 1990.

10.2 Earnings and Employment

10.2.1 Earnings, Standard Tables

10.2.1a Incomes and Wages

	1980	1981	1982	1983	1984	1985	1986	1987	1988	1989
	£	£	£	£	£	£	£	£	£	£
Full Time Male										
Solicitor										
General Practitioner	242.2	297.1	320.9	338.0			425.3	463.9	511.5	588.2
Police Constable	142.2	157.9	180.9	209.6	227.7	244.8	250.2	264.9	288.5	308.1
Teacher (secondary)	125.3	172.2	174.1	188.6	196.9	209.5	233.0	250.0	286.9	309.5
Nurse (Staff Nurse)	97.8	118.6	122.3	136.4	136.6	150.0	164.1	175.6	191.3	233.8
Train Driver	115.2	132.9	151.7	162.3	171.9	191.7	203.3	225.4	248.5	261.6
Coal Miner (face trained)	153.6	165.3	180.9	192.9		199.6	227.3	246.9	281.6	315.0
Fitter	121.4	139.9	141.5	151.9	165.4	185.1	197.1	204.4	228.7	291.8
Turner	122.5	143.5	129.3	141.2	151.2	170.0	177.3	198.9	216.6	235.3
Bricklayer	109.6	115.5	124.2	131.2	145.8	145.4	158.9	169.3	179.9	195.7
Labourer	93.6	101.4	109.1	117.3	126.3	131.6	140.9	151.9	164.2	182.9
Compositor	132.0	164.2	171.5	176.5	190.0	208.4	218.8	236.7	268.2	
Farm Worker	69.4	88.4	98.1	118.4	124.0	125.3	121.0	124.1	145.5	150.4
Numerical Clerk	97.6	114.3	123.3	132.8	144.7	160.1	169.3	171.6	189.3	195.2
Baker	98.2	112.0	117.7	122.9	132.8	137.3	149.6	152.3	158.9	176.9
Full Time Female										
Police Constable		132.8	152.1	178.9	196.0	210.2	218.6	240.5	259.9	264.7
Teacher (secondary)	109.8	148.5	150.4	163.2	171.6	181.5	201.7	218.3	250.1	270.9
Nurse (Staff Nurse)	82.2	93.9	101.7	115.8	118.4	129.4	143.7	151.0	167.1	214.2
Farm Worker		67.9	80.3	89.7	95.0	102.6	104.0	111.37	120.2	
Numerical Clerk	57.4	82.8	94.1	103.8	113.1	122.1	129.6	135.9	154.4	162.8
Textile Worker	61.3	66.4	71.5	77.6	82.3	89.6	96.4	101.5	110.1	117.2
Typist	68.5	76.9	86.3	94.4	102.3	110.0	116.5	126.9	138.7	152.8
Nursery Nurse	66.4	79.7	84.3	95.5	96.3	103.5	111.0	119.0	125.1	148.3
Hairdresser	47.7	51.5	56.0	60.5	67.4	74.5	101.3	108.2	116.7	128.1

New Earnings Survey.

All figures are weekly. Blank space denotes no available data.

10.2.1b Average Weekly Earnings

	Mining and Quarrying	Metal Goods Engineering and Vehicle Industries	Engineering and Allied Industries	Total Manufacturing	Food, Drink and Tobacco	Coal, Petroleum and Chemical Products	Gas, Electricity and Water	Public Administration and Defence	Misc. Services	All Industries
	£	£	£	£	£	£	£	£	£	£
Males										
1980	116.58	118.20	107.82	111.64	115.61	124.77	126.12	96.60	103.88	113.06
1981	126.08	132.96	118.72	123.23	126.36	140.02	142.28			125.58
1982	138.54	139.01	129.89	134.26	138.28	150.81	157.69			137.06
1983	150.14	154.23	140.70	147.23	148.85	196.68	169.12			149.13
Females										
1980		73.64	73.54	68.40	74.60	77.83	81.75	76.18	56.76	111.64
1981		79.07	81.54	75.71	83.06	87.75	99.07			76.44
1982		88.12	88.57	83.17	90.76	94.69	103.22			83.96
1983		99.16	99.14	90.29	99.56	108.61	111.72			91.18

	All Manufacturing Industries	Metals, Mineral Products and Chemicals	Metal Goods, Engineering and Vehicle Industries	Other Manufacturing	Construction	Distribution, Hotels and Catering	Transport and Communications	Banking and Finance	Other Services	All Industries
Males										
1984[1,2]	158.9	168.8	157.3	156.0	149.4	125.8	167.0	151.1	129.8	158.8
1985[2]	172.6	182.3	171.5	169.0	156.8	135.0	179.4	160.7	138.9	163.6
1986[2]	183.4	191.5	182.7	180.3	167.2	143.8	190.9	169.6	148.2	174.4
1987	222.3	233.6	222.0	216.5	198.6	188.1	226.9	284.5	224.1	224.0
1988	213.9	234.7	238.1	216.3	200.1					
1989	264.6	273.5	268.3	254.4	242.9	227.8	262.0	350.9	269.2	269.5
Females										
1984[2]	96.0	100.3	102.2	92.1		81.7	125.5	107.1	89.9	n/a
1985[2]	104.5	110.9	110.9	100.0		89.4	138.0	113.4	95.7	101.3
1986[2]	111.6	117.4	117.1	107.5		95.0	143.3	118.9	101.5	107.5
1987	133.4	142.3	137.0	128.3	134.8	118.3	158.2	160.8	160.1	148.1
1988	137.3	144.2	139.9	132.3						
1989	159.1	174.2	164.9	151.5	166.7	144.9	191.2	202.5	198.5	182.3

Regional Trends, 1980–1989.

Original sources, New Earnings Survey; Department of Employment; Department of Economic Development, Northern Ireland. Blank space indicates no available data. [1]From 1984 industry groups are based on the revised 1980 Standard Industrial Classification. [2]Earnings are for manual workers.

10.2.2 Regional Earnings

	South East	Greater London	Rest of South East	East Anglia	South West	West Mids	East Mids	Yorks and Humber	North West	North	England	Wales	Scotland	UK
	£	£	£	£	£	£	£	£	£	£	£	£	£	£
Full Time Male														
1980	134.6	143.8	125.7	116.0	115.9	118.2	117.8	118.6	120.8	120.2	124.7	119.1	124.7	124.5
1981	152.4	163.8	141.3	133.7	132.6	131.5	133.6	133.6	136.5	134.	141.0	132.7	140.0	140.5
1982	169.3	183.0	156.0	145.0	143.2	143.7	144.3	146.8	148.2	148.8	154.8	146.9	154.5	154.5
1983	184.9	200.1	169.9	157.4	156.2	155.2	155.0	158.6	160.1	159.3	168.1	156.3	167.5	167.5
1983	181.3	196.5	166.5	154.0	153.7	153.2	152.7	156.3	157.9	157.1	165.3	154.5	164.4	164.7
1984	198.2	214.7	182.3	166.9	166.1	167.0	164.6	167.4	171.9	167.5	179.4	165.8	178.7	178.8
1985	213.8	233.2	196.2	182.7	179.0	180.2	175.5	180.7	185.2	179.3	193.3	179.1	189.7	192.4
1986	232.8	255.0	212.8	195.1	193.1	193.9	190.9	193.2	198.4	192.7	209.0	190.5	201.3	207.5
1987	254.1	280.5	230.5	208.9	209.3	206.7	204.2	206.8	212.5	206.0	226.0	204.3	214.6	224.0
1988	283.0	312.8	255.8	229.6	227.6	225.8	222.5	224.1	231.1	223.0	248.4	217.8	233.3	245.8
1989	312.4	348.8	281.4	254.6	253.3	246.6	242.8	244.5	250.9	243.5	272.9	238.6	251.2	269.5
Full Time Female														
1980	86.4	93.6	79.0	74.4	75.2	75.4	72.3	73.4	75.3	76.5	79.5	75.4	74.7	78.8
1981	99.6	107.4	91.2	87.2	87.2	86.7	84.6	85.6	88.4	88.0	92.1	87.5	87.1	91.4
1982	109.5	118.9	99.4	93.9	93.5	93.4	90.8	92.3	94.8	93.0	99.8	92.6	95.0	99.0
1983	120.2	131.0	108.5	103.1	102.6	101.7	99.2	101.3	103.4	103.1	109.6	104.4	104.0	108.8
1983	121.0	131.8	109.3	103.3	103.4	102.5	99.8	102.2	104.4	103.6	110.3	105.0	104.8	109.5
1984	130.5	142.8	117.5	110.3	110.2	110.3	106.9	107.7	112.1	110.3	118.3	111.1	111.1	117.2
1985	140.9	154.4	127.1	118.6	119.4	117.6	114.3	117.3	121.0	119.7	127.6	118.8	119.1	126.4
1986	153.8	169.3	138.3	128.6	128.8	126.7	125.7	126.4	130.7	128.1	138.6	127.1	129.8	137.2
1987	167.6	184.9	149.6	137.2	137.6	136.4	132.1	135.5	138.0	137.0	149.5	137.5	139.9	148.1
1988	188.1	208.2	167.3	150.3	152.2	148.9	145.3	150.6	153.2	148.8	166.1	150.3	152.2	164.2
1989	209.1	232.3	186.2	168.3	169.9	165.1	158.8	164.2	171.0	161.9	184.4	168.0	169.6	182.3

New Earnings Survey

Earnings are averaged, before tax and include overtime.

10.2.3 Incomes, Miscellaneous

10.2.3a UK Pay: Highest and Lowest Full Time Weekly Earnings, 1983

	£
Ten Highest Paid Occupations	
Medical Practitioner	338.0
Finance, Insurance and Tax Specialists	311.2
Police Inspectors, Fire Officers	283.2
University Academic Staff	269.7
Personnel and HR Managers	265.0
Marketing and Sales Managers	253.4
Police Sergeants, Fire Supervisors	250.5
Mechanical Engineers	234.8
Journalists, Office Managers	234.4
Ships' Officers	233.4
Ten Lowest Paid Occupations	
Cleaners (female)	81.8
Counter Hands, Catering (female)	80.3
Receptionists (female)	80.1
Sewing Machinists (female)	77.6
Barmaids (female)	77.2
Kitchen Hands (female)	75.7
Check Out Operators (female)	74.9
Shop Assistants (female)	73.4
Waitresses (female)	72.5
Hairdressers (female)	60.5

Labour Research, November, 1983.

Original source, *New Earnings Survey*.

10.2.3b Top Directors' Pay, 1982

Director	Company	Financial Year End	Pay (£)	Number of Average Workers[1]
Richard Giordano	BOC	9.92	579,000	65
Patrick Sergeant	Associated Newspapers	9.92	302,596	33
Donald Reich	BOC	9.92	300,000	34
Gerald Ronson	Heron Group	3.92	288,000	50
Roland 'Tiny' Rowland	Lonhro	9.92	266,034	41
Russell Evans	Rank Organisation	10.92	250,250[2]	30
Donald Craig	BOC	.92	250,000	26
Peter Baxendell	Shell Transport	12.92	192,553	n/a
Warren Sinsheimer	Plessey	4.92	188,200	28
Peter Walters	BP	12.92	172,770	16
Stuart Cameron	Gallaher	12.92	168,027	28
Geoffrey Kent	Imperial Group	10.92	165,273	33
Robert Gross	Geers Gross	12.92	164,000	16
Trevor Chinn	Lex Service Group	12.92	152,747	15
Robert Wilmot	ICL	9.92	152,000	15
John Harvey-Jones	ICI	12.92	150,609[2]	16

Labour Research, October, 1983.

[1]Directors pay divided by average workers pay according to company accounts. [2]Annualised. Taken from *Labour Research* Fourth Annual Survey of top directors.

10.2.4 Employment

10.2.4a Unemployment by Region

	1980	1981	1982	1983	1984	1985	1986	1987	1988	1989
	000's	000's	000's	000's	000's	000's	000's	000's	000's	000's
Males										
United Kingdom	1,180.6	1,843.3	2,133.2	2,218.6	2,197.4	2,251.7	2,252.5	2,045.8	1,492.5	1,181.2
North	99.9	141.1	158.8	164.7	165.9	169.3	167.3	155.1	124.5	94.9
Yorkshire and Humberside	109.9	175.9	201.1	207.4	204.8	212.9	220.1	201.2	158.9	118.9
East Midlands	71.6	115.3	130.7	134.8	134.1	136.9	136.0	125.2	97.3	67.5
East Anglia	28.5	45.9	53.2	54.8	52.0	53.2	53.9	47.4	30.5	21.7
South East	241.0	407.5	490.8	514.5	511.0	527.1	524.7	460.8	328.1	240.3
South West	75.3	112.0	128.0	129.3	127.2	132.8	131.6	115.0	81.2	60.1
West Midlands	119.4	213.9	249.9	257.3	243.0	243.1	238.6	211.1	158.0	108.5
North West	171.5	257.9	298.6	315.7	313.2	317.1	313.2	284.3	228.5	175.4
England	916.8	1,468.9	1,711.1	1,778.5	1,751.3	1,792.4	1,785.4	1,600.1	1,405.0	887.3
Wales	72.0	106.8	120.9	122.9	123.2	127.7	126.1	111.8	87.6	63.9
Scotland	140.3	197.6	223.9	232.1	235.2	243.6	248.1	241.9	197.8	155.3
Northern Ireland	51.5	70.0	77.3	85.1	87.7	88.0	92.9	92.0	84.1	74.8
Females										
United Kingdom	484.3	677.0	783.6	886.0	962.5	1,019.5	1,036.6	907.6	681.2	454.5
North	40.8	50.9	55.8	61.0	64.6	68.4	67.6	58.0	47.9	32.4
Yorkshire and Humberside	44.7	61.3	72.0	81.3	87.0	92.9	95.8	84.8	69.2	43.6
East Midlands	27.1	39.9	45.9	53.2	60.2	65.3	66.8	58.7	45.6	27.8
East Anglia	10.7	15.5	19.0	22.6	25.3	28.1	29.5	25.1	17.5	9.5
South East	87.1	140.1	173.8	206.9	236.5	255.2	260.0	219.7	158.6	96.8
South West	31.6	43.6	51.0	59.3	66.5	72.2	74.2	63.9	46.4	27.6
West Midlands	50.7	76.6	87.9	97.4	102.4	106.6	108.0	94.8	75.0	44.3
North West	70.6	97.0	109.2	121.4	129.6	134.9	135.1	119.0	97.2	63.9
England	363.1	524.8	614.7	703.1	772.3	823.5	837.0	724.1	643.8	346.0
Wales	30.7	39.1	43.8	47.5	50.1	52.9	52.9	45.2	36.5	22.6
Scotland	67.6	85.2	94.1	103.4	106.4	109.3	111.8	103.8	87.3	58.8
Northern Ireland	22.9	17.9	31.0	32.0	33.7	33.8	34.9	34.5	33.4	27.1

Regional Trends, HMSO.

Figures are annual averages. Original source, Department of Employment.

10.2.4b Employment by Region

	1980	1981	1982	1983	1984	1985	1986	1987	1988	1989
	000's	000's	000's	000's	000's	000's	000's	000's	000's	000's
Males										
United Kingdom	13,045	12,562	11,760	13,320	13,212	11,949	11,881	11,887	12,240	11,975
North	729	654	636	592	574	571	598	599	621	587
Yorkshire and Humberside	1,155	1,083	1,027	1,025	1,008	1,008	999	987	1,011	954
East Midlands	892	855	821	809	797	800	861	852	884	837
East Anglia	404	400	369	399	402	404	415	458	495	409
South East	4,166	4,135	3,843	4,031	4,035	4,065	4,020	4,028	4,154	4,094
South West	906	883	841	863	862	870	873	865	886	892
West Midlands	1,290	1,199	1,100	1,128	1,121	1,132	1,151	1,155	1,202	1,116
North West	1,488	1,391	1,312	1,306	1,290	1,292	1,212	1,191	1,215	1,279
England	11,031	10,600	9,950	11,736	11,650	10,144	10,129	10,135	10,467	10,169
Wales	579	551	512	516	505	507	482	479	489	517
Scotland	1,154	1,128	1,058	1,068	1,057	1,054	1,032	1,066	1,020	1,018
Northern Ireland	280	283	240	250	246	244	238	257	262	268
Females										
United Kingdom	9,365	9,331	8,760	10,184	10,402	9,512	9,678	9,925	10,331	10,770
North	494	468	458	454	461	465	488	490	508	510
Yorkshire and Humberside	795	768	734	740	749	753	810	814	845	859
East Midlands	614	613	588	612	623	627	664	676	708	731
East Anglia	283	281	260	286	297	307	318	338	356	363
South East	3,063	3,128	2,886	3,103	3,175	3,255	3,295	3,420	3,584	3,718
South West	656	658	642	658	673	683	715	726	747	837
West Midlands	871	852	788	798	808	811	881	895	940	937
North West	1,102	1,075	1,014	1,050	1,072	1,092	1,051	1,071	1,097	1,165
England	7,878	7,845	7,370	8,943	9,130	7,993	8,222	8,432	8,785	9,120
Wales	391	389	364	388	398	400	378	385	402	462
Scotland	873	874	814	853	874	901	861	880	908	941
Northern Ireland	223	224	212	216	216	219	217	228	235	246

Regional Trends, HMSO.

Original source, Department of Employment.

10.2.4c Women in the Professions, 1988

Profession	Males	Females
	%	%
Architects	92.1	7.8
Barristers	78.8	21.2
Chartered Accountants	90.3	9.7
Dentists	76.8	23.2
Engineers	99.5	0.5
General Practitioners	77.6	22.4
Solicitors	78.6	21.4
Surgeons	96.8	3.2
Surveyors	94.3	5.7
Vets	73.5	26.5

Accounting, Organisations and Society, Vol.17, No.3/4, April/May, 1992, p.309.

10.3 Consumer Expenditure

10.3.1 Consumer Expenditure, Standard Table

	Food	Alcoholic Drink	Tobacco	Housing	Fuel and Power	Clothing and Footwear	House-hold Goods and Services	Transport and Com-muni-cation	Other Goods and Ser-vices	Recrea-tion, Entertain-ment and Education	Total Con-sumer Expen-diture
	£m	£m	£m	£m	£m	£m	£m	£m	£m	£m	£m
1980	22,873	10,153	4,867	20,443	6,413	9,750	6,469	5,211	22,788	27,421	135,738
1981	24,946	11,152	5,515	22,693	7,727	10,155	10,522	26,208	19,367	14,239	155,412
1982	26,490	12,003	5,881	26,058	8,696	10,925	11,104	28,827	21,634	15,647	170,650
1983	28,061	13,270	6,209	28,045	9,348	12,120	12,131	32,396	25,102	16,988	187,028
1984	29,274	14,316	6,622	29,603	9,492	13,186	12,861	34,365	28,568	18,365	200,261
1985	30,657	15,651	7,006	32,599	10,560	14,912	14,108	37,959	31,852	20,130	218,947
1986	32,561	16,404	7,471	36,173	10,885	16,661	15,765	41,495	37,835	22,364	243,030
1987	34,429	17,451	7,653	39,800	10,905	17,684	17,573	46,752	44,145	24,671	267,523
1988	36,587	18,754	7,945	44,500	11,115	19,034	20,112	54,094	53,590	27,624	302,057
1989	39,264	19,809	8,175	48,929	11,459	19,943	21,605	59,513	61,047	30,569	330,532

CSO Annual Abstract of Statistics, 1993.

10.3.2a Regional Household Expenditure

	Housing	Fuel and Light	Food	Alco-holic Drink	Tobacco	Clothing and Footwear	Durable House-hold Goods	Other Goods	Trans port, Vehicles, Services, Miscel-laneous	Total	Average Expendi-ture per Person
	£/wk	£/wk	£/wk	£/wk	£/wk	£/wk	£/wk	£/wk	£/wk	£/wk	£/wk
United Kingdom	18.22	6.83	26.22	5.71	3.54	9.11	8.58	9.11	30.97	118.30	43.46
North	14.84	6.43	25.43	6.47	4.03	8.98	7.78	7.88	28.11	109.94	40.57
Yorkshire and Humberside	13.89	6.05	24.63	6.13	3.96	8.83	6.95	7.87	24.45	102.77	38.01
East Midlands	15.60	6.53	25.06	4.89	3.34	7.66	10.59	9.44	30.35	113.45	41.66
East Anglia	17.51	7.06	25.89	4.52	2.92	7.90	7.78	9.66	29.22	112.45	40.06
South East	23.24	6.72	27.72	5.89	3.20	9.77	10.17	10.46	36.43	133.60	50.21
South West	18.91	7.39	24.21	4.79	2.71	7.83	7.00	8.99	30.67	112.51	43.17
West Midlands	19.67	6.39	25.99	5.63	3.47	9.62	8.15	8.74	30.16	117.82	42.23
North West	17.76	6.59	25.83	6.19	3.77	9.13	7.66	8.78	30.10	115.81	42.08
England	19.20	6.63	26.16	5.74	3.41	9.08	8.71	9.31	31.63	119.87	44.35
Wales	14.97	7.72	25.86	5.27	3.53	8.75	8.04	8.36	27.37	109.87	40.32
Scotland	12.74	7.32	26.54	6.08	4.51	9.56	8.46	8.21	28.14	111.56	39.55
Northern Ireland	11.16	10.86	28.47	4.02	4.56	9.52	4.91	6.85	26.45	106.81	34.56

Regional Trends.

Original Source, *CSO Annual Abstract of Statistics, 1993.* Figures are weekly averages.

10.3.2b Households with Certain Durable Goods

	Washing Machine	Tumble Drier	Dish-washer	Refrige-rator	Deep Freezer[1]	Tele-phone	Black and White TV only	Colour TV	Video	Home Com-puter	Total House-holds in Samples
	%	%	%	%	%	%	%	%	%	%	
1979–1980[2]											
Great Britain	75	20	3	92	43	69	28	68			23,210
North	85	17	1	89	37	57	28	70			1,400
Yorkshire and Humberside	82	21	2	88	35	63	28	68			2,135
East Midlands	83	20	3	92	41	65	27	70			1,564
East Anglia	80	21	4	93	53	70	27	70			843
South East	67	20	5	95	50	77	29	67			7,149
South West	71	21	4	93	51	68	29	69			1,810
West Midlands	76	20	2	91	39	66	30	67			2,193
North West	75	19	2	91	36	68	29	69			2,777
England	74	20	4	93	44	70	29	68			19,871
Wales	79	20	2	90	49	63	28	69			1,125
Scotland	81	21	3	89	33	71	25	72			2,214
Northern Ireland	66			82		51		91[3]			1,098
1984–1985[2]											
Great Britain	80	31	6	95	63	80	13	85	28	11	19,773
North	85	26	3	94	57	73	13	85	26	10	1,155
Yorkshire and Humberside	85	31	3	91	56	75	15	83	26	11	1,841
East Midlands	85	31	5	96	65	78	15	83	27	11	1,400
East Anglia	84	36	8	94	71	81	15	84	26	10	731
South East	75	33	9	97	70	86	12	85	32	12	6,015
South West	78	33	7	95	70	82	11	86	25	11	1,560
West Midlands	79	29	5	93	58	74	16	83	26	12	1,797
North West	82	29	4	93	60	79	12	86	26	13	2,325
England	80	31	6	95	65	81	13	84	28	12	16,824
Wales	81	28	3	95	63	71	13	85	24	8	997
Scotland	85	33	4	95	51	76	11	87	28	8	1,952
Northern Ireland	76	28	6	91	43	72	12	84	22	7	6,783

Regional Trends, HMSO, 1988.

Original sources, *Office of Population Censuses and Surveys, General Household Survey, Northern Ireland Department of Finance and Personnel, Family Expenditure Survey, Continuous Household Survey*. Blank space denotes no data available. [1]Fridge freezers are attributed to both Refrigerator and Deep Freezer except in Northern Ireland. [2]Average of figures for the two calendar years taken together. [3]Includes black and white TVs.

10.4 Prices

10.4.1 Food Prices

10.4.1a Food Basket

Article (per lb. unless otherwise stated)	1980	1981	1982	1983	1984	1985	1986	1987	1988	1989
	p.	p.	p.	p.	p.	p.	p.	p.	p.	p.
White Wheat Bread:										
Wrapped and Sliced (1¼ lb/800g)	34.3	36.7	37.0	37.7	38.3	39.4	42.0	44.0	46.0	48.0
Unwrapped and Sliced (1¼ lb/800g)	37.3	40.6	42.7	43.4	45.4	47.0	53.0	55.0	58.0	60.0
Other Bread (14oz/400g)	25.0	27.1	28.4	29.2	31.1	32.4	54.0	56.0	59.0	62.0
Flour, (wheat) white, self raising (3lb/1.5kg)	39.8	42.4	43.2	43.5	42.6	42.0	42.0	46.0	52.0	53.0
Rice (whole grain, polished)	29.0	29.6	32.2							
Beef, home-killed, first quality:										
Sirloin (without bone)	218.9	244.0	271.5	274.1	291.0	295.7	289.0	295.0	310.0	359.0
Brisket (with bone)						151.5	143.0			
Brisket (without bone)	109.4	127.3	140.3	142.9	147.2	148.9	155.0	156.0	165.0	181.0
Pork, home-killed:										
Leg (foot off)	91.9	99.7	103.2	104.4	106.7	113.2	111.0	113.0	109.0	115.0
Loin (with bone)	112.6	120.3	122.5	123.3	127.3	142.7	138.0	141.0	150.0	148.0
Ham (cooked, sliced, without bone)	166.7	177.2	190.8	192.6	201.4	213.5	51.0[2]	57.0	58.0	60.0
Bacon:										
Back, smoked	121.3	137.3	149.2	150.5	145.9	158.3	163.0	166.0	162.0[5]	170.0[5]
Streaky, smoked	83.1	90.7	99.6	99.6	107.4	105.0	102.0	105.0	158.0[5]	168.0[5]
Fish, fresh and fillets	112.3	113.4	122.6	129.8	140.5	146.5	162.0	195.0	213.0	213.0
Margarine (standard quality) (½ lb/200g)	16.2	16.8	16.9	17.1	19.0	21.5	23.0	18.0	38.0[6]	40.0[6]
Lard	28.3	28.9	30.4	31.1	31.7	37.7	18.0[3]	16.0	16.0	16.0
Milk (pint)	17.0	18.5	20.0	21.0	21.0	21.8	24.0	25.0	25.0[7]	27.0[7]
Butter	88.1	98.0	101.9	105.1	105.4	115.4	55.0[3]	57.0	57.0	62.0
Cheese	98.4	111.0	114.7	115.3	116.5	120.4	125.0	126.0	130.0	142.0
Eggs, fresh, home produced:										
Weight 63–70g size 2	72.6	81.1	79.0	78.2	91.1	96.9	109.0	105.0	114.0	106.0
Potatoes (white)	5.4	8.2	7.0	7.4	12.3	8.5	8.0	11.0	12.0	12.0
Potatoes (red)	6.2	8.9	7.9	8.2	13.2	9.1	10.0	12.0	11.0	11.0
Cabbage (green)	12.1	14.1	14.5	15.7	20.3	20.6	22.0	22.0	26.0	26.0
Onions (ripe)	13.3	13.8	13.3	13.2	17.4	16.4	15.0	18.0	21.0	20.0
Cauliflower				32.7	31.9	38.9	59.0	50.0	53.0	62.0
Carrots				11.4	15.8	17.7	15.0	19.0	21.0	20.0
Apples (eating)	20.6	26.8	23.0	24.2	31.3	30.0	31.0	35.0	34.0	35.0
Oranges	22.9	24.8	26.9	26.6	29.2	32.6	29.0	31.0	30.0	16.0 each

Continued

10.4.1 Food Basket *continued*

Article (per lb. unless otherwise stated)	1980 p.	1981 p.	1982 p.	1983 p.	1984 p.	1985 p.	1986 p.	1987 p.	1988 p.	1989 p.
Pears				28.3	31.2	31.6	34.0	41.0	37.0	41.0
Bananas				31.6	37.0	41.0	44.0	46.0	49.0	47.0
Sugar, white granulated (1 kg)	37.2	41.0	45.5	45.7	47.7	47.3	47.0	47.0	52.0	55.0
Coffee (pure roasted)	236.1	226.9	243.9	100.8[1]	113.8	135.3	129.0	147.0	134.0	134.0
Tea										
Higher priced	123.6	124.8	126.8	32.8	39.5	56.2	42.0 [4]	42.0	41.0	43.0
Medium priced	112.8	112.8	118.8	30.7	37.1	53.8	97.0 [4]	96.0	96.0	105.0
Lower priced	101.6	96.4	104.0	27.1	33.0	49.3				

Employment Gazette, 1980–1989.

Blank space denotes no data available. [1]Pure Instant, 100g. [2]per ¼ lb. [3]per 250g. [4]loose per 125g in 1986; tea bags per 125g in 1986. [5]Back vacuum packed, back not vacuum packed. [6]Low fat spread, 250g. [7]Skimmed

10.4.2 Prices, General Articles

	1980 p.	1981 p.	1982 p.	1983 p.	1984 p.	1985 p.	1986 p.	1987 p.	1988 p.	1989 p.
Aspirin (100)	30.0	36.0	39.0	44.0	49.0	54.0	51.0	53.0	54.0	56.0
Average House Price	£27,244	£28,028	£28,508	£31,678	£34,160	£37,304	£43,647	£51,290	£64,615	£74,976
Beer (1 pint)	40.5	49.0	54.5	56.5	65.0	70.0	73.5	76.0[1]	80.0	87.0
Cadbury's Dairy Milk chocolate (½ lb.)	68.0					84.0				
Cheddar Cheese	89.0				104.0	104.0				145.0
Colmans Mustard (113g.)	68.0		54.0	65.0 (4oz.)	69.0	76.0	80.0	85.0	89.0	94.0
Daily Mail	10.0	10.0	10.0							
Guinness Extra Stout (1 pint)	49.0					91.0				
Inland Letter Post	12.0	14.0	15.5	16.0	17.0	17.0	18.0	18.0	19.0	20.0
Mars Bar	13 to 14	14 to 15	16.0	16.0	17 to 18	18.0	20.0	20.0	20.0	20.0
Pears Transparent Soap (150g.)		39.0	45.0	47.0	49.0	51.0	53.0	53.0	43.0	38.0 (125g.)
Petrol (1 gallon)	120.0	133.0	162.5	168.0	180.0	192.0	193.0	175.0	169.0	36.0[2]
Pocket Money	99.0	113.0	95.0	122.0	105.0	109.0	117.0	116.0	123.0	140.0
Red Label Tea (1lb.)	88.0				124.0					
Scotch Whisky (standard bottle)	525.0	610.0	650.0	680.0	725.0	750.0		760.0	770.0	825.0
Swan Vestas Matches	5.0					7.0				
The Times	15.0	15.0								

The Boots Company; Birds Eye Walls Ltd; British Library; Burmah Castrol; Cadburys Ltd; Colmans of Norwich; Guinness Brewing GB; Halifax Building Society; Rowntrees; Royal Mail; Sainsburys Archives; The Scotch Whisky Association; Swan Hotel, Holmes Chapel and Unilever Historical Archives.

Blank space denotes no prices available. [1]From 1988, change of source to Swan Hotel, Holmes Chapel. [2]From 1989, all prices are quoted per metric litre for 4-star.

10.4.3 Prices, Selected

Item	Source	Description	Price £ p.
Alcoholic Drink			
Champagne	*Which*, 1981	Krug	20.85
		Moët & Chandon	7.69
		Marks & Spencer	6.29
		Bollinger	9.95
		JS Sainsbury	5.82
Liqueur	*Northwich Chronicle*, December 2, 1982	Baileys Irish Cream	4.49
Fortified Wine	*Which*, 1983	Harveys Bristol Cream	3.60
		Old Croft Original	3.50
Liqueur		Baileys Irish Cream	5.80
		Cointreau	9.70
Spirits		Martell 3-Star Cognac	9.85
		Smirnoff Red Label Vodka	6.75
		Bacardi White Rum	7.70
		Bells Whisky	7.40
		Gordon's Gin	6.80
		Lamb's Navy Dark Rum	7.50
Wine		Blue Nun	3.00
		Mateus Rosé	3.00
		Hirondelle Red	3.20 (litre)
		Lutomer Laski Riesling	2.10
Vermouth		Martini Dry	2.60
Wine	*Which*, 1984	Dom Crespo Vinho Verde	2.29 (Coop)
		Vinho Verde	2.15 (BHS)
Spirit	*Which*, 1985	Co-op Heatherdale Whisky	6.50
		Sainsbury's Highland Malt	12.50
		Teacher's Highland Cream	8.00
Wine	*Which*, 1986	Goldener Oktober	3.21
		Blue Nun	2.99
		Hirondelle	3.99 (litre)
Lager	*Which*, 1986	Carlsberg Pilsner	22½ (½ pint)
		Heineken	22
		Carling Black Label	22½
		Tennents Super	31½
Fortified Wine		Cockburn's Special Reserve	5.99
		Croft Triple Crown	4.39
		Tesco Ruby	3.65
Sparkling Wine		Touraine Blanc de Blancs Brut, Brou	3.99 (Oddbins)
		Crémant de Bourgogne Rosé Brut 1982	5.35
		Asti Spumante Fontanafredda	4.85
Appliances: Domestic and Electrical			
Cookers	*Which*, 1980	Belling Compact 430 TR	160.00
		Carron Capri 3	500.00
		New World Nova Q4	300.00
		Parkinson Cowan 4000	175.00

Continued

10.4.3 Prices, Selected *continued*

Item	Source	Description	Price £	p.
Cookers *cont.*		Main Marigold Auto 2	250.00	
Pressure Cookers		Prestige Auto 6167	27.00	
		Tower 2823	14.50	
Dishwashers		Miele G540	525.00	
		Colston Ariston	220.00	
Espresso Machines		Krups Espresso Mini	963.00	
Freezers (fridge)		Electrolux TR1241	250.00	
		Indesit CM360LI	245.00	
Heaters		GEC Xpelair FH3D	29.00	
		Bush Nelson Creole	59.00	
Television		Baird 8180	270.00	
		Mitsubishi CBI00	320.00	
Toasters		M.R.Harvest 44260	12.50	
		Kenwood A121	14.00	
Tuner Amplifiers		Rotel RX-1000L	140.00	
		Tandberg TR2045	300.00	
		Trio KR-2010L	100.00	
Cleaners	*Which*, 1983	Aquavac Super 40 Wet/Dry Vacuum Cleaner	37.00	
		Electrolux 560 Upright	60.00	
Freezers		Ariston DF235 Fridge Freezer	160.00	
		Electrolux TR901	220.00	
		Hotpint Iced Diamond 8630W	235.00	
Portable Stereo Radio Recorders		Aiwa CS360	90.00	
		Philips D8614	150.00	
		Sony CFS-5L	80.00	
Televisions		Pye 7228	255.00	
		Sanyo CTP4101	280.00	
		Toshiba C1625B	280.00	
Video Recorders		Akai VS5ER	470.00	
		JVC HR7650EK	650.00	
		Ferguson 3V2R	690.00	
Cleaner	*Which*, 1984	Electrolux 560 Upright	90.00	
Food Processors		Braun Multipractic	45.00	
		Moulinex Multichef	38.00	
Cleaners	*Which*, 1985	Philips Mini Pro	60.00	
		Numatic Charles Wet/Dry Vacuum Cleaner	100.00	
Cookers		Belling Compact 430TR	215.00	
		Tricity Contessa 1657A	265.00	
		Creda Carefree 49702	355.00	
		New World Nova	215.00	
		Canon Contour Electronic	330.00	
Food Processor		Braun Multipractic	43.00	
Freezers		Ariston RF225	180.00	
		Electrolux TR915	265.00	

Continued

10.4.3 Prices, Selected *continued*

Item	Source	Description	Price	
			£	p.
Freezers *cont.*		Hotpoint Iced Diamond 8630W	270.00	
		Bejam 231 Chest Freezer	135.00	
		Kelvinator CFG31	155.00	
Portable Stereo Radio Recorders		Aiwa CA30	170.00	
		Philips D8534	120.00	
		Sony FH3	300.00	
CD Players	*Which*, 1986	Philips CD350	250.00	
		Sony CDP102	400.00	
		Technics SL-XPT	230.00	
Cleaner		Elecrolux 560 Upright	85.00	
Cookers		Belling Compact 430TR	240.00	
		Tricity Contessa 1657A	270.00	
		Creda Carefree 49702	400.00	
		New World Nova	230.00	
Dishwashers		AEG Favorit 420	250.00	
		Mile G542	600.00	
		Ariston Aristella LS1054	250.00	
Freezer		Bejam VF123 Chest Freezer	120.00	
Personal Radios		Aiwa Cr05	40.00	
		Panasonic RF07	115.00	
		Boots TR45	15.00	
Refrigerators		Bosch KTL17202	270.00	
		Hotpoint Iced Diamond	170.00	
Stereo Cassette Decks		Aiwa AD-F350	125.00	
		Trio KX-54	100.00	
Televisions		Mitsubishi CT2101TX	445.00	
		Toshiba 212T	430.00	
		Panasonic TXC22	530.00	
Video Recorders		JVC HRD750EK	580.00	
		Ferguson 3V48	450.00	
CD Players	*Which*, 1989	Philips D6800	130.00	
		Sony CDPC50	200.00	
Camcorders		Sony CCD-F340	1,000.00	
		Bauer VCC 606AF	850.00	
Cleaners		Numatic Charles	103.00	
		Aquavac Super 40	90.00	
Computers		Amstrad PC2286	1,379.00	
		Compaq Deskpro	2,496.00	
		IBM Model 50	2,377.00	
Cookers		Belling Compact 430TR	290.00	
		Tricity Contessa 1657A	350.00	
		Creda Carefree 49702	480.00	
		New World Royale 600SBS	515.00	
		Canon Cambridge	425.00	
		Parkinson Cowan Strata	270.00	
Dishwashers		AEG Favorit 667	440.00	

Continued

10.4.3 Prices, Selected *continued*

Item	Source	Description	Price £ p.
Dishwashers *cont.*		Miele G572	550.00
Espresso Machine		Bialletti Cappuccino Super	60.00
		Krups Espresso Mini	53.00
		Tefal Espresso	45.00
Food Processors		Kenwood FP300	50.00
		Moulinex 531	20.00
Loudspeaker		Wharfedale Delta 5	100.00
Portable Stereo Radio Recorders		Aiwa CSWR66	90.00
		Philips AW7192	70.00
		Sony CFD60L	180.00
Refrigerators		Bosch KTR1541	220.00
		Hotpoint Iced Diamond	190.00
		Snowcap 150DL	90.00
Telephone Answering Machines		Answercall Apollo	90.00
		Betacom LR1500	90.00
		Saisho 5000	100.00
Television		Sanyo CBP2148	380.00
Toasters		M.R.Harvest 44210	18.00
		R.H.Microschip 5600	24.00
		Swan 20454	17.00
		Kenwood TT400	16.00
Tumble Dryers		Creda 37305	69.99
		Philips D153	69.00
Tuner Amplifier		NAD 3020E	120.00
Video Recorders		Akai VS425EK	300.00
		JVC HRD75OEK	500.00
		Ferguson FV395	1,000.00
Washing Machines		Hoover Computer Logic	400.00
		Philips Auto de Luxe	275.00
		Indesit 823	220.00
		Candy D4-104X	280.00
Cookers	*Traditional Homes*, November 1989	Rayburn Cookers, Oil Fired	815.00
		Rayburn Cookers, Gas Fired	750.00
Heating		Charnwood Fireflow Real Fire	1,000.00
Baby Equipment			
Push Chairs	*Mothercare*, 1981	High-Back Minit Pushchair	12.95
	Which, 1982	Boots Fold Flat	23.00
		Mothercare de Luxe Recliner	44.00
		Silver Cross Super Carnival	47.00
		Maclaren Baby Buggy	25.00
		Mothercare Everyway Stroller	50.00
Baby Carriers	*Which*, 1983	Baby Bjorn	13.50
		Easy Rider	12.50
		Boots Baby Carrier	11.00
		Karrimor Papoose 1V	30.00

Continued

10.4.3 Prices, Selected *continued*

Item	Source	Description	Price £ p.
Baby Car Safety Restraints	*Which*, 1984	Cindico Monarch	38.00
		Kangol Dreamseat	30.00
Carrycot Restraints		Britax AA3-199	12.00
		Mothercare 7474-51	7.00
Push Chairs	*Which*, 1986	Aprica Elle, Pushchair Birth Upwards	139.00
		Bebe Comfort Baby Bus	60.00
		Three-in-One Pushchair with Carrycot, Jane Janette	133.00
		Maclaren Cabrio Twin XO72	150.00
		Mothercare Twin Reclining Stroller	100.00

Clothing and Footwear:
Children's

Item	Source	Description	Price £ p.
Dungarees	*Northwich Chronicle*, April 22, 1982	St. Michael Cotton Dungarees from	7.99
Jacket		St. Michael Pin Stripe Cotton Jacket	9.99
Skirt		St. Michael Belted Skirt	5.99
T Shirt		Cotton T Shirts from	1.50
Jeans	*Woolworths*, 1983	Cotton Jeans from	7.99
Shirt	*MUFC Catalogue Collection*, 1989	Polo Shirts from	5.95
Tops		Sharp Hooded Tops	21.99
Bottoms		Sharp Hooded Bottoms	14.99
Knitwear		Cardigan	21.99
Sweat Shirt		Adidas Sweat Shirt	17.95
T Shirt		Adidas T Shirt	9.95

Men's

Item	Source	Description	Price £ p.
Jeans	*Which*, 1980	Lee Cooper	15.99
		Wrangler	14.99
		St. Michael	11.99
		Levi Unisex	15.99
Knitwear	*Liberty*, 1981–1982	Fisherman's Rib V-Neck Sweater	22.00
Shirt		Tana Lawn Shirt	24.50
Tie		Pure Silk Ties from	10.50
Shirts	*Which*, 1983	BHS Polyester Cotton	5.99
		Double Two	9.50
		Peter England Pride	7.99
		St. Michael	6.50
		Van Heusen All Cotton	13.95
		Selfridges (voile)	14.95
Jacket	*Next*, 1985	Tan Calf Suede Cardigan	99.99
Knitwear		Jade/Acqua Jacquard Knit Sweater	16.99
Shirt		Yellow Striped Shirt	12.99
		Cotton Abstract Print Shirt	14.99
Suit		Grey Marl Wool Suit	120.00
Shorts		Stone Cotton Fatigue Shorts	14.99
Tie		Diagonal Stripe Tie	9.99
Coat	*House of Fraser*, 1986	Single Breasted Classic City Coat	89.99

Continued

10.4.3 Prices, Selected *continued*

Item	Source	Description	Price
			£ p.
Jacket		Gabicci Blouson Wadded Jacket	59.99
Knitwear		Crew Neck Jacquard Jumper	18.99
Shirts		Cotton Shirt	12.99
		Plain Sweatshirt	14.99
		Rugby Shirt with Sleeve	16.99
		Heavy Cotton Interlock Long Sleeved Shirt	16.99
Suit		Pure Wool Pin Stripe Suit	120.00
Tie		Silk Tie	8.99
Trousers		Cotton Twill Trousers with Turnups	18.99
		Sweat Pants with Cord Tie Waist	16.99
	Which, 1986	BHS Polyester Wool	19.99
		St. Michael 2100 Polyester Wool	19.99
		House of Fraser J86 Dave	17.99
		C & A Maestro Polyester	14.99
		Debenhams Polyester Viscose	17.99
Blazer	*Selfridge Collection*, 1989	Classic Navy Blazer	150.00
Coat		Raincoat	89.95
Hosiery		Cool Cotton Socks	5.50
Jackets		Italian Wool Jacket	205.00
		Outdoor Jacket from Barbour	99.95
		Leather Jacket in Antique Look Finish	189.00
Jeans		Designer Jeans by Yves St. Laurent	34.95
Knitwear		Classic Crew Neck Pullover	57.50
Shirts		Harvie & Hudson Shirts	49.50
		Pure Cotton Shirt	22.95
		Blue Chambray Shirt	34.95
Shoes		Classic Oxford Shoes	115.00
Tie		Pure Silk Ties from	18.95
Trousers		Charcoal Grey Flannel Trousers	75.00
		Cord Trousers	42.50
Women's			
Jeans	*Which*, November 1980	Lee Cooper	18.95
		St. Michael	10.75
		Brutus Unisex	9.95
Shoes	*C & J Clark Ltd.*, 1980	Ramona Black Calf Look Torlon	13.99
		Sidewalkers Modern C Fit, Rich Brown Leather	21.99
		Sidewalkers Sandals	21.99
		New Pussyfoot Bump C Fit	23.99
Hosiery	*Which*, 1981	BHS Micromesh Tights	1.49 (pack of 4)
		Cindy by Dorothy Vernon	0.39
		Charnos Amy Plain Tights	0.85
Dress	*Liberty*, 1981–1982	Dress in Lightweight Printed Wool	76.95
		Classic Dress in Knitted Polyester	66.50
Hosiery		Funn Silk Stockings	7.95

Continued

10.4.3 Prices, Selected *continued*

Item	Source	Description	Price £ p.
Hosiery *cont.*		Funn Lisle Stockings	3.95
		Elbeo Wool/Nylon Lace Textured Tights	5.95
Jacket		Quilted Calico Jacket	59.50
Nightwear		Liberty Print Tana Lawn Nightie	16.95
		Soft White Towelling Robe	35.00
Scarves		36 ins. Pure Silk Twill Square	22.50
		27 ins. Pure Silk Twill Square	14.95
Shawl		54 ins. Shawl in Liberty Print Varuna Wool	14.95
Shirt		Green Wool Viscose Shirt	16.95
		Classic Liberty Print Tana Lawn Shirt	17.95
Skirt		Green Wool Viscose Skirt	27.95
Blazer	*Marks and Spencer*, 1984	Cotton Blazer Brushed Inside	29.50
Blouse		Tie Neck Silk Blouse	19.99
Jacket		Donegal Wool Blouson	45.00
		Lined Blouson Jacket	35.00
Knitwear		Pure Wool Cardigan	14.99
		Cowl Neck British Wool Aran Style Jumper	15.99
		Wool Cable Knit Cardigan	18.99
		Mohair Mixed Jumpers	18.99
Pinafore		Cord Pinafore	19.99
Skirts		Shetland Skirt	27.50
		Donegal Tweed Skirt	25.00
		Tartan Skirts	17.99
Suit		Zip Front Flying Suit	39.50
		Herringbone Pure New Wool Suit	47.50
Trousers		Basque Front Trousers	17.99
Blouse	*Next*, 1984	White/Tobacco/Grey Striped Blouse	13.95
Dress		Blue Chambray Sundress with Cross Overstrap	19.95
Jacket		Khaki Cotton Drill Jacket	21.95
		Blue Crushed Cotton Jacket	26.95
Skirt		White Cotton Skirt with Faggoting Detail	15.95
Vest		White Vest with Deep Back	5.95
Gilet	*Dorothy Perkins*, Summer 1984	Grey Button Through Gilet	13.99
Jeans		Black Cotton Jeans	11.99
Sweatshirt		Cap Sleeve Sweatshirt	4.99
T Shirt		Black Cotton T Shirt	1.99
Coat	*Dorothy Perkins*, Winter 1984	Cream/Beige Herringbone Coat	36.99
Jacket		Expressions Cream Jacket	29.99
Knitwear		Silk/Angora Dolman Sweater	16.99
		Red/Black Slipover	7.99
		Cable Knit Sweater	10.99
Skirt		Expressions Dirndl Skirt	14.99

Continued

10.4.3 Prices, Selected *continued*

Item	Source	Description	Price £ p.
Trousers		Black Trousers	13.99
Jacket	*Country Casuals*, 1984	Shoulder Emphasising Blouson, Open Rever Collar	69.00
		Large Double Breasted, Black Diagonal Tweed	69.00
		Oversized Corduroy Jacket	59.00
Blouse	*C & A*, Autumn 1985	Paisley Blouse	13.99
		Twill Blouse with Epaulettes	12.99
Coat		Pure New Wool Coat	65.00
Dress		Jacquard Dress	35.00
		Cocktail Dress	17.99
Jacket		Double Breasted Tweed Jacket	39.99
		Leather Jacket	125.00
Knitwear		Knitted Dolman Sleeved Jumper	25.00
		Chunky Knit Cardigan	17.99
Skirt		Paisley Skirt with Belt	15.99
		Fully Lined Soft Pleat Skirt	19.99
		Crêpe Button Through Skirt	19.99
Trousers		Leather Trousers	79.99
Blouse	*Miss Selfridge*, 1985	Leaf Print Top	21.99
		Striped Knitted Top	19.99
Coat		Check Coat	69.99
Dress		Printed Dress	34.99
Hosiery		Lace Tights	5.99
Jacket		Fleck Tweed Jacket with Paisley Lining	44.99
		Jacket with Nehru Collar	44.99
Knitwear		Heavy Knit Rib Sweater	16.99
		Polo Neck Sweater in Cotton Jersey	9.99
		V Neck Rib Sweater	16.99
Leggings		Panne Velvet Leggings	15.99
Shirt		Diamond Print Shirt	15.99
Skirt		Striped Skirt	19.99
		Skirt with Pleats at Hem	14.99
		Pencil Skirt	21.99
Trousers		Zuane Trousers	29.99
Shoes	*C & J Clark Ltd.*, 1985	Rosalinde Taupe Softee Leather	28.99
		Pop-Ons in Grey Grain Leather	22.99
		Natureveldt Light Brown Softee Leather	33.99
		Polyveldt Brown Grained Leather	28.99
Dress	*Lewis's*, 1986	Mini Dress	49.99
Knitwear		Cotton Knit Sweater	39.99
Leggings		Cotton Leggings in Colours	21.99
Lingerie		Camisole	8.99
Shirt		Print Shirt	22.99
Shorts		Cotton Striped Shorts	24.99

Continued

10.4.3 Prices, Selected *continued*

Item	Source	Description	Price £ p.
Trousers		Print Trousers	26.99
Blouse	*Country Casuals*, 1987	Jungle Print Open Rever Blouse	25.00
Hat		Lacquered Straw Hat	9.50
Jacket		White Piqué Jacket	59.00
Shoes		Bally Two Tone Shoe	45.00
Skirt		White Piqué Four Panel Skirt	39.00
		Soft Pleated Skirt	39.00
T Shirt		Cotton T Shirt	8.95
Beachwear	*Miss Selfridge*, 1988	Shoestring Bikini	8.99
		Bikini in Flower Print	6.99
		Matching Kanga	6.99
		Ruched Lycra Bikini	19.99
		Ruched Lycra One Piece	24.99
		Shorts and Matching Ruched Bandeau Top	11.99
Coat		Riding Mac	59.99
Dress		Black/White Cross Front Dress	29.99
Jacket		Embroidered Bolero Jacket	42.99
		Bright Red Swing Jacket	14.99
Knitwear		Lambswool Cardigan	21.99
Skirt		Pleated Culotte Skirt	29.99
Suit		Double Breasted Suit	62.99
		Wide Legged Trouser Suit	69.99
Waistcoat		Suede Waistcoat	34.99
Blazer	*Jaeger*, 1989	Wool/Cashmere Blazer	225.00
Blouse		Satin Blouse	89.00
Dress		Bright Pink Dress	99.00
Jacket		Edge to Edge Knitted Jacket	169.00
		Cropped Jacket with Velvet Collar	169.00
Knitwear		Lambswool Cardigan	69.00
Trousers		Pure New Wool Trousers	89.00
Waistcoat		Velvet Waistcoat	79.00
Coat	*Selfridge Collection*, 1989	Overcoat in Cashmere/Wool	139.00
		Selfridge's Raincoat	159.00
Dress		Chic Black Coat Dress	105.00
Jacket		Wool Cropped Jacket, Collarless	159.00
Knitwear		Cardigan by Betty Barclay	95.00
		Angora Wool Cardigan	125.00
Skirt		Classic Straight Black Skirt	39.95

Food Products

Item	Source	Description	Price
Bacon	*J Sainsbury*, 1980		89 (lb.)
Biscuits		McVities Digestive	25 (½ lb.)
Butter		Best Butter	42½ (lb.)
Cheese		Cheddar Cheese	89 (lb.)
Eggs		Six Medium Size	33½
Soup		Heinz Tomato Soup	15½ (15½ oz.)

Continued

10.4.3 Prices, Selected *continued*

Item	Source	Description	Price £ p.
Tea		Red Label Tea	88 (lb.)
Confectionery	*Cadbury Ltd.*, March 24, 1980	Bournville	90 (200 g.)
		Family Chocolate Buttons	35
		Milk Fruit and Nut	80 (200 g.)
		Large Old Jamaica	46
	Northwich Chronicle, December 16, 1982	Cadbury's Roses	7.61 (2 kg. tin)
		Quality Street	1.59 (1lb.)
		Terry's All Gold	2.29 (1lb.)
Bacon	*J Sainsbury*, 1984	Middle Unsmoked	1.12½ (lb.)
Beans		JS Beans	35 (15 oz.)
Beefburgers		Beefburgers	59 (4)
Breakfast Cereal		Kelloggs Corn Flakes	59½ (500 g.)
Butter		Best Butter	88 (lb.)
Cheese		Cheddar Cheese	1.45 (lb.)
Chicken		3 lb. Roasting Chicken	1.74
Coffee		JS Instant Coffee Refill	65 (4 oz.)
Jam		Strawberry Jam	42 (lb.)
Sugar		Sugar	47½ (2 lb.)
Tea		Loose Red Label	62 (½ lb.)
Tinned Fruit		Peach Slices	27 (14½ oz.)
Tomato Sauce		Heinz Tomato Ketchup	59½ (20 oz.)
Cheese	*J Sainsbury*, 1985		1.04 (lb)
Confectionery	*Cadbury Ltd.*, June 17, 1985	Bournville Dark Chocolate	86 (200 g.)
		Cadbury's Dairy Milk Chocolate	44 (100 g.)
		Chocolate Buttons Large	26
		Milk Fruit and Nut Chocolate	86 (200 g.)
		Milk Roast Almond Chocolate	47 (100 g.)
Cheese	*Which*, 1986	Sainsbury's Farmhouse Cheddar	1.98 (lb.)
		Coop Farmhouse Cheddar	1.50 (lb.)
		St. Michael Mature Farmhouse	2.49 (lb.)
Tea		Brooke Bond P.G.Tips	84 (250 g.)
		Coop 99	77 (250 g.)
		Twinings Earl Grey	1.40 (250 g.)
Confectionery	*Which*, 1986	St. Michael Luxury Assortment Chocolates	4.99 (1lb. 5 oz.)
		Thorntons Continental	2.59 (½ lb. pre-boxed)
		Tesco (made by Bruyerre)	3.49 (½ lb. sold loose)
Coffee (Instant, per 100 g. jar)	*Which*, 1987	Nescafé	1.59
		Nescafé Alta Rica	2.79
		Coop Medium Roast	1.29
		Maxwell House	1.55
		Asda Gold	1.69
Bacon	*J Sainsbury*, 1989	Middle Unsmoked	1.74 (lb.)
Beans		JS Beans	20 (15 oz.)
Beefburgers		Beefburgers	69 (4)
Breakfast Cereal		Kelloggs Corn Flakes	89 (500 g.)

Continued

10.4.3 Prices, Selected *continued*

Item	Source	Description	Price £ p.
Butter		Best Butter	1.15 (lb.)
Cheese		Cheddar Cheese	1.45
Coffee		JS Instant Coffee Refill	69 (4 oz.)
Jam		Strawberry Jam	54 (lb.)
Sugar		Sugar	59 (2 lb.)
Tea		Loose Red Label	65 (½ lb.)
Tinned Fruit		Peach Slices	35 (14½ oz.)
Tomato Sauce		Heinz Tomato Ketchup	64 (20 oz.)
Furniture Products			
Seating	*Queensway, Coop*, 1980	Three Piece Velour Suite	599.00
Bed	*Northwich Chronicle*, December 30, 1981	Melanie 4 ft. 6 ins. Orthopaedic Divan Bed	99.50 (sale price)
Floorcovering		100 % Wool Torbay Axminster	10.95 (sq. yard)
		Bedroom Luxury Carpet	3.99 (sq. yard)
Lounge		Meredew Wall Units in Teak Veneer from Wades	299.95
Seating		New Virginia Three Piece Suite in Dralon	299.95
	Northwich Chronicle, January 7, 1982	Dean Three Piece Suite with Dark Beechwood Frames	389.95 (sale price)
	Northwich Chronicle, January 14, 1982	Chesterfield Settee and Two Wing Chairs in Leather	699.00
Floorcovering		Wades All Wool Berber Carpet	5.95 (sq. yard)
Bedroom (Ready Assembled Furniture)	*Northwich Chronicle*, March 4, 1982	5ft. 6in. Wardrobe	99.00
		7ft. Wardrobe	119.00
		Drawer Divan from	79.00
Lounge		Schreiber Town and Country Wall Fitment	27.95
Bookcase	*Northwich Chronicle*, September 16, 1982	Haddow Teak Bookcase	49.95
Seating		Rio Three Piece Leather Suite	749.95
Dining	*Coop Superstore*, 1983	Atlas Table with Smoked Glass and 4 Metal Chairs	69.95
	Petcos Furnishers, Manchester, 1983	Stag Sideboard	295.00
		Stag Table and Four Chairs	395.00
Lounge		G Plan Coffee Table	85.00
Sofa Beds	*Good Housekeeping*, January 1984	Emma by Brecon Furniture from Queensway Superstore	249.95
		London Sofa Bed Centre's Oxford 3 Seater	599.00
Seating		Design Unlimited Settees from	520.00
	Family Circle, November 27, 1985	Laura Ashley 2 Seat Sofa covered in Cordelia	595.00
	Wesley Barrel, 1985	Three Piece Suite	895.95 (sale price)
Dining	*Sunday Times*, July 6, 1986	Habitat Lisa Pine Furniture Table and 4 Tom Chairs	129.75 (sale price)
Floorcovering	*Knutsford Guardian*, August 14, 1986	British Axminsters from	5.50 (sq. yard)
		Printed Lounge Carpet from	1.75 (sq. yard)
		Shadow Style Carpet	3.50 (sq. yard)

Continued

10.4.3 Prices, Selected *continued*

Item	Source	Description	Price £ p.
Floorcovering *cont.*		Cushion Floor Vinyl from	1.75 (sq. yard)
Bedroom	*MFI*, 1987	Single Teak Veneer Wardrobe	59.99
		Chest of Drawers from	9.99
Bed	*Traditional Homes*, September 1989	Hand Built Beds from	195.00 (inc. delivery)
		Hand Built Four Posters from	325.00
		Victorian Brass and Cast Iron Bed	500.00
Seating	*Traditional Homes*, November 1989	Scandecor Chesterfield Settees from	450.00 (2 seat)
			540.00 (3 seat)
Table		Squirrells Solid Oak Circular Table	99.95

Garden Equipment and Supplies

Item	Source	Description	Price £ p.
Mowers	*Which*, 1984	Small Electric Rotary Mower from	50.00
		Electric Hover Mower from	40.00
		Petrol Rotary Mowers from	148.00
		Hand Cylinder Mowers from	30.00
		Electric Cylinder Mowers from	81.00
		Petrol Cylinder Mowers from	226.00
Hedges (average price per 10 metres)	*Which*, 1986	Berberis x stenophylla	63.00
		Leyland Cyprus	30.00
		Common Laurel	35.00
Fertiliser	*Knutsford Guardian*, August 14, 1986	PBS Velvas Lawn Fertiliser from	3.49
Furniture		Padded Chair	35.54
		Relaxer Chair	42.56
		Futura Wheeled Lounger	90.32
		Futura High Back Chair	51.13
Fertiliser		P.B.I. Velvas Lawn Fertiliser from	3.49
Buildings		8ft. x 6ft. Garden Sheds with Floor	125.00
		16ft. x 6ft. Concrete Garages inc. Erection	422.00
		8ft. x 6ft. Greenhouses	118.00
Tools	*Which*, 1986	Bulldog Britannia Garden Fork	10.00
		Boots Garden Fork	9.50
		Wilkinson Sword Green Range	11.00
Barbecue	*Which*, 1986	Hibachi from	7.00
		Kettle Barbecues from	27.00
Furniture		Wooden Picnic Table and Bench from	26.00
	Traditional Homes, September 1989	Rustic Log Play Chalet from	399.00
Paving		Old York Stone Paving	15.00 (per yard)
Pumps		Traditional Cast Iron Working Pumps, Pump Barrel	65.00 (up to £135)
Summer House		Revolving SE Aperwood Summer House (8ft. x 8ft.)	1,500.00
Tools	*Which*, 1989	Jenks & Cattell One-Handed Shears	7.00
		Sandvik Pruning Saw	15.00
		Wilkinson Sword Hoe	17.00
		Coop Gardenmaker Border Fork	10.00
		Bulldog Britannia Digging Fork	12.00

Continued

10.4.3 Prices, Selected *continued*

Item	Source	Description	Price
			£ p.
Tools *cont.*		Boots Super Knife Cut Secateurs	6.00
		Spear & Jackson Neverbend Digging Spade	17.00
		Hozelock Courier 8 Garden Sprayer	26.00
Heat and Light			
Electricity	*Eastern Electricity*, April 1, 1980	Standing Charge per week (/£) 0.39	Price per Unit (/p) 3.80
	Eastern Electricity, August 1, 1980	0.39	4.18
	Eastern Electricity, April 1, 1981	0.45	4.44
	Eastern Electricity, April 1, 1982	0.49	4.83
	Eastern Electricity, April 1, 1983	0.49	4.83
	Eastern Electricity, April 1, 1984	0.49	4.94
	Eastern Electricity, April 1, 1985	0.49	5.13
	Eastern Electricity, April 1, 1986	0.49	5.42
	Eastern Electricity, October 1, 1986	0.49	5.16
	Eastern Electricity, April 1, 1988	0.53	5.61
	Eastern Electricity, April 1, 1989	0.57	5.94
Gas	*British Gas North Thames*, October 1, 1983	Standing Charge (£) 9.90	First 5,000 therms (p) 33.5
	British Gas North Thames, January 1, 1984	9.90	35.2
	British Gas North Thames, February 1, 1985	9.90	37.0
	British Gas North Thames, May 1, 1986	8.90	38.0
	British Gas North Thames, July 1, 1987	8.30	36.3
	British Gas North Thames, April 1, 1988	8.70	38.5
	British Gas North Thames, April 1, 1989	8.70	39.8
Coal	*Digest of UK Energy Statistics*, 1980	Coal delivered to Large Industrial Consumers	35.00 (per tonne)
	Digest of UK Energy Statistics, 1981		39.9
	Digest of UK Energy Statistics, 1982		47.9
	Digest of UK Energy Statistics, 1983		49.6
	Digest of UK Energy Statistics, 1984		49.6
	Digest of UK Energy Statistics, 1985		51.00
	Digest of UK Energy Statistics, 1986		49.64
	Digest of UK Energy Statistics, 1987		47.91
	Digest of UK Energy Statistics, 1988		42.63
	Digest of UK Energy Statistics, 1989		41.95
Hotel Rates			
St. Clears Lland-dowror Picton Country Club	*Farm Holiday Guide*, 1980	Full Board from	45.00 (per week)
Grove House, Killabeg, Ferns, Co. Wexford, Ireland		Dinner, Bed and Breakfast from	4.00 (nightly)
The Swan, Newby Bridge, Lake District	*Receipt*, 1981	Winter Weekend Rates from	36.00

Continued

10.4.3 Prices, Selected *continued*

Item	Source	Description	Price £ p.
Hotel Rates *cont.* Headland Hotel, Newquay	*Travel Brochure*, 1981	Weekly Terms from	69.00
Great Western Hotel, Newquay		Weekly Terms from	55.00
Hillthwaite House, Windermere, Lake District	*Sunday Times*, July 7, 1986	Any Two Nights	60.50 (p.p. inc.)
Ritz Hotel, London		Special Weekend Rates from	120.00 (p.p.)
Royal Oak, Appleby	*Cumbria Tourist Board*, 1989	Bed and Breakfast from	13.50
Balmoral Hotel, Oban, Scotland	*Guestacom Good Room Guide*, 1989	Dinner, Bed and Breakfast from	17.50

Household Goods

Item	Source	Description	Price £ p.
Cookware	*Northwich Chronicle*, December 30, 1981	Golden Harvest Deep Fryer from Tesco	5.99
		Tower Pressure Cooker	10.00
Bedding	*Northwich Chronicle*, January 7, 1982	Polyester Cotton Sheets Single	7.75 (pair)
		Polyester Cotton Sheets Double	10.25 (pair)
		Duvet Cover Single	15.95
		Duvet Cover Double	25.50
	Northwich Chronicle, May 27, 1982	Tesco's Single Bed Set	8.99
		Tesco's Double Bed Set	12.99
		Printed Duvet Cover Single	7.99
		Printed Duvet Cover Double	9.99
		Plain Sheets, Flat/Fitted Single	4.99
		Plain Sheets, Flat/Fitted Double	5.99
		Plain Cotton Pillowcases	1.49 (each)
Tableware		From Staffordshire Potteries 18 Piece Tea Sets	3.95
		30 Piece Dinner Sets from	9.95
		Mugs from	0.30 (each)
		World Cup Footfall Mugs from	0.40 (each)
Towels		Assorted Hand Towels	1.25 (each)
		Assorted Bath Towels	2.50 (each)
		Assorted Tea Towels	0.35 (each)
Cookware	*Northwich Chronicle*, September 16, 1982	1.2 Litre Prestige Saucepan with Lid	18.95
		1.7 Litre Prestige Saucepan with Lid	20.95
		2.4 Litre Prestige Saucepan with Lid	21.95
		Frypan	24.95
Tableware		Longchamps Sherry Glasses	8.50 (six)
		Longchamps Wine Glasses	8.99 (six)
		Flute Champagne Glasses	9.50 (six)
		Autumn Mist Tea Cup	1.65 (each)
		Autumn Mist Dinner Plate	2.65 (each)
Towels		Debenhams Plain Dyed Hand Towels	3.50
		Bath Towels	5.99

Continued

10.4.3 Prices, Selected *continued*

Item	Source	Description	Price
			£ p.
Towels *cont.*		Bath Sheet	8.99
Cookware	*Sunday Times*, July 6, 1986	Habitat Wok	8.95 (sale price)
Cleaners	*Knutsford Guardian*, August 14, 1986	Ewbank Sweepers	10.00
Lighting		Standard Lamps	9.50
Shelves		Radiator Shelves	3.19
Slicers		Salter Bread Slicers	9.95
Lighting	*British Home Stores*, 1987	Table Lamp and Shade	4.50
Table Linen	*Laura Ashley*, 1988	Rectangular Cotton Tablecloth reduced to	7.00
Window Blinds		Made to Measure Austrian Blinds in Jade Cotton	79.95
Coffee Machines	*Which*, 1989	Melitta Aroma Comfort	40.00
		Rowenta Fresco	33.00
Irons		Morphy Richards 42471	25.00
		Rowenta DA49	28.00
		Tefal Long Life 1641	23.00
Kitchen Maid	*Traditional Homes*, September 1989	Kitchen Maid Clothes Airer from	28.00
Glassware	*Traditional Homes*, November 1989	Recycled Wine Glasses from	1.35 (each)
		Recycled Storage Jars from	0.99
Lighting		Polished Brass Picture Lights from	29.95
Houses			
Cape Detached Homes in Croco Park, Holmes Chapel	*Northwich Chronicle*, December 30, 1981	Four/Five Bed Detached Houses from	42,000.00
Flat	*Sunday Times*, July 7, 1986	Luxury Flat in Putney	62,000.00
House		One/Two Bed Houses in Palmers Green from	44,000.00
Detached		Stone Built Period Country House in Wye Valley	78,500.00
Cottage	*Sunday Times*, July 13, 1986	Four Bed Cottage in Elkington	87,000.00
Detached	*Sunday Times*, July 20, 1986	Three Bed House in Ullswater, Ideal for Holiday Home	56,000.00
Flat		Converted Flat in Wooded Setting, Edinburgh	43,000.00
		Two Bed Flats in Teddington, Cheshire from	38,875.00
Jewellery			
Bracelet	*Liberty*, 1981	Titanium Coil Bracelet	10.75
		Brass and Mother of Pearl Bangle	4.25
		Silver Sacred Thread Bracelet	46.00
		Silver Open Ended Galla Bangle	50.00
Choker		Titanium Choker	11.50
Earrings		Silver/Ivory Earrings	10.50
		Gilt Drop Earrings	9.25
		Brass Earrings	14.95
Necklace		Turquoise and Lapiz with paste Pearl Beads	15.95
		Old Native Silver Necklace	100.00

Continued

10.4.3 Prices, Selected *continued*

Item	Source	Description	Price £ p.
Bracelet	*Northwich Chronicle*, May 27, 1982	9 ct. Gold Three Bar Bracelet from Weirs	44.95
Earrings		9 ct. Gold Creole Earrings	29.50
		9 ct. Gold Hoop Earrings	38.95
Pendant		9 ct. Gold Pendant with Garnets	19.95
Watches		Men's Watches from	14.95
Earrings	*Avon*, 1984	Stylish Goldrone Openwork Earrings	4.99
Necklace		Twisted Braid Necklace	7.99
Pendant		Initial Attraction Pendant	4.99
Ring		Victorian Style Antique Look Ring	3.99
		Gold Plated Glimmering Accent Ring	3.99
Earrings	*Which*, December 1986	9 ct. Gold Spiral Earrings	11.00
Watch		Seiko Automatic Man's Watch	35.00
Bracelet	*Country Casuals*, 1987	Wooden Bangle	6.50
Necklace		Leopard Print Necklace	11.50
		Ceramic Necklace	19.50
	H. Samuel, 1987	9 ct. Gold Chain	10.99

Musical Instruments

Item	Source	Description	Price £ p.
Piano	*Tostevin & Son*, 1980	Knight's Upright Piano	1,900.00
Strings	*Barnes & Mullins*, 1980	Barnes & Mullins Spanish Guitar from	75.00
Brass	*Which*, 1981	Trumpet from	80.00
Strings		Violin from	50.00
		Folk Guitar from	20.00
Woodwind		Clarinet from	100.00
		Saxophone from	280.00
		Flute from	100.00
		Recorder	10.00
Piano	*Which*, 1983	Hoffman 123	3,845.00
		Knight K-10	2,050.00
		Legnica Sonatina	1,000.00
		Schimmel 118T	3,400.00
Brass	*Boosey & Hawkes*, 1985	Trumpet, Beginners from	109.25 (inc. VAT)
		Saxophone, Alto	407.54 (inc. VAT)
Strings		Schrotter Violin	129.38 (inc. VAT)
Woodwind		Clarinet	142.38 (inc. VAT)
Harpsichord	*Sunday Times*, July 13, 1986	Harpsichord	925.00 (second hand)
Piano		Blüthner Grand Piano	1,250.00 (second hand)
	Sunday Times, July 20, 1986	Chappell Grand Piano	2,495.00 (second hand)
		Yamaha G2 Grand (ex-Chappell, 1984)	4,200.00 (second hand)

Personal Care Items

Item	Source	Description	Price £ p.
Chemists	*Which*, 1980	Boots Antiseptic Lozenges	0.22
		TCP Throat Pastilles	0.45
		Fisherman's Friend	0.15
Shaving Equipment	*Which*, 1980	Boots 2000	13.95
		Remington M3 Micro Screen Super	25.00

Continued

10.4.3 Prices, Selected *continued*

Item	Source	Description	Price £ p.
Shaving Equipment *cont.*		Philips Philishave Exclusive	33.00
Towels	*Which*, 1982	Dr. White's Size 1	0.93 (20)
		Sainsbury's Regular	0.43 (10)
		Vespré Press On Towels	0.83 (20)
		Tampax Tampons Super	1.15 (20)
Soap	*Liberty*, 1981	Box of Three Soaps	3.50 (75)
		Packet of 12 Bath Jellies	2.50
		Moisturising Bath Oil	5.25
Toilet Preparations		Culpepper Herbal Shampoo	0.65 (each)
		Packets of Henna Powder	0.99 (each)
		Talcum Powder	2.25
		Eau de Toilette Vaporiser	14.70
		Fruit Flavoured Lip Balms	3.00 (six)
Shaving Preparations	*Northwich Chronicle*, September 16, 1982	Wilkinson Sword Swivel 10 Disposable Razors	0.75
Soap		Boots Glycerin and Cucumber Bath Soaps	0.42 (3)
Toilet Preparations	*Which*, March 1984	Boots Skin Cream	1.15 (265 ml.)
		Body Shop Jojoba Moisture Cream	4.90 (100 ml.)
		Revlon European Collagen Complex	33.17 (100 ml.)
Cosmetics	*Avon*, 1985	Rich Moisture Hand Cream	1.19 (100 ml.)
		Lash Mascara	1.79 (15 ml.)
		Avon Kajalstick	0.99 (1.5 g.)
		Avon New Lipstick	1.99
		Nail Enamel	1.49
		Eyeshadow Pot	0.99
Toilet Preparations		Aqua Shower Gel	1.49
		Avocado Body Lotion	1.99
		Eau de Cologne Spray	1.99
		Selective Moisturiser	3.25
		Avon Talcum Powder	1.99 (200 g.)
		Natural Performing Blow Dry Curling Mousse	2.49
		Anti Dandruff Shampoo	1.59
		Folding Brush and Comb	2.49
		Men's Refreshing Shower Gel	1.99
		Shampoo/Shower Soap with Cord	2.99
		Roll on Anti Perspirant Deodorant	0.99
Shaving Preparations		Electric Pre-Shave	1.79
Shaving Equipment	*Which*, December 1989	Braun System 123	52.50
		Braun Linear 235	21.25
Prescription Charges			
	Department of Health, April 1, 1980	Charge per Item	0.70
	Department of Health, December 1, 1980		1.00
	Department of Health, April 1, 1982		1.30

Continued

10.4.3 Prices, Selected *continued*

Item	Source	Description	Price £ p.
Prescription Charges *cont.*	*Department of Health*, April 1, 1983		1.40
	Department of Health, April 1, 1984		1.60
	Department of Health, April 1, 1985		2.00
	Department of Health, April 1, 1986		2.20
	Department of Health, April 1, 1987		2.40
	Department of Health, April 1, 1988		2.60
	Department of Health, April 1, 1989		2.80
Publications			
Magazine	*Woman's Own Features*, 1981	Woman's Own	0.22
Year Book	*Receipt*, 1981	*Whitaker's Almanack*	8.20
Magazine	*Good Housekeeping*, January 1984	Good Housekeeping	0.75
	Family Circle, November 27, 1985	Family Circle	0.49
Children's Books		Ladybird Disney Books	0.75 (each)
		Eagle Annual 1986	2.95
		Grange Hill Annual 1986	3.75
Books	*Sunday Times*, July 6, 1986	*A Matter of Honour*, J. Archer, Hodder & Stoughton	9.95
		Hold the Dream, D.T.Bradford, Grafton	3.50
		Paradise Postponed, J.Mortimer, Penguin	3.50
		A Taste of Death, P.D.James, Faber	9.95
		The Bourne Supremacy, R.Ludlum, Grafton	10.95
		Fellwalking with Wainwright, A.Wainwright, Joseph	12.95
		Floyd on Fire, K.Floyd, BBC	3.95
Magazine	*Receipt*, 1989	Traditional Homes	1.70
Services			
Cinema	*Reward*, 1980	Average Admission Price	1.49
	Reward, 1981		1.76
	Reward, 1982		1.92
	Reward, 1983		2.07
	Reward, 1984		2.13
	Reward, 1985		2.10
	Reward, 1986		2.07
	Reward, 1987		2.22
	Reward, 1988		2.39
	Reward, 1989		2.52
Licence	*Post Office Archives*, December 1, 1981	Black and White TV	15.00
		Colour TV	46.00
	Post Office Archives, March 28, 1985	Black and White TV	18.00
		Colour TV	58.00
	Post Office Archives, April 1, 1988	Black and White TV	21.00
		Colour TV	62.50
	Post Office Archives, April 1, 1989	Black and White TV	22.00
		Colour TV	66.00

Continued

10.4.3 Prices, Selected *continued*

Item	Source	Description	Price £ p.
Licence *cont.*	*DVLA*, March 1, 1980	Road Tax for 12 months	60.00
	DVLA, March 11, 1981		70.00
	DVLA, March 10, 1982		80.00
	DVLA, March 16, 1983		85.00
	DVLA, March 13, 1984		90.00
	DVLA, 1985		100.00
Telephone Tariffs	*British Telecom Archives*, January 2, 1980	Ordinary Lines	
Peak Rate (Mon to Fri, 9am to 1pm) (Local)		Dialled Direct Time Allowed: 2 minutes	3.5
Up to 56 km.		30 seconds	3.5
Over 56 km.		10 seconds	3.5
Standard Rate (Mon to Fri, 8 am – 9 am and 1pm-6pm)		3 minutes	3.5
Up to 56 km.		45 seconds	3.5
Over 56 km.		15 seconds	3.5
Cheap Rate (Weekends and all other times) Local		12 minutes	3.5
Up to 56 km.		3 minutes	3.5
Over 56 km.		1 minute	3.5
Revised Quarterly Rentals (exclusive service)	*British Telecom Archives*, 1983	Business Line	22.00
		Line other than a Business Line	14.15
		Exchange Line Connected to Customer's Own Apparatus	19.50
Dialled Calls Local	*British Telecom Archives*, November 1, 1985	Approx. cost to the Customer inc. VAT	
Cheap(6pm to 8am and weekends)		5 minutes	6
Standard (8am to 9 am)			17
Peak (9 am to 1 pm)			23
Dialled Calls Local	*British Telecom Archives*, September 1989	Approx. Cost to the customer inc. VAT	
Cheap (6pm to 8am and weekends)		5 minutes	5
Standard (8am to 9am and 1pm to 6pm)			20
Peak (9am to 1pm)			25
Parcel Postage Rates (National Rate)	*Post Office Archives*, June 13, 1981	1 kg.	1.10
		5 kg.	2.05
		10 kg.	2.65

Continued

10.4.3 Prices, Selected *continued*

Item	Source	Description	Price £ p.
Parcel Postage Rates *cont.*	*Post Office Archives*, February 1, 1982	1 kg.	1.20
		5 kg.	2.25
		10 kg.	2.90
	Post Office Archives, April 5, 1983	1 kg.	1.30
		5 kg.	2.35
		10 kg.	3.10
	Post Office Archives, September 3, 1984	1 kg.	1.33
		5 kg.	2.50
		10 kg.	3.25
	Post Office Archives, September 2, 1985	1 kg.	1.41
		5 kg.	2.65
		10 kg.	3.45
	Post Office Archives, September 1, 1986	1 kg.	1.50
		5 kg.	2.75
		10 kg.	3.60
	Post Office Archives, September 7, 1987	1 kg.	1.60
		5 kg.	2.90
		10 kg.	3.75
	Post Office Archives, September 5, 1988	1 kg.	1.70
		5 kg.	3.00
		10 kg.	4.00
	Post Office Archives, September 2, 1989	1 kg.	1.85
		5 kg.	3.30
		10 kg.	4.40
Conveyancing Solicitor's Fees on the Sale of a £35,000 House	*Which*, 1985		
		Shrewsbury	325.00 (maximum)
		Doncaster	350.00 (maximum)
		Hove	350.00 (maximum)
		Overall (10 towns)	350.00 (maximum)
Dental Fees	*Which*, 1985	Check Up	Free
		Routine Scaling and Polishing	4.20
		Simple Filling	3.30
		Porcelain Jacket Crown	30.00

Sewing Equipment and Supplies

Item	Source	Description	Price £ p.
Machines	*Which*, February 1980	Bernina Nova 900	245.00
		Singer Capri 167	70.00
		Viking Husqvarna 5710	190.00
	Which, 1983	Frister & Rossman 45 Mark 1V	100.00
		Jones M350	70.00
		Singer 247	120.00
		Toyota Atlantis 602	95.00

Sports Equipment and Hobbies

Item	Source	Description	Price £ p.
Life Jackets	*Which*, 1980	Avon Folding Air	25.00
		Beaufort Auto Jacket	54.00
Buoyancy Aids		Sealbuoy Commodore	17.50

Continued

10.4.3 Prices, Selected *continued*

Item	Source	Description	Price
			£ p.
Buoyancy Aids *cont.*		Avon Air	30.50
		Helly Hansen Paddler/Canoe Aid	16.00
Golf Clubs	*Northwich Chronicle*, July 15, 1982	Macgregor, Jack Nicklaus 3 Woods, 9 Irons	120.00
		Half Sets from Keele Golf Shop	49.00
Running Shoes	*Which*, 1984	Adidas Oregon	32.99
		Hi-Tec Runaway	11.99
		Reebok Classic	24.95
		BHS 7098	8.99
Footballs	*Which*, 1985	Dunlop Selected Pro	26.00
		Mitre Multiplex	28.00
		Airborne	5.00
		Mitre League	11.00
Sportswear	*Knutsford Guardian*, August 14, 1986	Brugi Italian Designer Sportswear Tracksuits from	24.95 (sale price)
		Kleim Sports Dresses	7.99
		Kleim Skirts	3.99
		Le Coq Sportif Sweaters	9.99
Golf Clubs	*Receipt*, 1987	Half Set of Slazenger Golf Clubs	75.00
Rackets		Jaguar Badminton Racket	9.99
		Grays Standard Model Squash Racket	12.99
		Olympus Sport Bronze Medal Junior Tennis Racket	8.95
Hobbies	*Which*, 1988	Winemaster Kwik Wine Kit	3.67
		Brewmaker Basic White, Medium Dry	1.99 (6 bottle kit)

Tobacco Products

Item	Source	Description	Price
Cigarettes (packet of 20)	*Gallaher Ltd.*, 1980	Benson & Hedges King Size Special Filter	0.74
		Silk Cut Ultra Mild King Size	0.73
		Park Drive	0.68
Cigars		Hamlet	0.72 (5)
Pipe Tobacco		Condor Long Cut	0.83 (25 g.)
		War Horse Ready Cut	0.83 (25 g.)
Cigarettes	*Gallaher Ltd.*, 1981	Benson & Hedges King Size Special Filter	0.97
		Silk Cut Ultra Mild King Size	0.96
Cigarillos		John Cotton Cigarillos tipped	1.02 (20)
Cigarettes	*Gallaher Ltd.*, 1982	Benson & Hedges King Size Special Filter	1.06
		Silk Cut Ultra Mild King Size	1.05
		Park Drive Tipped King Size	1.04
	Gallaher Ltd., 1983	Benson & Hedges King Size Special Filter	1.13
		Silk Cut Extra Mild King Size	1.12
	Gallaher Ltd., 1984	Benson & Hedges King Size Special Filter	1.27
		Silk Cut Extra Mild	1.26

Continued

10.4.3 Prices, Selected *continued*

Item	Source	Description	Price £ p.
Cigarettes *cont.*	Gallaher Ltd., 1985	Benson & Hedges King Size Special Filter	1.35
		Silk Cut Extra Mild King Size	1.34
		Senior Service	1.48
	Gallaher Ltd., 1986	Benson & Hedges King Size Special Filter	1.39
		Silk Cut Extra Mild King Size	1.38
		Sobranie of London Black Russian King Size	1.58
	Gallaher Ltd., 1987	Benson & Hedges King Size Special Filter	1.55
		Silk Cut Extra Mild King Size	1.54
		Senior Service	1.68
	Gallaher Ltd., 1988	Benson & Hedges King Size Special Filter	1.58
		Silk Cut De Luxe Mild King Size	1.58
		Senior Service	1.72
	Gallaher Ltd., 1989	Benson & Hedges King Size Special Filter	1.65
		Silk Cut King Size De Luxe Mild	1.65
		Senior Service	1.81

Toys

Item	Source	Description	Price £ p.
Soft Toys	*Northwich Chronicle*, April 7, 1982	Giant Teddy	9.00
Toys	*Northwich Chronicle*, December 2, 1982	Play Track Builder	5.99
		Missile Invader	10.95
		Mini Munchman	14.95
		My First Barbie	2.99
		Happy Days Building Bricks	4.99
Games (Electronic)	*Which*, 1984	Game & Watch Donkey Kong Multi Screen	20.00
		Game & Watch Mario's Cement Factory	17.00
		Frogger	25.00
Games (Board)	*Which*, 1984	Monopoly	5.00
		Scrabble	5.00
		Game of Life	9.00
		Mousetrap	7.00
		Sorry	5.00
		Trivial Pursuits	20.00
	Which, 1987	Spear's Go and Fetch It from Hamleys	10.99
Trikes	*Which*, 1988	Raleigh Little Lamb	13.00
		Triang 4110 Kiddy	17.00
		Raleigh Mini	13.00

Transport and Vehicles

Item	Source	Description	Price £ p.
Air Fares	*Reed Travel Group*, 1980	London to Paris 1st. Class	82.50
		London to Paris Economy	42.50
		London to New York 1st. Class	594.00

Continued

10.4.3 Prices, Selected *continued*

Item	Source	Description	Price £ p.
Rail Fares	*National Railway Museum*, February 1980	Manchester to London 2nd. Class Return	27.50
Vehicle	*Northwich Chronicle*, January 14, 1982	Renault 5 GTL	4,100.00
	Northwich Chronicle, September 16, 1982	Peugeot 305, Special Drive Away Price	4,195.00
	Which, 1983	Rover 2000	7,750.00
		Ford Fiesta Popular Plus	3,743.00
Bicycles		Raleigh Colette Roadsters	92.00
		Elswick Ascot	110.00
		Falcon Super Pro Racing Bike	320.00
		Raleigh Zenith Sports	144.00
Vehicle	*Which*, 1984	Ford Fiesta Popular Plus	4,319.00
		Volkswagen Polo C 2 Door	4,025.00
		Vauxhall Cavalier 1.8	7,374.00
		Ford Escort 1.3L 3 Door	5,231.00
Air Fares	*Reed Travel Group*, June 1985	London to Paris 1st. Class	134.00
		London to Paris Economy	71.00
		London to New York	1,079.00
Rail Fares	*National Railway Museum*, July 1985	Manchester to London 2nd. Class Return	45.00
Vehicle	*Which*, 1985	Vauxhall Nova 1.0	4,011.00
		Ford Fiesta 1.1	4,490.00
		Ford Escort 1.3	4,929.00
		Vauxhall Cavalier 1600L	6,502.00
Car Replacements	*Which*, June 1985	Air Filter	4.05
		Oil Filter	3.80
		Set of Spark Plugs	3.60
		Shock Absorbers	39.00
		Water Pump	26.00
		Complete Engine	499.00
Vehicle	*Sunday Times*, July 7, 1986	BMW 528I SE	12,300.00
		Range Rover JS 1525	11,500.00 (second hand)
		Ferrari Mondial QV	19,600.00 (second hand)
	Complete Catalogue of Austin Cars since 1945	Montego 1.3 68 b.h.p. 4 Door Saloon	5,281.00 (price when introduced)
		Montego 2.0 102 b.h.p 4 Door Saloon	7,195.00 (price when introduced)
Bicycle	*Which*, 1988	Raleigh Budgie	40.00
		Raleigh Small Rider	40.00
Vehicle	*Which*, 1989	Volvo 240 GL	13,240.00
		Rover Montego 2.0 TD DL	11,260.00
		Vauxhall Carlton 2.3 LD	14,345.00
Travel			
Daily Sea Excursions	*Isles of Scilly Steamship Co. Ltd.*, 1981	Excursions to the Isles of Scilly from Penzance	10.00 (adults) 5.00 (children)
Holidays	*Sunday Times*, July 6, 1986	Cosmos Traveljet to Tenerife from	109.00
		16 Day Caribbean Cruise on Cunard Countess	1,280.00

Continued

10.4.3 Prices, Selected *continued*

Item	Source	Description	Price £ p.
Holidays *cont.*		Corsica with Cox & Knight	208.00 (per week)
		10 Day Tour of Egypt on a Sheraton Cruise	579.00
		Yugoslavia and Greece with Island Sailing Ltd from	70.00 (return)
		Disneyworld Special inc. Car	329.00 (7 days)
Coach Excursion	*Northwich Chronicle*, August 14, 1986	Holland Night Flyers, 3 Days, Duty Free Shopping	42.00
Miscellany			
Film	*Which*, June 1985	Boots Colourprint 100 HR	2.51
		Kodacolour VR1000	3.49
Home Computers	*Which*, 1986	Amstrad CPC6128	400.00
		BBC Micro	400.00
		Enterprise 128	250.00
Luggage	*Northwich Chronicle*, August 14, 1986	Allander Suitcase with Wheels	28.00
		Weekender Barrel Bags in Nylon	3.99
Pens	*Which*, December 1988	Papermate Monogram	4.50
		Sheaffer Triumph 440	12.50
		Parker Premier Silver Plated	115.00
Recorded Music	*The British Record Industry Year Book*, 1988	CD Single	5.16
		Vinyl Single	1.99
	The British Record Industry Year Book, 1989	CD Single	4.79

10.5 Finance and Economic Data

10.5.1 Finance, Personal

	1980 £	1981 £	1982 £	1983 £	1984 £	1985 £	1986 £	1987 £	1988 £	1989 £
Retirement Pension:										
Married	43.45	47.35	52.55	54.50	57.30	61.30	61.95	63.25	65.50	69.80
Single	27.15	29.60	32.85	34.05	35.80	38.30	38.70	39.50	41.15	43.60
Child Benefit:										
First	4.75	5.25	5.85	6.50	6.85	7.00	7.10	7.25	7.25	7.25
Subsequent	4.75	5.25	5.85	6.50	6.85	7.00	7.10	7.25	7.25	7.25
Unemployment Benefit: Men and Women	20.65	22.50	25.00	27.05	28.45	30.45	30.80	31.45	32.75	34.70
Income Tax Rate[1]	30%	30%	30%	30%	30%	30%	30%	29%	27%	25%
Base Interest Rate[2]	17%	14%	14%	11%	9%	10.50%	12.50%	11%	8.50%	13%

Bank of England; Department of Social Security; Inland Revenue Statistics.

[1]The rates apply to years ended 5th April. [2]The rates apply to January of each year.

10.5.2 Financial Markets

10.5.2a Closing Price of UK Major Stocks in January

	1980	1981	1982	1983	1984	1985	1986	1987	1988	1989
	p.	p.	p.	p.	p.	p	p.	p.	p.	p.
Barclays[1]	514	482	472	426	534	575	478	589	655	463
Boots	238	258	257	296	188	214	276	286	329½	259
Burmah Castrol[2]	197	249	190	160	187	240	318	419	620	582
Cadbury Schweppes	69	75	100½	132	131	163	276	196	291	429
Coats Viyella[3]	36½	19	17½	14½						
Courtaulds	122	87	83	96	130	160	194	326½	535	395
Guinness	213	97½	83	104	125	245	324	353	389	357
ICI[4]	415	402	342	360	660	746	883	£11¹¹⁄₁₆	£16½	£11¹¹⁄₁₆
Marks and Spencer	134	121	146	237	225	135	392	227	280½	190
Reckitt and Colman	263	216	308	400	450	578	650	900	£12½	969
Unilever	680	512	652	805	905	£10⅞	£13½	£22½	719	515
Whitbread	148	174	128	159	161	217	280	315	385	317

Financial Times, 1980–1989.

Blank space denotes no data. [1]Barclays Bank re-registered as Barclays in 1985. [2]Burmah Oil re-registered to become Burmah Castrol in 1981. [3]Vantona and Carrington Viyella merged in 1983 to form Vantona Viyella which in turn merged with Coats Paton in 1986 to form the present Coats company. [4]Imperial Chemical Industries

10.5.2b Commodities

	Coal (delivered to large consumers)	Raw Cotton (average typical day offering price)	Gold (average market price)	Sugar (annual average world price)	Wheat (ex-farm annual spot prices)[1][2]	Wool (annual average price)
	£ per tonne	pence per lb. CIF	£ per troy oz.[1]	£ sterling per metric ton	£ per tonne	pence per lb.
1980	35.0	n/a	263.74	291.524	117.50	63.20
1981	39.9	41.38	227.29	202.206	120.30	46.26[3]
1982	47.9[4]	41.38	215.67	118.917	135.90	45.30
1983	49.6	55.58	279.12	140.042	120.40	54.39
1984	49.6	56.99	269.68	103.561	130.40	62.91
1985	51.00	46.70	246.16	88.055	121.60	51.12
1986	49.64	33.04	251.33	103.990	121.40	52.94
1987	47.9	46.56	$446.44	107.923	121.40	60.72
1988	42.63	36.47	$437.12	148.913	136.60	61.86
1989	41.95	46.95	$381.64	196.325	119.20	49.71

British Wool Marketing Board; Cotlook Limited; Czarnikow Sugar; Digest of UK Energy Statistics, 1993; Home Grown Cereals Authority; World Gold Council. Blank space denotes no data.

[1]From 1987, prices in dollars. [2]Spot means delivery in month of contract. [3]Change of source. [4]From 1982, the prices are not strictly comparable with earlier data.

10.5.2c Foreign Exchange Rates

	Deutschmark per £1	French Franc per £1	United States Dollar per £1
1980	4.227	9.8250	2.3281
1981	4.556	10.9356	2.0254
1982	4.243	11.4846	1.7489
1983	3.870	11.5471	1.5158
1984	3.791	11.6349	1.3364
1985	3.784	11.5494	1.2976
1986	3.183	10.1589	1.4872
1987	2.941	9.8389	1.6392
1988	3.124	10.5969	1.7796
1989	3.079	10.4476	1.6383

CSO Financial Statistics.

Original source, Bank of England.

10.5.3 Balance of Payments and GNP

10.5.3a Balance of Payments

	Visible Balance	Invisible Balance	Current Balance	Total UK Investment Overseas	Total Overseas Investment in the UK	Net Foreign Currency Transactions of UK Banks	Net Sterling Transactions of UK Banks	Net Transactions in Assets and Liabilities	Balancing Item
	£m	£m	£m	£m	£m	£m	£m	£m	£m
1980	1,357	1,487	2,843	-8,175	5,786	669	266	-3,940	917
1981	3,251	3,496	6,748	-10,474	3,189	-137	-522	-7,436	530
1982	1,911	2,741	4,649	-11,656	3,016	3,422	433	-2,519	-2,130
1983	-1,537	5,302	3,765	-12,768	5,087	1,034	1,816	-4,562	797
1984	-5,336	7,134	1,798	-15,789	1,107	8,557	1,223	-8,414	6,616
1985	-3,345	6,136	2,790	-25,203	14,279	4,685	2,333	-3,733	943
1986	-9,559	9,625	66	-33,955	18,018	13,490	-369	-3,134	3,068
1987	-11,582	7,099	-4,482	-14,076	28,984	-2,301	4,234	4,334	148
1988	-21,480	5,302	-16,179	-32,183	27,570	5,383	9,015	9,369	6,783
1989	-24,683	2,956	-21,726	-57,001	33,170	6,649	9,478	19,259	2,467

CSO Annual Abstract of Statistics, HMSO, 1992.

10.5.3b GNP by Category of Expenditure and Factor Incomes

	Income from Employment	Income from Self Employment	Gross Trading Profits of Companies	Gross Trading Surplus of Public Corporations	Gross Trading Surplus of Government Enterprises	Rent	Stock Appreciation	Gross Domestic Product	Net Property Income from Abroad	Gross National Product	Capital Consumption	National Income
	£m	£m	£m	£m	£m	£m	£m	£m	£m	£m	£m	£m
1980	137,353	17,557	29,024	6,293	n/a	15,888	6,732	199,383	-219	199,164	27,900	171,264
1981	149,737	19,980	27,341	7,974	236	16,366	-5,974	218,755	1,251	220,006	-31,641	188,365
1982	158,838	22,140	31,176	9,502	216	17,700	-4,276	238,231	1,460	239,691	-33,653	206,038
1983	169,847	24,750	39,528	10,004	50	18,857	-4,204	261,083	2,831	263,914	-36,150	227,764
1984	181,406	27,909	43,906	8,381	-117	19,816	-4,513	280,758	4,345	285,103	-38,758	246,345
1985	196,858	30,404	51,287	7,120	265	21,875	-2,738	307,901	2,560	310,461	-41,883	268,578
1986	212,374	35,104	47,312	8,059	155	23,848	-1,790	328,130	4,974	333,104	-45,084	288,020
1987	229,836	40,122	59,177	6,802	-75	26,155	-4,725	360,599	3,754	364,353	-48,149	316,204
1988	255,625	47,612	63,375	7,354	-32	29,904	-6,345	401,127	4,423	405,550	-52,596	352,954
1989	282,919	54,093	67,142	6,418	199	33,795	-7,435	441,136	3,495	444,631	-56,632	387,999

CSO Annual Abstract of Statistics, HMSO, 1993.

10.6 Miscellaneous

10.6.1 UK Leisure Spending: Market Value by Activity

	1983 £m	1985 £m	1987 £m	1989 £m
Audio Equipment	980	1,273	1,622	2,165
Cinema	124	132	152	180
Eating Out	7,411	9,269	11,389	14,018
Foreign Visitors	4,003	5,442	6,260	6,775
Gambling	1,842	2,117	2,439	2,853
Gardening	664	893	1,033	1,398
Holidays Abroad	5,000	6,140	8,500	10,382
Holidays in UK	2,640	3,080	3,100	4,129
Sports	2,420	3,212	4,561	6,022
Television	2,119	2,314	2,618	3,026
Others	22,888	27,189	31,503	37,425

Financial Times, May 12, 1990, p. 6.

Original source, *Henley Centre for Forecasting*.

– Eleven –
1990–1993

Recession and Regression

PRIME MINISTER
John Major (Conservative), November 1990 to date

CHANCELLORS OF THE EXCHEQUER
Norman Lamont, November 1990–May 1993
Kenneth Clarke, May 1993 to date

After Thatcher's fall from grace and her subsequent resignation in 1990, the former Chancellor of the Exchequer John Major became Prime Minister. Major epitomized for much of the population proof that a 'working-class boy' could 'make good'.

Major's years in power have been centred around the severe recession that Britain has experienced since the late 1980s. Britain's economy suffered greatly from 1990 to 1993, as did the economies of western Europe generally. Chronic unemployment, a high rate of house repossession, cuts in social security benefits and the National Health Service remain dominant issues. The number of homeless people living on the streets, and the number of people living below the poverty line have increased as the gap between rich and poor has continued to grow.

Despite a period of political intrigues and scandals, Major won the 1992 election. Since then the Labour Party, which for most of the 1980s was struggling to define changes in its policies and therefore presented a relatively weak opposition, has gained strength and popularity. Recent reshuffles and redirections in policy have made it a much more formidable adversary. The death of John Smith led to the election of Tony Blair as the leader of the Labour Party.

At the same time, the government has brought about a reduction in, and stabilization of, inflation. Interest rates have also been radically reduced, due in large part to Britain's withdrawal from the European Exchange Rate Mechanism. After this withdrawal, the exchange rate of the pound against the strong European currencies slipped dramatically, raising the price of imports and travel abroad, but encouraging exports. Public sector pay increases have also been kept low, relatively closely inline with inflation, during this period. However, the 'green shoots of recovery' which the government repeatedly claimed to be emerging took time to detect.

In recent years the Conservatives have launched a 'Back to Basics' campaign which advocates community/family care as opposed to the system of government safety-nets created by the Welfare State. Part of this campaign has been an attack on the general level of morality including criticism by some against single mothers. The campaign has been viewed with a good deal of irony as a spate of scandals has caused a number of leading Conservatives to resign.

The rise of neo-nationalism as personified in the British National Party (BNP), and other similar factions around the world, has raised the profile of racialism and intolerance in general. The celebration of democracy in Eastern Europe has been followed by uncertainties and tensions in the area. Ethnic divisions have sparked off civil war in the former Yugoslavia.

In Britain the 'Poll Tax' was replaced by the Council Tax in April 1993, loosely based on the old Rates system. The most vociferous objectors were pensioners. Despite signs of economic recovery, consumer confidence has remained shaky. Around a million home owners are reported to be caught in the negative equity trap; and job insecurity is another factor which has stifled growth.

11.1 Historical Snapshots

11.1 Historical Snapshots

1990   UK in a serious and deepening recession.

Housing and commercial property prices fall.

Unemployment continues to rise and industrial output to fall.

AIDS claims 1,612 victims.

London Borough of Wandsworth sets the lowest poll tax (per capita council tax) of £148.

Margaret Thatcher resigns as Prime Minister. John Major is her successor.

Guinness takeover scandal ends with fines and prison sentences for Britain's top businessmen.

UK become members of the Exchange Rate Mechanism (ERM) of the European Monetary System (EMS).

1991   Bank of England closes the Bank of Commerce and Credit International (BCCI).

Retailers defy the Sunday trading laws.

Longest post-war recession continues to grip UK.

Unemployment rises to more than 2.5 million.

Housing repossessions rise to 80,000.

Robert Maxwell dies at sea.

Jaguar, the country's biggest maker of luxury cars, loses 1,000 jobs.

John Major unveils the Citizens Charter promising a better deal for consumers of public services.

Journalist John McCarthy, held hostage in Beirut for five years, flies home. Religious envoy Terry Waite is released also.

1992   John Major returns to office with a much reduced majority.

Membership of the TUC falls from 47 per cent of the workforce in 1979 to 40 per cent in 1992.

Linford Christie wins gold medal in the 100 metres at Barcelona Olympics.

UK leaves ERM because it cannot manage foreign exchange markets.

ICI dissolves into two companies.

1993   Inflation at its lowest level since 1967 at an annual rate of 1.8 per cent.

Government forecasts growth of 3 per cent in GDP in 1994.

Chronicle of Britain, J.L. International Publishing, 1992.

11.2 Earnings and Employment

11.2.1 Earnings, Standard Tables

11.2.1a Incomes and Wages

	1990 £	1991 £	1992 £	1993 £
Full Time Male				
Solicitor	502.8	584.2	623.6	621.9
General Practitioner	619.2	657.6	755.6	780.0
Police Constable	335.9	383.7	419.0	431.4
Teacher (secondary)	338.1	380.8	435.5	443.8
Nurse (Staff Nurse)	244.2	300.6	320.2	321.9
Train Driver		321.8	339.4	389.2
Coal Miner (face trained)	310.9	379.1	404.6	421.0
Fitter	323.2	301.8	308.5	326.3
Turner	245.4	224.3	285.6	296.6
Bricklayer	227.9	228.2	237.7	242.0
Labourer	200.2	224.3	233.8	226.2
Compositor	307.0	332.4	352.3	363.8
Farm Worker	180.8	186.7	198.4	211.8
Numerical Clerk	217.6	249.8	268.1	279.6
Baker	199.0	211.1	219.5	230.0
Textile Worker	202.3	212.5	240.5	250.4
Full Time Female				
Solicitor[1]		479.9	459.3	478.3
General Practitioner	447.7	524.4	615.1	626.5
Police Constable	288.6	329.6	360.1	378.0
Teacher (secondary)	300.6	337.6	382.4	391.1
Nurse (Staff Nurse)	258.5	270.8	293.2	295.7
Farm Worker[2]		137.4		143.9
Numerical Clerk	179.9	202.9	205.8	223.0
Baker	141.6	149.4		160.2
Textile Worker	130.8	142.6	150.6	157.4
Typist	168.9	184.2	196.6	206.5
Nursery Nurse	158.5	177.9	181.1	188.1
Hairdresser	139.4	126.8	127.7	138.3

New Earnings Survey.

All figures are weekly. Blank space denotes no available data. [1]Legal Professionals. [2]Other occupations in farming, forestry and fishing.

11.2.1b Average Weekly Earnings

	All Manufac-turing Industries	Metals, Mineral Products and Chemicals	Metal Goods, Engineer-ing and Vehicle Industries	Other Manufac-turing Industries	Construc-tion	Distribu-tion, Hotels and Catering	Transport and Communi-cations	Banking and Finance	Other Services	All Industries
	£	£	£	£	£	£	£	£	£	£
Males										
1990	289.2	295.4	292.9	280.3	277.3	247.8	281.2	390.5	293.4	295.6
1991	308.1	316.3	311.6	298.7	294.9	264.3	302.7	412.8	327.3	318.9
1992	328.3	340.1	331.2	318.3	315.6	278.5	325.4	436.4	349.9	340.1
1993	n/a	364.6	350.9	340.0	326.8	301.5	344.5	519.7	374.0	360.4
Females										
1990	177.1	193.3	180.3	170.5	178.5	157.2	207.7	227.2	218.4	201.5
1991	192.9	211.7	197.8	184.6	195.5	174.1	229.8	244.7	242.9	222.4
1992	207.1	229.5	211.6	198.3	205.7	184.8	249.9	260.1	266.0	241.1
1993	n/a	251.0	225.4	218.4	221.0	198.8	261.7	284.5	282.2	258.5

Regional Trends, HMSO, 1990–1993.

Original sources, *New Earnings Survey*; Employment Department; Department of Economic Development, Northern Ireland.

11.2.2 Regional Earnings

	South East	Greater London	Rest of South East	East Anglia	South West	West Mids	East Mids	Yorks and Humber	North West	North	England	Wales	Scotland	UK
	£	£	£	£	£	£	£	£	£	£	£	£	£	£
Full Time Male														
1990	344.4	383.1	310.6	281.1	277.3	269.3	269.7	266.9	274.7	265.2	299.5	258.6	276.4	295.6
1991	368.7	408.7	333.4	300.2	297.1	291.1	292.6	286.6	300.3	289.3	322.8	280.1	299.5	318.9
1992	391.9	434.4	355.0	321.4	315.2	312.1	306.1	307.5	320.1	314.3	343.6	299.2	324.6	340.1
1993	419.7[1]			332.8	339.7	331.0	323.4	323.1	341.1	328.1	364.9	314.3	339.5	360.4
Full Time Female														
1990	232.5	258.9	207.0	185.6	188.2	181.1	181.6	181.2	186.9	180.2	204.1	180.3	187.2	201.5
1991	256.1	284.9	228.1	202.7	207.7	202.2	199.4	200.2	206.8	196.4	225.2	199.1	206.5	222.4
1992	277.2	308.6	246.9	221.8	225.0	216.6	215.9	218.1	224.0	220.6	244.2	218.7	221.9	241.1
1993	297.5[1]			232.3	242.1	235.1	226.4	235.0	242.6	230.5	261.3	237.0	243.0	258.5

New Earnings Survey.

Earnings are averaged, before tax and include overtime. Blank space denotes no available data. [1]South East figures include Greater London and rest of South East.

11.2.3 Incomes, Miscellaneous

11.2.3a Women's Earnings, 1992

	Females	Males
	£/week	£/week
Cleaners and Domestics	151.60	199.40
Sales Assistants	149.00	190.20
Launderers, Dry Cleaners and Pressers	141.40	178.80
Kitchen Porters and Hands	134.50	157.80
Bar Staff	129.70	172.80
Waitresses and Waiters	138.30	169.00

Financial Times, September 1, 1993, p.16.

Average weekly earnings before tax of full time employees on adult rates. Original source, *New Earnings Survey*.

11.2.3b UK Pay: Highest and Lowest Full Time Weekly Earnings, 1993

	£
Ten Highest Paid Occupations	
Treasurers and Company Financial Managers	745.60
Medical Practitioners	736.40
Management Consultants, Business Analysts	631.00
Underwriters, Claims Assessors and Brokers	586.10
General Managers and Administrators in Companies	577.60
Computer Systems and Data Processing Managers	562.90
Solicitors	559.80
Bank, Building Society and Post Office Managers	551.40
Actors, Entertainers, Stage Managers and Producers	540.30
Taxation Experts	528.20
Ten Lowest Paid Occupations	
Petrol Pump Forecourt Attendants	145.90
Kitchen Porters, Hands	147.30
Retail Cash Desk and Checkout Operatives	156.00
Counterhands, Catering Assistants	156.10
Bar Staff	156.20
Launderers, Dry Cleaners, Pressers	156.30
Sewing Machinists, Menders and Darners	157.70
Waiters/Waitresses	159.70
Sales Assistants	172.90
Cleaners, Domestics	173.70

Labour Research, September, 1993, p. 7.

The earnings of self employed workers in these occupations are not taken into account. Original source, *New Earnings Survey*.

11.2.3c Company Directors Earning £500,000

Director	Company	Financial Year End	Pay (£)
David Dworkin	Storehouse	3.93	3,290,474
Mark Knopfler	Chariscourt	3.92	2,664,051
Highest Paid Director	Morgan Stanley	12.91	2,170,995
Mark Knopfler	Straitjacket Songs	3.92	1,994,000
Mohammed Pervez	Bestway Holdings	6.92	1,482,000
Robert Mills	Regency International	2.92	1,359,156
Dan Doyle	Danka Business Systems	3.93	980,657
Highest Paid Director	Robert Fleming	3.93	950,000
Barrie Stephen	Siebe	3.93	620,643
Cyril Stein	Ladbroke	3.93	586,000
Highest Paid Director	Eskenazi	12.92	568,000
Barrie Endean	Xtrac	6.92	563,864
Gordon Layton	National Parking Corporation	6.92	558,421
Lord Weinstock	GEC	3.92	514,000
Highest Paid Director	Hambros	3.93	513,000
Robert de Wynter	Dewynters	3.93	509,162

Labour Research, September, 1993, p. 6.

Taken from a survey published in the August 1993 edition of Labour Research.

11.2.4 Employment

11.2.4a Unemployment by Region

	1990[1]	1991	1992	1993
	000's	000's	000's	000's
Males				
United Kingdom	1,230.4	1,480,771	2,045,371	2,353,826
North	93.3	104,725	123,461	138,100
Yorkshire and Humberside	120.4	141,863	180,725	201,911
East Midlands	72.1	89,041	128,208	149,296
East Anglia	27.2	36,754	54,899	67,896
South East	272.8	365,003	592,310	727,480
South West	69.7	98,708	152,408	179,458
West Midlands	111.5	132,544	197,400	227,122
North West	176.2	199,066	249,966	267,982
England	943.2	1,167,704	1,679,377	227,122
Wales	65.6	78,938	101,149	110,016
Scotland	148.5	158,840	184,108	201,258
Northern Ireland	73.2	75,289	80,737	83,307
Females				
United Kingdom	431.4	478,976	628,493	708,239
North	29.4	30,857	34,535	33,864
Yorkshire and Humberside	40.6	43,248	52,365	57,263
East Midlands	27.1	30,359	40,264	44,974
East Anglia	10.2	12,620	18,208	22,069
South East	99.0	122,079	191,914	233,211
South West	27.5	34,607	48,921	57,143
West Midlands	41.1	44,520	61,392	68,385
North West	58.4	61,372	71,990	75,708
England	333.3	379,662	519,589	594,617
Wales	20.6	22,514	27,606	29,421
Scotland	53.6	53,821	57,243	59,499
Northern Ireland	24.0	22,979	24,055	24,702

Regional Trends, HMSO.

Original source, Department of Employment. [1]Annual average.

11.2.4b Employment by Region

	1990	1991	1992	1993
	000's	000's	000's	000's
Males				
United Kingdom	11,980	11,599	11,257	10,911
North	590	566	557	541
Yorkshire and Humberside	944	978	957	915
East Midlands	829	814	798	762
East Anglia	413	428	415	401
South East	4,086	3,772	3,639	3,556
South West	894	903	873	852
West Midlands	1,116	1,080	1,051	997
North West	1,279	1,249	1,189	1,147
England	10,154	9,791	9,480	10,636
Wales	527	509	489	473
Scotland	1,028	1,031	1,023	992
Northern Ireland	272	269	265	275
Females				
United Kingdom	11,241	10,635	10,480	10,510
North	532	513	514	516
Yorkshire and Humberside	895	902	891	892
East Midlands	770	742	726	751
East Anglia	381	379	364	361
South East	3,898	3,491	3,436	3,353
South West	872	852	844	845
West Midlands	976	930	895	920
North West	1,209	1,147	1,137	1,160
England	9,533	8,956	8,816	10,239
Wales	482	474	462	464
Scotland	972	949	956	977
Northern Ireland	254	256	254	271

Regional Trends, HMSO.

Original source, Department of Employment.

11.2.4c Childless Women in Employment

	Females aged 16–59					Males aged 16–64	Ratio
	All	With Children	Without Children	Full-Time	Part-Time		
	000's	000's	000's	000's	000's	000's	%
All in Employment	10,617	3,828	6,788	5,910	4,604	13,301	1.3
Managers and administrators	1,190	378	812	966	223	2,492	2.1
Corporate managers and administrators	763	228	535	623	140	1,726	2.3
Managers/proprietors in agric. and services	427	150	277	343	83	766	1.8
Professional occupations	918	388	529	674	243	1,476	1.6
Science and engineering professionals	62	17	45	57	1	582	9.5
Health professionals	58	26	32	39	19	111	1.9
Teaching professionals	590	280	310	413	176	335	0.6
Other professional occupations	208	66	143	165	44	448	2.1
Associate professional and technical	1,044	397	647	692	346	1,111	1.1
Science and engineering professionals	99	29	69	75	23	434	4.4
Health associate professionals	540	231	309	322	217	78	0.1
Other associate professionals	405	137	268	295	106	599	1.5
Clerical and secretarial occupations	2,784	903	1,881	1,770	985	902	0.3
Clerical occupations	1,848	621	1,227	1,189	641	879	0.5
Secretarial occupations	935	282	654	581	345	24	0.0
Craft and related occupations	341	107	234	238	98	2,904	8.5
Skilled construction trades	1	1	1	1	1	536	68.1
Skilled engineering trades	22	1	17	18	1	967	43.2
Other skilled trades	311	99	212	215	91	1,401	4.5
Personal and protective service occupations	1,574	634	940	634	913	804	0.5
Protective service occupations	56	13	42	41	14	425	7.6
Personal service occupations	1,518	621	897	593	899	379	0.2
Sales occupations	1,231	432	799	373	848	682	0.6
Buyers, brokers and sales reps	107	38	69	76	31	314	2.9
Other sales occupations	1,124	394	731	297	816	368	0.3
Plant and machinery operatives	465	151	314	339	125	1,835	3.9
Industrial plant and machine operators	436	140	296	322	113	946	2.2
Drivers and mobile machine operators	29	11	18	17	12	889	30.3
Other occupations	1,018	423	594	202	810	998	1.0
Other occupations in agriculture and forestry	59	19	40	25	31	141	2.4
Other elementary occupations	959	404	555	177	779	856	0.9
No answer/does not reply	52	14	38	22	13	98	1.9

Employment Gazette, November, 1993, p. 500.

Original source *Labour Force Survey*. [1]Fewer than 10,000 in cell; estimate not shown .

11.3 Consumer Expenditure

11.3.1 Consumer Expenditure, Standard Table

	Food	Alcoholic Drink	Tobacco	Housing	Fuel and power	Clothing and Foot-wear	Household Goods and Services	Transport and Commu-nication	Other Goods and Services	Recrea-tion, Entertain-ment and Education	Total Consu-mer Expen-diture
	£m	£m	£m	£m	£m	£m	£m	£m	£m	£m	£m
1990	41,869	21,738	8,683	47,593	12,321	20,875	21,907	62,732	68,168	33,458	350.411
1991	44,053	23,555	9,746	51,614	14,272	21,034	22,796	62,579	71,002	34,915	367.853
1992	45,264	24,612	10,104	57,598	14,404	21,246	24,266	64,358	73,542	37,674	382,696
1993[1]											

CSO Annual Abstract of Statistics 1994.

[1] Figures for 1993 not available.

11.3.2a Regional Household Expenditure

	Housing	Fuel, Light and Power	Food	Alcohol and Tobacco	Clothing and Foot-wear	House-hold Goods and Services	Motor-ing and Fares	Leisure Goods and Services	Misc. and Per-sonal Goods and Services	Average House-hold Expen-diture	Average Expendi-ture per Person
	£/wk	£/wk	£/wk	£/wk	£/wk	£/wk	£/wk	£/wk	£/wk	£/wk	£/wk
United Kingdom	47.3	11.7	45.5	15.4	15.9	32.7	39.9	33.5	11.2	253.1	103.4
North	36.2	11.3	41.2	16.3	14.1	26.3	32.0	24.4	8.9	210.5	86.4
Yorkshire and Humberside	39.3	11.9	41.7	15.7	13.9	27.8	32.6	28.4	10.1	221.4	89.6
East Midlands	47.9	11.7	45.7	15.0	16.0	32.3	44.3	33.7	10.7	257.3	103.5
East Anglia	48.8	11.7	45.3	11.9	13.2	32.7	34.6	31.2	12.4	241.7	101.1
South East	58.4	11.6	50.1	15.3	17.3	39.0	44.9	41.6	13.5	291.5	119.5
Greater London	59.9	11.3	51.1	16.4	17.0	39.7	41.6	42.0	13.1	292.1	126.1
Rest of South East	57.5	11.7	49.5	14.6	17.5	38.6	46.7	41.4	13.6	291.2	116.0
South West	51.7	11.6	45.3	13.8	15.3	33.7	46.4	36.1	12.4	266.2	111.0
West Midlands	48.4	11.3	44.3	14.7	15.2	30.3	41.4	27.0	9.8	242.3	97.6
North West	43.9	11.8	43.2	18.5	17.0	29.7	38.4	33.2	10.2	245.9	100.5
England	49.6	11.6	45.9	15.4	16.0	32.8	41.1	33.4	11.6	257.3	137.7
Wales	36.5	11.7	42.3	15.2	14.3	29.6	35.7	28.9	10.2	224.4	91.4
Scotland	33.7	11.8	42.7	16.0	16.0	30.1	31.7	28.5	9.1	219.6	92.1
Northern Ireland	34.0	14.8	46.2	13.4	18.6	26.4	36.1	24.5	8.4	222.3	78.3

Regional Trends, HMSO.

Original sources, Department of Environment; Family Expenditure Survey.

11.3.2b Households with Certain Durable Goods

	Micro-wave Oven	Washing Machine	Tumble Drier	Dish-washer	Refri-gerator	Deep Freezer[1]	Tele-phone	Black and White TV only	Colour TV	Video	Home Com-puter	Central Heating	Total
	%	%	%	%	%	%	%	%	%	%	%	%	
UK	52	87	47	13		82	88	4	94	66	20	81	19,578
North	53	91	44	7		78	81	5	94	66	22	90	1,128
Yorkshire and Humberside	53	89	47	9		80	85	5	93	64	18	74	1,760
East Midlands	52	90	47	12		82	86	4	95	65	22	85	1,427
East Anglia	50	87	49	14		83	90	3	95	63	21	87	708
South East	53	84	48	18		85	92	4	94	69	22	84	5,939
Greater London	46	79	42	14		80	91	5	93	66	19	81	2,182
Rest of South East	57	87	52	21		88	93	3	95	70	24	86	3,757
South West	54	84	48	17		85	90	4	94	64	20	80	1,710
West Midlands	52	87	46	10		80	85	5	93	67	19	76	1,817
North West	53	86	44	10		81	85	5	94	66	20	76	2,249
England	53	86	47	14		83	88	4	94	66	21	81	16,738
Wales	59	88	44	11		85	84	4	95	66	20	82	1,025
Scotland	47	91	49	10		76	85	4	94	64	17	78	1,815
Northern Ireland	44	88	35	13	98	67	80	5	92	56	15	83	6,273

Regional Trends, HMSO, 1993.

Original sources, *Office of Population Censuses and Surveys*, *General Household Survey*, *Northern Ireland Department of Finance and Personnel*, *Family Expenditure Survey*, *Continuous Household Survey*. [1]Fridge freezers are attributed to both Refrigerator and Deep Freezer except in Northern Ireland.

11.4 Prices

11.4.1 Food Prices

11.4.1a Food Basket

Article (per lb. unless otherwise stated)	1990	1991	1992	1993
	p.	p.	p.	p.
Bread:				
White Loaf Sliced (800g.)	50.0	53.0	54.0	55.0
White Loaf, Unwrapped (800g.)	64.0	70.0	71.0	75.0
Brown Loaf, Unsliced (800g.)	64.0	73.0	75.0	79.0
Flour, Self Raising, (per 1.5kg.)	55.0	59.0	64.0	63.0
Beef, home-killed:				
Best beef mince	152.0	158.0	160.0	160.0
Topside	281.0	268.0	276.0	278.0
Brisket without bone	193.0	193.0	195.0	203.0
Pork, home-killed:				
Leg (foot off)	137.0	137.0	156.0	145.0
Loin (with bone)	175.0	160.0	193.0	173.0
Ham (per 4oz.)	70.0	78.0	75.0	75.0
Bacon:				
Back, vacuum packed	210.0	223.0	236.0	220.0
Back, not vacuum packed	196.0	200.0	215.0	208.0
Fish, fresh cod fillets	242.0	282.0	306.0	312.0
Margarine (low fat spread)	41.0	49.0	47.0	49.0
Lard (per 250g.)	17.0	17.0	18.0	n/a
Milk, skimmed (per pint)	29.0	31.0	33.0	33.0
Butter (per 250g.)	70.0	71.0	70.0	74.0
Cheese	152.0	151.0	165.0	176.0
Eggs:				
(65–70g) size 2 (per dozen)	122.0	119.0	126.0	124.0
Potatoes, red	15.0	14.0	15.0	15.0
Potatoes, white	14.0	14.0	17.0	11.0
Cabbage	32.0	36.0	23.0	45.0
Onions	23.0	25.0	25.0	22.0
Cauliflower	71.0	77.0	72.0	84.0
Carrots	22.0	26.0	22.0	19.0
Apples, eating	39.0	45.0	56.0	41.0
Oranges (each)	17.0	20.0	21.0	20.0
Pears	49.0	55.0	52.0	47.0
Bananas	49.0	50.0	51.0	42.0
Sugar, granulated (per kg.)	59.0	65.0	66.0	68.0
Coffee:				
Pure instant (per 100g.)	143.0	128.0	130.0	125.0
Ground filter fine (per 8 ozs.)	135.0	140.0	137.0	137.0
Tea:				
Loose (per 125g.)	48.0	57.0	61.0	65.0
Tea bags (per 250g.)	114.0	134.0	156.0	136.0

Employment Gazette, 1990–1993.

11.4.2. Prices, General Articles

	1990	1991	1992	1993
	p.	p.	p.	p.
Aspirin (100)	62.0	74.0		
Average House Price	£78,917	£76,442	£73,093	£76,408
Beer (1 pint)	97.0	105.0	113.0	119.0
Cadbury's Dairy Milk Chocolate (200g.)	93.0	95.0	99.0	102.0
Cheddar Cheese	164.0		149.0	225.0
Colmans Mustard (113g.)	101.0	101.0	121.0	125.0
Daily Mail	25.0		30.0	32.0
Guinness Extra Stout (1 pint)	126.0			
Inland Letter Post	22.0	24.0	24.0	25.0
Mars Bar	21.0	22.0	23.0	25.0
Pears Transparent Soap	82.0			85.0
Petrol (1 litre)	58.5	41.8	44.2	46.7
Pocket Money	149.0	169.0	182.0	187.0
Red Label Tea (1lb.)	392.0			74 (250g.)
Scotch Whisky (Standard Bottle)		£10.50	£10.80	£10.69
Swan Vestas Matches	10.0			14.0
The Times	30.0			30.0

The Boots Company; Birds Eye Walls Ltd; Burmah Castrol; Cadburys Ltd; Colmans of Norwich; Guinness Brewing GB; Halifax Building Society; Rowntrees; Royal Mail; Sainsburys Archives; The Scotch Whisky Association; Swan Hotel, Holmes Chapel and Unilever Historical Archives.

Blank space denotes no available prices.

11.4.3 Prices, Selected

Item	Source	Description	Price £ p.
Alcoholic Drink			
Wine	*J Sainsbury*, 1990	Sainsbury's Orvieto	3.49
		Sainsbury's Muscadet	2.59
	Which, December 1990	Maison Deutz Brut Cuvée Arroyo Grande	9.99 (from Oddbins)
		Antinori Extra Brut Spumante Classico	10.59
Champagne	*Threshers*, 1991	Moët et Chandon	14.99
Beer	*Coop Pricefighter*, 1993	Stone's Draught Bitter	3.99 (4 pack)
Fortified Wine		Harvey's Bristol Cream	5.09
Lager		Carlings Black Label	2.79 (4 pack)
Spirits		Smirnoff Vodka	10.49
		Teachers Scotch Whisky	10.69
		Bacardi Rum	10.89
Vermouth		Martini Extra Dry	3.59
Wine		Lambrusco	2.69 (1.5 litres)
		Granleve Portugese Wine	1.99
Champagne		Chemevaux Champagne	8.99
Appliances Domestic and Electrical			
Camcorders	*Which*, 1990	Sony CCD-TR55E Video 8	1,000.00
		Ferguson FC15 VHS-C	800.00
		Nikon VN-9500 HI8	1,300.00
		JVC GR-S77 Super VHS-C	1,100.00
Car Radio Cassettes		Aiwa CT-Z3601	199.00
		Hitachi CSK492E	200.00
		Sharp RG F8342	170.00
Cleaners		Electrolux Electronic 616	110.00
		Hoover V1284 Sprite	65.00
		Moulinex Major 830	85.00
Dishwashers		AEG Favorit 420	300.00
		Hotpoint Super Plus 7822	310.00
		Miele G572	550.00
		Servis Secret Compact 4400	240.00
Fax Machines		Amstrad FX9600T	630.00
		BT CF10	685.00
		Ferranti Rhapsody	720.00
		Sharp FO-220	980.00
Food Processors		Braun MC1000	35.00
		Kenwood FP300	50.00
		Magimix 5000	140.00
		Tefal 8612	47.00
Freezers		Frigidaire FV1260	150.00
		Lec V3825	165.00
		Philips Whirlpool	200.00
Kettles		Boots Cordless	25.00
		Haden Autojug	19.00

Continued

11.4.3 Prices, Selected *continued*

Item	Source	Description	Price £ p.
Kettles *cont.*		Swan Elegance 10546	21.00
		Russell Hobbs 3076	17.00
Satellite Television Systems		Ferguson SRB1	380.00
		ITT Nokia SAT1200	400.00
		Philips STU902	370.00
		Tatuna TRX2801	400.00
Stereo Radio Recorders		Sony CFS903L	80.00
		Boots SRR33T	40.00
		JVC RC-W210	80.00
Video Recorders		Akai VS75EV VHS Nicam HI-FI	550.00
		Ferguson FV31R Standard VHS	300.00
		Toshiba Standard VHS	340.00
Washing Machines		AEG Lavomat 280	460.00
		Hotpoint Electronic De Luxe 1000	370.00
		Indesit 823	250.00
CD Players	*Which*, 1991	Akai CD 55	200.00
		Kenwood DP3020	140.00
		Rotel RCD855	280.00
Camcorders		Sony TR55E	750.00
		Panasonic NV-S1	800.00
Cleaners		Electrolux Electronic 616	120.00
		Hoover Turbolite	60.00
		Moulinex Major	110.00
Coffee Filter Makers		Cordon Bleu 5550	16.00
		Krups Compact Aroma 10	40.00
Computers		Commodore PC20111	800.00
		IBM PS/1	840.00
		Apple Mac Classic	1,050.00
Cookers (electric)		Belling Format 600X/T	700.00
		Leisure 3020	350.00
		Creda Hallmark Double Oven	420.00
Cookers (gas)		Leisure Silhouette	550.00
		New World Royale 600SBS	525.00
		Parkinson Cowan Continental	400.00
Microwave Ovens		AEG Micromat (compact)	225.00
		Frigidaire FCL600/60	100.00
		Bosch HMG726B	409.00
Dishwashers		Hotpoint Super Plus 7842	369.99
		Zanussi DW401	329.99
Food Processors		Braun MC200	42.00
		Kenwood Chef KM201	132.00
Freezers		Electrolux Fridge/Freezer	300.00
		Iceline CB28C	270.00
		LEC V3825	165.00
		Norfros	96.00
Gas Fires		Flavel Chalfont	260.00

Continued

11.4.3 Prices, Selected *continued*

Item	Source	Description	Price £ p.
Gas Fires *cont.*		Jetmaster Convector 16"	430.00
		Verine Zephyr	430.00
Refrigerators		AEG Santo Larder Fridge	215.00
		Electrolux RF593	200.00
		Frigidaire Elite	145.00
Televisions		Boots CTV1414R	160.00
		Matsui 1455	160.00
		Sony KUM1420	230.00
Tumble Dryers		Bosch WTA2710	300.00
		Indesit TD1000	160.00
		Creda Sensair 37549	230.00
Washing Machines		AEG Lavamat 280	470.00
		Hotpoint Electronic De Luxe 1000	420.00
		Indesit 823	220.00
Washer Dryers		Candy Turbomatic 22WD	400.00
		Hoover Logic 1300	460.00
Word Processing Packages		Word Perfect V5.1	320.00
		Word Star 2000 V3.5	270.00
Cleaners	*Which*, 1993	Electrolux Airstream	180.00
		Electrolux Lite De Luxe 1860	90.00
		Hoover Junior VI426	122.00
Computers		Amstrad Notepad NC100	165.00
		Hewlett Packard HP95LX	400.00
		Toshiba T1850	1,105.00
		Compaq 3/25	1,230.00
Printers		Epson LQ-100 Dot Matrix	180.00
		IMB 2390-001 Dot Matrix	300.00
		Canon BJ10 Inkjet	200.00
		Epson SQ-870 Inkjet	470.00
Refrigerators		AEG Santo 1732TK	300.00
		Electrolux ER1622T	340.00
		Frigidaire TR1521	150.00
Stereo Radio Recorders		Sony CFD204	150.00
		Sharp WQCD220L	150.00
		JVC RCX720	190.00
Stereo Systems		Goodmans 1250 Micro System	190.00
		Aiwa NSX220 Mini System	230.00
		Bush MS772 Midi System	180.00
Washing Machines		Electra 170206	380.00
		Elecrolux 1130B	480.00
Baby Equipment			
Bouncers and Rockers	*Mothercare*, 1993	Fisher Price Hop Skip Jumper	29.99
		Circular Baby Walker	39.99
High Chairs		Pine Folding Highchair	49.99
		Cube Highchair	84.99
Pram		Silver Cross Combination	339.99

Continued

11.4.3 Prices, Selected *continued*

Item	Source	Description	Price £ p.
Push Chairs		Silver Cross Wayfarer Push Chair	134.95
		Mothercare Stroller	29.99
		Maclaren E-Type	39.99
Car Seat		Britax Baby Sure Car Seat	29.99
Cot		Martine Cot in Natural Beechwood	145.00
		Junior Convertible Cotbed	189.00
Sterilisers		De-Luxe Six Bottle Steriliser	17.50
		Steam Sterilisers	29.99

Clothing and Footwear:
Children's

Item	Source	Description	Price £ p.
Dress	*Laura Ashley*, Spring 1992	Fine Cotton Loose Slip Dress	19.95
Dungarees		Fine Cotton Dungarees	14.95
T Shirt		Cotton Jersey T Shirt	6.95
Trousers		Fine Cotton Trousers	13.95
Dress	*Clothkits*, Summer 1992	Baby's Print Dress in Cotton	8.99
		Girl's Striped Cotton Dress 12 years	15.99
		Print Sundress 2–6 years	13.99
Jog Pants		Boy's Jog Pants in Cotton Jersey	16.99
Knitwear		Cardigan in Cotton/Polyester	9.99
		Aran Cardigan in Acrylic/Cotton 12 years	14.99
Jeans		Boy's Claret Jeans 12 years	14.99
Jumpsuit		Front Print Jumpsuit in Cotton/Polyester	12.99
Leggings		Elasticated Waist Leggings 12 years	11.99
		Pack of Two Leggings 4–6 years	8.99
Shorts		Boy's Shorts in Cotton	12.99
		Boy's Chino Shorts 12 years	11.99
		Children's Cotton Shorts 4–6 years	8.99
Socks		Pack of 4 Socks 12 years	6.99
Sweatshirt		Boy's Sweatshirt 12 years	15.99
		Elephant Sweatshirt in Cotton/Polyester	8.99
Swimsuit		Print Swimsuit 2–6 years	12.99
T Shirt		Child's T Shirt 4–6 years	9.99
		T Shirt 12 years	11.99
Trousers		Chino Trousers 12 years	14.99
Body	*Next*, 1993 (all 3–4 years)	Navy Velour Body	9.99
Dress		Deep Rose Taffetta Dress	24.99
Jeans		Dark Blue Denim Jeans	11.99
Knitwear		Emerald Base Tartan Hand Knit Sweater	19.99
		Jacquard Tapestry Sweater	12.99
		Navy Base Hand Knit Tunic Sweater	24.99
Leggings		Ribbed Leggings	11.99
Shirt		Blue Denim Shirt	10.99

Continued

11.4.3 Prices, Selected *continued*

Item	Source	Description	Price £ p.
Shirt *cont.*		Navy & Ochre Stars Print Shirt	11.99
Ski Pants		Navy Velour Ski Pants	9.99
Slippers		Dog Novelty Slippers	12.99
Waistcoat		Red and Navy Tartan Waistcoat	14.99
Blouse	*Laura Ashley*, 1993 (6–18 months)	Cotton Poplin Blouse in White	10.95
Dress		Frilled Collar Dress	21.95
Dungarees		Fun Dungarees with Bows on Pockets	25.95
Knitwear		Embroidered Cardigan	13.95
Pinafore		Simple Pinafore with Lined Bodice	17.95
Trousers		Fine Needlecord Trousers with Elasticated Waist	11.95
Men's			
Shirts	*Which*, February 1990	Allander House of Fraser Poly/Cotton Shirt	9.00
		St. Michael Poly/Cotton Shirt	16.00
		Top Man Poly/Cotton Shirt	8.00
		Van Heusen AS2000 Poly/Cotton Shirt	15.00
		Debenhams Classic Cotton Shirt	15.00
		Littlewoods Cotton Shirts	9.00
		Jaeger Cotton Shirts	33.00
Socks		Sock Shop City Men's Wool Blend	3.99 (pair)
		Littlewoods Wool Rich Blend	2.99 (pair)
		BHS Patterned Argyle Cotton Socks	2.50 (pair)
		Woolworths Cotton Blend	2.99 (2 pairs)
Suit	*Receipt*, 1990	Christian Dior Suit from Rackhams	120.00 (sale price)
Blazer	*Complete Essentials, Freemans plc*, 1992	Double Breasted Blazer in New Wool Gaberdine	95.00
Knitwear		Nautical Effect Jumper	34.99
Shirt		White Poplin Short Sleeved Shirt	16.99
		Long Sleeved Shirt with Slub Finish	21.99
Suit		Linen Mix Lined Jacket and Trousers	99.00
Trousers		Wool Trousers	49.99
Boots	*Next*, 1993	Black Double Buckle Boot	44.99
Jacket		Black Pure New Wool Jacket	89.99
Jeans		Black Leather Jeans	149.99
Knitwear		Merino Wool Turtle Neck Sweater	32.99
Nightwear		Navy/Blue Stone Check Towelling Robe	49.99
		Navy/Blue Marl Stripe Jersey Pyjamas	34.99
Shirt		Spot Print Shirt	29.99
		Blue Chambray Shirt	24.99
Tie		Black Geometric Spot Silk Tie	15.99
Trousers		Grape Textured Mélange Trousers	39.99
Waistcoat		Merino Wool Knitted Waistcoat	32.99
Jeans	*Xtend*, 1993	5 Pocket Western Style Jeans	25.00

Continued

11.4.3 Prices, Selected *continued*

Item	Source	Description	Price £ p.
Shirts		Bleached Chambray Shirt	18.00
		Long Sleeved Washed Twill Shirts	20.00
T Shirt		Heavy Jersey T Shirt	12.00
Shorts		Rugby Shorts in Washed Cotton	16.00
Trousers		Classic Safari Style Washed Cotton Trousers	29.00
Women's			
Shoes	*C & J Clark Ltd.*, 1990	Melody Black Kid Leather	29.99
		Piazza Solitaire in Tan Leather	29.99
		Piazza Ludo in Fuchsia Leather	27.99
		Piazza Dice in Jade Leather	27.99
Bodysuit	*Laura Ashley*, Spring 1992	Bodysuit in Cotton Jersey	24.95
Dress		Fine Cotton Loose Slip Dress	34.99
Dungarees		Fine Cotton Dungarees	38.95
Espadrilles		Cotton Espadrilles with Rubber/Jute Soles	7.95
Jacket		Jacket in Wool	54.95
Shoes		Shoes in Nubuck Leather	36.95
Shorts		Cotton Shorts with Half Elasticated Waist and Sash	18.95
Swimsuit		Swimsuit with Square Neckline and Low Back	19.95
T Shirt		Casual T Shirt with 5 Mother of Pearl Buttons	14.95
Trousers		Wool Crêpe Trousers	54.95
Bodysuit	*Clothkits*, Summer 1992	Bodysuit in Cotton/Lycra	19.99
Dress		Voile Dress in Viscose/Cotton	37.99
Jacket		Lightweight Jacket with a Textured Outer Shell	39.99
		Casual Jacket in Natural Mix of Ramie/Cotton	29.99
		Sandwashed Silk Jacket	59.99
Knitwear		Cardigan in Ramie/Cotton	37.99
		Crochet Cardigan in Ramie/Cotton	37.99
Leggings		Matisse Print Leggings in Cotton	21.99
		Plain Leggings in Cotton	16.99
Sarong		Sandwashed Silk Sarong	54.99
Shorts		Print Shorts in Cotton	19.99
Skirt		Shapely Short Skirt in Stretch Jersey	16.99
		Flared Skirt in Sandwashed Silk Crêpe de Chine	49.99
Sweatshirt		Fleece Backed Jersey Sweatshirt	21.99
Swimsuit		Print Swimsuit in Cotton Elastane	19.99
Blouse	*Laura Ashley*, Winter 1993	Pure Silk Blouse in Plum	49.99
		Classic High Neck Blouse in Cream Cotton	39.95
Boots		Leather Victorian Style Leather Ankle Boots	59.95
Coat		Double Breasted Duffle Coat in Wool	160.00

Continued

11.4.3 Prices, Selected *continued*

Item	Source	Description	Price £ p.
Dress		Elegant Dupon Dress with Shawl Style Collar	130.00
		Classic Soft Velvet Dress	120.00
		Classic Riding Dress in Wool Crêpe	110.00
Jodhpurs		Corduroy Jodhpurs	54.95
Knitwear		Two Tone Jumper in Grey/Black	54.95
		Longline Cardigan in Grey Marl Lambswool	49.95
		Hand Knitted Cardigan	90.00
Leggings		Printed Jersey Leggings	29.95
Ski Pants		Black Ski Pants	29.95
Skirts		Short Fine Needlecord Skirt	29.95
		Fully Lined Long Pleated Viyella Check Skirt	64.95
Shoes		Leather Walking Shoe with Lace Up Front	44.95
		Classic Style Suede Court Shoe	39.95
		Casual Slip on Brogue Shoe	44.95
		Stylish Loafer in Navy Suede	42.95
Trousers		Tailored Trousers in Navy Polyester/Wool	59.95
Underwear		Cambric Petticoat in White	34.95
Blouse	*Next*, Winter 1993	Floral Embroidered Georgette Blouse	39.99
Body		Black Scoop Neck Body	24.99
		Luxury Underwired Body	32.99
Coat		Pure Wool Navy Coat	125.00
Dress		Black Metallic Knitted Sleeveless Dress	49.99
Jacket		Red Crêpe Jacket	54.99
Knitwear		Patchwork Patterned Hand Knitted Sweater	59.99
		Charcoal Sweater with Fair Isle Pattern	49.99
Nightwear		Luxury Satin Long Nightdress	29.99
Trousers		Black Georgette Palazzo Pants	49.99
Underwear		Black Velvet and Stretch Satin Briefs	6.99
		Luxury 30's Style Deep Briefs	12.99

Food Products

Item	Source	Description	Price
Bacon	*J Sainsbury*, 1990	Unsmoked Back	2.58 (lb.)
Biscuits		McVities Digestive	31 (½ lb.)
Breakfast Cereal		Shredded Wheat	63 (12's)
Butter		Best Butter	71 (lb.)
Cheese		Cheddar Cheese	1.64 (lb.)
Eggs		Six Medium Size	61
Soup		Heinz Tomato Soup	34 (15½ oz.)
Squash		Kia Ora Squash	74 (20 oz.)
Tea		Red Label Tea	3.92 (lb.)

Continued

11.4.3 Prices, Selected *continued*

Item	Source	Description	Price £ p.
Confectionery	*Cadbury Ltd.*, June 1990	Cadbury's Bournville	95 (200 g.)
		Cadbury's Dairy Milk	93 (200 g.)
		Chocolate Buttons Large	35
		Cadbury's Fruit and Nut	95 (200 g.)
Biscuits	*Coop Pricefighter*, 1993	Coop Assorted Biscuits	2.79 (kg.)
Cheese		Cheddar Cheese	1.39 (lb.)
Chicken		4 lb. Whole Fresh Chicken	3.99
Confectionery		Cadbury's Milk Tray	3.99
Drinks		Robinsons Whole Fruit Drink	82 (litre)
		Coca-Cola	85 (2 litres)
Mincemeat		Coop Mince Meat	69 (413 g.)
Pudding		Mrs. Peaks Christmas Pudding	1.99 (454 g.)
Salmon		Princes Red Salmon	1.09 (213 g.)
Bacon	*J Sainsbury*, 1993	Middle Unsmoked	2.58 (lb.)
Beans		JS Beans	42 (15 oz.)
Breakfast Cereal		Kelloggs Corn Flakes	1.05 (500 g.)
Butter		Best Butter	1.30 (lb.)
Cheese		Cheddar Cheese	1.49 (lb.)
Chicken		3 lb. Roasting Chicken	1.85
Coffee		JS Instant Coffee Refill	1.30 (4 oz.)
Jam		Strawberry Jam	45 (lb.)
Sugar		Sugar	1.34 (lb.)
Tea		Loose Red Label Tea	74 (½ lb.)
Tinned Fruit		Peach Slices	35 (14.5 oz.)
Tomato Sauce		Heinz Tomato Ketchup	54 (20 oz.)
Vegetable Oil		JS Vegetable Oil	53 (litre)
Confectionery	*Cadbury Ltd.*, April 26, 1993	Cadbury's Bournville	1.02 (200 g.)
		Cadbury's Dairy Milk	1.02 (200 g.)
		Cadbury's Fruit and Nut	1.02 (200 g.)
		Cadbury's Milk Tray	4.79 (lb. Box)
		Wispa	24
		Crunchie	25
		Roses	3.39 (lb.)

Furniture

Item	Source	Description	Price £ p.
Bedroom	*Index Catalogue Shop*, 1993	Silentnight Double Firm Support Divan	149.99
		Silentnight Classic Standard Divan	199.99
		Perfecta Single Divan Set	84.99
		Two Door Wardrobe	49.99
		Three Drawer Tallboy	59.99
		Five Drawer Chest	49.99
Bookcase		Addspace Large Bookcase	34.99
Dining		Butterfly Dining Set in Real Wood Veneer	169.99
Lounge		Tower Hi-Fi Stacker Unit	36.99
		Video Storage Unit	27.99

Continued

11.4.3 Prices, Selected *continued*

Item	Source	Description	Price
			£ p.
Lounge *cont.*		Nest of Tables	29.99
		Long John Occasional Table	24.99
		Coffee Table with Undershelf in Real Wood Veneer	59.99
		Addspace Display Wall Unit	149.99
		Addspace Low Hi-Fi Cabinet	89.99
Seating		Two Seater Settee and Two Chairs	299.97
		Kensington Foam Sofa Bed	99.99
		Multi Coloured Swivel Chair	24.99
Bedroom	*Ikea*, 1993	Arnadel Swedish Double Bed	264.00
		Forsmo Swedish Single Bed	134.00
		Nils Wardrobe with Foiled Particleboard	39.00
Dining		Turku Table in Clear Lacquered Solid Pine	199.00
		Turku Clear Lacquered Solid Pine Chair	64.00 (each)
Lounge		Kalix Coffee Table	57.00
		Cabina Hi-Fi Storage	45.00
		KOL Video/TV Storage	18.00
		Consul Storage Unit in Beechwood	145.00
		ELO Desk in Antique Stained Wood	64.00
Seating		Ljusdal Three Seater Sofa	485.00
		Ljusdal Two Seater Sofa	375.00
		Lingbo Natural Black Leather Two Seater Sofa	755.00
		Lingbo Natural Black Leather Armchair	535.00
		Billdal Sofa Bed	495.00

Garden Equipment and Supplies

Item	Source	Description	Price
Hedge Cutter	*B & Q Catalogue*, Spring 1992	Qualcast HC35 Hedge Cutter	59.45
Mowers		Flymo Chevron RE300 Twin Electric Rotary Mower	108.95
		Qualcast Suffolk Turbo 40 Petrol Rotary Mower	299.99
		Qualcast Hover Safe 25 Electric Hover Mower	49.45
Tools		Spear & Jackson Digging Spade	18.99
		Black Forge Notched Shears	15.99
		Wilkinson Sword Small Anvil Pruner	12.25
Garden Buildings		Abberley Summerhouse	525.00
		Kids Klubhouse	99.00
Wheelbarrows		Hozelock Ballbarrow 4320	49.99
		Beldray Spartan	22.99
Hedge Cutter	*Index*, 1993	Qualcast HC35 Hedge Cutter	49.50
Mowers		Flymo XE250 Hover Mower	99.50
		Qualcast Hover Safe 25 Electric Mower	54.50
Tools		Rolcut Garden Rake	7.99

Continued

11.4.3 Prices, Selected *continued*

Item	Source	Description	Price £ p.
Tools *cont.*		Bulldog Six Piece Garden Tool Set	29.95
		Bulldog Edging Knife	6.99
		Wilkinson By-pass Pruner	9.99
Wheelbarrow		Galvanised Steel Wheelbarrow	18.99
Heat and Light			
Electricity	*Eastern Electricity*	Standing Charge per Week /£	Price per Unit/p
	Eastern Electricity, 1990	0.61	6.50
	Eastern Electricity, 1991	0.70	7.17
	Eastern Electricity, 1992	0.70	7.42
	Eastern Electricity, 1993	0.70	7.42
Gas	*British Gas North Thames*,	Standing Charge £	Unit Charges in Pence per Therm (first 5000)
	British Gas North Thames, March 1, 1990	9.40	42.8
	British Gas North Thames, November 1, 1990	9.40	44.3
	British Gas North Thames, April 1, 1991	9.40	45.9
	British Gas North Thames, October 1, 1991	9.40	45.9
Coal	*Digest of UK Energy Statistics*, 1990	Coal per Tonne to Large Consumers	42.36
	Digest of UK Energy Statistics, 1991		41.53
	Digest of UK Energy Statistics, 1992		40.99
	Digest of UK Energy Statistics, 1993		n/a
Hotel Rates			
Crown & Mitre Hotel, Carlisle	*Cumbria Tourist Board*, 1990	Daily Bed and Breakfast Rates per Person from	46.00
Swallow Hilltop Hotel, Carlisle (near M6)			60.00
Roxburghe Hotel, Edinburgh	*Edinburgh Accommodation Guide*, 1991		40.00
George Hotel, Edinburgh			73.50
The Gore, Kensington, London	*Best Western International Hotel Guide*, 1991		83.00
The Phoenix, Bayswater, London			55.00
Crickdale Hotel, Swindon	*Sunday Times*, June 7, 1992	Two nights inc.	87.00 (p.p.)
Craig Manor Hotel, Windermere		Two nights inc.	98.00 (p.p.)
Charterhouse Hotel, Manchester	*Sunday Times*, December 12, 1993	Single Occupancy of Twin/Double Room from	100.00
Savoy Hotel, London			158.00
Town House Hotel, Glasgow			50.00
Household Goods			
Knives	*Which*, 1991	Kitchen Devil Paring Knife	6.73

Continued

11.4.3 Prices, Selected *continued*

Item	Source	Description	Price £ p.
Knives *cont.*		Kitchen Devil Sure Grip Cooks Knife	13.44
		Sainsbury's Chef Bread Knife	6.45
		Sabatier Carving Knife	10.00
Bedding	*Argos*, 1993	Starlight 10.5 tog Duvet Single	8.99
		Starlight 12.0 tog Duvet Double	14.99
		Dunlopillo Golden Lullaby	11.99
		John Cotton Pack of Four Pillow Cases	12.49
		Burlington Blue Stripe Duvet Cover Double	14.99
Cookware		Swan Four Piece Cookware Set	36.99
Cutlery		Spencer Forge "Eton" 24 Piece Cutlery Set	5.99
		Viners "Dubarry" 44 Piece Cutlery Set	58.99
Kitchenware		Viners Kitchen Tool Set	9.99
		Eternal Beam Pedal Bin	9.89
		Brabantia Five Piece Gadget Set	9.89
Tableware		Wood & Sons Alpine Meadow 30 Piece Dining Set	44.99
		Fine Bone China Mugs	6.99 (each)
		Kilncraft Coffee Mugs	3.49 (each)
		Set of Six Wine Glasses	15.99
Bedding	*Index*, 1993	Slumbalux Hollow Fibre Polyester Duvet 13.5 tog	14.99 (single)
			21.99 (double)
			29.99 (king size)
		Plain Dyed Cotton/Polyester Sheets Single	5.99
		Plain Dyed Cotton/Polyester Sheets Double	6.99
		Flannelette Fitted Sheet Single	6.50
		Flannelette Fitted Sheet	7.50
		Starburst Duvet Cover Single	8.99
		Starburst Duvet Cover Double	13.99
		Dunlopillo Latex Foam Pillow	12.99
		Ariel Feather Pillows	6.99 (pair)
Cookware	*Ikea*, 1993	Gourmet Casserole with Lid	33.00
		Gourmet Lasagne Oven Dish	6.90
		Terracotta Mixing Bowls	7.50 (set of 2)
Cutlery		Stainless Steel City Cutlery Set	11.00 (3 piece set)
		Fiesta 24 Piece Cutlery Set	24.00
Kitchenware		Lex Five Piece Utensil Set	16.00
Knives		Drabant Kitchen Knives: Bread	12.00
		Cooks	11.50
		Paring	7.50
		Meat	10.00
Tableware		Marcella 4 Pack Dinner Plates	16.25
		Marcella 4 Pack Side Plates	11.75

Continued

11.4.3 Prices, Selected *continued*

Item	Source	Description	Price £ p.
Tableware *cont.*		Marcella 4 Pack Soup Plates	16.25
		Novett 20 Piece Dinner Set	16.50
		Syntes 18 Piece Coffee Service	7.00
		Lorry 12 Wine Glasses	4.00
		Spurt Glazed White Stoneware Mugs	3.30 (set of 8)
Towels		Kaitun Terry Towels Hand	2.50
		Kaitun Bath Towel	5.00
		Kaitun Bath Sheet	7.50
Houses			
Terrace	*House Beautiful*, December 1991/ January 1992	4 Bed Terrace with Garage in London Docklands	220,000.00
Apartment		2 Bed Apartment with Parking Space in Docklands	290,000.00
Terrace		Barratt Walpole 4 Bed Terrace with Garage	315,000.00
Semi	*Sunday Times*, July 1, 1990	2 Bed Stone Built Cottage in Saddleworth	54,775.00
		3 Bed Bungalow in Rural Northumberland	120,000.00
Detached	*Nationwide Estate Agents*, 1992	Mature 3 Bed House in South Cheshire	120,000.00
Mews		2 Bed Mews Type Cottage in South Cheshire	69,950.00
Detached	*Sunday Times*, June 7, 1992	4 Bed Houses in Kent from	199,950.00
Flat		1 Bed Flat in Oxford	65,000.00
Terrace		3 Bed Mid Terrace in Wembley	79,950.00
Semi	*Bridgfords Estate Agents*, 1993	3 Bed Semi in Alsager, Cheshire	49,950.00
New Detached		4 Bed Jones Homes in South Cheshire from	84,950.00
Jewellery			
Necklace	*House Beautiful*, December 1991/ January 1992	Coloured Dragees from The General Trading Company	3.85
		Metallic String of Baubles from Woolworths	4.99
Diamonds	*Good Housekeeping*, October 1992	Alan Wayne Designs from	5,610.00
Rings	*Argos*, 1993	9 ct. Gold Bevelled Edge Plain Wedding Ring	14.95
		18 ct. Gold Bevelled Edge Plain Wedding Ring	47.99
		9 ct. Three Coloured Gold Russian Wedding Ring	49.95
		18 ct. Gold 10mm Wide Wedding Ring	129.99
		9 ct. Gold Diamond Ring Set	189.99
		Genuine 22 ct. Gold Full Sovereign Coin	189.00
Bracelet	*H.Samuel*, 1993	9 ct. Gold Charm Bracelet	39.99
		9 ct. Gold Bracelet, 3 Hearts of Gold	89.99
Chain		9 ct. Gold 20 ins. Curb Chain	299.00

Continued

11.4.3 Prices, Selected *continued*

Item	Source	Description	Price £ p.
Chain *cont.*		9 ct. Gold St. Christopher with Chain	69.50
Cufflinks		Janet Reger 9 ct.Gold Cufflinks	59.95
Earrings		9 ct. Gold Wedding Band Earrings	39.50
		Amethyst Drop Earrings	29.99
Lighter		Colibri Quantum Windproof Lighter	29.95
Rings		Diamond Cluster 9 ct. Gold Ring	199.50
		Diamond Solitaire 20 Points 18 ct. Gold	299.50
		Ruby & Diamond Eternity Band 9 ct. Gold	199.50
		Channel Set Diamond Eternity Band 18 ct. Gold	299.50
		Oval Diamond Cut 9 ct. Gold Signet Ring	49.99
Watch		Lorus Gold Plated Case and Expanding Bracelet	29.99
		Seiko Gold Plated Case and Bracelet	185.00
		Accurist 2 Tone Gold Plated Case and Bracelet	54.90
		Rotary Stainless Steel and Gold Plated Sports	149.00
		Swatch Sophomore, Leather Strap	27.50
		Zeon the Official Barbie Watch	15.99
		Men's Rotary Watch, 9ct.Gold Swiss Quartz Movement	299.50
Gifts		Silver Plated and Crystal Rose Bowl	11.95
		Classic Design Quartz Carriage Clock	13.95
		Musical Jewellery Box with Revolving Ballerina	5.95
		Jacobean Style Pewter Tankard	19.95
		Braun Quartz Travel Alarm	17.95

Musical Instruments

Item	Source	Description	Price £ p.
Pianos	*Tostevin & Son*, 1993	Knights Upright Piano	4,000.00
		Steinmann Baby Grand	26,000.00
Guitars	*Barnes & Mullins*, 1993	Barnes & Mullins Spanish Guitars from	100.00
Brass	*Boosey & Hawkes*, 1993	Trumpet, Beginners	199.00 (inc. VAT)
		Saxophone, Alto	725.00 (inc. VAT)
Strings		Schrotter Violin	199.00 (inc. VAT)
Woodwind		Clarinet	635.00 (inc. VAT)
Electronic Keyboard	*Argos*, 1993	Yamaha PSS-31 Electronic Keyboard	84.50
Guitars		Encore Student Classic Guitar	29.50
		Hohner Concert Classic Acoustic Guitar	32.99
Guitar Strings	*Receipt*, 1993	American String Packet Co. Ltd. Classical Strings	4.95

Continued

11.4.3 Prices, Selected *continued*

Item	Source	Description	Price £ p.
Personal Care Items			
Toilet Preparations	*J Sainsbury*, 1990	Colgate Toothpaste	0.79 (standard)
		Andrex Toilet Rolls	0.79 (2's)
	Which, February 1991	Dixcel Killensoft Toilet Tissue	1.29
		Sainsbury Revive	1.25
		Andrex Family Size Tissues	0.97
		Superdrug White Tissues	0.42
Sunscreens		Boots Soltan Sun Lotion	5.41 (125 ml.)
		Superdrug Family Sunblock	3.39 (150 ml.)
		Uvistat Sun Cream	6.52 (100 ml.)
Travelling Appliances	*Which*, June 1991	Pifco Worldwide Travel Iron	13.00
		Babyliss Travel Pro 815	20.00
		Pifco Worldwide Travel Jug	13.00
Soap	*House Beautiful*, 1991/1992	Morny Luxury English Soap	4.95
Cosmetics	*Good Housekeeping*, October 1992	Rimmel Rich Moisture Lipstick	1.99
		Shadow Sweep by Max Factor	2.95
		Chanel Black Fluid Eye Liner	14.00
		Eau Tonique Body Splash by Elancyl	16.50
		Eau de Parfum Eternity by Calvin Klein	29.00 (50 ml.)
Toilet Preparations		Estee Lauder Advanced Night Repair Cream	26.00 (30 ml.)
		Guerlain Issima Aquaserum	49.50 (30 ml.)
		Calvin Klein Bath and Shower Gel	20.50
		Body Shop Frequent Wash Shampoo	0.80
		Klorane Almond Milk for Fine Hair	3.15
		Silkience Frequent Use Shampoo	1.69
		Herbal Vosene	1.11
		Vidal Sassoon Wash and Go	21.17
Hair Dryers	*Which*, 1993	Babyliss	24.00
		Boots 1600	16.00
		Clairol Professional	20.00
Cosmetics	*Argos*, 1993	Luxury Cosmetic Collection	9.49
		Set of 10 French Perfumes	9.79
Shaving Equipment		Philishave HS825 Mains/Rechargeable Shaver	58.50
		Remington XLR1110 Micro Screen Mains/Rechargeable	36.50
		Hitachi AV72/10P Mains Shaver	19.95
Solaria		Trilec Foldaway Full Body Solarium	149.00
		Slimtan Finesse Foldaway Full Body Solaria from	249.00
Prescription Charges			
	Department of Health, April 1, 1990	Charge per Item	3.05
	Department of Health, April 1, 1991		3.40
	Department of Health, April 1, 1992		3.75
	Department of Health, April 1, 1993		4.25

Continued

11.4.3 Prices, Selected *continued*

Item	Source	Description	Price £ p.
Publications			
Books	*Sunday Times*, July 1, 1990	*Sandstorm*, L.Gough, Gollancz	12.95
		Last Loves, A.Sillitoe, Grafton	12.95
		Rosemary Conley Complete Hip & Thigh Diet, Arrow	3.50
		A Year in Provence, P.Mayle, Pan	4.50
		A Time to Die, W.Smith, Pan	4.99
		Around the World in 80 Days, M.Palin, BBC	15.00
		Mozart the Dramatist, B.Brophy, Libris	9.95
Magazine	*House Beautiful*, December 1991/ January 1992	*House Beautiful*	1.20
Books		*Instant Gardening*, A & J Caplin, Chatto & Windus	3.99
		Simple Country Style & How to Achieve It, Conran	16.99
		Decorated Dolls House, J.Ridley, Macdonald	17.50
Magazine	*Good Housekeeping*, October 1992	*Good Housekeeping*	1.60
Books		*Possessing the Secret of Joy*, A.Walker, Cape	13.99
		The Queen and I, S.Townsend, Methuen	9.99
Magazines	*Womans Own Publications*, 1993	*Woman's Own*	0.46
		Woman	0.46
		Woman's Journal	1.70
		Practical Gardening	1.90
Books	*Sunday Times*, December 12, 1993	*Taken on Trust*, T.Waite, Hodder	14.99
		Life in the Freezer, A.Fothergill, BBC	18.99
		The Queen and I, S.Townsend, Mandarin	4.99
		The Copper Beech, M.Binchey, Orion	4.99
Services			
Cinema	*Receipt*, 1990	Regal Cinema, Northwich Admission Price	1.50
	Receipt, 1991		2.00
	Receipt, 1992		2.50
	Receipt, 1993		3.00
Licence	*Post Office Archives*, 1990	Colour TV	72.00
	Post Office Archives, 1991		77.00
	Post Office Archives, 1992		80.00
	Post Office Archives, 1993		83.00
	DVLA, March 11, 1992	Road Tax	110.00 (12 months)
	DVLA, March 16, 1993		125.00 (12 months)
Telephone Tariffs			
Cheap: Mon to Fri 6pm to 8am	*British Telecom*	5 minutes	
Local:			10

Continued

11.4.3 Prices, Selected *continued*

Item	Source	Description	Price £	p.
Telephone tariffs *cont.*				
Up to 56.4 km.				20
Over 56.4 km.				30
Standard: Mon to Fri 8am to 9am and 1pm to 6pm				
Local:				20
Up to 56.4 km.				46
Over 56.4 km.				51
Peak: Mon to Fri 9am to 1pm				
Local:				25
Up to 56.4 km.				61
Over 56.4 km.				66
Cheap: Mon to Fri 6pm to 8am	*British Telecom*, April 2, 1991	5 minutes		
Local:				10
Up to 56.4 km.				19
Over 56.4 km.				29
Standard: Mon to Fri 8am to 9am and 1pm to 6pm				
Local:				19
Up to 56.4 km.				43
Over 56.4 km.				48
Peak: Mon to Fri 9am to 1 pm				
Local:				24
Up to 56.4 km.				58
Over 56.4 km.				63
Parcel Postage Rates (National Rate)	*Post Office Archives*, September 17, 1990	1 kg.	2.00	
		5 kg.	3.60	
		10 kg.	5.00	
Parcel Postage Rates (Parcelforce Standard)	*Post Office Archives*, July 1, 1991	1 kg.	2.50	
		6 kg.	4.65	
		10 kg.	6.25	
	Post Office Archives, 1992	1 kg.	2.50	
		6 kg.	4.65	
		10 kg.	6.25	
	Post Office Archives, November 1, 1993	1 kg.	2.65	
		6 kg.	5.00	
		10 kg.	6.75	
Sewing Equipment and Supplies				
Machine	*Which*, September 1991	Bernina 1015 Sport	500.00	
		Brother VX1095	160.00	

Continued

11.4.3 Prices, Selected *continued*

Item	Source	Description	Price £ p.
Machine *cont.*		Frister & Rossman Star 114	200.00
		Husqqvarna Classica 105	295.00
Furnishing Fabric (per metre)	*House Beautiful*, December 1991/ January 1992	Pure Glazed Cotton Chintz	2.90
		Ticking (80 ins. wide)	4.90
Fabrics (per metre)	*Singer Sewing Shop*, 1993	Handwoven Silk Dupion	9.95
		Polyester Cotton	8.95
		Tartans from	6.25
		Polyester/Cashmere Georgette	9.95
Haberdashery		Sylko Mercerised Cotton Thread	4.40 (1000 metres)
		Guterman Sew-All thread	0.89 (100 metres)
		Polysew Elastic	0.99 (metre)
		Newey Dorcas Dressmaking Pins	1.95 (25 g.)
		Butterick Shoulder Pads	3.50 (small)
		Polysew 20 Assorted Snap On Fasteners	0.99
Machines		Singer Festival	499.95
		Singer Concerto 3	399.95
		Singer Professioanl XL-10	1,199.00
		Alfa Electric	36.00 (secondhand)
Paper Patterns		McCalls Paper Patterns from	1.75
		Phildar Knitting Patterns from	2.50
Scissors		Fiskars Dressmaking Scissors	16.75
		Singer Dressmaking Scissors	6.95
Wool		Arkansas Double Knit Yarn	0.99 (50 g. balls)
		Spectrum Aran	1.69 (100g. ball)
Needles		Milward Hand Sewing Needles	1.25
Sports and Hobbies			
Photographic Equipment	*Which*, 1990	Canon Snappy V	50.00
		Miranda Solo	10.00
		Olympus Trip Fixed Focus	35.00
		Chinon Auto Focus	50.00
	Which, 1991	Canon EOS 10 SLR Auto Focus	350.00
		Olympus OM-4Ti Manual Focus	500.00
		Leica RF Manual Focus	1,200.00
Sports Shoes	*Good Housekeeping*, October 1992	Nike Cross Trainer Low	49.99
		Reebok AXT Plus	54.95
		Dunlop Juno	21.99
Sports Equipment	*Argos*, 1993	Slazenger Half Set of Golf Clubs	99.99
		Slazenger Golf Balls	14.99 (12)
		Mitre Delta League Football	9.50
		Airborne Leather Football	6.99
		Slazenger Panther Cup Badminton Racket	7.99
		Dunlop Power Play Senior Tennis Racket	15.99
		Slazenger "Challenge 70" Squash Racket	29.50

Continued

11.4.3 Prices, Selected *continued*

Item	Source	Description	Price £ p.
Sports Equipment *cont.*		DP "Trac 20" Multi Gym and Butterfly Unit	299.99
Tobacco Products			
Cigarettes (packet of 20)	*Gallaher Ltd.*, 1990	Benson & Hedges King Size Special Filter	1.75
		Silk Cut King Size De Luxe Mild	1.75
		Park Drive Tipped King Size	1.74
		Senior Service	1.91
	Gallaher Ltd., 1991	Benson & Hedges King Size Special Filter	2.08
		Silk Cut King Size De Luxe	2.08
		Park Drive Plain	2.15
Smoking Equipment		Benson & Hedges Pipes	13.95
Cigarettes	*Gallaher Ltd.*, 1992	Benson & Hedges King Size Special Filter	2.21
		Silk Cut Extra Mild	2.21
		Senior Service Plain	2.40
Cigarettes	*Gallaher Ltd.*, 1993	Benson & Hedges King Size Special Filter	2.41
		Silk Cut Extra Mild	2.41
		Senior Service Plain	2.62
Smoking Equipment		Benson & Hedges Pipes	13.95
Toys			
Games	*House Beautiful*, December 1991/ January 1992	Colourful Floor Puzzle	6.95
		Travel Game Set from Littlewoods	15.99
		Badger Chalkboard	11.95
Toys	*Toys R Us*, 1992	Mattel Barbie Magic House	32.87
		Paint and Dazzle Barbie Doll	13.87
		Fisher Price Baby Activity Table	21.78
		Bantel Scooter	9.97
		Barval D. Formula One Pedal Car	54.99
		Baby Walker with Bricks	17.99
		Hasbro Action Man	13.87
	Index, 1993	Lego Large Playcase	24.50
		Technic Multi Model Motor Set	28.50
		Meccano Set 2	19.99
Games	*Argos*, 1993	Scrabble	16.99
		Monopoly	9.25
		Game of Life	13.75
		Trivial Pursuits	31.50
Transport and Vehicles			
Air Fares	*Reed Travel Group*, June 1990	London to Paris 1st. Class	180.00
		London to Paris Economy	120.00
		London to New York	1,634.00
Rail Fares	*National Railway Museum*, February 1990	Manchester to London 2nd. Class Return	69.00

Continued

11.4.3 Prices, Selected *continued*

Item	Source	Description	Price £ p.
Vehicles	*Sunday Times*, July 1, 1990	4WD Subaru Legacy from	10,999.00
		Lotus Esprit Turbo 89	25,950.00
		Porsche 944 2.7	19,950.00
Bicycles	*Which*, August 1991	Apollo Colorado Mountain Bike	100.00
		Falcon Cheetah/326 Mountain Bike	225.00
		British Eagle Touristique Sports Bike	430.00
		Falcon Team Banana 302	185.00
Vehicles		Ford Escort Popular 1.3	8,123.00
		Vauxhall Sierra XR4i	15,895.00
		Vauxhall Nova Trip 1.0	6,480.00
		Volvo 440SE	10,620.00
		Land Rover Discovery V8	20,895.00
Metro Fares	*Metro Link*, 1992	Weekly Travel Pass	5.70
Air Fares	*Reed Travel Group*, June 1993	London to Paris 1st. Class	247.00
		London to Paris 2nd. Class	173.00
		London to New York	1,935.00
	Delta Travel, July 1993	Manchester to Athens Cheap Return	147.00
		Manchester to Brussels Return	125.00 (Apex Ticket)
Metro Fares	*Metro Link*, April 26, 1993	Single Adult to Cross 7 Zones	2.60
		Adult Peak Return to Cross 7 Zones	4.90
Rail Fares	*National Railway Museum*, January 1993	Manchester to London 2nd. Class Return	90.00
	Receipt, 1993	Crewe to London Cheap Return	29.00
Bicycles	*Argos*, 1993	Raleigh Outland All-Terrain Bike	174.99
		Falcon Arctic Fox Mountain Bike	189.99
		Falcon Fat Track Boy's Mountain Bike	99.99
Vehicles	*Congleton Guardian*, December 9, 1993	Ford Escort LX	10,890.00
		Metro 1.4Si CTV 5 Door	9,180.00
		Peugeot 106 Kid	6,195.00
		Proton Persona 1.6 SEi 5 Door	11,479.00
Travel			
Tours	*Sunday Times*, July 1, 1990	9 Day Escorted Tours of Jordan with Jasmin Tours from	449.00
Villas		Beach Villas in Menorca from	179.00 (inc. flight)
Air Flights		Travel Bug Discounted Flights to Bangkok	386.00
Ferries		Return fares to France with Brittany Ferries from	78.00 (2 adults + car)
Holidays	*Sunday Times*, June 7, 1992	Q.E.2 Holidays to New York	595.00
		Trailfinders to New York from	255.00
		Morocco with Inspirations from	194.00 (1 week)
		Ultimate Sailing Holiday, Caribbean & Florida	699.00 (14 nights)
		PGL Children's Adventure Holidays	159.00 (week)
	Good Housekeeping, October 1992	14 Day Caribbean Holiday with Airwaves from	1,586.00 (all inc.)

Continued

11.4.3 Prices, Selected *continued*

Item	Source	Description	Price £ p.
Holidays *cont.*		2 Weeks in Cyprus with Olympic Holidays from	79.00
	Sunday Times, December 12, 1993	Xmas in Jamaica with Hayes & Jarvis from	995.00
		7 Nights in Austria, Italy or France with Crystal	109.00
		7 Nights in the South Pacific from	2,998.00 (all inc.)
		2 Nights in Vienna from	199.00 (inc. flights and accom.)
Miscellany			
Answering Machines (without telephone)	*Which*, December 1990	Answercall TAM90	60.00
		Panasonic Easa-Phone KX-TI446BE	90.00
Answering Machines (with telephone)		Audioline 890	80.00
		Dialatron 961	125.00

11.4.4 Prices, Miscellaneous

11.4.4a Cost of Driving, 1993

	1993 £
12 horse power car (Mini Metro)	6,000.00
Road Tax	130.00
Insurance Comprehensive	338.76
Petrol (gallon)	2.50
Battery (12 volt)	25.00
Labour Charges (per hour)	15.00
Tyres (each)	35.00

Small car sales and garage in South Manchester.

Road tax excepting, all prices are approximate. See Chapter 7, table 7.4.4b for 1947 and 1957 prices.

11.5 Finance and Economic Data

11.5.1 Finance, Personal

	1990 £	1991 £	1992 £	1993 £
Retirement Pension				
Married	75.10	83.25	86.70	89.90
Single	46.90	52.00	54.15	56.10
Child Benefit				
First	7.25	8.25	9.65	10.00
Subsequent	7.25	8.25	7.80	8.10
Unemployment Benefit: Men and Women	37.35	41.40	43.10	44.65
Income Tax Rate[1]	25%	25%	25%	20%
Base Interest Rate[2]	15%	14%	10.50%	6%

Bank of England; Department of Social Security; Inland Revenue Statistics.

[1]The rates apply to years ended 5th April. [2]The rates apply to January of each year.

11.5.2 Financial Markets

11.5.2a Closing Price of UK Major Stocks in January

	1990 p.	1991 p.	1992 p.	1993 p.
Barclays	574	428	489	410
Boots	322	348	445	571
Burmah Castrol	705	698	614	738
Cadbury Schweppes	495	378	440	499
Coats Viyella			193	231
Courtaulds	402	291	443	562
Guinness	689	824	538	644
Imperial Chemical Industries (ICI)	1,352	1,263	1,381	1,410
Marks and Spencer	225	272½	361	348
Reckitt and Colman	1,323	1,334	741	709
Unilever	738	738	902	1,129
Whitbread	409	489	516	499

Financial Times, 1990–1993.

Blank space denotes no available data.

11.5.2b Commodities

	Coal (average price delivered to large consumers)	Raw Cotton (average typical daily offering price)	Gold (average market price)	Sugar (annual average world price)	Wheat (ex-farm annual spot prices)	Wool (annual average price)
	£ per tonne	pence per lb.CIF	$ per troy oz.	£ sterling per metric ton	£ per tonne	pence per lb.
1990	42.36	45.82	383.69	177.846	112.10	27.94
1991	41.53	42.88	361.21	132.535	122.30	28.40
1992	40.99	32.38	343.45	133.127	133.30	28.40
1993	n/a	38.70	354.67[1]	172.657[2]	142.60	36.29

British Wool Marketing Board; Cotlook Limited; Czarnikow Sugar; *Digest of UK Energy Statistics*, 1993; Home Grown Cereals Authority; World Gold Council.

[1]January/19 October, 1993. [2]January/25 October, 1993.

11.5.2c Foreign Exchange Rates

	Deutschmark per £1	French Franc per £1	US Dollar per £1
1990	2.8760	9.3160	1.61400
1991	2.8860	9.8040	1.93000
1992	2.8430	9.6900	1.86950
1993	2.4410	8.3250	1.51450

CSO Financial Statistics.

Original source, Bank of England.

11.5.3 Balance of Payments and GNP

11.5.3a Balance of Payments

	Visible Balance	Invisible Balance	Current Balance	Total UK Investment Overseas	Total Overseas Investment in the UK	Net Foreign Currency Transactions of UK Banks	Net Sterling Transactions of UK Banks	Net Transactions in Assets and Liabilities	Balancing Item
	£m	£m	£m	£m	£m	£m	£m	£m	£m
1990	-18,809	1,778	-17,029	-25,397	23,910	-2,448	8,820	11,091	5,938
1991	-10,920	3,969	-6,321	-41,169	28,672	12,592	-4,385	5,249	1,072
1992	-13,406	4,766	-8,620	-42,242	31,733	6,465	-8,002	8,319	301
1993[1]									

CSO Annual Abstract of Statistics, HMSO, 1993.

[1]1993 data not available at time of going to press.

11.5.3b GNP by Category of Expenditure and Factor Incomes

	Income from Employ- ment	Income from Self Employ- ment	Gross Trading Profits of Compa- nies	Gross Trading Surplus of Public Corpora- tions	Gross Trading Surplus of Gov- ernment Enter- prises	Rent	Stock Appre- ciation	Gross Domes- tic Product	Net Property Income from Abroad	Gross National Product	Capital Consump- tion	National Income
	£m	£m	£m	£m	£m	£m	£m	£m	£m	£m	£m	£m
1990	311,745	59,971	65,588	4,342	12	39,363	-6,288	479,452	2,094	481,546	-61,126	420,420
1991	329,808	57,507	60,674	3,119	119	44,092	-2,825	497,001	328	497,329	-63,968	433,361
1992	341,009	58,060	64,574	1,813	89	46,846	-2,216	514,594	5,777	520,371	-63,984	456,387
1993[1]												

CSO Annual Abstract of Statistics, HMSO, 1993.

[1] 1993 data not available at time of going to press.

11.6 Miscellaneous

11.6.1 Trustee Savings Bank Balance Sheet

	1990 000's	1991 000's	1992 000's
Total Assets	30,799	29,934	32,182
Advances (net of provisions)	17,206	17,190	16,301
Current and Deposit Accounts	23,047	21,727	23,403
Shareholders' Funds	1,814	1,742	1,638

Report to Shareholders, 1992, Annual Review, TSB Group PLC.

In 1992, TSB had 7 million customers. See also tables 2.6.1 for 1914/18 figures and 4.6.1 for 1930/37 figures.

APPENDICES

1. Purchasing Power of the Pound, 1900 – 1993

Year	Value	Year	Value
1900	35.87	1947	15.32
1901	35.58	1948	14.82
1902	35.02	1949	14.17
1903	34.75	1950	13.70
1904	34.48	1951	13.19
1905	34.75	1952	11.70
1906	36.76	1953	11.22
1907	33.70	1954	11.08
1908	32.95	1955	10.65
1909	32.95	1956	10.13
1910	32.71	1957	9.73
1911	32.23	1958	9.39
1912	31.11	1959	9.21
1913	31.11	1960	9.24
1914	31.33	1961	9.06
1915	27.64	1962	8.67
1916	23.07	1963	8.45
1917	18.90	1964	8.29
1918	16.67	1965	7.94
1919	14.26	1966	7.62
1920	13.91	1967	7.36
1921	11.89	1968	7.18
1922	16.25	1969	6.78
1923	17.51	1970	6.47
1924	17.65	1971	5.99
1925	17.38	1972	5.55
1926	17.76	1973	5.17
1927	17.76	1974	4.65
1928	18.59	1975	3.95
1929	18.67	1976	3.23
1930	18.82	1977	2.81
1931	20.36	1978	2.58
1932	21.22	1979	2.38
1933	21.95	1980	2.06
1934	21.95	1981	1.85
1935	21.74	1982	1.68
1936	21.25	1983	1.61
1937	20.64	1984	1.55
1938	19.65	1985	1.49
1939	20.08	1986	1.42
1940	17.93	1987	1.38
1941	15.97	1988	1.34
1942	15.63	1989	1.27
1943	15.69	1990	1.18
1944	15.69	1991	1.08
1945	15.47	1992	1.02
1946	15.42	1993	1.00

Bank of England Retail Price Index.

2. Decimal Currency Converter, 1971

Old	New	Old	New	Old	New	Old	New	Old	New	Old	New	Old	New	Old	New	Old	New	Old	New
		2/0	10	4/0	20	6/0	30	8/0	40	10/0	50	12/0	60	14/0	70	16/0	80	18/0	90
1d.	½	2/1	10½	4/1	20½	6/1	30½	8/1	40½	10/1	50½	12/1	60½	14/1	70½	16/1	80½	18/1	90½
2d.	1	2/2	11	4/2	21	6/2	31	8/2	41	10/2	51	12/2	61	14/2	71	16/2	81	18/2	91
3d.	1	2/3	11	4/3	21	6/3	31	8/3	41	10/3	51	12/3	61	14/3	71	16/3	81	18/3	91
4d.	1½	2/4	11½	4/4	21½	6/4	31½	8/4	41½	10/4	51½	12/4	61½	14/4	71½	16/4	81½	18/4	91½
5d.	2	2/5	12	4/5	22½	6/5	32	8/5	42	10/5	52	12/5	62	14/5	72	16/5	82	18/5	92
6d.	2½	2/6	12½	4/6	22½	6/6	32½	8/6	42½	10/6	52½	12/6	62½	14/6	72½	16/6	82½	18/6	92½
7d.	3	2/7	13	4/7	23	6/7	33	8/7	43	10/7	53	12/7	63	14/7	73	16/7	83	18/7	93
8d.	3½	2/8	13½	4/8	23½	6/8	33½	8/8	43½	10/8	53½	12/8	63½	14/8	73½	16/8	83½	18/8	93½
9d.	4	2/9	14	4/9	24	6/9	34	8/9	44	10/9	54	12/9	64	14/9	74	16/9	84	18/9	94
10d.	4	2/10	14	4/10	24	6/10	34	8/10	44	10/10	54	12/10	64	14/10	74	16/10	84	18/10	94
11d.	4½	2/11	14½	4/11	24½	6/11	34½	8/11	44½	10/11	54½	12/11	64½	14/11	74½	16/11	84½	18/11	94½
1/0	5	3/0	15	5/0	25	7/0	35	9/0	45	11/0	55	13/0	65	15/0	75	17/0	85	19/0	95
1/1	5½	3/1	15½	5/1	25½	7/1	35½	9/1	45½	11/1	55½	13/1	65½	15/1	75½	17/1	85½	19/1	95½
1/2	6	3/2	16	5/2	26	7/2	36	9/2	46	11/2	56	13/2	66	15/2	76	17/2	86	19/2	96
1/3	6	3/3	16	5/3	26	7/3	36	9/3	46½	11/3	56	13/3	66	15/3	76	17/3	86	19/3	96
1/4	6½	3/4	16½	5/4	26½	7/4	36½	9/4	46½	11/4	56½	13/4	66½	15/4	76½	17/4	86½	19/4	96½
1/5	7	3/5	17	5/5	27	7/5	37	9/5	47	11/5	57	13/5	67	15/5	77	17/5	87	19/5	97
1/6	7½	3/6	17½	5/6	27½	7/6	37½	9/6	47½	11/6	57½	13/6	67½	15/6	77½	17/6	87½	19/6	97½
1/7	8	3/7	18	5/7	28	7/7	38	9/7	48	11/7	58	13/7	68	15/7	78	17/7	88	19/7	98
1/8	8½	3/8	18½	5/8	28½	7/8	38½	9/8	48½	11/8	58½	13/8	68½	15/8	78½	17/8	88½	19/8	98½
1/9	9	3/9	19	5/9	29	7/9	39	9/9	49	11/9	59	13/9	69	15/9	79	17/9	89	19/9	99
1/10	9	3/10	19	5/10	29	7/10	39	9/10	49	11/10	59	13/10	69	15/10	79	17/10	89	19/10	99
1/11	9½	3/11	19½	5/11	29½	7/11	39½	9/11	49½	11/11	59½	13/11	69½	15/11	79½	17/11	89½	19/11	99½